Unfurling The Divine Standard

Bahá'í
Publications
Australia

Unfurling
The
Divine Standard

Vignettes in the Lives of the Hands of the Cause of God

By
Barron Harper

Unfurling The Divine Standard

Published by Bahá'í Publications Australia

ISBN: 1-876322-47-0

Distributed by:
Bahá'í Distribution Services
P.O. Box 300
Bundoora Vic 3083
Australia

Email: bds@bahai.org.au
www.bahaibooks.com

Cover Design & Book Layout: Massoud Tahzib

Vignettes

is dedicated to the memory of

Mr David Hofman

Former member of the Universal House of Justice
writer, administrator, teacher

Who widened my horizons,
bestowed upon me a glimpse of his brilliance,
and inspires me in my striving for scholarship

Contents

Preface 3
Acknowledgements 5
Introduction 7
The Standard-bearers of the Cause of God 11

Patterns of Bahá'í Life:

Backbiting 15
Beauty 19
Courage 27
Distinction 39
Firmness in the Covenant 43
Happiness 55
Humility 63
Love 71
Loyalty 81
Obedience 87
Sacrifice 91
Steadfastness 97
Trust and Trustworthiness 107

Inspiring the Heart:

Calamities 119
Death 127
Grief & Sorrow 135
Guidance 145
Pilgrimage 153
Prayer 161
Reflections 167
Spiritual Birth 175
Supreme Concourse 189
Unity 195
Youth 199

Serving the Cause of God:

Administrative Order 203
Contributions and the Right of God 211
Education 221
Martyrdom 229
Perseverance 235
Pioneering 245
Proclamation 263
Scholarship 269
Teaching 283

Endnotes 305
Bibliography 327
Origins 335
Appointments of the Hands of the Cause 345
Addendum 353

Preface

> ***The attainment of any object is conditioned upon knowledge, volition and action. Unless these three conditions are forthcoming there is no execution or accomplishment.***[1]

Many years ago when the writer as a Christian regularly attended church, he longed one Sunday to know the Apostle Peter. Pre-eminent among the disciples, he was the 'rock' upon whom Christ would build His church. Now, twenty centuries later, Christ's church has long since been built and the historical Peter obscured by time and relevance.

As a young Bahá'í in 1970, the writer chanced to attain the presence and experience the love of the Hand of the Cause of God William Sears. Deeply affected by the encounter, he later learned upon reading *God Loves Laughter* that Mr Sears had been called 'Peter' by the shiny man he had seen in childhood dreams and in a waking moment at a train station. Mystified by these visions, he discovered as a young adult that the Shiny Man was 'Abdu'l-Bahá.

Christ had appointed 12 disciples whom He called to be 'fishers of men'. Eleven of these earliest Christians that included the Apostle Peter took the healing message of their Lord into the Pagan Roman world. 'Abdu'l-Bahá has stated that they sacrificed themselves for the Cause of Christ. Had they not found faith following the horrific crucifixion of their Leader and the consequent shattering of their hopes for leadership and prestige, Christianity would never have emerged from an obscure movement to embrace the generality of mankind.

In His *Will and Testament*, 'Abdu'l-Bahá challenges us to emulate them. Throwing light on the manner in which they sacrificed themselves, He writes:

> "The disciples of Christ forgot themselves and all earthly things, forsook all their cares and belongings, purged themselves of self and passion and with absolute detachment scattered far and wide and engaged in calling the peoples of the world to the Divine Guidance, till at last they made the world another world, illumined the surface of the earth and even to their last hour proved self-sacrificing in the pathway of that Beloved One of God. Finally in various lands they suffered glorious martyrdom. Let them that are men of action follow in their footsteps!"[2]

The disciples upheld a standard that acted as a mainspring in the evolution of the eternal Cause of God. They were the Standard-bearers of Christianity whose example 'Abdu'l-Bahá has validated for the Bahá'í Dispensation.

In this Dispensation, the Standard-bearers of the Cause of God are the Hands of the Cause. They hold aloft the standard of the Faith's laws, teachings and principles before the gaze of all mankind in general and the Bahá'ís in particular. In referring to the Hands as Standard-bearers, the Guardian would have intended that the Bahá'ís emulate them.

As an institution, the Hands were charged to protect and promote the Cause of God. As individuals, they carried out their dual roles according to their respective qualities and requirements. United in their common devotion to the Heads of the Faith, these remnants of the Guardian bequeathed a truly historic legacy of services and sayings.

The fortitude of Rúḥíyyih Khánum, the fearlessness of Mullá Riḍá, the devotion of Amelia Collins, the long-suffering of George Townshend, the trustworthiness of Shu'á'Alá'í, the renunciation of Martha Root, the ardour of Rahmat Muhájir, the courage of Hermann Grossmann, the scholarship of Ḥasan Balyúzí, the insight of Abu'l-Qásim Faizi, the sacrifice of Corinne True, the humility of Zikrullah Khadem, the generosity of Siegfried Schopflocher, the talent of William Sutherland Maxwell, the perseverance of Ugo Giachery, the distinction of Valíyu'lláh Varqá, the intrepidity of Hyde and Clara Dunn, and the stout-heartedness of William Sears – these and so many more living examples from our Standard-bearers must surely arouse in any crusading Bahá'í a yearning to follow in their footsteps.

So that the reader better appreciates the pathways trodden by these chosen ones, the stories compiled in this little book have been arranged in three broad categories: *'Patterns of Bahá'í Life'* (knowledge), *'Inspiring the Heart'* (volition) and *'Serving the Cause of God'* (action).

Whatever the inspiration that may be drawn, these divinely appointed Hands of His Cause are they who followed their Lord in this Day and became the first *quickeners of mankind*[3]. Little wonder the Universal House of Justice should have written: *'Their deeds are such as to eclipse the acts of the apostles of old . . .'*[4]

Acknowledgements

Deny not My servant should he ask anything from thee . . . [5]

The effort to produce this work of vignettes in the lives of the Hands of the Cause of God was enhanced through the generous and willing help of contributors. First the writer must acknowledge the late Mr David Hofman who both encouraged the writer in his quest to complete the book and kindly reviewed every article on George Townshend not many months before his passing. *Unfurling the Divine Standard* is dedicated to his loving memory.

Former Counsellor Donald Witzel, who in his advanced years continued as a mighty pillar to the Cause in Venezuela and a sterling example of service to present and future generations of believers, generously assented to review and comment on several articles in the book, provided some invaluable insights into Covenant-breaking and other subjects, and submitted reminiscences of Raḥmat'u'lláh Muhájir and Agnes Alexander.

Javidukht Khadem kindly consented to be interviewed and recorded at the annual Social and Economic Development Conference for the Americas, Orlando, in 2000. The writer was emboldened to raise numerous questions about her beloved husband due to the loving-kindness and patience this regal lady showered upon him.

Dr Khazeh Fananapazir, a scholar of wide repute, considered the writer's lengthy article on the Varqá family, provided several sources on Persian Hands of the Cause, and translated an article on Valíyu'lláh Varqá from the *Mu'assisiy-i-Ayádiy-i-Amru'lláh.*

Special thanks to the Universal House of Justice for its response to the question concerning individual qualities of the Hands of the Cause and to Dr 'Alí-Muḥammad Varqá for his comments on the qualities of his distinguished father. The writer is grateful to former Universal House of Justice member Mr 'Alí Nakhjávání for clearing up several points about Músá Banání and Enoch Olinga.

Other distinguished friends who contributed articles or to articles: Universal House of Justice members Ian Semple (Agnes Alexander) and Hartmut Grossmann (Hermann Grossmann); Brigitte Beales Ferraby (John Ferraby); Ben Levy (Ugo Giachery); Shomais Afnan (Shu'á'u'lláh

'Alá'í); Shirley Macias (Abu'l-Qásim Faizi); Nancy Coker (Dr 'Alí-Muḥammad Varqá); Richard Detweiler from Pedro Reis (William Sears); Gilbert and Donja Murray, Don Letbetter and Barbara Taylor (the family); Fuad Izadinia (Abu'l-Qásim Faizi); Orval Minney (Zikrullah Khadem); unknown contributor (Jalál Kházeh); and Susanne Pfaff-Grossmann (Hermann Grossmann).

Other special thanks to Ramin Khadem for clarifying background details of his father, to Paul Vreeland for contributing poetry of and responding to questions about Horace Holley, to Mary Gregory for providing a special letter to her from Mr Faizi, to Ursula Grossmann for assistance in reviewing an article on the courage of Hermann Grossmann, to James (Bud) Humphries at American Bahá'í for permission to use an article by Sophie Loeding, to Leila Harper for her encouragement and help, to Amelia Pawlak for sending a Tablet of Bahá'u'lláh addressed to the Hands of the Cause, to Elisabeth Mühlschlegel for responding to queries, to May Hofman for commenting on my Dedication, to Dr Wendi Momen with whom is always a pleasure and learning experience to work, and to my beloved wife Dr Nancy Lee Harper for continuous encouragement, helpful suggestions and manuscript reviews.

Barron Harper
Portugal 2009

Introduction

In the early Adrianople period (1863 – 1868), Bahá'u'lláh in the *Súriy-i-Haykal* anticipated the emergence of Hands of the Cause:

> ***"Ere long will God raise up through Thee conquering Hands and subduing Helpers who will come forth from behind the veils and will arise to win victory for the Manifestation of God, the All-Merciful, amongst all mankind. They will raise such a cry as to purify all hearts . . ."*** [6]

Prior to His appointing these *Chosen Ones*, Bahá'u'lláh had instructed certain outstanding souls to travel as knowledgeable teachers. Their role was to speak in the meetings about the Faith, to deepen and enthuse the believers. In 1881, He instructed three believers to consult together in order to establish a resident teacher in every locality in Persia. The naming of four Hands by the Blessed Beauty near the end of His life consolidated this process.

Following these appointments, the services of these four appointees were unchanged with the result that the believers did not readily understand the role of Hands of the Cause. Gradually they were perceived as spiritual leaders of the community. Charged by the Supreme Manifestation with teaching and protecting His Cause, these sanctified ones held consultative meetings for the purpose of facilitating the growth and development of the Bahá'í community. Eventually their gatherings evolved at the instruction of 'Abdu'l-Bahá in 1899 into the first Spiritual Assembly in the entire Bahá'í world in Ṭihrán. Following the passing of Bahá'u'lláh, the stewardship of these devoted and vigilant Hands was such that the believers were protected from Covenant-breaking, encouraged to acquire knowledge, defended from attacks on the Faith, and aroused to intensify their teaching activities.

After the appointment of the first four Hands around the late 1880s, there were no more living appointments announced until 1951. 'Abdu'l-Bahá referred to four outstanding believers posthumously as Hands of the Cause. During the first 30 years of his ministry, Shoghi Effendi also made posthumous appointments. Then, between 1951 and 1957, the beloved Guardian named 32 living Hands of the Cause: twelve in December 1951, seven in February 1952 and eight in October 1957. Also, in this period, five appointees died and were replaced by him. Thus, at the time of the Guardian's passing, there were 27 living Hands of the Cause. They were from all continents and ranged in age from 31 to 96.

Through his constant care and loving encouragement, Shoghi Effendi developed in his stewards at the World Centre and in the five continents a strong sense of loyalty and devotion to the Guardianship. On 4 June 1957, Shoghi Effendi in a cable stated that the primary obligation of the Hands of the Cause in the World Spiritual Crusade was to insure the protection of the Bahá'í world community *in close collaboration* with National Spiritual Assemblies.[7] Subsequently, in his final message to the Bahá'í world four months later, he referred to the Hands of the Cause as the 'Chief Stewards of Bahá'u'lláh's embryonic World Commonwealth, who have been invested by the unerring Pen of the Centre of His Covenant with the dual function of guarding over the security, and of insuring the propagation, of His Father's Faith.'[8] These two messages assured that the National and Regional Spiritual Assemblies as well as the rank and file of believers would cling to the Institution of the Hands after the sudden passing of the beloved Guardian on 4 November 1957.

During their five and one-half years of stewardship from November 1957 to April 1963, the Hands of the Cause managed the affairs of the Faith in Shoghi Effendi's stead. They elected in accordance with the *Will and Testament of 'Abdu'l-Bahá* nine among their number to serve as Custodians of the Faith at the World Centre. These Custodians would respond to attacks upon the Faith, maintain correspondence with and coordinate the work of the continental Hands, assist National Assemblies in the prosecution of the Ten Year Plan, work with those same Assemblies in resolving administrative questions, act through the International Bahá'í Council in dealings with local and national Israeli authorities, and assume authority for expelling violators of the Covenant.[9]

On the occasion of their first Conclave, however, the 25 Hands of the Cause who gathered together in the upper hall of the Mansion of Bahá'u'lláh on 18 November 1957 were overwhelmed with grief at the passing of their beloved Commander and alarmed by their frightening responsibility for the Cause of God. Hour after hour, morning and afternoon, day after day their consultations proceeded, hindered by the need for painstaking translations between the Persian and Western Hands who insisted on understanding the opinions voiced in their respective languages. Wholly consecrated to the Cause of God and to their beloved Guardian, the Chief Stewards, lacking the certainty of divine guidance as was assured the Guardian, determined the only safe course was in firmly adhering to the instructions and policies of Shoghi Effendi. The decisions reached by the Hands in this first historic Conclave were announced in a momentous Proclamation dated 25 November 1957.

This Proclamation to the Bahá'ís of the East and West stated that Shoghi Effendi had left no will and no heir. It shared with the believers the initial despair of the Hands at these discoveries. Nevertheless, they recalled the Guardian's legacy of translations and interpretations bequeathed; of institutions and Shrines at the World Centre established; of the Faith in 254 countries and territories opened; of the foundations of the Divine Plan built up; of the guidance of the World Crusade to 1963 laid out; of the International Bahá'í Council, Auxiliary Boards and Chief Stewards raised up; and of their determination to carry out the Guardian's expressed wishes and hopes.

The Hands of the Cause in this historic Proclamation went on to announce the formation and functions of the Custodians, the evolution of the International Bahá'í Council into the Universal House of Justice, the holding of Intercontinental Conferences in 1958, an appeal to the Bahá'ís to distinguish themselves by firmness in the Covenant and by devoting themselves to the work of the Cause, and the reassurance that the Supreme Body once established would examine anew all the conditions of the Faith.

In the brief but difficult years ahead, the Custodians succeeded in safeguarding the assets of the Faith, solved critical issues concerning the raising of funds and practiced rigid economy. The Hands of the Cause overcame attacks on the Faith from a new generation of Covenant-breakers and addressed issues concerning the Guardianship. They attended the five Intercontinental Conferences in 1958. They assured that the cornerstones of three Temples were laid and that two of these Houses of Worship were completed and dedicated to worship. They brought about a demonstration of international Bahá'í solidarity in defence of 14 believers wrongly imprisoned in Morocco in a case which weighed on the Hands for 20 months. They arranged for the elections of the International Bahá'í Council in 1961 and the Universal House of Justice in 1963. They helped bring into existence by the end of their Interregnum 30 new National Spiritual Assemblies and 7,010 new localities where Bahá'ís resided. In consultation with Dr Muhájir, they developed a teaching plan which formed the basis of the Nine Year Plan. And in a document dated 7 June 1963, they officially relinquished their authority to the Supreme Body.

In 1968, the Universal House of Justice appointed Continental Boards of Counsellors in order to extend the functions of the Hands of the Cause into the future. In 1973, the House of Justice established the International Teaching Centre which they said: '... brings to fruition the work of the Hands of the Cause residing in the Holy Land and provides for its extension into the future, links the institution of the Boards of Counsellors even more intimately with that of the Hands of the Cause of God, and powerfully reinforces the discharge of the rapidly growing responsibilities of the Universal House of Justice.'[10] As permanent members of the Teaching Centre, the Hands were free to take part in consultations and activities there.

As these and other institutions evolved and the Hands found themselves increasingly freed from administrative cares, they went out into the Bahá'í world to lend their support to teaching activities. Regarded as '. . . one of the most precious assets the Bahá'í world possesses,'[11] the Chief Stewards protected the Cause of God, proclaimed its truths, deepened the knowledge of the believers, galvanized the rank and file to increase their services, awakened an appreciation of the Faith in the public, and presented Bahá'í literature to prominent persons and leaders. According to the wishes of 'Abdu'l-Bahá, they '. . . diffused widely the Divine Fragrances, declared His Proofs, proclaimed His Faith, published abroad His Law, detached themselves from all things but Him, stood for righteousness in this world, and kindled the Fire of the Love of God in the very hearts and souls of His servants . . .'[12]

What will be the effect of the services of the Hands of the Cause as the Faith advances in coming decades and centuries? With the passing of the last surviving link to this beloved institution on 22 September 2007, it is instructive that the House of Justice in its eulogy to Dr 'Alí-Muḥammad Varqá recorded: '. . . his love for the teaching work inspired countless believers across the globe.'[13] Such a statement well applies to all the Hands of the Cause whose teaching exploits have exerted immeasurable influences throughout the world. If 11 Disciples of Christ made the world another world by their sacrifice to the Cause of their Lord, imagine the fruits of these 49 Disciples of Bahá'u'lláh in this world in coming ages and centuries.

The Standard-bearers Of The Cause Of God

> ***The obligations of the Hands of the Cause of God are to diffuse the Divine Fragrances, to edify the souls of men, to promote learning, to improve the character of all men and to be, at all times and under all conditions, sanctified and detached from earthly things. They must manifest the fear of God by their conduct, their manners, their deeds and their words.***[14]

Adib Ṭaherzadeh in *Revelation of Bahá'u'lláh,* vol.4, states that the role of the Hands of the Cause of God can be understood by considering a Tablet revealed by Bahá'u'lláh in honour of Ḥájí Amín where He declares that movement results from heat and heat from the Word of God. A believer arises to serve the Faith because his heart is warmed by the fire of the love of God. Nothing is more potent than the Word of God to create this warmth of love in the heart of a believer.[15]

Next to the Word of God is the influence which an enkindled believer can exert on the hearts of other people. For this reason Bahá'u'lláh has written:

> "You must be so ablaze in this day with the fire of the love of God that the heat thereof may be manifest in all your veins, your limbs and members of your body, and the peoples of the world may be ignited by this heat . . ."[16]

While this remarkable statement reveals the potential of a believer to impart the quickening power of his faith to others, the Hands of the Cause occupy a very high station. Considerably exhilarated by their love for Bahá'u'lláh, they warmed the hearts of the friends and aroused them to serve the Faith. 'The Hands of the Cause are such blessed souls,' relates 'Abdu'l-Bahá, 'that the evidences of their sanctity and spirituality will be felt in the hearts of people.'[17] He praises them as . . .

> ". . . holy personages, the rays of whose holiness and spirituality throw light on the minds of people. Hearts are attracted by the beauty of their morals, the sincerity of their intentions and the sense of equity and justice. Souls are involuntarily enamoured of their praiseworthy morals and laudable qualities; faces turn spontaneously to their manifest signs and traces."[18]

Enoch Olinga possessed a beautiful smile that revealed much love. He was like a light wherever he went. People would crowd around him like moths to light. He deeply affected those who met him. He could *bear hug you into paradise.*[19] Once he entered a large hall packed with people in a little village and just smiled, not saying a word. The people there were so affected that they all stood up as one body, and commenced cheering and shouting.

So lofty is the station of the Hands of the Cause that the Supreme Pen has illumined their excellence in the following wondrous revelation:

> "Through them the standards of Thy oneness were raised in Thy cities and realms, and the banners of Thy sanctity were uplifted in Thy Kingdom. They utter not a word on any subject ere Thou hast spoken, for their ears are attuned to hear Thy Command, and their eyes are expectant to witness the effulgence of Thy Countenance. They are servants who have been well-favoured, have attained Thy good-pleasure, and have arisen in Thy Cause. The people of the world, the denizens of the Kingdom, and the dwellers of Paradise and the Realm on High, and beyond them, the Tongue of Grandeur send salutation upon them. Praise be to Thee, O my God, that Thou hast aided me to make mention of them and to praise them and their stations in Thy Cause and in Thy days."[20]

Shoghi Effendi referred to the Hands of the Cause as standard-bearers[21], because as conspicuous leaders of our Faith they hold aloft the standard of the Cause of God. They help to quicken our love for God, inspire us to teach our own selves so that our words will influence the hearts of seekers and enable us to summon to our assistance '. . . the hosts of a praiseworthy character and upright conduct, the influence (of which) will, most certainly, be diffused throughout the whole world.'[22] Therefore we would do well to study their lives, heed their exhortations and follow their example.

> *"He that seeketh to commune with God, let him betake himself to the companionship of His loved ones; and he that desireth to hearken unto the word of God, let him give ear to the words of His chosen ones."*[23]

PATTERNS OF BAHÁ'Í LIFE

Backbiting

> ***. . . backbiting quencheth the light of the heart, and extinguisheth the life of the soul.*[24]**

Doris McKay was an early American believer who knew Louis Gregory. She described him as having *long legs, long arms, long neck*[25] and a head very much above her own. She felt that his physical size reflected high integrity, resolution and courage. At his request, she described for him the community's group Bahá'í activities but then complained against a particular member.

At that moment Louis jumped to his feet, snapped his fingers and retired to his room without saying a word to her. Doris realized she had been backbiting and feeling superior. Later she encountered Louis in prayer. When he spoke to her, he made no mention of her omission. She never forgot the lesson he taught her about backbiting.[26]

* * *

> "If you defame the character of a person with your tongue, the effect lasts for centuries. If you murder, at least the person passes over in the state he was in."[27]
>
> – Rúḥíyyih Khánum

* * *

> ***Breathe not the sins of others so long as thou art thyself a sinner. . . How couldst thou forget thine own faults and busy thyself with the faults of others?*** [28]

In a deepening class on *The Hidden Words,* Abu'l-Qásim Faizi told his audience that the worst of all things ever explained in the Writings of all the religions of God is backbiting. So hideous is this fault that the *Qur'án* describes it as eating the flesh of your own brother's dead body. Mr Faizi explained:

> "... when you backbite, the thing is divided between you and the one who listens to you. But when you suspect something in people, (or) you are suspicious about people, what do we do? We are backbiting against somebody to ourselves. Therefore, both things are committed by one person. You see, many of the families are ruined because of suspicion.

> Many commercial houses have been absolutely demolished because of suspicion of one against the other, without any reason. Especially when it is not revealed, the slightest movement of the other side strengthens the suspicion in man's heart. Please let's pray and pray and pray that God will give us enough courage that if we suspect or have suspicion against anyone, to have enough courage to go to him or her and say, 'This is what I think. Please relieve me from it.' And then perhaps the problem will be solved immediately. Let's never fall into this spiritual disease of backbiting and suspicion against others. These are spiritual diseases, the consequences of which will be insanity, madness and incurable diseases."[29]

Mr Faizi pointed out something 'Abdu'l-Bahá said. The friends should realize that their conversations create a certain spiritual atmosphere in the house. Just as a child is nurtured in the atmosphere of the mother's womb, the atmosphere in the house should be conducive to the spiritual birth of the child.

> ". . . the most detrimental factors of this atmosphere is backbiting. . . We think that the child is not listening, but the child's spirit is like crystal clear water. (Backbiting) is like a drop of ink. It's no more clear. It's dirty. Now the child reaches 15. You say, 'Now Johnny, will you register here as a Bahá'í child?' He doesn't accept it. Whose fault is it? You have killed the spirit of the child and he doesn't want to. If you had not done that backbiting in the house, he would have readily accepted at the age of 15 . . . "[30]

* * *

> ***O beloved of the Lord! If any soul speak ill of an absent one, the only result will clearly be this: he will dampen the zeal of the friends and tend to make them indifferent. For backbiting is divisive, it is the leading cause among the friends of a disposition to withdraw.***[31]

Horace Holley offered this perspective on backbiting:

> "The sign of true faith is spiritual health – health of the individual Bahá'í and of the Bahá'í community. In this condition thoughts and activities are exalted above personality and are characterized by universal attributes

and purposes. The individual believer finds himself fulfilled in unity with his fellow Bahá'ís; the community becomes fulfilled in service to humanity through demonstrating the power of the Divine Teachings.

Spiritual disease, on the contrary, dividing the minds and hearts, imprisons the individual within narrow confines of inconstant, varying impulses, either aggressive or timid in his relationship to others.

In this condition he cannot judge aright either himself or his fellow believers. To relieve the pressure of uneasiness he becomes prone to exaggerate the words and actions of others and to indulge in the sin of rumour and backbiting. Moreover, he tends to believe without proof in the rumour and suspicion spread by other negative souls. The result is a community which becomes unable to serve the constructive programs of the Bahá'í Teachings.

Gossip and backbiting stand as the most sinister and destructive evils of any society. At all costs they must be eliminated from the Bahá'í community."[32]

* * *

The worst human quality and the most great sin is backbiting; more especially when it emanates from the tongues of the believers of God. If some means were devised so that the doors of backbiting were shut eternally and each one of the believers unsealed his lips in praise of the others, then the teachings of His Holiness Bahá'u'lláh would spread, the hearts be illuminated, the spirits glorified, and the human world would attain to everlasting felicity.[33]

'Alí-Akbar Furútan has written that backbiting . . .

". . . is a social disease and spreads like the plague, destroying its victims, extinguishing the flame of love in their hearts, veiling their intellects and harming their souls. Experience has shown that the lower nature of man strongly inclines him towards this habit; when people are overcome by worldly desires, or by the 'fire of self', they blame others, slander them, spread malicious comments, and backbite - and in so doing, derive from it a form of satisfaction."[34]

Since parents exert a strong influence on their children, they should be extremely careful that no backbiting emanate from their lips. He wrote:

> "(C)hildren should never hear or see any trace of backbiting or fault-finding in the home. And, since shunning all forms of backbiting conforms with the will of God, then unquestionably those people who make the effort to remove this stain from the mirrors of their hearts will be assisted and strengthened."[35]

* * *

Beauty

Every created thing in the whole universe is but a door leading into His knowledge, a sign of His sovereignty, a revelation of His names, a symbol of His majesty, a token of His power, a means of admittance into His straight Path.[36]

In his youth William Sutherland Maxwell studied at the *École des Beaux Arts* in Paris and worked in the studio of Paschal. Later he partnered with his brother, Edward, in a Canadian architectural firm which prior to the First World War had the largest offices in the country. Edward possessed engineering and business skills whereas W.S., a highly talented artist, could paint beautifully as well as '. . . model and carve anything with his hands.'[37] Together the talented duo produced many famous Canadian landmarks such as 'The Regina Parliament Buildings; Palliser Hotel, Calgary; Chateau Frontenac Hotel, Quebec; the Art Gallery, Church of the Messiah, and Nurses Wing of Royal Victoria Hospital, in Montreal . . .'[38] When Sutherland Maxwell worked on the Chateau Frontenac, he '. . . designed not only the lines of the twenty-story modern structure, but practically every detail of the interior: wrought-iron railings, furniture, grills, lamps, ceilings, elevator interiors, etc.'[39]

Sutherland Maxwell was also known as a man of integrity for his truthfulness, trustworthiness, courtesy, judgement, friendliness and graciousness. On the occasion of his being in Haifa for the marriage of his daughter to the Guardian on 25 March 1937, Shoghi Effendi had been drawn to the older man's *sterling qualities*.[40]

Following the death of May Maxwell in Argentina where she travelled in 1940 to render some service to the Cause both out of gratitude for the unexpected union of her daughter to the sign of God on earth and also to be more worthy of her beloved daughter whom she greatly missed, Shoghi Effendi invited Mr Maxwell to transfer his residence to Haifa. Once Mr Maxwell was ensconced in the Western Pilgrim House, father-in-law and son-in-law evolved an intimate relationship not only familial but consistent with their stations and circumstance.

A time of momentous developments at the World Centre, Shoghi Effendi found in Mr Maxwell a devoted believer who could render a sympathetic and beautiful interpretation of his vision. Thus he turned increasingly to Sutherland Maxwell for designs: stairs, walls, pillars, lights, lamp-posts, vases and eagles, entrances to Mt Carmel gardens, and many other embellishments to the Shrine gardens. When Shoghi Effendi asked the older man to design the Sepulchre of the Báb, Mr Maxwell not only had the talent, the genius and the long years of experience for such a project but also possessed certain qualities of nobility which no doubt attracted this favour from God.

To prepare the architectural plans for the outer structure of the Shrine, Mr Maxwell worked in a studio he had set in a smaller room of the Western Pilgrim House at 10 Persian Street. When Dr Ugo Giachery some years later saw the smallness of this studio, he was impressed by the magnitude of the architect's output. Dr Giachery made this touching observation:

> ". . . the varied collection of drawings, sketches, plans and water-colour paintings testified (to Mr Maxwell's) genius for detail; there was not even the most minute particular of his project that did not become the object of special care, illustrated with skill and precision, to show how it would look in actuality. There was at that time such an abundance and variety of sketches and studies as would have graced the collection of an art lover."[41]

Under the guidance of the Guardian, Mr Maxwell incorporated the spiritual meaning of the Islamic prophecy: '. . . on that day eight shall bear up the throne of thy Lord'[42]. The Master referred to the Shrine, the casket of the Báb and the Holy Dust as the Throne. One day, Shoghi Effendi explained to Dr Giachery that this prophecy concerned followers who were associated with the construction of the Shrine and with the Faith.

Abu'l-Qásim Faizi threw light on this distinction between direct and indirect association with the Shrine at a conference in which he was the honoured speaker:

> ". . . when the body of the Báb was buried on Mt Carmel, the beloved Master named five of the doors in the names of outstanding friends of His time. He said I name them because some of them worked in the Shrine and some of them had spiritual affiliation with the Shrine. 'Abdu'l-Bahá rewarded Amín, Trustee of Huqúq, who was always in Ṭihrán and never in Haifa. And He named one of the doors the door of Amín. He named another door by the greatest scholar who has ever come to the Cause of God: Mírzá Abu'l-Faḍl. . . . And he was in Egypt teaching. He did not even have money to come to Haifa. But he had spiritual affiliation with this great undertaking of 'Abdu'l-Bahá."[43]

These five individuals so honoured by 'Abdu'l-Bahá were: Ḥájí Amín (Báb-i-Amín), second Trustee of Ḥuqúqu'lláh and Hand of the Cause; Mírzá Abu'l-Faḍl (Báb-i-Faḍl), greatest Bahá'í scholar of the East; Ustád Áqá 'Alí-A<u>sh</u>raf and Ustád Áqá Bálá (Báb-i-A<u>sh</u>raf and Báb-i-Bálá), master masons; Ustád 'Abdu'l-Karím (Báb-i-Karím), mason; and Ḥájí Maḥmúd Qaṣṣáb<u>ch</u>í (Báb-i-Qaṣṣáb<u>ch</u>í), major contributor. The three remaining doors designated by the beloved Guardian: William Sutherland Maxwell (Báb-i-Maxwell), immortal architect and Hand of the Cause; Ugo Giachery (Báb-i-Giachery), logistical supervision and Hand of the Cause; and Leroy Ioas (Báb-i-Ioas), construction supervision and Hand of the Cause.[44]

The Guardian also guided Mr Maxwell to '. . . testify to (the Báb's) exalted station, to honour eternally the Martyr-Prophet enshrined in the Sepulchre, and to emphasize how closely the Báb's Revelation was connected with the expectations of the Islamic world.'[45] After several attempts at designing the Sepulchre, Mr Maxwell submitted a design based on the style of dome that he had originally submitted in 1920 at the annual convention of Bahá'í Temple Unity for the Wilmette Temple and that mostly pleased the Guardian. At Shoghi Effendi's request further modifications were made to the upper part of the clerestory, with the design finally being approved by the Guardian on 25 December 1943. Mr Maxwell then completed a model of the design for the Guardian, which was finished and displayed in time for the Declaration of the Báb in 1944. The model had required much patience and ingenuity on Mr Maxwell's part in making paper resemble marble and in creating the illusion of the actual building. On 23 May 1944, Shoghi Effendi cabled America:

> "... ANNOUNCE FRIENDS JOYFUL TIDING HUNDREDTH ANNIVERSARY DECLARATION MISSION MARTYRED HERALD FAITH SIGNALISED BY HISTORIC DECISION COMPLETE STRUCTURE HIS SEPULCHER ERECTED BY 'ABDU'L-BAHÁ ON SITE CHOSEN BY BAHÁ'U'LLÁH. RECENTLY DESIGNED MODEL DOME UNVEILED PRESENCE ASSEMBLED BELIEVERS. PRAYING EARLY REMOVAL OBSTACLES CONSUMMATION STUPENDOUS PLAN CONCEIVED BY FOUNDER FAITH AND HOPES CHERISHED BY CENTRE HIS COVENANT."[46]

Time passed without any further progress owing to the world war. Then, on the sixth anniversary of the bombing of Pearl Harbour - December 7, 1947, Shoghi Effendi wrote the Haifa Local Building and Town Planning Commission of his intention to embellish the original Tomb of the Báb with a building of great beauty. He introduced W.S. Maxwell as the architect and included drawings of the completed structure with his letter. However, owing to difficulties associated with the approaching end of the British Mandate in 1948, Mr Maxwell was unable to place contracts locally for quarrying stone. So the Guardian in deciding to look to Italy for available stone asked Dr Giachery to help Mr Maxwell locate nearly 800 tons of suitable marble for the arcade and make the necessary contracts.

On his way to meet Dr Giachery, Mr Maxwell took with him to Italy a photograph of his two foot high Shrine model. Fortuitously this photograph provided a convincing argument for the contracting firm of Guido M. Fabbricotti to accept the project. It readily demonstrated the prestige and subsequent business which would come to them once the project was done.

The building of the Shrine between 1948 and 1953 was contracted in stages. In consequence of limited funds and the political situation, the arcade was all that was initially contracted. Mr Maxwell's search for appropriate marble in consultation with the Fabbricotti firm eventually took them to the Chiampo quarries between Verona and Vicenza. The arches, capitals, walls, corners and balustrade of the arcade would subsequently contain Chiampo marble. Granite also had to be located for the columns, pilasters and bases, which was found in the north-western Italian Alps. Contracts were signed on 29 April and 5 May 1948, and the monumental work then got underway. Close collaboration between Mr Maxwell and the Fabbricotti firm would coincide with the work in progress.

When W.S. Maxwell returned to Haifa on 15 May with news that the erection of the Sepulchre of the Báb was assured, the Guardian was overjoyed. Over the next two years work on the arcade progressed with 9 July 1950 desired by the Guardian for completion. Upon completion Shoghi Effendi was so overwhelmed by the beauty of the arcade that he called the Bahá'í world to the timeliness of the erection of the octagon and trusted in divine assistance to confirm this next bold step. Rising immediately above the arcade, the eight-sided octagon was contracted with Fabbricotti on 21 October 1950. Then, before the octagon was finished, Shoghi Effendi called for an estimate of the cost of the drum and dome with the result that a contract was made on 24 March 1951. The octagon was finished in the early spring of 1952, the drum at the end of the same year, the dome with its 12,000 gilded tiles around July 1953 and remaining cosmetic work to the Sepulchre by the closing weeks of the Holy Year.

To the attendants at the New Delhi Intercontinental Conference the Guardian announced the completion of the Shrine of the Báb – an announcement which includes the now well-known description:

> ". . . QUEEN CARMEL ENTHRONED GOD'S MOUNTAIN CROWNED GLOWING GOLD ROBED SHIMMERING WHITE GIRDLED EMERALD GREEN ENCHANTING EVERY EYE FROM AIR SEA PLAIN HILL."[47]

He called upon that gathering to 'PAY TRIBUTE HAND CAUSE SUTHERLAND MAXWELL IMMORTAL ARCHITECT ARCADE SUPERSTRUCTURE SHRINE.'[48] Mr Maxwell had died on the 15th anniversary of his daughter's marriage to the Guardian: 25 March 1952, and Shoghi Effendi obviously missed this collaborator whose resourcefulness he had respected and whose life he had called *saintly*.[49]

Concerning the completed mausoleum, Dr Giachery observed of Mr Maxwell's work:

> "The whole edifice displays a great variety of architectural and artistic gems, products of the inventiveness and refined taste of Mr. Maxwell; Shoghi Effendi highly valued and admired every expression of such taste, which manifested itself in the ornamental details abounding throughout the edifice. Nearly every stone shows the gracefulness of the Maxwell artistic talent; in some instances the delicacy of the design is like a beautiful piece of embroidery or hand-made jewelry. It would require much space and time to enter into the details of all the motifs which beautify every frieze, festoon, moulding, garland, arabesque, finial, leaf, flower, rosette and chaplet, with which the appearance of every component piece of marble, or granite, or iron-work, or glass, is enriched. . . . Before deciding on the final design, Mr. Maxwell had made many sketches to develop the main motif, each of which is a little gem of artistry in tempera, revealing over and over his boundless love for beauty and precision."[50]

* * *

The Egoist

She has no soul.
Her almond eyes diminish to a spark
And change the sun to amber.
When she looks at me
I draw without myself and pass, unwilled,
The strange lids of her eyes, and enter

A garden that knows no law.
Sowed with imaginations like a god's
I enter and become
Another self, drunken
By new thoughts and hot-pulsed danger.
I long to sing, to prove my madness,
Dancing away from habit,
Responsibility and grave laws of soul.
A woman has no right to perilous thoughts.
She has no soul, and O,
I lose my own, and all my satisfied past,
Desiring her.[51]

Horace Holley, 1913

* * *

> ***. . . in every aspect of life, purity and holiness, cleanliness and refinement, exalt the human condition and further the development of man's inner reality. Even in the physical realm, cleanliness will conduce to spirituality, as the Holy Writings clearly state. And although bodily cleanliness is a physical thing, it hath, nevertheless, a powerful influence on the life of the spirit.***[52]

Zikrullah Khadem once described Keith Ransom-Kehler, whom he met as a young man in Iran, as being . . .

> ". . . the most stylish woman he had ever met. She had a beautiful and elegant mink coat cut in the latest fashion. Her dresses were so exquisite they would attract the attention of onlookers. Yet they were also very dignified and tasteful. . . Though she had a regal bearing and never failed to impress all who encountered her, she was also a lesson in humility."[53]

When Rúḥíyyih Khánum was leaving the Holy Land for the Wilmette Conference in 1953, a young pilgrim (Violette Nakhjávání) who was privileged to meet her was . . .

> ". . . struck at once by her innate grace, her regal presence and disarmed by her spontaneous vitality, her direct, unflinching gaze. She had eyes that shifted colour with her clothes, sometimes appearing to be green and sometimes

> blue. . . . In Wilmette, she rose to speak like the queen she was, her delicate, gauzy mantilla framing her lovely young face, and even from the photographs it is easy to see how she would have made an unforgettable impression on the Bahá'ís, as well as on the non-Bahá'í seekers and distinguished speakers."[54]

* * *

Louis Gregory accepted privation to be a Bahá'í race amity worker. Yet he did not appear impoverished. Paying careful attention to his appearance and conscious that he was representing the Faith, Louis could appear quite fashionable and well-groomed. 'By careful brushing and pressing,' his friend Roy Williams observed, 'Louis Gregory made the most of even one suit.'[55]

* * *

'Abdu'l-Jalíl Bey Sa'ad was an imposing man. He was always well dressed, particularly at Bahá'í functions and could often be seen wearing a beautiful red fez.[56]

* * *

John Henry Hyde Dunn typically sported a neat bow tie and an immaculately laundered shirt. He was spotlessly clean and tidy.[57]

* * *

In a letter to the writer in 1989, Rúḥíyyih Khánum enclosed on a 9 x 16 cm sheet the following endorsement, as follows:

> "Excerpt from the message of the Universal House of Justice to National Spiritual Assemblies, 4 November 1988, urging the Bahá'ís to further the objectives of WWF (World Wide Fund for Nature), the most prominent organization for the protection of life on this planet and the world's atmosphere. I think all of us should take to heart and act upon these words:
>
> > **'OUR SPIRITS STIRRED BY POWERFUL INDICATIONS THUS GIVEN OF GREAT POTENTIALITIES FOR SERVICE WHICH BAHÁ'Í COMMUNITY WORLDWIDE CAN AND**

MUST RENDER IN MAKING ITS DISTINCTIVE CONTRIBUTIONS TO CONSERVATION AND ENRICHMENT PHYSICAL ENVIRONMENT FOR BOUNTIFULLY ENDOWED PLANET.' [58]

# # #

Courage

***The source of courage and power is the promotion of the Word of God, and steadfastness in His Love.*[59] *Strive as much as ye can to turn wholly toward the Kingdom, that ye may acquire innate courage and ideal power.*[60]**

Abu'l-Qásim Faizi once emphasized to friends at a conference in Hawaii the Hidden Word: 'Ponder and reflect. Is it thy wish to die upon thy bed, or to shed thy life-blood on the dust, a martyr in My path . . .'[61] He told the friends that this particular passage reminded him of the four Hands of the Cause appointed by Bahá'u'lláh. He said that they never had their own home and never had any comfort in their lives. Instead they visited the homes of the believers from town to town. Always they wore all their clothes even at night because, as they said: 'When the government officials come for the Bahá'ís, we want to be ready always, not to keep them waiting for us.'[62]

Mr Faizi explained that '. . . whenever there were any difficulties in Persia, that they wanted to persecute the Bahá'ís, these Hands would immediately go to the government and say, "We heard that you wanted the Bahá'ís. We are here."'[63] In this way did they protect the believers and the Cause of God.

* * *

In His second and last Tablet, to George Townshend, dated 19 December 1920, 'Abdu'l-Bahá expressed a hope to which George would devote the remaining 36 years of his life. 'It is my hope,' the Master wrote, 'that thy church will come under the Heavenly Jerusalem.'[64] An ordained Episcopalian priest, George at the time of receiving this Tablet was settled with his wife Nancy as rector in the Galway village of Ahascragh in the beautiful rectory.

He struggled with whether to resign his clerical position or work within the Church in order to realize the desire of the Master. Many Bahá'ís in those early days of the Faith believed that the Revelation of Bahá'u'lláh would reform existing institutions; they did not feel any need to dissociate themselves from their various confessions. Lacking the benefit of the Guardian's as yet undisclosed exposition of the World Order of Bahá'u'lláh and consequently having no perception of the independent character of the Faith, George decided that he could best fulfil his mission within the

Church by bringing Christians back to the reality of Christ's teachings. By presenting the message of Christ from a Bahá'í point of view and relating the portents described by Christ to the time of His return, George felt that the prejudice and tradition of conservative Christian communities in his native land could be overcome.

'When people have become really Christian,' he wrote to the Guardian in 1925, 'they will find themselves Bahá'ís'[65]. To which the Guardian replied through his secretary: '. . . valuable work for the Bahá'í Cause can be done within the Christian Churches by promoting the 'Christianity of Christ'. 'Abdu'l-Bahá said that when people become true Christians, they will find themselves Bahá'ís.'[66]

Accordingly George prepared a booklet of prayers and meditations entitled *The Altar on the Hearth*. Incorporating the fundamentals of the Bahá'í Faith into his literary masterpiece in such a way as not to lift the veil too suddenly, he set out to draw his Christian audience closer to the New Jerusalem. Published in 1927, *The Altar on the Hearth* rapidly sold out, receiving acclaim in the Irish press and endearing him to the Church of Ireland. He next wrote five essays published in 1930 as *The Genius of Ireland* in which he proclaimed that a new day of God had dawned.

So as to avoid in the eyes of the Church too intimate an association with the Faith, George pleaded with the Guardian to neither acknowledge his unique and invaluable collaboration [67] in the translating of *The Hidden Words* (1926-7) nor his authoring the Introduction to *The Dawn-Breakers* (1930-1931). Possibly his greatest work, *The Promise of All Ages*, was published in 1934 under the pseudonym "Christophil" (a peace-offering to his wife) and, in the last half of the 1930s, he wrote a series of articles for *World Order* magazine under the initials A.G.B. and C.P.L.

Although Canon Townshend took these steps to avoid appearing eccentric and thereby jeopardize his efforts to convert the Church, he increasingly risked the prospect of being branded a heretic by stepping up his campaign of proclamation when his earlier literary masterpieces failed to achieve his purpose. 'He sent his book (*The Promise of All Ages*) to senior clergy; he spoke of 'Abdu'l-Bahá in Bible classes, and read a paper about Him to the Ballinasloe Clerical Union; he contributed articles to *The Bahá'í World*; *The Church of Ireland Gazette* published his article on the Christ-like character of 'Abdu'l-Bahá; he printed and circulated his Reflection on *The Hidden Words* of Bahá'u'lláh as well as the composite pamphlet of two essays; and finally he wrote and presented the paper,

Bahá'u'lláh's Groundplan of World Fellowship, to the World Congress of Faiths in London. . . His books (*The Promise of All Ages* and *The Heart of the Gospel*) were openly advertised and reviewed in leading newspapers; he engaged in a written dialogue with his Bishop, announced to him his association with the Bahá'í community and declared his allegiance to Bahá'u'lláh. He sought an interview with the Archbishop of Dublin and 'told him about Bahá'u'lláh and His Promise; he preached a sermon in St Patrick's Cathedral, Dublin, proclaiming Bahá'u'lláh by name; he addressed the Synod of the Church of Ireland to the same purpose.'[68] Finally he sent *God Passes By* to Bishops as well as the Dean of St Patrick's announcing the return of Christ.

While George's actions did not provoke Church authorities into forcing his resignation as he had hoped, he succeeded in bringing the Bahá'í Faith to the attention of his countrymen throughout Ireland. The clergy were personally informed. His books were read. Thousands of Irishmen read reviews of his books in *The Irish Times, Church of Ireland Gazette* and other leading papers. Many attended his lectures.

Meanwhile, as early as 1926, he was writing to the Guardian concerning his clerical position that to '. . . have to stay as I am seems an appalling and impossible fate.'[69] In coming years he would struggle to free himself '. . . from the shackles of an archaic and superseded system to which he had committed himself before knowledge of the New Jerusalem was given to him.'[70] Seeking alternative means of support, he looked forward in 1928 to taking over the directorship of the Geneva-based International Bahá'í Bureau. This proved abortive when promised support was withdrawn. He made other efforts as well. But most promising was an arrangement worked out with the British National Spiritual Assembly in 1936 to form a publishing company which would then '. . . acquire the rights and publish the works of Mr Townshend . . .'[71] However, his acceptance of this arrangement was postponed by Nancy's threat to leave him and denounce him; she would have no part in abandoning the financial security provided by her husband, as Archdeacon. For George the break-up of his home would spell disaster both for the Cause and his mission. Therefore he withdrew from the precipice, determined to maintain family unity.

The Guardian's letters to George were encouraging. When George wrote in 1933: 'I trust and pray that very soon God will release me from my clerical position and permit me to serve His Cause openly,'[72] Shoghi Effendi replied: 'I will . . . pray from the depths of my heart and will supplicate the Almighty to liberate you from anything that prevents you from proclaiming the Cause of God and from establishing its principles in the hearts and minds of your countrymen.'[73] While the Guardian looked forward as early as 1928 to appointing George a general at the Front,[74] he wrote around this same period:

> "God is no doubt preparing the way for the spread of His Faith in a strange and mysterious manner. You are, it seems, His chosen instrument and this should, alone, greatly encourage you in the crusade you are so bravely initiating for the proclamation of His Faith."[75]

By 1936, the height of Nancy's threat to denounce George if he left the Church, Shoghi Effendi was praising George's '. . . heroic determination to face the consequences of your fearless act on behalf of our beloved Cause . . .'[76] for his courageous stand in reading the Bahá'í paper to the World Congress of Faiths (George expected the Church authorities to force his resignation) and hoping that '. . . the day may not be distant when you will have been freed from every shackle that impedes your work in the Divine Vineyard.'[77] A year before George's resignation in 1946, the Guardian was writing to the NSA of the United States and Canada: 'He considers that our dear Bahá'í brother, George Townshend, can best serve the Faith at the present time where he is; he is now contacting many high ecclesiastics in his church . . .'[78]

The catalyst which finally paved the way for George's resignation was a complaint lodged in March 1947 to the Archbishop of Canterbury by an Anglican missionary against *The Promise of All Ages*. The complainant maintained that the book exalted Bahá'u'lláh over Christ. In his own defence, George stated that his book did not lower Christ, that he believed in Bahá'u'lláh as the return of Christ, and that he was prepared to leave the Church. The investigation being made against *The Promise of All Ages* placed Nancy in the equivalent or anomalous position of supporting her husband's resignation. Years before she had promised to support him if ever he were attacked for this book. Finally his resignation became effective on 30 September 1947, and the family resettled into a small bungalow in a Dublin suburb.

A man of outstanding courage, George manifested this quality through his resolute determination to achieve 'Abdu'l-Bahá's hope, his persistence in spite of unresponsiveness from the Church, his cheerfulness in the face of disappointments, his readiness to accept whatever consequences his unorthodox approach might incur, and his patience in the face of Nancy's opposition. '. . . a man of seventy,' writes David Hofman of George Townshend's heroism, 'with family responsibilities, holding high office in an honoured and well-rewarded calling, gave up all he had achieved, his beautiful country rectory – the scene of happy family life and long research – his position among the gentry, his future security in the form of pensions and other emoluments, to embrace poverty, indignity, the scorn and loss of friends, dependence on others . . . to serve his Lord.'[79]

As the hour of his resignation approached, the Guardian cabled:

> "THRILLED YOUR NEWS PRAYING MIGHTY RESULTS DEEPEST LOVING APPRECIATION COURAGEOUS STAND"[80]

* * *

When you hear of ancient heroes,
young man, know this:
A far loftier battle
looms in your own breast.
Once they skirmished for kingdoms
and castles long since decayed;
But this fight is for your fate:
torment of triumph eternal.
What is taken by sword
is lost by future generations.
What is won through character
remaineth undying wealth.[81]

Adelbert Mühlschlegel

* * *

When Paul Haney was elected by his fellow Hands at the first Conclave to be one of the Custodians (nine Hands in the Holy Land) following the passing of the Guardian, he bowed his head and said: 'You are only called once.'[82] He left behind a position in a prominent investment firm to which he had recently been promoted and through which he would have received generous financial rewards and retirement pension had he remained.[83]

* * *

For 12 years the Gestapo was the most feared organization of terror in Europe. Through torture, betrayal, executions and ruthlessness, the tyranny of the efficient police organization of the Gestapo and its 20,000 secret policemen maintained their rein of terror on the populations under Nazi control.

At the top of this horrific organization sat the Reichsführer-SS and chief of the German police Heinrich Himmler, a ruthless organizer who was obsessed with setting up a modern Teutonic order dedicated to eradicating what he believed were degenerate infiltrations of Slav or Jewish blood and with building up an intelligence service designed to create a police state. In Himmler's mind the SS was the '. . . imperial guard of the new Germany,'[84] whereas the Gestapo was the foundation of the Nazi police state. After the Nazis came to power in 1933, Germans soon learned that any suspected dissent could result in denunciation and arrest. Taken into 'protective custody', they could find themselves interred in a brutal concentration camp from which the only release might only be from this world. 'The Gestapo got the right of arbitrary arrest and 'protective custody' without any legal restriction or accountability . . . It became effectively a law unto itself and the German tradition of the *Rechtsstaat*, the state rooted in law and respect for the law, was torn aside.'[85]

On 21 May 1937 a special order issued by Heinrich Himmler interdicted the administrative institutions of the Faith. Persecutions quickly followed. The material of Bahá'í publications, the archives of the National and Local Assemblies and the Bahá'í literature of believers were confiscated. Hermann Grossmann lost the greater part of his valuable Bahá'í material, including historical information on the development of the Faith in Germany. The friends were denied the right to assemble. Arrests, interrogations, imprisonments, and fines of believers resulted on flimsy charges or false evidence. Under such circumstances mounting a defence was extremely difficult or highly unpredictable.

Dr Grossmann's daughter Susanne Pfaff-Grossmann in her German biography about her father writes of some of the stresses he courageously endured:

> "During Hitler's regime, Hermann Grossmann had difficulties not only because he was a Bahá'í. He was viewed with suspicion by the authorities and, in particular, was put under pressure in his professional life because he was not a member of the National Socialist German Workers' Party – the NSDAP. . . Several NSDAP party leaders plotted to remove him as a managing director . . . so as to be able to take over the company themselves. From 1934 to 1938 they were successful insofar as an interim managing director being appointed in his stead. In 1938 Hermann Grossmann succeeded in having the forced administration removed. . . Again the party leadership started to pressure him to join the

party. When he refused to comply, his rights as managing director were again infringed upon...

The next step taken by his opponents was to attempt to use his former activities as a Bahá'í against him. When this did not succeed, they initiated "penal proceedings for damaging the war economy" against him ... in 1944.... Thus the party leadership finally managed to achieve their goal. However, because by now the economic situation in Germany was so bad – the war now being all but lost after five years – every individual was urgently needed. So Hermann Grossmann did not have to go to prison after all; his six-month sentence being commuted."[86]

In 1944 seven believers (including Hermann's wife, Anna) and sympathizers of the Cause were falsely charged with 'having continued the organization of the dissolved and prohibited Bahá'í sect . . .'[87] in Darmstadt. In 1944 also Hermann Grossmann's sister Elsa Maria Grossmann (later a Knight of Bahá'u'lláh on the Frisian Islands) and other Bahá'ís of Heidelberg and nearby places were accused at Heidelberg and imprisoned. Acting in the role of witness in the defendants' favour, Hermann Grossmann was able to successfully defend the accused as well as the character of the Faith before the tribunals in Darmstadt and Heidelberg.

> "In a miraculous way the persecutions at that time were not targeted towards Hermann Grossmann. In this way he had the unique opportunity to act as witness for the defence of the believers and of the Faith of God before a number of tribunals. This he did e.g. in the case against Ruth Espenlaub, a Bahá'í in southern Germany. He confirmed above all the unconditionally non-political character of the Cause and the loyalty of the Bahá'ís towards the government of the country; and he was successful in this by convincing the State Attorney to drop the accusation of the Bahá'ís being dangerous to the state. What he could not hinder was the indictment of disregarding the prohibition of the Faith and the meeting of the friends; however, the

> former would have meant death by hanging or being sent to a concentration camp while the latter resulted in imprisonment for a time or a fine. The judges in the special court case in Darmstadt expressed their intention to extinguish the Faith of Bahá'u'lláh in Germany, but His all-powerful arm was superior to all the power of His enemies. On 22 September 1944 Hermann Grossmann received a punishment of a rather severe fine or six month imprisonment. Because of the war turning into a defeat he did not have to do his time. The driving force behind the persecutions, Kriminal-Assistant Gerst, received in a sensational court case after the war ten years in a penitentiary because of brutal torture of prisoners and was stigmatized as the most brutal GESTAPO representative in Baden."[88] (The part of Germany in which the Grossmanns lived).

The act of Dr Grossmann standing up for the defendants before the menacingly dictatorial court of the Gestapo in spite of himself having already suffered and being under threat was highly courageous in that extraordinary time of terror in Hitler's Germany.

* * *

Jalál Kh͟ázeh was very bold. Whenever he learned that a believer had been oppressed, he would '. . . not hesitate to reprimand even government officials if they neglected to fulfil their duty in favour of giving in to pressure from fanatical elements in the society.'[89]

* * *

Shoghi Effendi once described Keith Ransom-Kehler as '. . . very frank, very sensitive and very brave.'[90] She was absolutely fearless in saying her mind and could be particularly hard on men who were accustomed to submissive women. Sensitive to rejection, she nevertheless spoke and acted out what was to her right. When she prayed, she often became completely enraptured, sobbing and crying. She was a dynamic teacher of the Faith, travelling through the United States, Barbados, Japan, China, Australia, Burma, India and Iran. On a western tour in 1930-31, she gave 45 public talks in Seattle. In May 1931 the Bahá'ís of San Francisco reported that she had spoken 329 times in 11 months.

Later, during her 15-month stay in Persia when she repeatedly appealed to the Sháh to permit the publication and distribution of Bahá'í books, Keith travelled thousands of miles throughout the country, '. . . meeting the Bahá'ís, teaching administration, (and) encouraging Bahá'í women to take their rightful place in the work of the Faith.'[91] She literally gave up her life in service to the Cause and the friends of Bahá'u'lláh's native land.

The NSA of India and Burma reported on the effect of her visit following her passing:

> "Mrs. Keith Ransom-Kehler toured through India and Burma in the early part of 1932. She visited Rangoon, Mandalay, Myamo and Kanjangaon in Burma and Calcutta, Benares, Lucknow, Agra, Delhi, Aligarh, Amritsar, Lahore, Karachi, Bombay, Poona, Hyderabad (Deccan) and Bolepur in Northern and Western India and delivered lectures under the auspices of Indian Universities and met professors, students and religious leaders in various towns. On March 21st of the same year she performed the opening ceremony of the first Haziratu'l-Quds constructed on the Indian soil at Karachi. Her visit to the university towns of our country proved very fruitful and the message of Bahá'u'lláh was broadcast to the intelligentsia in the country. Her discourses were listened to with deep interest and she created a very great impression both by her learning as well as eloquence. As a matter of fact, many were attracted to the Cause. Her passing away in Isfahan has been deeply mourned by every one who came in touch with her."[92]

* * *

'Alí-Akbar Furútan wrote of Shu'á 'Alá'í:

> "I do not recall anyone to be so bold in the meetings with high officials and government authorities. He ('Alá'í) did not hesitate to state fearlessly and without the slightest ambiguity the importance of the Cause of God. I saw all this with my own eyes and heard this with my own ears. I admired in my heart his directness and his wise judgement in such occasions. He had a profound knowledge of the Cause of God. And this fact was well known to all, friends and foe alike."[93]

* * *

> ***Consider thou the lives of the former sanctified souls; what tests have they not withstood and what persecutions have they not beheld; while they were surrounded with calamities they increased their firmness and while they were overwhelmed with tests they manifested more zeal and courage.*** [94]

Mullá Riḍá was never at a loss for words when teaching the Cause. Whether an opportunity arose or he created one, the mullá would teach with unrestrained enthusiasm. However he often antagonized fanatical Muslims who heard his words with the result that he would bring much suffering on himself and friends in his company.

Once when Mullá Riḍá was imprisoned in 1896 in the Síyáh-Chál, his companions urged him to observe restraint in teaching the Faith, pointing out that his actions were bound to incur more sufferings. He replied that as the Cause is great it . . .

> ". . . is bound to encounter great opposition and that those who try to defile its fair name through abuse and vituperation surely will never succeed in doing it any harm. . . . (Their opposition) resembles that of a man who tries vainly to spit on the sun."[95]

Incurring the wrath of a gaoler, he was brutally flogged in the prison yard. He bore this punishment with a calm which astonished the friends imprisoned with him. When his ordeal was ended, one of them rushed to dress his wounds and extend his sympathy. Mullá Riḍá exclaimed to the friend:

> "Do you really think I am hurt? At the time of flogging I . . . never felt the slightest pain. I was in the presence of Bahá'u'lláh, talking to him."[96]

* * *

Mullá Ṣádiq was ordered to be scourged with a thousand lashes by the cruel governor of the province of Fárs. An eye-witness to this savage punishment did not believe the mullá would survive even 50 strokes as he was advanced in age and frail in body. Each stroke of the lash was fiercely applied, yet Mullá Ṣádiq remained serene throughout his ordeal. He was even seen with his hand before his mouth, concealing a smile. Later asked by this same witness why he had covered his mouth with his hand, he commented that the first strokes were very painful but to the remainder he had become indifferent:

> "I was wondering whether the strokes that followed were being actually applied to my own body. A feeling of joyous exultation had invaded my soul. I was trying to repress my feelings and to restrain my laughter. I can now realize how the almighty Deliverer is able . . . to turn pain into ease, and sorrow into gladness."[97]

* * *

In 1891 Ibn-i-Abhar was imprisoned for some four years. During these years he was brutally treated and tortured. He was cruelly flogged on the soles of his feet and pitilessly malnourished. Around his neck was placed the same chains as the Blessed Beauty had borne. When his loved ones despaired of his suffering, he wrote in very small characters on wrappers:

> "Would it be fitting for He who is the Ruler of all the nations and the Lord of all creation to accept tribulations in order that mankind might be freed from the fetters of prejudice, liberated from attachments to this mortal world and disentangled from animalistic evil passions, while this insignificant being, who considers himself as one of His servants, be exempt from similar sufferings?"[98]

When a photograph of Ibn-i-Abhar in chains reached 'Abdu'l-Bahá, He wrote:

> "By chance I came across thy photograph. As I beheld thy person standing poised and in the utmost dignity with chains around thy neck, I was so affected that all sorrow was turned into joy and radiance, and I praised God that the world's Greatest Luminary hath nurtured and trained such servants who, while tied in chains and under the threat of the sword, shine forth in the utmost exultation and rapture."[99]

# # #

Distinction

> ***I desire distinction for you . . . In the love of God you must become distinguished from all else. You must become distinguished for loving humanity, for unity and accord, for love and justice. In brief, you must become distinguished in all the virtues of the human world – for faithfulness and sincerity, for justice and fidelity, for firmness and steadfastness, for philanthropic deeds and service to the human world, for love toward every human being, for unity and accord with all people, for removing prejudices and promoting international peace. Finally, you must become distinguished for heavenly illumination and for acquiring the bestowals of God. I desire this distinction for you.***[100]

Asked why his father, Valíyu'lláh Varqá, was named the most distinguished Hand of the Cause, his son Dr 'Alí Muḥammad Varqá replied to the writer: 'Because Shoghi Effendi recognized in him this capacity, devotion and sincerity. From him there was a feeling of nothingness. He devoted his life, mind and health to the Faith. The Faith for him was above all.'[101]

Later in a letter dated 2 January 2003, Dr Varqá wrote the author:

> "Concerning your question about my memories of my beloved father's visits to various countries, I am sorry to say that I did not accompany him on his trips. In fact following my appointment at the Tabriz University, I was very busy with work, which was during the time that my father undertook to travel and visit the Bahá'í communities around the world.
>
> When he was appointed as a Hand of the Cause of God, I was not able to be with him, and my mother told me that this appointment unfolded for him a new horizon of service to our beloved Faith. Upon my transfer to the University of Tehran, I found him entirely occupied with the matters of the Faith, and he subsequently travelled extensively, and attended all four Intercontinental Conferences in 1953. Following the visits of the friends in Paris, Germany and Turkey, which was crowned by the visit of the Beloved Guardian in Haifa, he fell ill and travelled to Germany for

treatment in 1955, so I was deprived of spending much time with him during this period.

Among his outstanding qualities, which many of the friends and I witnessed, were his total dedication to the Faith, his extreme humility, his kindness, and the courtesy, respect and cordiality with which he treated everyone he met without exception. He influenced audiences during meetings and talks on his trips. I have heard from friends about his travel experience in the presence of the Blessed Master in 1912 and His historic trip to the West."[102]

* * *

Shoghi Effendi in a letter to the Bahá'í community of Australia wrote:

"Mr (Siegfried) Schopflocher . . . is truly one of the most distinguished believers in the West. He has a deep knowledge of the Cause, and specially of the Administration, and has contributed a unique share towards its establishment and consolidation in the States. For many years a member of the American N.S.A., he revealed such great qualities of heart and mind as very few of his fellow-members were able to manifest."[103]

* * *

Amatu'l-Bahá Rúḥíyyih Khánum laid the cornerstones of the Bahá'í Houses of Worship in Kampala (1958), Panama (1967), New Delhi (1977) and Samoa (1979), and represented the Bahá'í World Centre at the dedication ceremonies of the Houses of Worship in Wilmette (1953), Kampala (1961), Sydney (1961), Frankfurt (1964), Panama (1972), Samoa (1984) and New Delhi (1986).[104] Her frequent travelling companion, Violette Nakhjavání wrote:

"Standing on platforms on behalf of the Sacred Institution she served, in the course of Bahá'í Conventions at Riḍván, at youth conferences and Native gatherings, at inaugurations of Bahá'í Temples and other great historical events to which the Bahá'ís had streamed from all the quarters of the globe, she was erect and regal and forever memorable, the essence of dignity and beauty."[105]

* * *

John Esslemont was fluent in Esperanto, French, Spanish, German and of course English. He later learned Persian and Arabic. He graduated from Aberdeen University, honourable distinctions, with Bachelor degrees in Medicine and Surgery, having won a medal in clinical surgery. He was the first winner of the Phillips Research Scholarship as well. He was a member of the executive committee of the State Medical Service Association, which he helped set up – an association which produced a far-sighted document the recommendations from which became the foundation of the British National Health Service.[106]

* * *

William Sears was once a very public personality on radio and national television. His thirty-minute television program on CBS titled *In the Park* was very popular. He appeared twice on *The Ed Sullivan Show*, and was the only man to be listed in Edward R Murrow's *This I Believe.* He was invited because of his exemplary life.[107]

* * *

Martha Root was at a YMCA restaurant with a friend. Dorothy Baker was invited. Martha was dressed plainly and unassuming. Dorothy appeared in distinctive attire. As soon as Dorothy (who was normally quite talkative) caught sight of Martha, she perceived the latter's station and became humble and submissive. Dorothy's humility was an obvious attitude. [108]

* * *

John Henry Hyde Dunn was described as giving everyone '. . . a joyous welcome. He always had a sweet smile on his dear face. . . . (His) manner was at all times kind and gentle. He always had a good answer for enquirers.'[109]

* * *

Horace Holley wrote of Roy Wilhelm, who was treasurer of Bahá'í Temple Unity and later the National Spiritual Assembly of the United States and Canada:

> "As treasurer, the integrity of his character and the simple, direct humanness of his exposition of financial matters brought about a rapid development of the Bahá'í fund as an organic institution of the community."[110]

* * *

Muṣṭafáy-i-Rúmí was proficient in Arabic, Persian, Turkish, Gujarati, Bengali, Urdu and English. He was a scholar who knew the religious books of the Jews, Christians, Muslims and Buddhists. He translated many books into Burmese, including *The Hidden Words, The Kitáb-i-Íqán, Some Answered Questions* and *Bahá'í Prayers.*[111]

Honouring him, the Guardian wrote:

> "HIS RESTING PLACE SHOULD BE REGARDED FOREMOST SHRINE COMMUNITY BURMESE BELIEVERS."[112]

* * *

John Robarts was recognized for his competence and reliability with the result that he never had to apply for any job he ever held. The last position he was offered occurred when the family pioneered to Bechuanaland. After a three-week ocean journey, the ship docked at Cape Town. Such was his reputation that John was approached with two job offers before he had a chance to disembark the ship.[113]

* * *

Ugo Giachery, an aristocrat, once described Ḥasan Balyuzi as '. . . young, elegant, soft-spoken, gentle and graceful. His luxuriant black hair enhanced the handsomeness of his countenance; to me he appeared the embodiment of the perfect Persian aristocrat. His linguistic ability was truly superb . . .'[114] A young relative of Balyuzi who lived in the latter's household for 17 years said:

> "I was enraptured by his kindness, gentleness and understanding. As time passed, I came to realize more and more what a unique person he was. . . . He was like a many faceted precious jewel."[115]

* * *

Muḥammad Taqí Iṣfahání knew most of the general Tablets of Bahá'u'lláh and 'Abdu'l-Bahá by heart. As a member of the Publishing Committee, he assisted in translating into Arabic many works, including *The Kitáb-i-Íqán* and *Some Answered Questions.*[116]

# # #

Firmness In The Covenant

> ***The ordinances of God have been sent down from the heaven of His most august Revelation. All must diligently observe them. Man's supreme distinction, his real advancement, his final victory, have always depended, and will continue to depend, upon them. Whoso keepeth the commandments of God shall attain everlasting felicity.***[117]

Around the early 1990s, 'Alí Nakhjavání spoke of Dorothy Baker:

> "Dorothy was strong in the Covenant. Someone must have taught her very well about the Covenant. She was in love with every word of Shoghi Effendi. In front of an audience it was clear her motive was pure. She knew what she must do and her object was to help them see what they must do."[118]

* * *

Upon the passing of 'Abdu'l-Bahá, Louis Gregory had no difficulty transferring his allegiance to Shoghi Effendi. He continued his travels for the Faith, encouraging the believers with whom he met in an appreciation of the passing of the Master and an anticipation of the future. Louis manifested such firmness in his loyalty to the Heads and Institutions of the Faith as to discourage disunity and schism.[119]

* * *

> "The entire life of the Guardian was plagued and blighted by the ambition, the folly, the jealousy and hatred of individuals who rose up against the Cause and against him as Head of the Cause and who thought they could either subvert the Faith entirely or discredit its Guardian and set themselves up as leaders of a rival faction and win the body of believers over to their own interpretation of the Teachings and the way in which they believed the Cause of God should be run. No one ever succeeded in doing these things, but a series of disaffected individuals never ceased to try."[120]

> "It is difficult for those who have neither experienced what this disease (Covenant-breaking) is, nor devoted any consideration to the subject, to grasp the reality of the power for destruction it possesses. . . . The weakness of the human

heart, which so often attaches itself to an unworthy object, the weakness of the human mind, prone to conceit and self-assurance in personal opinions, involve people in a welter of emotions that blind their judgement and lead them far astray."[121] – Rúḥíyyih Khánum

* * *

Now some of the mischief-makers, with many stratagems, are seeking leadership, and in order to reach this position they instil doubts among the friends that they may cause differences, and that these differences may result in their drawing a party to themselves. But the friends of God must be awake and must know that the scattering of these doubts hath as its motive personal desires and the achievement of leadership. [122]

At a Bahá'í deepening session in California, William Sears told his audience that the Covenant is unique in religious history and a great protection to the Faith. Those who attack the Faith commit an unpardonable sin, endangering the foundation of mankind's future peace and security as well as the spiritual destiny of the antagonist. Providing an illustration of a spy who has tried to betray his own country, Mr Sears pointed out that the punishment for such treason is severe. So where betrayal is directed by a Covenant-breaker determined to undermine the faith of a believer and the Religion of God, the Bahá'ís must act to shun him or her as if that person had the bubonic plague.

Unfortunately lack of understanding of the true nature and significance of Covenant-breaking particularly among believers new to the Faith leaves them vulnerable to this danger. The warm-hearted, loving and hospitable nature of fledgling believers coupled with inexperience in the Faith means they can easily be misled by those who have broken the Covenant.

Mr Sears gave an example. Once in Europe, a stranger approached him and in an overly solicitous manner praised the greatness of the Cause and the beloved Guardian. Smiling he added that it was a pity the Universal House of Justice doesn't have the presence of the beloved Guardian so that the Bahá'ís can be assured of infallibility.

Now suppose, continued Mr Sears, that a new believer does not understand that infallibility of the Supreme Body on all things not recorded in the Book was given them by Bahá'u'lláh and does not depend on the presence of the Guardian? Covenant-breakers like to manipulate our teachings in order to cause doubts. Where a believer understands the Covenant and teachings, a Covenant-breaker has no chance.[123]

* * *

When Isobel Locke (Sabri) was a new Bahá'í in her last year of college, she encountered literature by Covenant-breakers in the school library. As the author of one such book lived nearby, she decided to meet this person and attempt to correct his views. Leroy Ioas learned of Isobel's intention and telephoned her to stay put so he could meet with her. Driving some 30 miles for the meeting, Leroy explained to her the Covenant of God and the importance of shunning Covenant-breakers. Covenant-breaking is a disease like leprosy. Isobel was impressed that a man in Leroy's position would leave work to see a university student, and realized that Leroy considered the matter of Covenant-breaking quite seriously.[124]

Leroy would have well understood this warning from 'Abdu'l-Bahá:

> "Thou hadst asked some questions; that why the blessed and spiritual souls, who are firm and steadfast, shun the company of degenerate persons. This is because, that just as bodily diseases . . . are contagious, likewise the spiritual diseases are also infectious. If a consumptive should associate with a thousand safe and healthy persons, the safety and health of these thousand persons would not affect the consumptive and would not cure him of his consumption. But when this consumptive associates with those thousand souls, in a short time the disease of consumption will infect a number of those healthy persons. This is a clear and self-evident question."[125]

* * *

At the close of the 1958 Intercontinental Conference in Chicago, John Robarts, in addressing that august gathering, recalled something Rúḥíyyih Khánum had told the Hands at Bahjí:

> "I think of the closing moments of the Bahjí Conference in November 1957 when twenty-six of us met there for that week to deliberate on the future of the Cause after the passing of our beloved Shoghi Effendi. We had seven days during which we consulted and prayed and supplicated to God to guide us in every step we took.

Finally, when all the decisions were made – and they were all made unanimously and in the greatest spirit of love – our conference came to a close. And, as it did, our dearly beloved Amatu'l-Bahá Rúḥíyyih Khánum said she would like to tell us just one thing:

> 'You know, when I first married Shoghi Effendi and came to live in this blessed spot, I felt that being here, being under the shade of this great tree, that the destiny of my soul would be safe and secure for all time. But, one day, Shoghi Effendi said to me: 'The destiny of your soul lies in the palm of your own hands.'

Rúḥíyyih Khánum told us that that rather shattered her illusions. But as she thought about it, she realized that it must be so – that the destiny of every soul must depend upon the service and devotion of each person to the Cause of God. So she then turned to us and said:

> 'You who are the Hands of the Cause must also remember that the destiny of your soul depends upon your service and your dedication to the service of the Cause. The station of a Hand is not in itself any guarantee of your own future.' [126]

* * *

Should any, within or without the company of the Hands of the Cause of God disobey and seek division, the wrath of God and His vengeance will be upon him . . .[127]

Charles Mason Remey declared his belief in Bahá'u'lláh in Paris, France on the last day of the 19th century through May Bolles (later Maxwell). He described his conversion as *the highest ecstacy.*[128] Returning homeward to Washington DC in 1903, he was soon in the forefront of Bahá'í teaching. His efforts to encourage the publication of a national newsletter in the years when the believers were struggling to build the Wilmette House of Worship may have exerted some influence on the creation of *Star of the West*. Remey personally published pamphlets on the Faith and in coming years produced several books, a compilation on the Covenant, a 56-volume set of his personal archives: *Bahá'í Reminiscences, Diary, Letters and Other Documents* and a 119-volume set called *Reminiscences and Letters.*

Following his visit in 1908 to the 'Ishqábád Temple, Remey wrote the most complete description in English of that magnificent edifice.[129] Inspired by his visit to Persia the same year, he asked the Chicago House of Spirituality whether two American Bahá'í women could travel there. He felt that they should be physicians, nurses and teachers. The result was that Dr Susan Moody settled there for many years where she rendered her historic services.

Remey was elected to the Executive Board of Bahá'í Temple Unity in 1909. The Board oversaw the work of the Wilmette Temple and acted as a national administrative institution for the publication of Bahá'í literature, the activities of teaching across the continent and the encouragement of isolated believers. An architect, Mason Remey would later play a part in the approval and some modification of Louis Bourgeois's Temple design. He would also design the memorial to Martha Root and the Temples in Australia, Africa and Mt Carmel (yet to be built).

Mason Remey carried on a correspondence with, and attained the presence of, the Master many times. 'Abdu'l-Bahá sent him the well-known eulogy on Thomas Breakwell. He outlined and explained for His young disciple the seven qualifications of the divinely enlightened soul: Knowledge, Faith, Steadfastness, Truthfulness, Uprightness, Fidelity and Humility.[130] Addressing Remey as 'O thou who art firm in the Covenant,'[131] He charged him to travel in the United States and Hawaii and call the friends to firmness in the Covenant. By 1918 Remey was so recognized for his position on the Covenant that he was appointed to a 'Committee of Investigation' to investigate Covenant-breaking.

In 1951 Shoghi Effendi appointed Mason Remey President of the newly constituted International Bahá'í Council (IBC), and later that year a Hand of the Cause of God. As an officer of the IBC, he helped forge links with government officials by calling on dignitaries. As a Hand of the Cause, he represented the Guardian in 1953 at the Intercontinental Conference in New Delhi and attended the conferences in Kampala, Wilmette and Stockholm. In March 1958 he attended the Intercontinental Conference in Sydney as the Guardian's representative where he presented the message from the Hands. Two months later he was present at the conference in Wilmette.

During the lifetime of the Guardian, the rank and file of believers expected that Shoghi Effendi would eventually clarify the question of his successor. This expectation was based on the *Will and Testament of 'Abdu'l-Bahá*:

> "He is the expounder of the words of God and after him will succeed the first--born of his lineal descendents. . . ."[132]

> "It is incumbent upon the guardian of the Cause of God to appoint in his own life-time him that shall become his successor, that differences may not arise after his passing. He that is appointed must manifest in himself detachment from all worldly things, must be the essence of purity, must show in himself the fear of God, knowledge, wisdom and learning. Thus, should the first-born of the guardian of the Cause of God not manifest in himself the truth of the words: 'The child is the secret essence of its sire', that is, should he not inherit of the spiritual within him (the guardian of the Cause of God) and his glorious lineage not be matched with a goodly character, then must he (the guardian of the Cause of God), choose another branch to succeed him."[133]

When Shoghi Effendi unexpectedly passed away on 4 November 1957, the Hands of the Cause were soon plunged into an abyss of despair upon discovering that the beloved Guardian had not appointed a successor. On 25 November 1957 they issued a Unanimous Proclamation stating that the Guardian had named no heir. In their Proclamation to the Bahá'ís of East and West of the same date, they declared: 'The Aghsán (branches) one and all are either dead or have been declared violators of the Covenant by the Guardian for their faithlessness to the Master's Will and Testament and their hostility to him named first Guardian in that sacred document.'[134] Thus Shoghi Effendi could not have appointed one to follow him. Mason Remey was a signatory to both proclamations.

Within a year of his signing those proclamations, Mason Remey was agitating for the appointment of a second Guardian. When his colleagues refused to comply, he called them violators at their 1958 Conclave. Recalling that Mason was known for his position on firmness in the Covenant from the earliest decades of the Faith in America, he must have read and pondered the *Will and Testament of 'Abdu'l-Bahá* following the Master's passing. There, 'Abdu'l-Bahá writes that the Hands must approve the choice of the Guardian's chosen successor:

> "The Hands of the Cause of God must elect from their own number nine persons. . . . The election of these nine must be carried either unanimously or by majority from the company of the Hands of the Cause of God and these, whether unanimously or by a majority vote, must give their assent to the choice of the one whom the guardian of the Cause of God hath chosen as his successor."[135]

This requirement of nine Hands in their role as Custodians voting their approval of a successor was divine protection vouchsafed by the Master because it validated their rejection of Mason's claim. Later in a letter dated 6 October 1963, the Supreme Body resolved once and for all the question of succession:

> "After prayerful and careful study of the Holy Texts bearing upon the question of the appointment of the successor to Shoghi Effendi as Guardian of the Cause of God, and after prolonged consultation which included consideration of the views of the Hands of the Cause of God residing in the Holy Land, the Universal House of Justice finds that there is no way to appoint or to legislate to make it possible to appoint a second Guardian to succeed Shoghi Effendi."[136]

Six years later, the Universal House of Justice further elucidated the issue of future Guardians. They wrote: 'Future Guardians are clearly envisaged and referred to in the Writings, but there is nowhere any promise or guarantee that the line of Guardians would endure forever; on the contrary there are clear indications that the line could be broken. . . . One of the most striking passages which envisage the possibility of such a break in the line of Guardians is in the Kitáb-i-Aqdas itself:

> "The endowments dedicated to charity revert to God, the Revealer of Signs. No one has the right to lay hold on them without leave from the Dawning-Place of Revelation. After Him the decision rests with the Aghsán (Branches), and after them with the House of Justice - should it be established in the world by then - so that they may use these endowments for the benefit of the Sites exalted in this Cause, and for that which they have been commanded by God, the Almighty, the All-Powerful. Otherwise the endowments should be referred to the people of Bahá, who speak not without His leave and who pass no judgement but in accordance with that which God has ordained in this Tablet, they who are the champions of victory betwixt heaven and earth, so that they may spend them on that which has been decreed in the Holy Book by God, the Mighty, the Bountiful."'[137]

> "The passing of Shoghi Effendi in 1957 precipitated the very situation provided for in this passage, in that the line of Aghsán ended before the House of Justice had been elected."[138]

Adib Ṭaherzadeh after considering this theme writes:

> "When Shoghi Effendi passed away, there was no House of Justice. So it can be seen that the above passage in the Kitáb-i-Aqdas was prophetic, in that a period of more than five years separated the passing of Shoghi Effendi from the establishment of the Universal House of Justice, and the Hands of the Cause during this period – 'the people of Bahá who speak not without His leave' – fulfilled the last provision stated in the above text. . . . The statement, 'The people of Bahá who speak not without His leave' is precisely applicable to the Hands of the Cause, because during the period of custodianship the Hands of the Cause faithfully carried out the instructions of the Guardian. They did not introduce any innovations in the Faith, nor did they express their own opinions or exert undue influence on the future development of the Bahá'í community throughout the world."[139]

Much loved by 'Abdu'l-Bahá, distinguished for his long years of service in the Cause and a close friend of Hands of the Cause Rúḥíyyih Khánum and Amelia Collins, Mason's '. . . extraordinary and sudden display of unexpected pride and conceit . . .'[140] was at first regarded by his fellow Hands as a *profound emotional disturbance*.[141] He was, after all, 84 years of age and would surely soon recover. And so the Hands remonstrated, admonished and then warned him.

In April 1960 Remey issued a proclamation in which he claimed for himself the rank of second Guardian. His claim to the Guardianship was that his appointment by the Guardian to the Presidency of the nominated IBC (1951) meant that he would automatically succeed to both the Presidency of the elected IBC (1961) and Chairmanship of the Universal House of Justice (1963) when both of these latter institutions came into existence. The Guardian was in effect naming Mason his heir. 'Abdu'l-Bahá had written that '. . . the guardian of the Cause of God is its (Universal House of Justice) sacred head and the distinguished member for life of that body.'[142]

In rapid succession Mason Remey sent out documents entitled "The Question of the Guardianship" and his first "Encyclical" to the Bahá'í world. In this "Encyclical" he classified '. . . all the Hands as violators, call(ed) upon the believers to abandon their activities in support of the plans announced by the Hands for the remainder of the beloved Guardian's Crusade, to withdraw their financial support of these activities, and direct(ed) them to turn to him alone for guidance and instructions.'[143] He was circulating these documents when the Hands, realizing that his campaign was both persistent and well thought out, announced their decision to expel him on 26 July 1960.

> ". . . the Will (Will and Testament) gives the Hands the authority to expel those who 'oppose and protest' against the Guardian and, by implication, those who 'disobey' him and 'seek division'. The Hands of the Cause concluded that the very advancing of a claim to the Guardianship in conflict with the spirit and letter of the terms of the Will was a repudiation of the terms of a sacred document, the very charter on which the institution of the Guardianship rested."[144]

By December, 1966, Remey had announced in a general letter:

> "The first Guardian (Shoghi Effendi) of the Faith so construed the Master 'Abdu'l-Bahá's Will and Testament that he formed his Administration upon the Bábí Faith and not upon the Bahá'í Faith. This mistake has caused so much confusion and misunderstanding and trouble that the only thing for the second Guardian (Remey) to do, to set matters aright, is to discard all which Shoghi Effendi did and to institute a New Faith which shall be the Orthodox Faith of Bahá'u'lláh under the Holy Name of ABHA in order to carry out the conditions that will lead to the establishment of the TRUE Bahá'í Faith (of Bahá'u'lláh) which Faith has not yet been established in the world."[145]

Why should a man so distinguished and honoured by 'Abdu'l-Bahá and Shoghi Effendi rise up against the Cause of God? According to Shoghi Effendi, the personal failings, which in varying degrees afflict and influence persons to break the Covenant, are 'blind hatred, unbounded presumption, incredible folly, abject perfidy, (and) vaulting ambition.'[146] Elsewhere Shoghi Effendi expatiates on this theme:

> "Do you think it is the teachers who make converts and change human hearts? No, surely not. They are only pure souls who take the first steps and then let the spirit of Bahá'u'lláh move and make use of them. If any one of them should even for a second think or consider his achievements as due to his own capacities, his work is ended and his fall starts. This is the fact why so many competent souls have,

after wonderful services, suddenly found themselves utterly impotent and perhaps thrown aside by the spirit of the Cause as useless souls. The criterion is the extent to which we are ready to have the will of God work through us."[147]

When Mason Remey passed away in extreme old age, the Universal House of Justice in few words recorded his legacy for the Bahá'í world:

> "CHARLES MASON REMEY WHOSE ARROGANT ATTEMPT USURP GUARDIANSHIP AFTER PASSING SHOGHI EFFENDI LED TO HIS EXPULSION FROM RANKS FAITHFUL HAS DIED IN FLORENCE ITALY IN HUNDREDTH YEAR OF HIS LIFE BURIED WITHOUT RELIGIOUS RITES ABANDONED BY ERSTWHILE FOLLOWERS. HISTORY THIS PITIABLE DEFECTION BY ONE WHO HAD RECEIVED GREAT HONOURS FROM BOTH MASTER AND GUARDIAN CONSTITUTES YET ANOTHER EXAMPLE FUTILITY ALL ATTEMPTS UNDERMINE IMPREGNABLE COVENANT CAUSE BAHÁ'U'LLÁH."[148]

According to the House of Justice, Covenant-breaking '. . . represents a spiritual contagion threatening the well-being of the individual believer because of its subtle appeal to the human ego. 'Abdu'l-Bahá called for the complete exclusion from the Bahá'í community of anyone found to be infected with the virus of Covenant-breaking, and urged all believers to shun any contact whatever with the persons involved.'[149] He emphasized: '. . . one of the greatest and most fundamental principles of the Cause of God is to shun and avoid entirely the Covenant-breakers . . . their breath is infectious, like unto poison.'[150] They '. . . will try to mislead the friends of the Divine Beauty through temptations which arouse the desires of self, and will cause them to follow the footsteps of Satan away from the right and glorious path . . . (Appearing) as sheep and in reality are ferocious wolves(,) they exercise every sort of oppression, endeavour(ing) to destroy the foundation of the Covenant – and claim to be Bahá'ís. They strike at the root of the Tree of the Covenant . . . Every hour they contrive new intrigues and fraud, and bring forth new calumny.'[151] Shoghi Effendi warned that they attempt '. . . to arrest the march of the Cause of God, misrepresent its purpose, disrupt its administrative institutions, dampen the zeal and sap the loyalty of its supporters.'[152]

'These do not doubt the validity of the Covenant,' the Master explained, 'but selfish motives have dragged them to this condition. It is not that they do not know what they do – they are perfectly aware and still they exhibit opposition.'[153] If unchecked Covenant-breaking would '. . . utterly destroy the Cause of God, exterminate His Law and render of no account all efforts exerted in the past.'[154] Because unity is the purpose of Bahá'u'lláh's Revelation, He warned: 'Were it not for the protecting power of the Covenant to guard the impregnable fort of the Cause of God, there would arise among the Bahá'ís, in one day, a thousand different sects as was the case in former ages.'[155]

* * *

Abu'l-Qásim Faizi informed the friends at a seminar in 1967 that 'Abdu'l-Bahá in His *Will and Testament* imposed four conditions on Shoghi Effendi for the appointment of a successor: 1) He said that the first born of Shoghi Effendi must be the Guardian. 2) If the first born does not qualify, Shoghi Effendi must appoint from another branch. 3) This branch must be in the lineage of the Guardian. 4) A majority of nine Hands of the Cause must approve his appointment.[156]

* * *

The Hands of the Cause in the Holy Land provided the following guidance concerning Covenant-breaking in a letter dated 15 October 1960 to all National Spiritual Assemblies:

> "The glorious Báb forbade association with Covenant-breakers. Bahá'u'lláh strictly forbade association with the Covenant-breakers, and even warned the friends against entering if possible a city where Covenant-breakers resided, as their poison polluted the entire area. 'Abdu'l-Bahá's teaching with regard to shunning and having no contact whatsoever with the Covenant-breakers is contained in hundreds of Tablets. The beloved Guardian forbade all association with Covenant-breakers and warned that their poison was so deadly, that is was not permissible to have even their literature in one's possession."[157]

* * *

In his diary, Dr Yúnis Khán wrote down something 'Abdu'l-Bahá said about the pernicious influence of Covenant-breakers in a community. 'Abdu'l-Bahá explained that . . .

> ". . . Covenant-breaking exerts an evil influence upon the conduct and morals of the public. The seed of sedition which the Covenant-breakers have sown among the people is capable of inclining the world of humanity towards ungodliness and

> iniquity. Therefore the believers must manifest righteousness and divine virtues in their lives, so as to remove the foul odour of this rebellion from the world. At the same time they will have to be vigilant and resourceful lest the Covenant-breakers influence public opinion because whenever their foul breath reaches a certain area, it impairs the spiritual nostrils of the people and obscures their vision. Consequently these people are unable to inhale the sweet savours of holiness or to behold the effulgence of the divine light . . . One of the important duties enjoined upon the loved ones of God is to make every endeavour to prevent the Covenant-breakers from infiltrating the Bahá'í community."[158]

* * *

The only prayers Dr Muhájir said on his own behalf was to remain steadfast in the Cause. His abnegation was genuine. He truly believed that all were in danger of failing spiritual tests, no matter their title or role in the Cause.[159]

# # #

Happiness

Rejoice in the gladness of thine heart, that thou mayest be worthy to meet Me and to mirror forth My beauty. [160]

At a seminar Mr Faizi told the attending friends that Bahá'u'lláh counsels his loved ones in *The Hidden Words* to rejoice with the joy of their own hearts. He then elaborated that this joy can only be found within ourselves. 'It is the miserable condition of the people of the world that they seek their happiness in material things. They think if they have more material luxuries, material comfort . . . they will feel happier (but) they never feel any happier.'[161] This happiness is within and must be brought out. Then will we find happiness.

Mr Faizi gave the story of one of the prisoners in the time of Bahá'u'lláh as told by 'Abdu'l-Bahá. Every day he would make tea for himself in a samovar. Although the conditions of the 'Akká prison were miserable, this believer was filled with happiness. He would praise the quality of the tea, the green trees in the desert, the air itself, and even his meagre possessions. His happiness made those who observed him happy.

Faizi told the story that when two of the Hands of the Cause appointed by Bahá'u'lláh were in prison for two years that they were fed dry pieces of bread soaked in castor oil and water. During this period two young people from noble families were also in the prison. Their food was brought to them and their needs were met from their homes. Still they were unhappy.

Meanwhile the two Hands (Ḥájí Amín and Ḥájí Á<u>kh</u>únd) were animated, cheering each other with stories, songs and chants. The two young persons were perplexed. Finally they asked: 'What is the matter with you? You are in chains. You are in a cellar. Your food is this, and you're always happy.' Ḥájí Amín replied: 'My dear, Bahá'u'lláh has trained us for this. You are not trained.'[162]

Mr Faizi went on to say that nowadays (1967) the Hands of the Cause are '. . . flying by plane, going to the best hotels, having such a beautiful congregation of friends, the most comfort, and believe me, there are Tablets and prayers that the travelling teachers should read every morning, and one of them says, "O God, I am forsaking all my comfort." And I never read this.'[163] (laughter)

***

Enoch Olinga used to ask the believers if they are happy. He told the friends that they should be happy because they have recognized Bahá'u'lláh as the Lord of this Day. In reality very few people are happy; only those who know and love God for today can be happy. Enoch then said that a higher station than happiness is joyfulness. To be joyful one must become familiar with the will of God and then obey His Law. The twin inseparable duties of man - recognition and obedience - are what bring happiness and joy.[164]

* * *

A SONG OF THE DAWN

O God, O God, the dawn of joy is broken!
The flood gates of light are open,
and joy descends in torrents on the earth.
The frosts of life melt in the sunshine of Thy joy.
Thy kiss of joy has touched all, sweetened all!
Thy joy triumphant conquers the heart of man,
and in the depth of our being joy awakes.
There is no room for sadness, for doubt.
Within, without, joy fills all space, all time, all thought.
The prophet's voice, the lover's heart,
proclaim the victory of joy.
Far and wide, in every clime, in every land,
the soul of man wakens to join at last that triumph song of praise
which for long ages Truth unheard of men,
has sung to God in solitude.[165]

- George Townshend

* * *

May everyone point to you and ask, 'Why are these people so happy? I want you to be happy . . . to laugh, smile and rejoice in order that others may be made happy by you.[166]

Enoch Olinga possessed the endearing quality of laughter that cheered his fellow Hands during the otherwise serious drama unfolding at the World Centre during their annual Conclaves. His laugh was joyous and contagious. The other Hands would save up funny stories to tell him at the Conclaves. Enoch would chuckle and then convulse with laughter, thus affecting and lightening everyone's hearts.[167]

Audrey Robarts recalled:

> ". . . there were times when John (Robarts) and Enoch were together (at the Conclaves), and they were absolutely hopeless. Enoch was one who when something tickled him he literally rolled and rolled on the floor. He was such fun. He came to stay with us when we were living in southern Rhodesia. And what a joy. And we also went to stay with him in Nairobi with Elizabeth and the family who as you know were the ones who lost their lives later."[168]

* * *

A new Auxiliary Board Member at a banquet found herself seated between two Hands of the Cause: William Sears to her left and John Robarts to her right. She was quite nervous to find herself thus situated and so excitedly whispered to John that she was afraid she would spill her dinner. Mr Robarts spontaneously replied: 'Spill to the left!'[169]

* * *

Louis Gregory possessed a charming sense of humour. He and his wife Louise who formed at 'Abdu'l-Bahá's request the first marriage between a black and white Bahá'í encountered many racial obstacles over the years. They often could neither travel nor live together. Louis who had infinite patience said of those years that his friends were *none too many.*[170] Once he spoke of their years of enforced separation as they went their own ways in service to the Cause that they would find eternal reunion in the worlds of God. He said 'We have had but one spirit, one purpose and one purse.'[171]

* * *

William Sears was widely known for his humour. In its eulogy to him, the Universal House of Justice referred to this quality as 'DISARMING'[172], which means that in tense situations he could *disarm* the opposition. To better appreciate something of the flavour of his humour, the following passage relating to his childhood from *God Loves Laughter* will suffice:

> "As I went upstairs to bed I noticed that the new linoleum had not been put down. It was still rolled up against the wall in the living-room. I had the big hollow cardboard tube in which it had come; I kept it in my room and used it for my experiments in summoning spirits. I'd been using it to frighten Ella (his sister). One day I took off the warm-air

ventilator which connected our two rooms. I placed the long tube under my bed and pushed it through the opening until it was under Ella's bed. Then when she would say her prayers I would talk to her in an eerie, far-off voice. She never knew where the voices were coming from.

That very night I crawled under the bed and waited for Ella to go into her room. When she kneeled down to say her prayers I called softly through the long tube in a high sing-song voice: 'Ella Sears! Ella Sears! Can you hear me?' She could. She stopped dead in the middle of her prayers. There was a long silence. Ella started to pray again, uncertainly, weaker.

'Ella Sears!' She stopped. 'Can you hear me?' Her voice was a timid squeak. 'Yeess.' 'I'm watching you! My eyeballs are looking through the ceiling. From heaven. Are you a good girl?' She sounded as though she were starting to cry. 'I – I don't know.' 'Otherwise I'm coming down to get you.'

That was too much for Ella. If anyone was coming she didn't want to be there. She straightened up, shot out of the room and rushed down the stairs. Father and Mother were still arguing . . . when Ella zoomed out on to the kitchen floor, shrieking: 'God hollered down the wall! God hollered down the wall!'

. . . A few days later, having nothing to do, I tried another experiment with my spirit-summoning tube. . . . I heard Ella giggling at her book in the next room. Why should she be so happy, I asked myself, and set about remedying this injustice right away. I crawled under the bed, put my head up the long tube, and called to her.

'Ella Sears!' I intoned mournfully. Her giggling stopped. 'The end has come,' I warned her. 'This is St. Paul coming for you.' Ella didn't answer, so I added a nice touch: 'Ella Gertrude Helen Sears! Your time is up! Prepare for the journey!'

Then Ella Sears answered me with a deep man's voice. 'Ella Sears is not here. This is her father, St. Peter.' Father! . . . Quickly I hollered up the tube, 'I'll never appear to you again, Ella Sears. I'm going back to heaven – farewell!' 'Oh, no, you don't!' Father called out. 'You appear in here at the double before I come in there and get you by the wings.'

I sighed, crawled out of the tube, and slowly went in to appear at the judgement seat before St. Peter."[173]

* * *

One day when 'Abdu'l-Bahá was meeting the friends in the Pilgrim House, He appeared very sad and withdrawn. Naturally the friends were affected and wondered what they could do to bring Him happiness. Usually there was a core of three or four believers who inevitably arose to the challenge.

'I don't know where the friends have learned the art of backbiting,' He abruptly said. Clearly He had heard this blameworthy act being committed in the Bahá'í community. One of those responsive friends from the core group got up and said: 'Beloved Master, from God Himself.' 'How can you say such a thing,' 'Abdu'l-Bahá admonished. 'I have proof my beloved Master,' the friend said. 'Adam ate one apple in paradise and God mentioned this act in the Old Testament, the New Testament and the Qur'án. Isn't this backbiting?' The beloved Master laughed and the matter was forgotten.[174]

* * *

Once, when Dr Muhájir was in the Philippines, he needed to travel to a particularly difficult country. As Mr Samandarí was at the time visiting, Raḥmat approached him and said: 'Samandaríján, today I have received an invitation to go to (country). As it is on your way I want to write to them that they will have the bounty of your visit instead of mine.' Mr Samandarí laughed and exclaimed: 'You young people think you can put something over on this old man? . . . I think they should again have the bounty of your visit this time.' The two Hands bargained and then Mr Samandarí out of his love for Raḥmat consented to go.[175]

* * *

One day, when he was walking in the village near his Rectory, George Townshend genially greeted one of his parishioners: 'Hello, Mrs . . ., you old sinner; how are you?' Unfortunately this woman could not grasp the joke, and was sure for some time that the Rector was *impugning her moral character.*[176]

* * *

Circa 1883, Prince Kámrán Mírzá, Governor of Ṭihrán and third son of Náṣiri'd-Dín Sháh, detained a number of Bahá'ís. Mullá Riḍá was among those gaoled. In those days it was the custom of the authorities, besides incarceration and execution, to hold debates with and seek miracles from the believers. One night the prince entertained the mullá with dinner in his apartments. After dinner he asked Mullá Riḍá whether he considered Bahá'u'lláh a Prophet or an Imám. The mullá replied by boldly praising and elaborating the lofty station of Bahá'u'lláh.

When the prisoners were brought before the authorities the following day for interrogation, the prince challenged them because in his view they were claiming Bahá'u'lláh to be the return of the Imám Ḥusayn whereas Mullá Riḍá had claimed Him to bear the Light of the Invisible Godhead.

Replying mildly to this accusation, Ḥájí Ákhúnd said: 'Your Royal Highness! Mullá Muḥammad-Riḍá is the Ṣúfí of the Bábís, waxing extravagant.'[177] Perhaps not to be outdone, Mullá Riḍá rejoined: 'Your Royal Highness! You listen to me. What I had said is the truth. These are the samovar-centred Bahá'ís: when the samovar is boiling and they are seated somewhere safe and secure, they all say the same as I have told you. That is the belief of all; but now, at the time of testing, they draw a veil over it all and follow the dictates of circumspection.'[178]

* * *

Leroy Ioas was at a meeting with believers in 1931 to meet Martha Root. Those attending were eating ice cream. Leroy whispered to a believer who had barely recovered from Martha's spiritual impact: 'The Master said that the Bahá'ís should all eat with one mouth.'[179]

* * *

When Ḥájí Amín arrived in Paris on his way to London to meet the Master, he found himself back in the French capital after crossing the Channel owing to his inability to speak any European language and undoubtedly due to confusion in travel. When he eventually found his way to the presence of the Master on 19 December 1913, 'Abdu'l-Bahá '. . . laughingly told him that no doubt the Ḥájí could not forsake the delights of Paris and had to hurry back there.'[180]

* * *

Martha was aboard the *Tatsuta Maru* from Hawaii to San Francisco where she would arrive 22 January 1931. As the crossing was anything but smooth, Martha struggled with her typewriter to get a letter off to the National Spiritual Assembly of the United States and Canada and the National Teaching Committee. As she typed her letter, she wrote: 'Please let me explain that this ship is doing far more than its 'daily dozen' exercises. The tywrter (sic) lurches from side to side and I am obliged to stop and hold the machine and hold on to my chair and I do this typing when I can hit the keys.'[181]

She was inclined to rely on guidance or inspiration in her services to the Faith. During her travels and at the request of the Guardian, she would share with Shoghi Effendi her teaching services. The Head of the Faith would reply that her news brought him *joy, encouragement, comfort,*[182] etc. When she asked for his approval to travel to Portugal, Shoghi Effendi replied: 'Do as Divine guidance inspires you.'[183]

Once in Belgrade, Martha was staying in the same hotel as Howard and Marzieh Carpenter (later Gail). They were several floors removed from each other. Howard was ill but Martha insisted they should all go meet the editor of a local paper. Acting as courier Marzieh took Martha's message up the several flights of stairs to Howard, who did not wish to leave the hotel. 'She (Martha) says it's the Will of God that you should go', Marzieh said to her husband who retorted: '(Y)ou run down and tell her I'm nearer to God up here than she is down there, and it isn't (the Will of God).'[184]

Some years later when Marzieh told Horace Holley why they would be living in Europe, Horace laughed and said: 'Reasons are never believable, Marzieh. Only excuses are plausible.'[185]

* * *

Once, late at night, the members of the American NSA were consulting. One of the exhausted friends apologized if he was not successful in expressing himself lucidly. Horace Holley retorted: 'I assure you, my dear boy, you have more capacity to give than we have to receive.'[186]

* * *

Clara Dunn was fun loving, possessing a sense of humour. She would say that age improves your "forgettery". She compared the Faith to measles; it was catching.[187]

* * *

As a speaker Dorothy Baker touched many hearts. She had a way of expressing herself which painted word pictures. Once when she mentioned 'girdles of immorality around South America,' her colleagues on the National Spiritual Assembly teased her about it. Her readiness to laugh at herself no doubt encouraged them to find other expressions to teach which she had coined.[188]

# # #

Humility

The ones in real authority are known by their humility and self-sacrifice and show no attitude of superiority over the friends. . . . Let the servant be known by his deeds, by his life! To be approved of God alone should be one's aim. [189]

At a Bahá'í gathering in America in 1974, William Sears introduced Abu'l-Qásim Faizi as one of the learned in Bahá. He spoke of how Mr Faizi as a pioneer in the Arabian Peninsula was unable to teach the Cause in that hostile country. But he would go from place to place, visiting the isolated friends, teaching the children and deepening the believers. He exemplified in his personal life those distinguishing characteristics of the Faith. The friends had such tender love for him. They would have his picture along with the Shrine on a wall in their home.

Mr Faizi collected stories during those years from the descendents of the Dawn-breakers, from children and grandchildren of martyrs, from anyone who had anything to share in the Cause of God. He collected them and now the world is reaping the bounty because he shared them to console the hearts of the friends throughout the world.

After Mr Sears had said so many wonderful things about Mr Faizi to that audience, Abu'l-Qásim Faizi stood up and the two beloved Hands embraced. At the podium Mr Faizi was weeping that anyone could say such things about him. In his humility he then said to that audience that anyone who serves the Cause of God is a Hand of the Cause.[190]

***

Shu'á 'Alá'í
by Shomais Afnan
October 2003

"I once asked him (Shu'á 'Alá'í) what was the station of a Hand of the Cause. His reply was (to) look at this hand, showing me his hand. He said: 'The hand has no power of distinction, has no power of reason, has absolutely nothing. Whatever the brain orders it to do, the hand does. The brain is the beloved Guardian, and we are his obedient servants. We have the responsibility to keep the hand in good working conditions spiritually as well as physically.' This made a great impression on me."[191]

***

Upon learning by cable of his appointment as a Hand of the Cause, Jalál Kházeh said: 'God knows the state I entered when I read this cable. On the one hand I saw my weakness and on the other hand I saw the arduousness of my future task, and the fire of hopelessness began to consume me.'[192] He sent a supplication to the Guardian: '. . . the future lies in the hands of this servant. I will either find a spot in the paradise of nearness to Him by attracting the bounty of the incomparable Protector, or I will be neglectful and careless and fall into the fire of remoteness from Him. Thus I ask you for your support and help so that the feeble back of this nonentity will be enabled to carry this heavy load and will come to a good end in this passing world.'[193] Seeing the future, Shoghi Effendi replied: 'REST ASSURED CONFIDENT GREAT SUCCESS. SHOGHI.'[194]

***

Louis Gregory once wrote a friend:

> "I know it is all the Will and Power of 'Abdu'l-Bahá which brought success. Every day I ask 'Abdu'l-Bahá not to let me forget that I am dust, and to acknowledge my absolute nonexistence in that Court."[195]

A humble and self-effacing man, Louis admitted that as a young man he was guilty of the sin of pride. He said:

> "We have to look at ourselves first and bring ourselves to account so that we will know when we are "standin' in need of prayer".[196]

***

On the final day of the Banání's pilgrimage in February 1952, the Guardian informed them of his announcement of Músá Banání's appointment as a Hand of the Cause. Mr Banání protested: 'I am not worthy. I cannot read or write. My tongue is not eloquent.' Shoghi Effendi replied: 'It is your arising that has conquered the continent.'[197]

***

Leroy Ioas came to an NSA meeting in Canada not long after his being appointed a Hand of the Cause. When the members gazed at him, he said with tears in his voice 'Oh, don't look at me like that! You know, we used to think that the Hands of the Cause were these glorious beings, before whom we would have to bow down, and now we find that they're just – they're just like I am!'[198] Leroy broke down and wept.

***

Enoch Olinga was in Uganda to fetch his wife and children now that he seemed permanently established in West Africa. Summoned to the Banání home in October 1957, he was handed a cable from the Guardian notifying him of his elevation to the rank of Hand of the Cause. When he read the message, Enoch prostrated himself on the floor in the African way of submission to one's *Liege*.[199]

* * *

When Shoghi Effendi bestowed on William Sutherland Maxwell the honour of being named a Hand of the Cause, he was *deeply touched* and said: 'I did not do it all alone; there were so many others who helped.'[200] Such was the humility of the man.

* * *

On Friday morning during the Fast of 1952, a cablegram arrived from the Guardian dated 28 February and addressed to Zikrullah Khadem: 'MOVED CONVEY GLAD TIDINGS YOUR ELEVATION RANK HAND CAUSE.'[201] Unbelieving and thinking the cable a ruse, Mr Khadem told no one except his wife and mother of his appointment until the official announcement. He could not possibly be a Hand of the Cause, he thought. He would spend the rest of his life praying fervently to become worthy of his appointment.

In an interview with Javidukht Khadem in 2000, the writer asked:

> "Many of us struggle to achieve some degree of humility in our lives. Within this struggle there is the desire to be recognized for what we achieve. But, in our quest for recognition, we want to be at the centre of attention or even manipulate circumstances in our favour. Mr Khadem was a very humble man and I only had the blessing of being in his presence once 30 years ago. But his humility was very evident. The friends were making a big fuss when he entered the meeting room, which embarrassed him. In your thinking how did Mr Khadem achieve his remarkable humility?"[202]

Mrs Khadem, who was delighted to speak of her husband even to my unworthy person, replied:

> "Because of his love for the Guardian, he thought there (was) nothing in the world at that time or even to his thinking in the larger human society. The Guardian was the representative of 'Abdu'l-Bahá and the representative

> of this Faith. And (he) has the authority to be the centre of the Covenant. And nothing can ever take the place of his words and his command. So he (Mr Khadem) wanted all the attention for the Guardian and not for himself. So you say he was embarrassed. Yes he was embarrassed. He thought that whatever there is of the Guardian who are they (the Hands). They are just the servant of the threshold of the Guardian. That was his feeling.
>
> He acquired this from the time he was 18 years old. The very first letter that he sent to the Guardian for a visit. The Guardian didn't immediately answer his letter. He (Mr Khadem) was crying and crying. Because I have his own letter that he sent to the Guardian. And I have his own letter that he sent to the father of the Guardian, beseeching him to please have mercy on him. . . . He was in such agony and crying that his (own) father thought that he would die. (For him) meeting the Guardian was out of this world. It revived him."[203]

For Mr Khadem, obeying and pleasing the Guardian was precious to him. Asked what sort of legacy her husband would convey to the friends about himself, Mrs Khadem said: 'If the Bahá'ís recognize the station of the Guardian.'[204]

When the Khadems came to the United States to live in 1960, she felt that there was neither an understanding of nor respect for the beloved Guardian. Little by little Mr Khadem helped the friends to appreciate and approach the high station of his utter humility toward the Sign of God on earth.

Mrs Khadem said that her husband educated her. 'I was trained by my husband. He affected me. I thought, even if I look at the Guardian straight, I'm not respectful.'[205] On a pilgrimage when she found herself with the Guardian, she felt: 'I'm in the presence of someone (who has) the world society in his hands. I (thought), but who am I? I'm just a drop.'[206]

* * *

In December 1951, Edna True telephoned Dorothy Baker from the National Bahá'í Centre and read her the cable from the Guardian announcing the first contingent of appointments of living Hands of the Cause. Dorothy was stunned when Edna read out her name; she thought Edna must have made a mistake. When the news was confirmed, Dorothy lost her voice for three days. Edna reported: 'All her modesty, all her humility, came to the top and she just couldn't conceive that this could be true.'[207]

* * *

When Shoghi Effendi informed Rúḥíyyih Khánum that he was naming her a Hand of the Cause to replace her father who had recently died, all her tears and begging him to change his mind had no effect. She wrote that Shoghi Effendi was *singularly uninfluenceable.*[208]

* * *

Raḥmatu'lláh Muhájir received a cable in Jakarta in October 1957 from the NSA of Iran relaying a telegram from the Guardian which read that he had been appointed a Hand of the Cause. He wife related:

> ". . . His first reaction was absolute perplexity. He shut himself in a room for hours and wept constantly. It took two days of continuous prayer before he could emerge, pale and wan, to cable his obedience to the beloved Guardian."[209]

* * *

Siegfried (Fred) Schopflocher learned of his appointment as a Hand of the Cause directly from the Guardian during one of his visits to Haifa. Rúḥíyyih Khánum was present at the Pilgrim House when Shoghi Effendi informed him. 'Freddie turned so white I thought he was going to faint!'[210] she later wrote.

* * *

Horace Holley was away on Bahá'í assignment when the news of his appointment as a Hand reached his wife Doris. Meeting him at the airport, she gave Horace the news. He responded by throwing up his hands and saying: 'No, not that.'[211]

* * *

In her 91st year, Corinne True was appointed a Hand of the Cause. Upon receiving the cable of her appointment, she was only concerned with how she could serve the Cause more effectively. She understood that she had not been elevated to the station of a figurehead but rather that service to the Cause in whatever capacity required hard work.[212]

* * *

In mid-March 1954, Shoghi Effendi had cablegrams sent to Paul Haney and the Bahá'í world announcing Paul's appointment as a Hand of the Cause. Astonished and doubting the veracity of the cable, he flew to Wilmette to confer with Corinne True and Horace Holley concerning the historic developments recently announced in the Guardian's message of 6 April 1954. Paul was *dazed* by the responsibility so unexpectedly handed him.[213]

* * *

Mother Dunn was *humbled to the dust* and taken by surprise upon being appointed a Hand of the Cause.[214]

* * *

Collis Featherstone was shocked when he was informed of his elevation to the rank of Hand of the Cause. Leaving his office he went to sit in his car to regain his composure. Afterward he telephoned his wife and then informed his business partner that he was taking the remainder of the day off owing to his having received some disturbing news.[215]

* * *

On 5 October 1957 – the morning of the launching of the first Sputnik – John Robarts received a cable addressed to him in Rhodesia: 'LOVING CONGRATULATIONS ELEVATION HAND CAUSE GOD.'[216]

John looked at the cable, saw the name Robarts and handed it to his wife. He thought she had been appointed a Hand of the Cause.

* * *

John Robarts once heard Músá Banání say that some years before he was appointed a Hand of the Cause the Guardian pointed to a stone and said: 'You know, God could activate that stone so it would rise up and teach the Cause if He wanted to.' Mr Banání pondered the Guardian's words for some years before he concluded: 'Now I know. I am that stone. God has raised me up to do a little something in the way of teaching His Cause.'[217] The Guardian wrote that Mr Banání was the *spiritual conqueror of Africa.*[218]

* * *

Nabíl-i-Akbar was famous through Persia as an outstanding man of learning. In a spoken chronicle he recalled how his attitude of superiority in about 1860 was changed to humility when he heard Bahá'u'lláh's profound explanations on a question. He related:

> "It was through my vain imagining that in the gatherings of the friends I always used to occupy the seat of honour,

assume the function of the speaker and would not give an opportunity to... anyone else to say anything. One afternoon, Bahá'u'lláh arranged a meeting in His house . . . Again, I occupied the seat of honour. Bahá'u'lláh sat in the midst of the friends and was serving tea with His own hands.

In the course of the meeting, a certain question was asked. Having satisfied myself that no one in the room was capable of tackling the problem, I began to speak. All the friends were attentively listening and were absolutely silent, except Bahá'u'lláh Who occasionally, while agreeing with my exposition, made a few comments on the subject. Gradually He took over and I became silent. His explanations were so profound and the ocean of His utterance surged with such a power that my whole being was overtaken with awe and fear. Spellbound by His words, I was plunged into a state of dazed bewilderment. After a few minutes of listening to His words – words of unparalleled wonder and majesty – I became dumbfounded. I could no longer hear His voice. Only by the movement of His lips did I know that He was still speaking. I felt deeply ashamed and troubled that I was occupying the seat of honour in that meeting. I waited impatiently until I saw that His lips were no longer moving when I knew that He had finished talking. Like a helpless bird which is freed from the claws of a mighty falcon I rose to my feet and went out. There three times I hit my head hard against the wall and rebuked myself for my spiritual blindness."[219]

Nabíl-i-Akbar attained such a station of servitude that he wandered homeless and in poverty as a result of his courageous teaching and subsequent persecutions. 'Abdu'l-Bahá called him 'A sign of guidance (and) an emblem of the fear of God (who became) the recipient of heavenly grace.'[220]

# # #

Love

In the world of existence there is indeed no greater power than the power of love. When the heart of man is aglow with the flame of love, he is ready to sacrifice all – even his life.[221]

O Thou! whence God's Beauty shineth,
I know Thee.
Would my being, my soul Thy ransom be,
I know Thee.
Shouldst Thou behind a hundred-thousand veils cover seek,
By God, O Thou, the Visage of God,
I know Thee.
Shouldst Thou a King choose,
or a Servant appear to be,
Apart – at the crest of each Station – apart,
I know Thee.[222]

'Alí-Muḥammad Varqá, the martyr

* * *

Amelia Collins was in possession of a treasure. She possessed a profound love for Shoghi Effendi. On her pilgrimage in 1923 when she first laid eyes on the divine countenance of the Guardian, she marvelled at his beautiful and expressive eyes which she felt were so full of eagerness and expectation. Being childless she adopted Shoghi Effendi in her heart and soul as her own son. '. . . In the world of faith and spirit (I) enthroned him on the throne of certitude,' she said, 'where he reigned as the sole sovereign of my soul, the ruler of my destiny and the fashioner of my life. In whatever direction he willed, I would go, with the utmost joy and assurance.'[223] Such was her devotion that she would often say that a lifetime of suffering was worth just one smile from the Guardian.

In succeeding years Milly rendered historic services to the Faith, including special missions entrusted her by the Head of the Faith. Because of her great love for and complete obedience to the Guardian, she became the recipient of many accolades from him. Expressing in letters to her his gratitude, admiration, affection, encouragement and love, Shoghi Effendi praised her steadfast service, self-sacrificing devotion, exemplary spirit, beneficent influence and unfailing solicitude.

In a cable dated 22 November 1946, Shoghi Effendi confidentially appointed her a Hand of the Cause and in 1947 informed her that she would be in '. . . the category of the Chosen Nine who (would be) associated directly and intimately with the cares and responsibilities of the Guardian of the Faith.'[224] In 1951 he announced her appointment as Vice-President of the newly-constituted International Bahá'í Council, precursor of the Universal House of Justice.

Amelia Collins came to occupy a very high station in the Faith of God through the light of her love. From the *Will and Testament of 'Abdu'l-Bahá* she memorized a sentence that the friends should make Shoghi Effendi happy. In the later years of her life, she said:

> "Whatever step I took in my life, any vote cast in the Assemblies, any trip taken, even any thought, I would first ask myself whether my vote, words, trip or thought would make him happy. When I was sure, then I would take action without fear."[225]

Of her Rúḥíyyih Khánum wrote:

> "So great and tender was her love for Shoghi Effendi . . . that she almost never wrote to him directly but addressed her letters to me in order to spare him the necessity of writing to her direct. Well she knew that some believers had, in their innocent egotism, amassed as many as fifty, sixty or more letters from that over-burdened pen! She was determined never to add her share to such a weight and her every thought was directed to sparing him, in any way she could, the slightest extra effort and to serving him in any way that could bring some happiness to his heart. So great was her concern in these matters that, although she lived in his house, when the time came for him to go out or come in she would return to her room so as not to oblige him to expend a moment of his overtaxed time and tired mind on greeting her and feeling he should stop to talk to her for a few minutes."[226]

One cannot imagine her reaction to the passing of her beloved Shoghi Effendi. She had returned to Haifa after spending several months in Arizona where the dry heat helped her arthritis. She had looked forward to welcoming him back from London only to receive news that she would never again behold his blessed countenance in this world. She left at once for London to lend her support to her beloved Rúḥíyyih Khánum. Herself ill, aged and prostrated with grief, she became the greatest comfort to the Guardian's widow.

Eight months later at the Intercontinental Bahá'í Conference in Frankfurt, she gave a marvellous talk about the Guardian. She spoke of his enthusiasm, his suffering, his qualities, his accomplishments, his guidance, his translations, his encouragement, and his vision. Revealing for that audience the majesty, custodianship and loving care of the recently-deceased Guardian, she brought him closer to the consciences of the participants in that Conference. She captured their hearts, and then called upon them as Shoghi Effendi's heirs to build a memorial to him through active participation in the World Crusade. She appealed:

> "Let us love him more now than ever before and through the power of our love attract his love to us, and bring his blessing on our labours. Let us not fail him, for he never failed us. Let us never forget him, for he never forgot us."[227]

Less than two and one half years later, Amelia Collins passed from this world in the arms of her beloved Rúḥíyyih Khánum.

* * *

Muḥammad Taqí Iṣfahání made many visits to the Holy Land where he attained the presence of 'Abdu'l-Bahá and received His blessings. He was very sincere in his devotion to the Centre of the Covenant. Upon the passing of the Master he became distressed and disoriented. He proceeded to Haifa where he shared in the grieving. When 'Abdu'l-Bahá's *Will and Testament* was read revealing the appointment of Shoghi Effendi as Guardian, the atmosphere of sadness was dispelled and Muḥammad Taqí Iṣfahání returned home to Egypt where his activities brought about the entry of many souls into the Faith.[228]

* * *

In January 1955, John Robarts together with his wife Audrey, son Patrick and daughter Nina, made a pilgrimage to the Holy Land where he met the Guardian. In reply years later to a question posed him by Douglas Martin as to the impression Shoghi Effendi made on him during pilgrimage, Mr Robarts replied: 'He made an impression on me that seized my heart. I loved him so much . . .'[229] Mr Martin commented: 'I often remember, John, your saying that to know Shoghi Effendi was to want to make him happy, to serve him in any way you could . . .'[230]

On another occasion John Robarts in speaking of the Guardian said: 'To meet with the Guardian was one of those joys one cannot describe. One felt the power of the Holy Spirit, the love, the power of the Guardian, of God.'[231] He believed that if the Bahá'ís prepared talks on the life of Bahá'u'lláh, their love for Him would increase and, consequently, they would be inspired and prepared to teach.[232]

* * *

"The Message
Bahá'u'lláh

O manifested Sun of Man
Thy sheen the reign of peace began.
Thine exile proved to man his home.
Thy shackles freed the souls to roam
The universe of God's great love
Directed by the Heavenly Dove.
The kings, their homage due to thee,
Enthroned, ethereal majesty,
Shall bring the treasures of the earth
Memorial to thy cycle's birth.
The sweetest carols angels sing
Proclaim the oneness of our King.
O deathless Flame of Beauty bright
Set fire our souls, bestow thy might!"[233]

-Louis Gregory (From *The Message*)

* * *

Abu'l-Qásim Faizi
by Shirley Macias
23 August 2002

"I met Mr Faizi for the first time in 1963 while pioneering in Honduras. As secretary of that National Spiritual Assembly, one of my duties was to greet visitors when they arrived at the airport in Tegucigalpa. One day in February, 1963, we received word that Mr Faizi would be visiting our community for a few days. When I greeted him at the airport, it was truly love at first sight. It was as if I had found a long-lost relative. I really cannot describe the feeling, except to say that being in his presence filled me with the utmost joy and happiness.

He spent several days with the Bahá'ís in Tegucigalpa, sharing with us wonderful and deeply moving stories as he showed us photographs from his "black notebook" of the early heroic believers and martyrs in Iran and Iraq. His next stop on his journey was to the neighbouring country of Guatemala. With sadness at his departure, the small contingent of Bahá'ís (we were only a small handful then) went to the airport to bid him farewell. While waiting for his plane to arrive, we sat on the terrace of the terminal, had some coffee and took photographs. Suddenly Mr Faizi became very concerned and said that he had misplaced his "black notebook". I immediately telephoned the hotel where he had stayed; they found the notebook and sent it to us by taxi. When they paged me to go to the front desk to retrieve it, he insisted on walking downstairs with me. As we were walking, he spoke about the beloved Guardian, Shoghi Effendi, and said that all of the Hands of the Cause whom the Guardian had appointed had so many talents and qualities, and that each of them had one quality of the Guardian. He then began to speak of them (there were then twenty-seven living Hands of the Cause), describing their qualities and attributes. Then he said, 'But I have no talent.' I looked at him with amazement and said, 'But, Mr Faizi, you have the greatest talent of them all; you have the talent of love.' He then looked at me and said, 'Yes, I guess I do.'

He wrote to me a few days later saying, 'I could get my black notebook, but what about my poor heart which is always hovering over all these places where our precious friends work for the beloved Faith? . . . There is nothing more in the world which possibly can make me happy except the little bit of chance of serving the friends in this very limited capacity that I have.' This was the beginning of a correspondence spanning some seventeen years. His letters were always a source of joy to me and sustained me through many tests and trials.

I saw Mr Faizi a few months later in Haifa. (I was privileged to attend the first International Convention as a delegate from Honduras to elect the Universal House of Justice.) One evening at the Pilgrim House, as the friends were sitting around, he walked toward me with an old torn string bag filled with many delightful gifts. He took them out of a string shopping sack, one by one, placing them in my hands.

In the bag was a box of Persian sweets from his mother (who lived in Iran), which he said the doctors had forbidden him to eat (he suffered from diabetes). Also included were some photographs of dancers and postcards from India containing paintings and verses from Persian poets, a lovely green silk scarf from Iran, a few handkerchiefs, and the most wonderful gift of all, four photographs of Shoghi Effendi as a child and young boy (later published in Rúḥíyyih Khánum's *The Priceless Pearl*). My arms were full and I was not able to carry all these precious gifts, so he said that I should take the sack to carry them in. I don't know why, but I asked him where the sack was from, and he said, 'Oh, I just picked it up at the Master's house.' Then I saw him again in London for the Centenary of the Declaration of Bahá'u'lláh. He was the last speaker at that historic World Congress. Among his words to the 6,000 Bahá'ís at Royal Albert Hall were these:

> 'A hundred years ago when Bahá'u'lláh was in Baghdád, one day He was pacing up and down in front of His House and rows of people were standing near Him. Some were Persian princes and some were from Arab noble families. Bahá'u'lláh asked, 'What is the news of the town? What is the news of the martyrs?' And one of the Persian princes said, 'How is it that when you are with your own people, you speak to them of such exalted subjects, but when you are with us, you only ask us of the news of the town and of the martyrs?' Bahá'u'lláh paced up and down and said, 'People who can hear my words are not yet created.' He again paced up and down and started to tell them something. One of the things He said at that time was this: He said, 'If there are pearls beneath seven seas, I will bring them out.' Who could ever realize in that hour what these words meant? But today we see with our eyes the fulfilment of these words. Bahá'u'lláh brought out pearls from seven seas, and brought jewels from beyond seven mountains and brought them all here, from the Pacific, the Atlantic, the mountains of Bolivia, all countries of the world. These are the pearls and jewels which Bahá'u'lláh desired to have.

> 'One of the greatest prophecies about the Manifestation of Bahá'u'lláh ever mentioned in the Qur'án is this. He said, 'On that day friends would be sitting on benches facing each other.' Here is the fulfilment of that great prophecy. All of you are sitting in absolute love and perfect harmony under the Tabernacle of Bahá'u'lláh on benches facing each other.'"²³⁴

* * *

Let each one of God's loved ones centre his attention on this: to be the Lord's mercy to man . . . ²³⁵

Jalál K͟házeh was meeting with a group of some 100 believers in Dallas, Texas. He had just finished speaking and he was surrounded by friends wanting to shake his hand, ask a question or just be near him. One of the African American friends was a new believer. Reluctant to join the group around the Hand of the Cause, she retreated to the back of the room for refreshments.

Through the encouragement of a veteran believer who offered to hold her hand, however, she timidly approached the crowd which by now had formed circles around Mr K͟házeh four rows deep. Doubting she had made the right decision, she suddenly found herself the focus of Mr K͟házeh's attention as he reached up and over those four rows and hugged her with a full and loving embrace.

> 'I love you more than the rest!' Mr K͟házeh said to her. 'But why me?' she responded in a tiny fearful voice, her eyes averted toward the floor. 'Because Bahá'u'lláh says you are the pupil of the eye.'²³⁶

At that moment the other believers in that room saw something magnificent they had not seen before. Truly 'Abdu'l-Bahá illumined the world on the importance of the black race when He said:

> "Bahá'u'lláh once compared the coloured people to the black pupil of the eye surrounded by the white. In this black pupil you see the reflection of that which is before it, and through it the light of the Spirit shines forth."²³⁷

* * *

Agnes Parsons was an American aristocrat who became a believer in her middle years. On her second pilgrimage to 'Akká in early 1920, 'Abdu'l-Bahá turned to her at the supper table one evening and charged her with arranging an amity convention between the coloured and white races in Washington DC. Although she had neither organized a major event nor been accustomed to associating with people outside her immediate social circle, she arose to the challenge in spite of herself.

A time when racial segregation was deeply engrained in the psyche of white Americans, Mrs Parsons was able to organize a committee on which she was a member and which in turn planned the convention. Held in the spring of 1921 and attended by about 2,000 people, the gathering garnered praise from 'Abdu'l-Bahá and became a pattern for future amity conventions.

Agnes Parsons' approach to racial amity was to avoid controversy; yet she managed to be controversial. In 1926 she was appointed by the National Spiritual Assembly to a National Bahá'í Committee on Racial Unity. At the outset she was upset by the committee's ambitions, and let her feelings be known of favouring a cautious approach. Her stance exasperated several fellow members, and one appealed to Horace Holley, the national secretary, for help.

Louis Gregory, who had been appointed the executive secretary of the committee, had long been unfailingly kind to Agnes. In the present circumstances he recognized her devotion coupled with her sense of timing in amity work. His loving attitude helped Mrs Parsons embrace the committee's wider horizons.[238]

***

Zikrullah Khadem, in recalling *The Beloved of All Hearts – Shoghi Effendi* at an annual conference of the Association of Bahá'í Studies in 1984, told the audience:

> "According to Bahá'u'lláh, nothing is sweeter than to be with the friends."[239]

***

Fred Schopflocher was in the habit of buying bunches of ties when visiting New York City. A member of the National Spiritual Assembly of the Bahá'ís of the United States and Canada, he would present his colleague John Robarts with a tie whenever a meeting went particularly well. Meanwhile John's mother-in-law always gave him a tie for his birthday and for Christmas.

Whenever the NSA meeting was held in Montreal, John stayed in the home of his mother-in-law where he would wear one of her ties. However, on his way to the NSA meeting, he would switch to a tie Fred had given him. John was careful in this matter because he understood the importance of showing *such small signs of love.*[240]

* * *

Dr 'Alí-Muḥammad Varqá was attending a conference at the Louhelen Bahá'í School in the late 1980s. A believer in attendance acting as program coordinator was waiting in the dining hall for her chance to approach the beloved Hand, who was encircled by admirers. As she distanced herself by tidying up, she wondered in observing him that he must be in need of rest. She wrote:

> "He was watching me after a bit. I felt his love and appreciation across two rooms. I was awed by his understanding of my staying away. It wasn't imagining on my part. It was a powerful eye message from Dr Varqá."[241]

# # #

Loyalty

Their deeds must prove their fidelity, and their actions must show forth Divine light. [242]

At the Third Intercontinental Conference on 4 May 1958 at the 8th Street Theatre in Chicago, Illinois, the Guardian's special representative Dr Ugo Giachery gave the closing address following comments by Leroy Ioas, Mason Remey, Horace Holley and John Robarts. Unflinchingly loyal in all his prodigious services to his dearly-loved Guardian, Dr Giachery from an aching heart said:

> "To start something is very easy. But to end it is the most difficult one because it must end well. I wish this task had been spared to me because I have been under a terrific emotional strain for many many months. . . . (Six months ago) Shoghi Effendi disappeared. He (was) a unique figure in the history of mankind. There will never be one like him. There can't. He was the sign of God among men. . . . From the moment he made the great renunciation in 1921 when to his great dismay and surprise he discovered that he was going to be the first Guardian of the Faith, his life was that of the utmost devotion and service to the Faith. There was no repose for him. There was no holiday. There was work, work, work for the service of the friends; the friends throughout the world and to humanity as he was forging in his delicate hands, the still powerful hands, the instrument of the foundation of the World Order of Bahá'u'lláh.
>
> We say, how did he look, Shoghi Effendi, the friends often ask. Sorry there are no pictures to be seen of him. All the pictures are from his infancy or from his early days in school. He had a beauty in his face. Those of you who have had the privilege of seeing the pictures of the Báb and Bahá'u'lláh can combine the two pictures together. He had the great(ness) and delicacy of both of them. . . . Those of you who lived in Holy Land knew that his day started very early, at sunrise, sometimes before sunrise. And he worked uninterrupted up to the very end of the day and through the night, sometimes past midnight, always in the service of the Faith, of the friends, of humanity. His masterly translations will never be equalled no matter what scholar will come along. Never. His vision . . . was not belong to a human being. His vision

> was far beyond our vision . . . He saw into the future. He saw in the great future. That is why he warned us all the time. That is why he pointed out the perils that were around us. That is why he spurred and urged . . . He was pointing the way . . . to a spiritual salvation.
>
> His vision was one of a seer. He plotted, charted the way for every individual . . . so that they could follow the right course. That was Shoghi Effendi. We can only honour his memory by doing until our last breath what we have not yet done, what we are undertaking to do, what we feel we cannot accomplish. . . .
>
> Friends, I told you it was very difficult to close this meeting. I have had the privilege today for the last few moments to be featured as Shoghi Effendi's representative. I (hope) next time we meet together I'll be my old self again. Shoghi Effendi will be a bond between myself and you."[243]

* * *

During a 17 year period from 1943 to 1960, Ḥasan Balyuzi served on many national committees: 'Reviewing, *New World Order*, Literature (secretary), Archives (11 years), National Contacts and Public Relations, National Scripts, Summer School Management and Programme, Assembly Development, Persian, Consolidation, National Centenary (1953, chairman), Visual Aids, European and Asian Teaching (chairman for four years), Installation and Maintenance plus Reception Committees for the Ḥaẓíratu'l-Quds (1955-1956), and Ḥaẓíratu'l-Quds (1956-1957)'.[244]

During these years, he also served on the National Spiritual Assembly of the British Isles, regularly attended Summer Schools and in 1957 joined the ranks of the Hands of the Cause.

How he handled so many responsibilities was in part due to his subjecting himself to many sleepless nights at his desk. Asked why he was so hard on himself, Mr Balyuzi replied:

> ". . . Whenever I think of what our beloved Guardian is doing for us I am ashamed of how little we are doing in response and sleep escapes my eyes."[245]

* * *

John Ferraby
by Brigitte Ferraby Beales
18 August 2002

"Shoghi Effendi described John Ferraby as *the Horace Holley of the British Isles.* An efficient Bahá'í administrator, Mr Ferraby wanted to pioneer during the Ten Year Crusade. But the Guardian felt that his work as National Secretary was more important. While many believers went to virgin pioneer posts and won the accolade *Knight of Bahá'u'lláh*, the Guardian wrote of John Ferraby: 'He is giving a service no Knight of Bahá'u'lláh can give . . .'

Following his pilgrimage to the Holy Land in 1955 where Shoghi Effendi told him he should write for the Faith, John Ferraby worked on *All Things Made New* evenings, mornings and weekends after full days of work as National Secretary. He would often read long passages to his wife for her comments, who said that he '. . . worked as a man inspired.' This work went on for quite some time.

He was always keen that his daughter should do things according to the teachings. When she was quite small, he gave her a copy of *Pattern of Bahá'í Life*, underlining some passages for her to learn. She wrote of his loving training: 'Of course these passages I learned so young stay with me better than anything I have memorised as an adult so there was a wisdom in it. He also made sure that I could have Holy Days off school, so that the Faith would be recognised.

According to his wife Dorothy, he was frequently able to obtain the necessary visas during the Crusade for pioneers travelling to foreign countries. He was good at dealing with government officials. While John Ferraby could be very vocal concerning something he felt strongly about, he was perceived as reticent. During discussions he might say nothing for some time, only to introduce some thought which would put matters in a different light.

The beloved Guardian made wonderful comments in letters to John Ferraby, such as the following on 26 September 1957: 'May the Almighty, whose Cause you serve with exemplary devotion, perseverance and loyalty, reward you abundantly for your highly meritorious achievements, and graciously assist you to widen the scope of your activities, and win great victories in the days to come."[246]

* * *

Dorothy Ferraby wrote of her beloved husband:

> "John's (Ferraby) whole life as a Bahá'í was one of activity and intense devotion. From the moment of his declaration the Faith came absolutely first with him and nothing else mattered, and this was true until the end of his life, whatever his circumstances and condition."[247]

* * *

> ***(A principle) which the Guardian wishes the friends to always bear in mind and to conscientiously and faithfully follow (is that) of unqualified and whole-hearted loyalty to the revealed Word. The believers should be careful not to deviate, even a hair-breadth, from the Teachings. Their supreme consideration should be to safeguard the purity of the principles, tenets and laws of the Faith. It is only by this means that they can hope to maintain the organic unity of the Cause.***[248]

Following the untimely passing of the beloved Guardian on 4 November 1957, the bereaved Hands of the Cause maintained the unity of the Bahá'í world community. Watchful not to deviate from their conferred responsibilities of protection and propagation and from the Guardian's World Crusade goals, they guided the Bahá'ís through this uncertain time until the election of the Universal House of Justice on 21 April 1963. Mentioned in the *Kitáb-i-Aqdas* as '. . . the people of Bahá who speak not except by His leave and judge not save in accordance with what God hath decreed . . .'[249], they rallied the believers and institutions in their role as *Chief Stewards of Bahá'u'lláh's embryonic World Commonwealth.*[250]

While the historic acts accomplished by these noble souls do not reveal the struggles they underwent in unexpectedly being called upon with *neither premonition, warning nor advice* [251] to assume responsibility for the Cause of God, the Universal House of Justice placed their heroism into perspective in one of their messages:

"From the very outset of their custodianship of the Cause of God the Hands realized that since they had no certainty of Divine guidance such as is incontrovertibly assured to the Guardian and to the Universal House of Justice, their one safe course was to follow with undeviating firmness the instructions and policies of Shoghi Effendi. The entire history of religion shows no comparable record of such strict self-discipline, such absolute loyalty, and such complete self-abnegation by the leaders of a religion finding themselves suddenly deprived of their divinely inspired guide. The debt of gratitude which mankind for generations, nay, ages to come, owes to this handful of grief-stricken, steadfast, heroic souls is beyond estimation."[252]

* * *

"The greatest achievement of the Hands (during the Interregnum) is that they did not deviate a hair's breadth from the teachings and guidance of Shoghi Effendi. For more than five years they held the reins of the Cause in their hands - a period that may be regarded as the most critical stage in the history of the Faith of Bahá'u'lláh. From the day the Faith was born until the passing of Shoghi Effendi divine protection had been vouchsafed to the community. For 113 years, the infant Faith of Bahá'u'lláh had been nurtured by the infallible guidance of its Central Figures and its Guardian. Now it was entrusted to the care of a number of religious leaders, the Hands of the Cause, who did not have this promise of divine guidance.

It was a period fraught with dangers. In the same way that a newly-built airplane is subjected to a series of rigorous tests in order to be sure that it works properly, the Covenant of Bahá'u'lláh was severely tried during these six years and found to be absolutely impregnable. The custodianship of the Hands was itself a proof of the invincibility of the Covenant, in that, unlike the leaders of former religions who introduced many man-made practices into the teachings of their Prophets, the Hands of the Cause did not add even a single dot to the Cause, nor did they introduce any innovation into the workings of its institutions. They guided the Bahá'í community strictly in accordance with the holy text and the writings of the Guardian. Their responses to questions from National Spiritual Assemblies and individuals were based on the holy writings and if they could not find the answer in the Tablets of Bahá'u'lláh or 'Abdu'l-Bahá or in the letters of Shoghi Effendi they strictly refrained from making any pronouncement. Such questions were left to be determined by the Universal House of Justice in the future.

The Hands acted with such loyalty that when they handed over the Cause of God, pure and unadulterated, to the elected body of the Universal House of Justice in 1963 the whole Bahá'í world acclaimed their devotion. This generation and those yet unborn owe the Hands of the Cause an immeasurable debt of gratitude. Through their faithfulness they took the Ark of the Covenant from the hands of the Guardian, steered it for over five years through treacherous waters, brought it safely to the shores of salvation and humbly delivered it into the hands of the Universal House of Justice."[253]
– Adib Ṭaherzadeh

###

Obedience

Wert thou to speed through the immensity of space and traverse the expanse of heaven, yet thou wouldst find no rest save in submission to Our command and humbleness before Our Face. [254] ***Whoso keepeth the commandments of God shall attain everlasting felicity.*** [255]

In a revealing lesson in the study of *The Hidden Words*, Abu'l-Qásim Faizi demonstrated from this gemlike book the evolution of the laws and principles of the Faith. He gave an example of Bahá'u'lláh's counsel that a wise man of spiritual power will not imbibe wine.[256] But Bahá'u'lláh did not forbid the drinking of wine until later in the *Kitáb-i-Aqdas*. Mr Faizi referred to a passage in *The Hidden Words* which mentions an unknown covenant.[257] This covenant was not understood until the revelation of the Book of Laws where He says that after His passing everything must be referred to the Centre of the Covenant, 'Abdu'l-Bahá.

In yet another example of the evolution of the Laws of God, the Manifestation commands the recitation of the Greatest Name 95 times in the *Kitáb-i-Aqdas*. However this law was only made universally applicable by the Supreme Body in a letter to the Bahá'ís of the world on 28 December 1999. The Law of Ḥuqúqu'lláh is also mentioned in *The Kitáb-i-Aqdas*. But, preliminary to the application of the Right of God (Ḥuqúq) on the Western believers at Riḍván 1992, the Universal House of Justice had the text relating to this Law translated in 1986 for the understanding of the friends. Elucidating further Faizi explained: 'Study the education of mankind. (The teachings of the Prophets) never came with an abrupt order. They made the people ready so that when the time comes, they will understood (sic) the clear commandment of God.'[258]

Bahá'u'lláh sheds further illumination on this evolutionary process:

> "... if the Sun of Truth were suddenly to reveal, at the earliest stages of its manifestation, the full measure of the potencies which the providence of the Almighty hath bestowed upon it, the earth of human understanding would waste away and be consumed; for men's hearts would neither sustain the intensity of its revelation, nor be able to mirror forth the radiance of its light."[259]

Mr Faizi, who devoted many years of his life to education and who emphasized the importance of nurturing people toward spiritual maturity, said that the Faith is best understood gradually and not abruptly.

***

On a visit to New York City in 1912, 'Abdu'l-Bahá summoned Roy Wilhelm to His room at the Hotel Ansonia. Upon arriving, the Master placed Roy in the middle of a room in which other believers including Persians were seated. He then began to reprimand Roy on the importance of obedience, even waving His finger. Although Roy was puzzled, he submitted to the tongue-lashing without flinching because he was very firm in his obedience to the Master.

The purpose of 'Abdu'l-Bahá was to reach a Persian believer also present in the room that was drifting toward Covenant-breaking. Fortunately the individual was rescued by this indirect reprimand and stood firm in the Faith.[260]

***

In *Priceless Pearl* Rúḥíyyih Khánum writes about an incident of disobedience:

> "Tonight a man came here. He left (refusing to obey the Guardian, becoming a Covenant-breaker). I wanted to cry out to him. 'Do you leave your soul behind so easily?' After all these years, reared in the Faith, he throws it away so lightly! And what else has life to offer man except his soul? And the most precious gift of God he drops by the wayside because it is inconvenient and difficult to obey at the moment."[261]

***

In the early days of Shoghi Effendi's ministry, the believers in the West, generally unaware of the independent character of the Faith, could see nothing wrong in continuing to affiliate themselves with their respective churches after declaring themselves Bahá'ís. George Townshend was no exception to this lack of awareness. When he learned during his early days in Ahascragh that the Guardian had expressed confidence that he would eventually leave the Church, he was surprised and confused by the remark.

After George had been settled in his country rectory in Galway for more than a decade, he was exposed to Shoghi Effendi's *The Goal of a New World Order*. Dated 28 November 1931, this letter was addressed to the adherents of the Faith of Bahá'u'lláh. While not prohibiting membership in churches, mosques and the like, George must have realized from his study of it that the Faith would supersede rather than purify the Church as he had hoped. By now his struggle to free himself from his clerical duties had already begun.

During Their ministries, Bahá'u'lláh and 'Abdu'l-Bahá had frequented the mosques and had warm relations with the more liberal Muslim and Christian clergy of Their times. Indeed Bahá'u'lláh had counselled His followers to consort in a friendly manner with the followers of all religions.[262] However, from the outset of his ministry, Shoghi Effendi did not attend the mosque or spend as much time visiting Muslim clergy as had his Grandfather. When the family of 'Abdu'l-Bahá remonstrated with him for his dissociation, he merely commented that he had to devote his energies to the promotion of the Faith of Bahá'u'lláh. In actuality he was already taking steps to bring about the independence of the Faith.

As the Cause of God matured, Shoghi Effendi, in a letter written in his behalf on 11 December 1935 to the National Spiritual Assembly of the United States and Canada, reconciled dissociation with consorting: 'There should be no confusion between the terms affiliation and association. While affiliation with ecclesiastical organizations is not permissible, association with them should not only be tolerated but even encouraged.'[263] There is no better way to demonstrate the universality of the Cause than this. In this and other letters relating to non-Bahá'í organizations, Shoghi Effendi educated the believers to understand that membership in ecclesiastical organizations, secret societies and partisan politics was not sanctioned in the Faith.

Nine years after George had severed his affiliation with the Church of Ireland, Shoghi Effendi praised his act in a letter written on his behalf to the National Spiritual Assembly of the United States dated 19 July 1956:

> "As he has already informed you, the Guardian feels that the time has now come to ask any ministers still affiliated with churches, but who consider themselves practicing Bahá'ís, to withdraw from the church openly. This is following the example of the Hand of the Cause, former Archdeacon Townshend, who courageously defied the opinion of his fellow clergymen, his relatives and the public, and stepped forth from his high office as a Bahá'í. When the friends realize that many of the first to accept the Báb were priests

> and suffered martyrdom for their act, it does not seem to be asking much that they should rally openly to the Kingdom of the Father which they believe in and for whose advent they cannot very well go on encouraging people in their churches to pray."[264]

* * *

Rúḥíyyih K͟hánum told an audience at a youth conference that the believers must obey the laws of the government because we don't support anarchy, civil trouble or revolution. We believe in law and order, which is not possible where every person sits in judgement about the government. 'One of the greatest maladies of the world, why (there is) . . . so much unrest, (is) because everyone thinks he has the right to decide what is right or wrong. What does (anyone) know to decide what is right from wrong?'[265] She observed that everyone thinks he has the right to impose his personal opinions on society. Bahá'u'lláh says no one does.

In another talk at a teaching conference in 1971 on the subject of *Obedience to the Laws of Bahá'u'lláh*, Rúḥíyyih K͟hánum said that we should strive to have a successful Bahá'í life because what we build into ourselves here is what we take with us into the next world. Since no one knows when or how his own end shall be, we must give more attention to developing our characters.[266]

* * *

> "I once had to pick up Hand of the Cause Mr Khadem at the airport to drive him to a large public meeting at which he was the speaker. The airplane was late and so once on the road I decided to make up the time and get him to the meeting on time. Soon I noticed that he was sitting with his arms folded in the passenger's seat. He leaned over toward me and then leaned back into his seat. With a little smile he said: 'Bahá'ís obey ALL the laws.'
>
> My foot eased off the gas pedal and we still arrived at the meeting on time for his talk."[267]

# # #

Sacrifice

> ***One of the requirements of faithfulness is that thou mayest sacrifice thyself and, in the divine path, close thine eye to every pleasure and strive with all thy soul that thou mayest disappear and be lost, like unto a drop, in the ocean of the love of God.*** [268]

In *The Advent of Divine Justice* the Guardian encouraged pioneering, saying that the provision to take is reliance upon Bahá'u'lláh. The example he gave was Father and Mother Dunn. When the Dunns heard the stirring call from the *Tablets of the Divine Plan* where 'Abdu'l-Bahá mentions the American Bahá'ís will sit on the throne of eternity when they open the Pacific, they were inspired. Lacking financial means and not knowing about their destination, they nevertheless made a sacrifice. Relying upon Bahá'u'lláh they went in their advancing years to far off Australia. Because of their sacrifice explained the beloved Guardian, they opened the whole of Australia and New Zealand to the Faith and raised up one of the pillars of the Universal House of Justice. Bahá'u'lláh's prophecy concerning the middle of the ocean was fulfilled through them.[269]

Addressing His countrymen, the Manifestation had prophesied:

> "Should they attempt to conceal His light on the continent, He will assuredly rear His head in the midmost heart of the ocean and, raising His voice, proclaim: 'I am the Life-giver of the world'"[270]

* * *

During the Great Depression, Louis Gregory slipped $5.00 into the hand of a believer who was in difficult straits. Before she realized what he had done, Louis was on the other side of the room. Astonished she asked herself: 'By what power of intuition had he read my problems so sympathetically?' Louis's own economic situation was precarious and no doubt he would go without dinner for some days because of his gift to her. She wondered that too.[271]

* * *

Martha Root's great teaching journeys and her outstanding qualities endeared her to Shoghi Effendi. Paying her such glowing tributes over some years as the *star servant of the Faith of Bahá'u'lláh,*[272] the *archetype of Bahá'í itinerant teachers,*[273] *the indomitable and zealous disciple of 'Abdu'l-Bahá,*[274] *the peerless herald of the Cause,*[275] and *Leading Ambassadress of Bahá'u'lláh's Faith,*[276] he wrote Martha again and again for news of her remarkable teaching exploits which he longed to receive.

She sailed from San Francisco on her last world teaching trip on 20 May 1937, taking her to Japan, China, India, Burma, Australia, New Zealand and Hawaii. She set an astonishing pace. On her way to Japan when her ship docked for a few hours in Honolulu, Martha went ashore and was interviewed by the *Honolulu Advertiser*, met with a professor of Chinese History at the University of Hawaii, and attended a lecture on the progress of the Faith. Back aboard ship, she gave a talk on 'What is the Bahá'í Movement' before Class I and II passengers, placed copies of *Bahá'u'lláh and the New Era* in the ship's libraries, and wrote an article, which was translated and given out to the press upon her arrival in Yokohama.

During her three-week stay in Japan, she had 15 interviews by reporters representing publications with circulations in the millions and managed to see nearly every Bahá'í in that country. Following her arrival in Tokyo on 3 June, she sent *Gleanings* and other new Bahá'í books to the 'Magazine King of Japan'. She had three meetings with the Bahá'ís in her hotel and others in Bahá'í homes. She met with 18 blind students, attended a dinner in her honour at the home of the American Consul, and spoke at the English Speaking Club of the Y.M.C.A. She gave out Bahá'í books to editors, educators, pastors and several libraries. She interviewed a well-known writer for *World Order* magazine and *The Bahá'í World*, and gave him *Gleanings, Bahá'u'lláh and the New Era* and some other literature. And she visited the leader and some disciples of the Dokai Church.

In Kyoto Martha had meetings with acquaintances, lectured in Esperanto at a meeting, and visited a modern movement group. In Kobe she saw a Buddhist priest who had translated *Bahá'u'lláh and the New Era* into Japanese, lectured at her hotel, met Japanese friends, and attended a gathering of believers and seekers. In Osaka on one afternoon, she called on the editor of a newspaper with circulation of three and a half million, gave him *Bahá'u'lláh and the New Era*, and sent an article to Japanese newspapers. She was the last Bahá'í to visit Japan until after the Second World War.

On 6 July 1937 Martha mailed out a circular letter from Shanghai of her experiences in the Orient, and looked forward to months of teaching work. She set about distributing Bahá'í books, setting up broadcasting and speaking dates, lecturing at a university, and meeting with the believers. She had hardly gotten settled in when war broke out. Caught by deadly bombings in Shanghai, she barely managed to escape as a refugee aboard an over-crowded steamship bound for Manila. Upon arriving in Manila on 20 August, she had to contend with the worst earthquake the city had known in a century. This was followed by a typhoon. Still she managed to give the message.

On 31 August she sailed for Bombay, arriving in Colombo, Ceylon (Sri Lanka) in mid-September where she recuperated for a month. Hardly inactive she tried to establish the Faith in that island country through meeting the Mayor of Colombo, speaking on radio on three occasions, and lecturing at the League of Nations Union and to university students.

She arrived in Bombay on 15 October 1937 for the start of 15 months of indefatigable teaching work in India and Burma. She delivered the Message in colleges, universities, conferences, societies and institutes. She visited all the big towns in India. She gave many lectures in Burmese communities. She gave talks that were broadcast throughout India. Ultimately she was responsible for the whole of the intelligentsia and millions of literate people receiving the Teachings through her lectures, literature and newspaper publicity. She completed and published her book, *Ṭáhirih the Pure*, which was then presented to all the libraries in India and Burma as well as distinguished personages.

Leaving from Bombay Harbour on 29 December 1938, Martha reached Perth on the western coast of Australia on 10 January 1939. There she aroused interest in the Faith and stimulated the believers. In Adelaide she did radio broadcasts and lectures. In Tasmania considerable interest and publicity resulted from her visit. She made several broadcasts and spoke at three high schools, eight organizations and three public meetings. At Melbourne she addressed ten groups, made broadcasts and attended informal talks. In Sydney, broadcasts, receptions, interviews and public meetings were arranged for her.

On 29 May 1939 Martha left Australia aboard the *Mariposa* bound for San Francisco. She was very ill and on the voyage suffered from severe pain in her neck and leg, terribly inflamed muscles, difficulty in swallowing and nausea. When her ship docked in Honolulu for a few hours on 7 June 1939, Martha had a full program of activity arranged for her by the Spiritual Assembly. Instead she had to be assisted to disembark the ship. She would never leave Hawaii. Diagnosed with hopeless carcinoma of the breast with metastasis to the bones, she was given morphia hypodermics to alleviate her pain and kept as comfortable as possible. Her condition continued to deteriorate until on 28 September 1939 she passed away.

Twenty-seven years before her passing, Martha had disclosed to 'Abdu'l-Bahá on His visit to America her discovery of one or two lumps in her breast. The Master had recommended a treatment with the likely result that the cancer was kept in remission for many years. While Martha's health was never robust, she began to suffer physical problems probably related to advancing cancer beginning when she suffered a fall in Sweden on 6 December 1934. In Oslo early in 1935, she was bedridden with influenza and possibly near death. Her recovery required three months, during which she suffered fainting spells. Although she resumed a Herculean schedule as soon as she was able to do so, Martha's health waxed and waned. In her ten-month stay in America from 27 July 1936 to 20 May 1937, three members of the National Spiritual Assembly set about monitoring her health and activity in accordance with Shoghi Effendi's wishes for her care and rest.

While in America Martha did rest and keep to a reduced though occasionally daunting schedule, she had periods of weakness, chronic pain and another attack of influenza, which threatened her life. When her next world tour approached, friends expressed their concern over her precarious state of health. Even her close friend and supporter Roy Wilhelm admonished her to use caution and wisdom.

Nevertheless, her face lined by evidences of pain, she set sail from San Francisco with her 17 pieces of luggage in tow. On this final two-year trip, she would manage her astonishing schedule in spite of waning resistance, worsening pain, ceaseless headaches, difficulty in breathing and eating, and a mild heart attack. Eventually in Australia she would be unable to reach down to open her suitcase, have to stand in order to do her typing and require the frequent care of a Bahá'í chiropractor to help relieve her discomfort. The excruciating pain and decreased mobility she suffered were the result of the cancer affecting her bones.

What inspired this heroic woman to carry on, willing herself not to think about her physical suffering and so overcoming formidable physical impediments? According to Amatu'l-Bahá Rúḥíyyih Khánum:

> "Martha Root was firmly convinced that in her possession was the most priceless gem the world had ever seen – the Message of Bahá'u'lláh. She believed that in showing this gem and offering it to anyone, king or peasant, she was conferring the greatest bounty upon him he could ever receive. It was this proud conviction that enabled her, a woman of no wealth or social prestige, plain, dowdily dressed and neither a great scholar nor an outstanding intellectual, to meet more kings, queens, princes and princesses, presidents

> and men of distinction, fame and prominence and tell them about the Bahá'í Faith than any other Bahá'í in the history of this Cause has ever done."[277]

In paying tribute to her sacrifice, the Guardian unerringly evaluated the magnitude of her indomitable fortitude in *God Passes By:*

> "Neither age nor ill-health, neither the paucity of literature which hampered her early efforts, nor the meagre resources which imposed an added burden on her labors, neither the extremities of the climates to which she was exposed, nor the political disturbances which she encountered in the course of her journeys, could damp the zeal or deflect the purpose of this spiritually dynamic and saintly woman. Single-handed and, on more than one occasion, in extremely perilous circumstances, she continued to call, in clarion tones, men of diverse creeds, color and classes to the Message of Bahá'u'lláh, until, while in spite of a deadly and painful disease, the onslaught of which she endured with heroic fortitude, she hastened homeward to help in the recently launched Seven Year Plan, she was stricken down on her way, in far off Honolulu. There in that symbolic spot between the Eastern and Western Hemispheres, in both of which she had labored so mightily, she died, on September 28, 1939, and brought to its close a life which may well be regarded as the fairest fruit as yet yielded by the Formative Age of the Dispensation of Bahá'u'lláh." [278]

* * *

Keith Ransom-Kehler could suffer from self doubt, feel *stranded without centre* [279] and witness for a light she could barely see. In such a darkened mood, she prayed, meditated, cried out to heaven, and pondered upon the *dark night of the soul* [280] ere she took it upon herself to try and attract people to the Faith; whereupon the atmosphere improved. While she was in India on a challenging tour and feeling ill, she received a cable from the Guardian requesting her presence in Haifa in preparation for an '. . . extended summer tour of Persia'.[281] In Haifa the Guardian charged her with a delicate mission to petition Reza Sháh of Persia to permit the entry of Bahá'í literature. She spent over 15 months in Iran where she brought much encouragement to the believers. During this period she made repeated and strenuous efforts to fulfil her mission, meeting with suave government officials, petitioning the government, writing to every cabinet minister and even to the Sháh himself, championing the Bahá'í principles of loyalty to government, and reiterating the sanctity of Islam.

Horace Holley, who would have appreciated masterful arguments presented in the English language, praised her efforts in this way:

> ". . . the eyes of the friends were constantly on the alert for encouraging news from the Orient where our beloved Keith was labouring with such remarkable fortitude and zeal to secure the admission of the Bahá'í literature into Persia . . . The masterly correspondence of Keith, copies of which were sent to every Court Minister and to the President of the Parliament, in addition to her epistles to the Shah . . . will ever stand out as monuments to her brilliancy, her tact, her intense zeal and her perfect command of language . . ." [282]

Gradually her health weakened until, exhausted and disappointed by her failed efforts, she wrote:

> "I have fallen, though I never faltered. Months of effort with nothing accomplished is the record that confronts me. If anyone in future should be interested in this thwarted adventure of mine, he alone can say whether near or far from the seemingly impregnable heights of complaisance and indifference, my tired old body fell. The smoke and din of battle are to-day too dense for me to ascertain whether I moved forward or was slain in my tracks." [283]

Following her passing in her 57th year apparently succumbing to smallpox, Shoghi Effendi assayed the value of her sacrifice:

> "The intrepid defender and illustrious herald of God's Cause has risen triumphant from depths of darkness to her heavenly home; her magnificent deeds were hidden from the negligent in that land; the Supreme Concourse knew her worth; she possesses the rank of martyrdom and is one of the Hands of the Cause." [284]

# # #

Steadfastness

> ***I swear by God! So great are the things ordained for the steadfast that were they, so much as the eye of a needle, to be disclosed, all who are in heaven and on earth would be dumbfounded, except such as God, the Lord of all worlds, hath willed to exempt.*** [285]

Corinne Knight True found steadfastness through tragedy and suffering. Married on 24 June 1882 to Moses Adams True, she incurred the wrath of a father she dearly loved and respected when she did not obtain his blessing on her marriage. They had been very close but for the next eight or nine years Moses Knight would refuse to speak to or see his daughter. Even when Corinne gave birth to their first child Harriet in 1883, the elder Moses would not see her. Meanwhile the Trues added to their growing family when Corinne gave birth to four more children: Laurence Knight, Charles Gilbert Davis, Edna Miriam and Arna Corinne.

Eventually reconciliation occurred. The Trues moved into the Knight's former home in Chicago circa 1891. Then tragedy struck when Harriet fell down the basement stairs in June, 1892. Just two months shy of her ninth birthday, she had been a delight to her mother; full of life, curiosity and adventure. Corinne who could thank her father for an inner strength based on faith in God, found no comfort in the sudden loss of this much cherished daughter. Instead she had only questions with no ready answers.

Unable to satisfy her questions in traditional Christianity, she explored several modern movements with her husband. Unsatisfied, the pain of Harriet's sudden death gradually subsided with the rhythm of life. The older children attended private school. Play-acting in the home based on current vaudeville held the attention of the family. Around October 1893, Corinne gave birth to twins: Katherine and Kenneth. In January 1896, her eighth and final child Nathanael was born.

In 1898 diphtheria struck Chicago. Nathanael who had a *sparkling personality*[286] was most severely affected. In an era that preceded vaccines and antibiotics, the disease could affect breathing, damage the heart or cause suffocation. Four of the children were stricken. Moses and Corinne valiantly laboured over them, but on the night of 31 May 1899 Nathanael died.

The crisis prompted Corinne to renew her religious quest. She yearned for guidance as to why her children were so inexplicably wrenched from her care. So she prayed for help even as she intensified her search. Then, mercifully within months of Nathanael's death, she was led to the Bahá'í message. A friend who was aware of Corinne's suffering urged her to attend a lecture by some men from the East who might be able to assuage her pain. In 1899 'Abdu'l-Bahá had sent Ḥájí 'Abdu'l-Karím, Mírzá Asadu'lláh and Mírzá Abúl-Faḍl to the United States and these men were at the time in Chicago. At the meeting Corinne recognized the Message as from God and started attending weekly meetings. Deepening her understanding of the Faith in excerpts from the available writings and Tablets of the day, she found an assurance she wanted to share with her family. Encouraged to write to 'Abdu'l-Bahá, she complied perhaps reluctantly because she felt Him too busy to reply. But on 12 October 1900 a Tablet from 'Abdu'l-Bahá did reach her which touched the core of her sorrow and uncertainty concerning Nathanael's passing:

> "Be not grieved nor troubled because of the loss which hath befallen thee – a loss which caused the tears to flow, sighs to be produced, sorrow to exist and hearts to burn in great agony; but know, this hath reference only to the physical body, and if thou considerest this matter with a discerning and intelligent eye, thou wilt find that it hath no power whatsoever, for separation belongeth to the characteristics of the body. But concerning the spirit, know that thy pure son shall be with thee in the Kingdom of God and thou shalt witness his smiling face, illumined brow, handsome spirit and real happiness. Accordingly, thou wilt then be comforted and thank God for His favour upon thee." [287]

The cooling rain of 'Abdu'l-Bahá's caressing message was rapidly followed three months later by the loss of another child - Kenneth - again to that scavenger diphtheria. His death was soon followed by another Tablet from 'Abdu'l-Bahá, comforting Corrine on the condition of this son in the after-life and encouraging her to endure every trial and commit her affairs to God. Thanks to the Faith and to 'Abdu'l-Bahá's Tablets, over fifty of which she received from Him, Corinne did gradually develop the kind of calmness which enabled her to be more accepting about life's vicissitudes.

Nine months after Kenneth's passing, Corinne's mother unexpectedly died on vacation. She was 62 and her husband, 20 years older and now confined to a wheelchair, was devastated. Although the reconciliation with his daughter some ten years earlier had not included his son-in-law, the Trues invited him to stay with them. The old man accepted and soon Moses Knight and Moses True were fast friends. Two years after his wife's death, Mr Knight followed her.

Meanwhile Corinne was confronted by dissension among the believers even as her services to the Faith increased. The Master in a Tablet pointed to the importance of remaining unmoved in times of violent tests as these unsettling events are followed by fruition and joy. '. . . (B)lessed art thou,' He wrote, 'for thou art steadfast in the Cause of God, firm in His Covenant.'[288]

In August 1906, Laurence who was athletic and competed on a sailing team passed through Fruitport to be near his fiancée and on to Saginaw Bay to join his team-mates. During the race he was knocked overboard and drowned. The family was shocked when news reached them at Fruitport that evening. Moses grieved for days. Corinne believed in the will of God but also grieved. One can only guess the state of Laurence's fiancée. As always Corinne turned to 'Abdu'l-Bahá; only this time she sought to attain His presence in 'Akká. The Master sent her permission to come and another Tablet to console her:

> "Do not grieve on account of the death of thy son, neither sigh nor lament. That nightingale soared upward to the divine rose-garden; that drop returned to the most great ocean of Truth; that foreigner hastened to his native abode; and that ill one found salvation and life eternal.
>
> Why shouldst thou be sad and heartbroken? This separation is temporal; this remoteness and sorrow is counted only by days. Thou shalt find him in the Kingdom of God and thou wilt attain to the everlasting union. Physical companionship is ephemeral, but heavenly association is eternal. Whenever thou rememberest the eternal and never ending union, thou wilt be comforted and blissful." [289]

In December 1909 Moses True died suddenly of a heart attack. Devoted to each other throughout their 29 years of marriage, Moses was 52 when he died. Following his death Corinne continued her active work for the Cause without allowing herself a period of mourning. Death was a process and a natural phenomenon to her. Being busy must also have acted as a tonic for her.

Next year Corinne received news that Davis had been diagnosed with tuberculosis. By 1911 he was in a sanatorium in Denver, Colorado.

Corinne wrote to a close friend: 'It is a fiery ordeal to fight that awful disease tuberculosis. For almost a year now I have tried doing the things advised by the most skilled physicians and nurses. God alone knows how the battle will result. Through these hot fires our souls are to be refined.'[290] By Christmas Davis was weaker. A doctor reported his condition hopeless.

Davis returned to Chicago by March 1912 to be with his family. When 'Abdu'l-Bahá arrived in Chicago 29 April on his western tour, Corinne longed for Him to see her ailing son. Next day her longing was realized when the Master arrived at the True home and saw Davis for some time in his room. After seeing the young man, He emerged to say that Davis was much better than expected and exclaim that the calamities in the house must cease. Indeed Corinne suffered no more deaths in her immediate family through the rest of her long life.

Corinne was overjoyed. Feeling assured of Davis's recovery she spent the afternoon and evening at meetings in which 'Abdu'l-Bahá was present. While she was out, however, Davis passed peacefully away. Only then did she realize that the Master earlier that day had meant Davis's spiritual condition was better than expected.

Corinne was present for the dedication of the Temple site the following day much to the surprise to those in the crowd who knew of Davis's death the previous day. When 'Abdu'l-Bahá arrived in a taxi, however, He motioned to Corinne to accompany Him in the car. What the Master said to her during those brief moments together is not known. No doubt His loving presence must have quickened her soul and calmed her troubled heart.

Davis was buried on 2 May. 'Abdu'l-Bahá visited his gravesite where He prayed for him, for Moses and for the other children who were all buried nearby. At His invitation later, Corinne and her three surviving children attained His presence. Then He assured eternal reunion and the nearness of the spiritual world.

Later during 'Abdu'l-Bahá's visit to Chicago in September, Corinne sought further reassurance. She had borne her heartache alone and buried questions she had been unable to answer. Would she be reunited with her husband in the next world? Had he accepted Bahá'u'lláh? To both these questions, 'Abdu'l-Bahá responded assuredly. 'I have had a great many sorrows,' she said to Him one day. 'I have had a sad life – sad things to bear.' 'I know, I know, Mrs True,' 'Abdu'l-Bahá replied, 'because I have sent them to you.'[291]

Corinne found peace in His response. Her spiritual strength was now such that she could grasp the wisdom of her suffering. And the Master knew she could receive this great truth. Some years later the Guardian testified to her inner strength in this tribute:

> "My heart is filled with gratitude for the fresh evidences of untiring activity, of exemplary loyalty, of steadfastness and devotion that you have so powerfully manifested . . . You are truly a tower of strength in these days of stress and trial, worthy of the unquestioning confidence reposed in you by 'Abdu'l-Bahá."[292]

* * *

Nabíl-i-Akbar was a learned man whose erudition was said to be unsurpassed. Mistaken for and arrested as a Bábí, he subsequently studied the writings of the Báb and was converted. Following this he began teaching the Faith and converting people in the area of Qá'in. In an uproar the clergy rose up against him, spreading their calumnies to Ṭihrán and antagonizing the populace against him. Hunted by the authorities he became a fugitive. Homeless and eventually penniless, he wandered throughout the country, guiding souls to the water of life.

'Abdu'l-Bahá writes of this illustrious soul:

> "He . . . continuously (taught) the Faith . . . Like a candle, he was using up his life; but in spite of his sufferings he was never dispirited, rather his joy and ardour increased with every passing day. He was eloquent of speech; he was a skilled physician, a remedy for every ill, a balm to every sore. He would guide the Illuminati by their own philosophical principles, and with the mystics he would prove the Divine Advent in terms of "inspiration" and the "celestial vision." He would convince the Shaykhí leaders by quoting the very words of their late Founders, Shaykh Aḥmad and Siyyid Káẓim, and would convert Islamic theologians with texts from the Qur'án and traditions from the Imáms, who guide mankind aright. Thus he was an instant medicine to the ailing, and a rich bestowal to the poor.
>
> . . . because he stood steadfast in this holy Faith, because he guided souls and served this Cause and spread its fame, that star, Nabíl, will shine forever from the horizon of abiding light."[293]

* * *

In 1905, George Townshend experienced his spiritual awakening in consequence of his perusing the Bhagavadgita. Entering the Church as a deacon, he was assigned responsibility for a Mission in Provo, Utah. The next year he was ordained a priest of the Episcopalian Church. There, nestled near the magnificent Rocky Mountains and remote from civilization, George could contemplate the majesty of the Creator while carrying out his priestly functions. Eventually he realized that the church in its claim to be the *guardian* of the truth was inflexible, and so he left the Mission in 1909.

At this time he associated himself with 'The Great Work'. A mystic, George may have been attracted to the *oriental flavour* [294] of the movement with its teachings on Universal intelligence, karma, natural laws and immortality. Devoting himself to the 'Work', George supported himself teaching. The first year he taught high school at Salt Lake City and then moved on to the Extension Department of the University of the South, in Sewanee, Tennessee, as Assistant-Director and English professor.

In 1910 he met Nellie Roche. She was a highly intelligent woman with whom George established a highly spiritual relationship. Within three years they decided to marry and George set out for Ireland in July, 1913, to make arrangements for the ceremony. The marriage would take place in his mother's home in Enniskerry after which the couple would honeymoon in Ireland before returning to Sewanee for the fall term.

Instead Nellie, who had an intimation of George's spiritual destiny, broke off the engagement by cable to her fiancée. Convinced that she would merely be a hindrance as his wife, she nevertheless believed that the two of them were *partners in a Divine plan.*[295] Having divined that George's destiny was to *lead the Anglican Churches and British people into the promised Day of God,*[296] she would in later years play practical and spiritual parts in helping George realize his destiny. At this time neither of them were aware of the Bahá'í Faith and over three years would go by before George received 'Abdu'l-Bahá's second Tablet in which He wrote: 'It is my hope that thy church will come under the Heavenly Jerusalem.'[297]

So George, having turned forty, found himself without his spiritual and career orientations. He had been rejected by his bride. And now his sight was uncertain. But George was never defeated by disappointments, difficulties or frustrations. Instead he overcame these challenges with persistence, resilience and optimism. Since he felt that spiritual growth or overcoming weaknesses was the key to resolving difficulties, he would have seen suffering as opportunities for growth. Not surprisingly, therefore, we find him writing in *The Altar on the Hearth*: 'When I am fit to bear the burden Thou wilt lay it on my shoulders.'[298]

* * *

Clara Dunn suffered many difficulties in her life. English by birth, she was raised in Canada under circumstances of poverty and in-harmony in the home. Her parents had different religious persuasions and so created a disagreeable home life. Moreover her father was restless and unstable occupationally. Clara's solution to the resulting unhappiness was to marry in her 16th year. But within a year of her marriage, her husband was killed in a railway accident, leaving her with an infant child for whom she was unable to care. An elder brother assumed the responsibility. But Clara regretted being unable to bring him up and worried over his well-being. While still in Canada she became ill with Typhoid fever, enduring a *long and debilitating illness.*[299] Following her recovery at 33 years of age (she was born in 1869), she migrated to Walla Walla, Washington where she found employment as a nurse.

In 1907 Hyde Dunn appeared at the medical centre where Clara worked and introduced her to the Faith. She accepted the Cause and then spent the next five years struggling to spread the teachings. No one responded. She was forced to give up her job when one of the doctors at the medical centre called her a quack. Her anguish was so severe that she was hospitalized with a nervous breakdown. Afterward Clara was bereft of funds but a kindly woman offered her an attic room where she could sleep. Then the woman warned away all Clara's acquaintances, saying that Clara '. . . was mad and belonged to a crazy religion about which she wanted to tell everyone.'[300]

She married Hyde Dunn in 1917 and within three years they arrived in Sydney, Australia as pioneers. She had doubted the wisdom of this venture and it was only 'Abdu'l-Bahá's encouragement in a cable that had reassured her on the eve of their departure. Upon their arrival, however, customs fined her husband all the spare money they had. Father Dunn had neglected to declare jewellery he had brought into the country, which represented part of their survival plan. He then became ill and for the first six months of their pioneering venture Clara provided their income.

When he had recovered, Hyde obtained a job with Nestle's Milk Company as a travelling salesman. The job enabled the couple to move about over the continent and attempt to establish the Faith. They met with many disappointments while persevering in their efforts to establish Local

Assemblies and elect a National Assembly in 1926 and 1932. When Martha Root visited them in 1924, Clara wept and she said: 'I have failed.' [301] And Hyde said to Martha: 'Never mention us in writing about Australia, I wish that I could do something for Australia.'[302] Keenly suffering a sense of failure, Clara, on her pilgrimage in 1932, begged the Guardian to replace them. She felt '. . . clumsy and awkward and uneducated.'[303] The Guardian reminded her of the illiteracy of Peter the Apostle; then encouraged her to go back and form the National Assembly. The National Spiritual Assembly of Australia and New Zealand was formed in 1934. Supporting it were the Local Spiritual Assemblies of Sydney, Adelaide and Auckland.

At a conference some years later and near the time of the death of her son, Clara was asked to recount her difficulties. Unselfconsciously, she declared that she had no difficulties.

* * *

In 1935 a campaign of Bahá'í persecution was being waged in Iran, compelling the National Spiritual Assembly to petition the Sh̲áh and government authorities. Bahá'í meetings were suppressed. Ḥaẓíratu'l-Quds were closed. Petitions for justice were impeded. Bahá'ís were imprisoned or abused. Negative publicity was disseminated. The Cause in Ahváz was denounced. Bahá'í correspondence was confiscated. Bahá'í schools throughout the country were closed. Bahá'í employees at the Department of Highways in a town were dismissed. The registration of Bahá'í marriage certificates in registry offices was refused. Employment of Bahá'ís by departments of the Ministry of Finance was denied. And Bahá'í pocket calendars as well as the book *Mysterious Forces of Civilization* were seized. The Tarbíyat Schools in Ṭihrán were closed the year before.[304]

Apparently, in 1936, a conscripted officer 'Alí-Muḥammad Varqá was accused of insubordination and imprisoned. The cause of his arrest was that his marriage was declared illegal by the Ministry of Justice. At the time in Iran, there were only four bureaus for four religions, none of which were Bahá'í. Consequently no registry would register the marriage. In defence of his son, Valíyu'lláh Varqá petitioned the Sh̲áh:

> "I have the honor to submit that my eldest son 'Alí-Muḥammad Varqá after the completion of advanced studies entered the Officers' Training College last year to finish his term of military service; having concluded his studies there he served as a 3rd lieutenant in the artillery until on the 31st of Murdád his term of service was completed. On

> the 4th of Shahrívar he was summoned to Headquarters and although he was no longer in the army and was seeking work in order to support his family, he was arrested and imprisoned by the military authorities. It appears that the cause of his arrest was his marriage, which the Ministry of Justice has declared illegal although it conformed to all the regulations, as is proved by his marriage certificate which was officially submitted to the Registry Office. A Bahá'í can never act against the country's laws and the Imperial will, and his conscience forbids him falsely to represent himself as Muslim, Christian, Jew or Zoroastrian and to register his marriage on the certificates and at the bureaus reserved for them. Such an act would be disloyalty to the Government and is forbidden by the Bahá'í Faith; a Bahá'í is obliged to conform to the Bahá'í marriage requirements and to seek the registration of Bahá'í certificates by the officials concerned; and since hundreds of such marriages have taken place all over Irán, and being in conformity with the law have led to no incidents, my son likewise has proceeded according to the laws of his faith and also of his country. It is certain that in view of imperial justice and favor, it will not be permitted that a young man of education, who has completed his military service under the law, has married and with a thousand hopes made ready to serve his country; should at the outset of his career for no fault or disloyalty be subjected to such difficulties. I humbly beg His Majesty's order for a thorough investigation of the legality of this marriage, and, if it agrees with the desire of His Majesty, the order for his release."[305]

Summoned for interrogation by the Assistant Chief of Police, Valíyu'lláh Varqá was warned to cease publicly declaring his faith. The Government, while respecting the rights of the Bahá'ís, cannot give official recognition. Varqá replied that his son had '. . . married according to the laws of his religion and . . . also made out a marriage certificate in conformity with the laws of his country; to what bureau must he take this certificate to be registered?'

The police chief continued the same argument. Valíyu'lláh Varqá said that according to Shoghi Effendi 'both public avowals of faith and concealment of faith are blameworthy.'[307] So the believers neither declare nor conceal their religion. Varqá asked him to '. . . consider that both the grandfather and the twelve-year-old uncle of this boy ('Alí-Muḥammad Varqá) – that is, my father and brother – were hacked to pieces forty years ago in Náṣiri'd-Dín Sháh's prison because they refused to conceal their belief; obviously my son who is a fourth generation Bahá'í will likewise refuse to do so.'[308]

* * *

In the last ten years of his life, Músá Banání suffered debilitating health problems. In 1960 he had a stroke which paralyzed one side of his body. His condition continued to deteriorate. At the Kampala Intercontinental Conference in October 1967 Mr Banání . . .

> ". . . was carried down the stairs and into the auditorium in the arms of a loving friend, was gently placed in his wheelchair and taken to the speakers' platform. Every believer rose to his feet in spontaneous, deeply sincere love, respect and honor. Here was the hero of Africa, scarred but unbent and unwavering. Mr. Banání, sixteen years a pioneer to Africa, and in the twilight of his life, ill and almost blind with diabetes, paralyzed on his right side by a devastating stroke, and now straight from bed, his left leg amputated above the knee three weeks ago to arrest the angry thrust of gangrene. . . . (W)e admired his stern self-control as he sat in obvious physical discomfort throughout the talks of his fellow-Hands. An era seemed to have ended; we sensed it. Would he ever come amongst us like that again?" [309]

# # #

Trust and Trustworthiness

Place thy trust in God, and commit thine affairs unto Him . . . [310]

Ḥájí Á<u>kh</u>únd was frequently persecuted for his devotion to teaching the Cause of God. He converted a multitude and was often arrested and imprisoned. Once he was taken away after only three days of marriage. His sufferings were such that Bahá'u'lláh Himself testified that the Concourse on High lamented. Nevertheless the Manifestation encouraged him to rejoice as he had borne hardships in the path of God. Indeed he remained thankful to his Lord in spite of his imprisonment.

In *Memorials to the Faithful*, 'Abdu'l-Bahá wrote that . . .

> ". . . whenever there was an uproar Mullá 'Alí would put on his turban, wrap himself in his 'abá and sit waiting, for his enemies to rouse and the farráshes to break in and the guards to carry him off to prison. But observe the power of God! In spite of all this, he was kept safe. 'The sign of a knower and lover is this, that you will find him dry in the sea.' That is how he was. His life hung by a thread from one moment to the next; the malevolent lay in wait for him; he was known everywhere as a Bahá'í – and still he was protected from all harm. He stayed dry in the depths of the sea, cool and safe in the heart of the fire, until the day he died." [311]

Once during a particularly fanatical period, he had been advised to conceal himself from his enemies. He gave a reply which exposed their ignorance concerning reliance upon God:

> "It is true that in the Holy Tablets we are commanded to observe wisdom. By wisdom is not meant to be fearful or to have no reliance upon God. It means to act with thoroughness, and to conduct oneself with truthfulness, benevolence and patience; it means to sow the seeds of the teachings of God in the pure and goodly soil of the hearts. It does not mean fear or hiding.
>
> When I was a child, I fell into a river and was carried down the stream for a few miles. People were sure that I was drowned, but somehow I was thrown on the bank almost lifeless, and in the end I recovered. God saved me. On another occasion, I fell twice on a mountain, from a height

of about one hundred metres. I survived, for it was meant that I should live. Besides, I have been captured many times, and from periods of six months up to three years I have been imprisoned, chained and fettered. On each of these occasions there was no hope of freedom. And yet many souls who were not as famous as I, but were worthy to lay down their lives in the path of God, have been martyred. But so far I have not. If it is the will of God, and if this incomparable bounty of laying down my life becomes mine, imagine what a great gift that would be! Furthermore, is it possible or conceivable to be able to run away from God's decree? On the contrary one has to speed up towards Him." [312]

* * *

When Dr Muhájir and his wife pioneered to the Mentawai Islands in 1954, Raḥmat had no experience in mass teaching. The Guardian had called for entry by troops and so Dr Muhájir confidently set about gaining the experience which would enable him to be so successful in later years among the indigenous peoples around the world. Following his intuition he repeatedly visited their villages, painstakingly deepened the new believers, affectionately welcomed the Mentawais, respectfully treated them and generously shared what he had. Through his love for them did he attract them to the Faith. Thus did he become a great mass teacher.[313]

* * *

Agnes Alexander lived a life of faith which she might well have inherited from her maternal grandmother. Mrs Dwight Baldwin possessed a strong spirit of faith described as follows: 'I leave the future all in the hands of our good heavenly Father. He has never left or forsaken us – in Him we trust.'[314] Characterized by *extraordinary steadfastness* and *unwavering certitude* [315] Agnes completely submitted herself to the Will of God.

"Anyone who knew her would soon become aware of her complete reliance on what she called her "guidance" and her unqualified obedience to it once she had prayed for and received it. She was so fully confident in the outpouring of guidance that would come as a result of earnest prayer, that she never worried about the consequences of following it, never wavered in the face of opposition to it, never questioned or doubted or rebelled against it. Many who tried beforehand to get a decisive answer from Agnes

> would be frustrated by her reply, "If it is God's plan." But the moment she received what she felt was guidance in answer to her prayer, the action was decisive. All through her life Agnes's sensitivity to the Divine Will was to be confirmed by messages or cables from both the Master and the beloved Guardian . . ." [316]

Thus over the years Agnes would quite naturally write or say: 'I was guided to go directly . . .'[317] 'In such an environment . . . God destined me to be placed.'[318] 'For 3 months I was alone in Italy with only God to teach me.'[319] 'God used this means to teach me to depend only on Him.'[320] 'Thus, in God's plan, my stay lengthened to two months . . .'[321] 'Through God's bounty, I was guided to meet many glorious souls . . .'[322] 'God granted me the privilege of seeking . . .'[323] 'God had revealed His truth to me!'[324] 'God opened his heart that he might understand.'[325] 'God put this in my heart . . .'[326] 'During those days an inspiration came to me . . .'[327] 'Suddenly the guidance came to me to . . .'[328] 'I moved into a Japanese house which I had been guided to find . . .'[329] Very simply Agnes would often say that '. . . one must never worry, but must always trust in God and then everything would turn out right.'[330]

Agnes grew up in a Christian home in Hawaii. Descended from Christian missionaries from both sides of her family, who had migrated and settled there in the days when ship travel was uncertain and survival arduous, Agnes was brought up in a home accustomed to prayers and worship. Possessing an unusual intuitive quality, she was troubled in that atmosphere with the Christian teaching that one must be born again. When she failed according to her understanding to experience a *rebirth*, she concluded something must be wrong with her. She wrote: 'From childhood I had loved and wished to serve Christ, but His life seemed far away from me, and I always felt that something was lacking, that I had never been reborn.'[331]

Perhaps recognizing in his child this inner intuitive quality, Agnes's father in 1900 sent his 25 year old daughter on a trip to Europe. This beautifully regal and delicate young woman who was innately gentle and timid embarked on a journey not usually embraced by women of her experience and background. After arriving in Europe and at her father's urging she set out for Rome. As the train on which she had embarked approached the Italian capital, she sensed with a thrill of anticipation that somehow her goal was approaching.

In a pension in the Holy City, Agnes came into contact with Mrs Charlotte Dixon who together with her two daughters had just returned from pilgrimage to the Holy Land. Agnes saw them in the dining room and was unable to avert her eyes. The trio had attained the presence of 'Abdu'l-Bahá and exuded a happiness which was compelling to young Agnes. Embarrassed at her own hopeless gaping, she finally mustered the courage to enquire as to the cause of their joy. From Mrs Dixon she received a handwritten copy of a Bahá'í prayer, which calmed her restless heart. 'Abdu'l-Bahá had cautioned not to give the Message except to those thirsty for the water of life, and so Mrs Dixon had said nothing to Agnes about Him. Nevertheless, on the third evening, Agnes realized as in a great illumination the truth that Christ had returned. Next morning she confronted Mrs Dixon and announced her revelation to her: 'Christ is on this earth!'[332]

Convinced that God's will was for Mrs Dixon to come to that pension, Agnes also felt that her instant recognition was a gift from the Creator. Alone in Italy she took to reading the Bible. Day by day she would pray and open the good Book. As proof after proof of the new Revelation was revealed to her, she became so interested in the Bible that she preferred it to any other reading.

After three months she felt that Bahá'í contact was necessary. Finding May Bolles of Paris to be the nearest believer, Agnes went at May's invitation to the French capital and was soon immersed in May's love and surrounded by closely-unified believers. Over a three-and-half-month period she was confirmed in the Faith. Reborn a Bahá'í Agnes at last understood what Christ had meant when He said: 'Ye must be born again.'[333]

Sensing the time propitious for her return to Hawaii where she was restless to proclaim her newfound Faith, she was on the verge of setting out when a Tablet arrived from 'Abdu'l-Bahá. The Master validated the remarkable way in which she had heard the Message and charged her to proceed to her native country. For Agnes the Tablet would have reaffirmed her conviction that guidance of God was ever present in her life.

> "O maid servant of God! By God, the Truth, the Spirit of Christ from the Supreme Concourse doth in every time and aspect announce to thee this Great Good News. Be therefore a divine bird; proceed to thy native country; spread the wings of sanctity over those spots and sing and chant and celebrate the Name of thy Lord, that thou mayest gladden the Supreme Concourse and make the seeking souls hasten unto thee as the moths hasten to the lamp and thus illumine that distant country by the Light of God." [334]

Confirmed by 'Abdu'l-Bahá's Tablet in her decision to return to her native land, Agnes reached Hawaii as that land's first Bahá'í and remained there for 12 years during which the Faith was established. In *Tablets of the Divine Plan*, 'Abdu'l-Bahá praised her efforts:

> "Consider ye, that Miss Agnes Alexander, the daughter of the Kingdom, the beloved maid-servant of the Blessed Perfection, traveled alone to Hawaii . . . Reflect ye how this daughter was confirmed in the Hawaiian Islands. She became the cause of the guidance of a gathering of people. . . . (H)ad this respected daughter founded an empire, that empire would not have been so great!" [335]

Sometime during this period of her early Bahá'í life in Hawaii, Agnes heard a lecture about Japan in her father's home and became inspired to study the country. She perused every available book, and developed a big folder with notes about Japan's history, religions and culture. Little did she dream that '. . . God was preparing me to teach His Cause in that country.'[336] Years later in a recorded talk she said: '. . . It was all in God's plan my going to Japan because God does have a plan of our lives.'[337]

With the death of her parents and the breaking up of her home, she felt guided to proceed to the home of her spiritual mother May Maxwell in Montreal, Canada. After a month in the Maxwell home she journeyed to Brooklyn and there she received a wonderful Tablet from 'Abdu'l-Bahá:

> "This light of guidance which is ignited in the lamp of thy heart must become more brilliant day by day and shed its light to all parts. Therefore if thou travelest toward Japan unquestionable Divine confirmations shall descend upon thee." [338]

In 1937 on her pilgrimage she would speak to the Guardian about her inspirations. He said to her: 'It is the Master.'[339]

She sailed from New York for Italy in May, 1914 to first visit relatives and then the Holy Land. But, at the outbreak of the First World War on 1 August 1914, she was delayed in Switzerland with her trunk in Germany and her funds tied up in drafts. She received the following guidance from 'Abdu'l-Bahá:

> "It is now more advisable for thee to depart directly to Japan and while there be engaged in the diffusion of the fragrances of God. . . . I hope that thou mayest be like unto the realm-conquering army and a farmer, therefore thy voyage to Japan is preferred to everything else." [340]

The Master afforded her the freedom to make her pilgrimage. In spite of the longing Agnes must have felt to meet 'Abdu'l-Bahá, she made her way to Japan and forewent her pilgrimage. Such was her unquestioning obedience to His slightest wish. Confident in the spiritual power to reach her goal, she was miraculously able to obtain her trunk and arrange her money affairs. 'How great are the favors of God,' she later wrote of that time, 'if only we have faith and obey!'[341] Arriving in Japan on 1 November 1914 after a crossing considered precarious, she would spend altogether 32 years there until 1967 when she returned as an invalid to Hawaii.

She arrived in Tokyo and began immediately to teach and win wide publicity for the Faith. Through her study of Esperanto and joining the Universal Esperanto Association, she launched the translation of *The Hidden Words* into that language and spread the Message in Japan through Esperantists. Within months she was writing: 'It is such a wonderful life God has permitted me to have here in Japan and how grateful I should be.'[342] Dedicating her room to 'Abdu'l-Bahá, contacts came every week. 'God surely leads me to those who need me . . . I woke up the other morning with such joy.'[343]

Wishing to use every opportunity to spread the teachings, she set up a Bahá'í lending library; gave the Message at schools and universities; attended conferences on religion; worked with Martha Root in Japan and China; learned English and Esperanto Braille as an aid in teaching the blind of Japan; wrote articles on the Faith; helped care for earthquake orphans; introduced the Faith in Korea; contacted many student groups; visited Taiwan, Hong Kong, and the Philippines; assisted in the process of mass conversion in the Philippines; and gave the Faith to hundreds of prisoners over a three year period at a prison in Manila.

Her services won praises from both the Master and the Guardian. 'Abdu'l-Bahá wrote: 'Praise be to God, that in Japan thou hast been assisted in the accomplishment of a distinguished service. Thou hast raised the Call of the Divine Kingdom, and hast led the people to an illumined world and a heavenly Cause; thou hast become the cause of enlightenment and the wisher for the education of human souls.'[344] And Shoghi Effendi from whom she received some 100 letters paid her this tribute: 'Your name will forever remain associated with the rise of the Faith and its establishment in Japan, and the record of your incessant and splendid endeavors will shed on its annals a lustre that time can never dim.'[345]

Agnes was remembered by Donald Witzel, future member of the Continental Board of Counsellors for South America, who in 1953 was attached as an officer to the US Army in Tokyo. He wrote:

> "One Sunday I requisitioned a jeep for personal use to take Miss Agnes Alexander teaching in the Tokyo area. . . . We visited a number of people interested in the Faith and attended a meeting. I wanted to take her home and started out, but she could not explain how to reach her house. She knew how to take the train there, so I decided to follow the train tracks. At one point the tracks entered a dark tunnel. I had stopped and questioned Agnes about where we were in relation to her house. She did not know and asked me to enter the tunnel following the tracks. I did so and after a short time I saw the headlights of a train coming in our direction in this single track tunnel. I quickly reversed the car and backed out in haste. On leaving the tunnel I swerved backwards to the left and hit another car outside coming from the opposite direction. . . . The driver of that car . . . had borrowed the car without permission, and we had to wait for the traffic police to fill out papers. This was still the time of the Occupation of Japan, and I had to respect these formalities. Agnes urged me to go back into the tunnel to find her house, which I couldn't do. She would not wait, picked up her water cooler (which contained her food, water, etc.) and walked away into the night. . . . She was detached from all material things. She had her own goals and things to accomplish for the Faith. Nothing else really mattered." [346]

In her 75th year Agnes returned to Japan in 1950 after a 13 year absence owing to circumstances of the Second World War. As a prominent Bahá'í, she was soon seen at meetings of the Annual World Religion Day in Tokyo, the World Federalist Conference in Hiroshima, the Japanese Unitarian church in Tokyo, a Conference of World Religionists, and the International Congress of World Fellowship of Faiths. In 1954 she was appointed to the Auxiliary Board. Three years later in 1957 she was named a Hand of the Cause and the same year elected to the National Spiritual Assembly of the Bahá'ís of North East Asia. She continued to be re-elected to the National Assembly until 1963.

Not long before his being elected to the International Bahá'í Council in 1961, future Universal House of Justice member Mr Ian Semple remembered a luncheon with Agnes. He and Mrs Marian Mihaeloff, later the first English-language secretary of the Universal House of Justice, were working at the London Ḥaẓíratu'l-Quds. Mr Semple wrote that one day he and Marian . . .

> ". . . took (Agnes Alexander) out to lunch at a little self-service restaurant we used to eat at. The three of us sat at a table for four. During our lunch, three other people came successively and occupied the fourth chair to eat their lunch. We were eating much more slowly, and talking a lot about the Faith. Nevertheless, Agnes was able to mention the Faith to each of those three people. That was a profound lesson to two reticent Britons on how to teach the Faith!" [347]

In 1965 Agnes Alexander fell and broke her hip. Intending to attend the World Congress of Esperantists in Tokyo, she went instead into a Tokyo hospital where she was confined for two years. She never complained. A companion believer who kept a worried vigil through that time was comforted when Agnes uttered something consistent with her deep faith: 'Dearie, nothing happens by chance.'[348]

***

> ***Trustworthiness is the greatest portal leading unto the tranquillity and security of the people. In truth the stability of every affair hath depended and doth depend upon it. All the domains of power, of grandeur and of wealth are illumined by its light.*** [349]

Shu'á 'Alá'í had a reputation for personal integrity, honesty and reliability. He was held in such high esteem that parties to lawsuits would often entrust funds to him while their cases were being tried in court to decide who was entitled. He was often named as trustee of estates in last wills and testaments of Bahá'ís.

An accountant by training, General 'Alá'í was just 19 years of age when appointed financial officer of the National Police (army) responsible for a worthless treasury. In the course of a year through various taxation schemes, the resourceful young man was able to substantially increase the treasury such that a modern police force could be trained. As a consequence the resulting law and order brought an end to rebellion and highway robbery. Between 1914 and 1919 he was treasurer of the Ministry of Justice.

Following the World War the Iranian government borrowed heavily from British banks. In 1921 the salaries of soldiers in the bitterly cold region along northern fronts had not been paid. Shu'á 'Alá'í was sent to pay these men. His efficiency in handling this difficult responsibility resulted in his being promoted to Chief Controller of army finances, a post he held for 25 years. During this time he brought organization to various departments and wrote manuals for procurement officers and quartermasters.[350]

Among his outstanding services was his work in helping to reorganize and modernize the Ministry of Post and Telegraph. He served on the boards of directors of Bank Sepah and Bank Melli Iran for many years where he protected the financial interests of Iranians irrespective of background. He set up the former bank to safeguard military pensions.

As he rose in stature and rank General 'Alá'í became known even in the highest circles for his integrity. The Sháh himself came to rely on 'Alá'í whom he knew to be truthful and trustworthy. The royal family turned to him to make an inventory of the Crown jewels, valued at $7 billion.

Concerning his services to his native country, Ugo Giachery mentioned General 'Alá'í's qualities:

> "Shu'á'u'lláh Alá'í's integrity greatly influenced developments in his native country. Such incomparable examples of a divinely guided, long, active life, reflecting all Bahá'í virtues will enrich the history of the Faith eternally." [351]

Following the fundamentalist revolution in 1979, the property and finances of General 'Alá'í's family were confiscated.

Shu'á 'Alá'í was elected to the National Spiritual Assembly of Iran in 1934, often serving as chairman. He completed delicate assignments entrusted him by the Guardian. Following his appointment as a Hand of the Cause, he was responsible for the management of properties of the Faith within Iran. In his world travels as a Hand of the Cause, he was able to make appointments and negotiate with government officials for the safety and security of the Bahá'ís '(b)ecause of his position as a financier and general of the army, and by the sheer force of his personality and worldwide reputation for his accomplishments . . .'[352]

His nephew Colonel Serreddin 'Alá'í wrote of him:

> "Everyone respected him and gave praise for his high character traits, noble qualities and divine attributes. Those coming to meet him felt in him greatness and became calm and humble. His judgements were invariably correct and all

> those who worked with him and for him carried out his wise instructions without question as they felt them best to be put into practice."[353]

When he passed away in 1984, the Universal House of Justice in its eulogy to all National Spiritual Assemblies made mention of Mr 'Alá'í's '. . . EXEMPLARY COURAGE REPRESENTING INTERESTS FAITH HIGH PLACES HIS INTEGRITY PERFORMING OFFICIAL DUTIES ENHANCED PRESTIGE BELOVED FAITH . . .'[354]

# # #

Inspiring The Heart

Calamities

> ***In the spiritual development of man a stage of purgation is indispensable, for it is while passing through it that the over-rated material needs are made to appear in their proper light. . . . The present calamities are parts of this process of purgation, through them alone will man learn his lesson. They are to teach the nations, that they have to view things internationally, they are to make the individual attribute more importance to his moral, than his material welfare.***[355]

Mr Faizi, in a letter dated 6 March 1979, wrote about how the beloved Guardian would acquaint the pilgrims with the prospect of wars and cities being on fire. When his listeners became saddened, he would then say that he wanted them to be happy. Mr Faizi continued: 'When the world reaches the very depths of miseries of wars, etc., man will open his eyes to the horizon full of effulgence of the new Day when they will agree to stop the devilish wars. We, as Bahá'ís must be more than ever before ready to spread the message. This is the time for every adherent to open his or her mouth and refresh the minds of the contacts with the glad tidings.'[356] In another letter he explained that everything in this transient life will vanish except the efforts of the friends to elevate the Cause of God.

Faizi was asked to speak about the term *catastrophe*. He said:

> "We shouldn't waste our lives, our precious lives to think what the catastrophe means and what the calamity means and what will happen, so on and so forth, because it is detrimental to our spiritual growth. There are so many beautiful things in the Bahá'í literature which are the food of life, and we must consume those things rather than these which are detrimental. Bahá'u'lláh has said a sudden calamity will come to the world because of the disobedience. He didn't mean that God is revengeful, that God is retaliating. He explains the law of God on this earth. . . . Bahá'u'lláh wrote letters to all these leaders and kings and sovereigns of the world and told them, 'I am giving you the divine advice. If you seek My advice and tread the path of God, you will be on the safe side. Otherwise the results will be so great that it will be beyond your control. . . . 'Abdu'l-Bahá says that the whole body of humanity is deaf, the eyes cannot see, the ears cannot hear, the blood is poison and the people are utterly

broken and exhausted. The only thing which will bring this thing back to life is the spirit of this divine religion which is the quickest and earliest and most urgent need of this dead body of humanity." [357]

Faizi went on to explain something 'Abdu'l-Bahá said concerning a mitigation of these calamities. He said: 'If you knew how much the world is in need of these teachings, you will never sleep, never drink water, never take food, and instead teach and teach and teach.'[358] Mr Faizi continued:

"The more we teach, the more army of light we will have in this world and the less of these calamities. This is what He meant. And please don't depend so much on the pilgrim notes, because the Guardian told each pilgrim and said according to circumstances, according to their questions. We don't know what the questions were, but some of the answers, therefore, fall into these pitfalls which will ruin our happiness, our joy, our life." [359]

* * *

Concerning a future cataclysm, Leroy Ioas wrote:

"Why people should worry about these things and make them a major consideration in their thinking and way of life, I don't know. God surely is able to direct and assist His chosen ones in all circumstances, and to think of running away, or speculating on the punishment of humanity, is wrong. It is a Christian residue, stemming from the belief that the world would be destroyed, the chosen would be lifted up above the earth while the destruction takes place, and then return here to enjoy what is left." [360]

* * *

In his scholarly work on the life of George Townshend, David Hofman states that Townshend brilliantly summarizes in his last great work the forces which have contributed to disturbances afflicting modern-day Europe. The work is *Christ and Bahá'u'lláh* and the chapter is *The Rise of Modern Europe.*[361] Townshend exposes as false the modern-day Christian view of having raised-up a superior civilization. Rather the Church's long history of resisting civilizing ideas and practices in consequence of *flagrant breaches of Gospel ethics*[362] has wrought an unchristian European civilization which today is dominated and torn apart by oppression, conflict, hatred and discontent.

Writing in mid-20th century, George Townshend, whom Shoghi Effendi described as the greatest Bahá'í scholar in the West and who served for many years as a parish priest in the Church of Ireland, unequivocally states that the main concern of Church leaders has been the preservation of orthodoxy rather than of moral righteousness. Acknowledging the Christianizing influence of the early Church by the time of Constantine, Townshend writes that the enthusiasm of religious authorities since the Dark Ages . . .

> ". . . has been confined largely to insistence on teachings, doctrines, speculations which, like their own structure were devised by themselves, and around which controversies were raised which none could finally settle. About the main ethical injunctions of Christ and actual obedience to them there was no such insistence. No church, for example, has ever adopted the challenging test for membership used by Jesus Himself for His disciples: 'By this shall all men know that ye are my disciples, if ye have love one to another.' [363] Europe in consequence has never been tranquil, full of good will, united, but rather full of oppression, misery, strife and turbulence."[364]

The real debt of Western civilization and its material power is owed firstly to the influence of Islám and lastly to a secular movement springing from the emancipation of the human spirit. Therefore whatever strides European and ultimately Western peoples have made in the civilizing process have been won in spite of and not because of the influence of the Church.

* * *

At the 1954 Annual US Bahá'í Convention, Horace Holley read the Guardian's cable directing the Hands of the Cause to appoint Auxiliary Board Members. Following the reading, Mr Holley gave a wonderful talk elucidating the crisis of our modern age.

> "Down through all the grievous years of the struggle of the human race, there's been a separation between the two most important collective forces at the disposal of humanity. To put it in its simplest terms, this separation has been that which has existed always between religion and government. You've had the government maintained by different types of states, by kings, by monarchs, by emperors, by aristocracies, by presidents, by all types

of executive jurisdictions and legislative branches. But (you've had) in the function of government the predominant element of the self-preservation of the nation or the empire. And therefore this great collective and creative force, the basis of civilization as the outer worldly government, has been committed always to the necessity of defence or the necessity of attack. And the combination of this unmoral character (of) government . . . is the crisis which has overtaken the world today. We have come to the end of that evolution. It can go no farther than the invention of the atomic bomb."[365]

***

Paul Haney was once asked whether the Bahá'ís should move out of unsafe places. Reminding his audience of Bahá'u'lláh's statement, '. . . there is no place to flee to except Thee,'[366] he said that the motivation of the friends should not be personal safety. Rather they should strive to serve the Faith in places where Bahá'ís are needed, turning to their National Spiritual Assembly and Universal House of Justice for guidance on home front and international goals.

In response to another question concerning the extent to which the world situation would adversely affect the believers, the Shrines and personnel in Haifa, Mr Haney said:

"I think the way to begin answering that is to say that the beloved Guardian made it very clear to us that these things were going to happen in the world, that we should not pay too much attention to them, and that our task is to concentrate on teaching the Cause and not worry too much about the calamities or whatever will befall mankind until the people of the world become sufficiently purified to enter the kingdom of God.

But developments in the world could have some adverse effect in breaking down communications. The World Centre itself conceivably might at some point be cut off temporarily from the rest of the Bahá'í world. But we just shouldn't dwell upon it. Certainly the Shrines and holy places and the buildings at the World Centre are certainly in danger. It's a very dangerous part of the world. Whatever happens provisions have been made so that the work of the Faith will be carried on regardless.

> We will just hope that conditions won't reach a point where the World Centre itself becomes the centre of war or other calamity." [367]

* * *

On 1 September 1923 two-thirds of Tokyo was destroyed by an earthquake. Thousands of the city's inhabitants lost their lives while several millions were made homeless. Agnes Alexander was at home when the house began to shake with increasing violence. Fleeing to the street she saw the roofs of neighbouring houses falling. At first opportunity Agnes rushed back into the house in order to retrieve her hand bag in which she carried a prayer for protection. Back on the street, she said this prayer each time the earth shook.

In spite of the terrible destruction, the believers were safe. Letters of condolence poured in from friends in other parts of the world as well as contributions to help relieve the suffering. Three days after the earthquake, Louis Gregory wrote Agnes:

> "I have felt especially anxious for you, our dear sister, Mrs. Finch, Prof. Monroe and that dear circle of illumination whom you have trained and gathered about you, all of whom I seem to know. Yet my hope for you is above all; for I know that you are unshaken in your faith in the Supreme Power of the Covenant and rely at all times upon its Guidance and Protection. This is indeed the only safety for any soul. Physical calamities affect only our bodies. The real calamity, in 'this gloomy, disastrous age,' is not knowing God. I thank God that you and your associates, in reality, live in a world above the realm of dust. I hope that you will at once communicate with us and let us know, aside from the general measures of relief in which all the friends will join, what we can especially do for you and your associates, who are so dear to our hearts through the eternal bond. Meantime, may our kind and merciful Lord comfort you and yours!" [368]

What did Agnes have to say concerning this catastrophe? She wrote a letter to the Bahá'ís of India describing the great Kanto earthquake:

> "That day our beloved Lord protected His servants in these parts. . . . On the street this servant met a delivery man passing. He grasped her hand and kept her standing. The earth shook and quaked, tiles rolled from the neighboring

houses, and then a fierce gust of wind swept darkening the atmosphere with the dust it carried. Through it all, this servant repeated aloud the Greatest Name. Her first apprehension was that Tokyo would be consumed by fires. . . . Then this servant rushed back into the home to get her Tablets, her money, etc., for safety. The walls of the little house had been shaken and broken and everything was scattered on the floor. She grasped Abdu'l-Baha's Tablet for Protection, and each successive time the earth shook, she read it aloud on the little street. Three more times the earth shook with terror, but as the Tablet was read it calmed and His Power was felt. The frightened people came from their houses and gathered on the street. We little knew then, the terrible things which were happening not only in Tokyo, but the destruction of Yokohama, the sea port, an hour's train ride from Tokyo, and the destruction of many places along the coast." [369]

Agnes felt that crisis brings growth, and that the earthquake was the means of guiding her . . . No stranger to adversity, she had lost her possessions in a hotel fire a few years before and written:

"My heart was not burned . . . and the Reality could never be taken from it. His words are eternal and will remain when all else perishes, and He came near to me for His love is beyond our knowledge. There was a great meaning in that fire . . ." [370]

* * *

At the 1967 Intercontinental Conference in Chicago-Wilmette, Ṭarázu'lláh Samandarí . . .

". . . quoted Shoghi Effendi as saying that all the peoples of the world must pass through three stages: they must suffer for what their hands have wrought; they will awaken after a punishment which will burn away the drunken fumes from their brains; and then they will come into the Cause of God in troops." [371]

Mr Samandarí added:

"It will take strength to meet the great upheavals which the Guardian has said were certain to take place; first in the Holy Land; second in Persia; and third in America. The friends must be steadfast and detached, they must *be* the Teachings, and must immediately obey the commands of the Universal House of Justice." [372]

* * *

William Sears was seriously ill. On his way to the United States for major surgery, he left his bed to briefly attend the final day's session of the 1967 Kampala Intercontinental Conference in the Mashriqu'l-Adhkár. There he reminded the attendees of the circumstances in which humanity was struggling and of their calling:

> "The beloved Guardian told us that we were being swept into the vortex of unprecedented disasters, undreamed of afflictions and sufferings. The world around us is suffering. It is tragic, but the real tragedy is that the Bahá'ís within the community may fail to respond to His exhortations to accomplish the task before them.... Unless we are Bahá'ís outwardly and within, we cannot win the victories.... Sometimes we appear outwardly devoted and active, but inwardly we lack dedication; we go through the motions but our hearts are not in it, the fire seems to have gone out. We can fool other people, but we cannot fool Bahá'u'lláh. Sometimes we can fool ourselves, but not for long. No man is happy without the love of God in his heart.... 'one thing and only one thing,' said Shoghi Effendi, 'will unfailingly and alone secure the undoubted triumph of this sacred Cause, namely the extent to which our own inner lives and private character mirror forth in their manifold aspects the splendour of those eternal principles proclaimed by Bahá'u'lláh." [373]

* * *

Half a world away at the 1967 Chicago-Wilmette Intercontinental Conference, John Robarts said:

> "A power has been infused into the world by the Universal House of Justice by which the Faith will advance on the unknown seas of proclamation, but the results depend ultimately on the efforts of the individual Bahá'ís." [374]

* * *

Dr Giachery once explained that the Guardian was aware of the material progress of the United States even though he had never visited there. He saw a great danger in that progress because two things never go together: comfort and spirituality.[375]

* * *

Keith Ransom-Kehler was once asked to write down her favourite quote in the guest book of a friend. She wrote:

> "O our God! Lead us to the ocean of Thy graciousness and immerse us in Thy Name, that our thought may not grieve us and whatever happens to us in Thy Cause may not afflict us." [376]

# # #

Death

Live . . . the days of thy life, that are less than a fleeting moment, with thy mind stainless, thy heart unsullied, thy thoughts pure, and thy nature sanctified, so that, free and content, thou mayest put away this mortal frame, and repair unto the mystic paradise and abide in the eternal kingdom for evermore.[377]

I HAVE A RENDEZVOUS WITH DEATH

I have a rendezvous with death –
Sweet death, dear death,
Soon or late I come to thee.

My ancestors were wild folk,
Highland folk, deep, keen,
They plied the sword
For those they loved,
They grinned and parried,
Spilt their blood,
Died for lost causes
Counting not the cost!

The same blood flows in me,
I'll race fate one last course
About the green,
Give destiny a run
For its black money –
And then, my friends,
I have a rendezvous with death –
Dear death, sweet death,
I'll come to thee. [378]

-Rúḥíyyih Khánum

***

Ismu'lláhu'l-Aṣdaq was one of the survivors of Shaykh Ṭabarsí. In his long life, he suffered much abuse. He was scourged with a thousand lashes. His beard was burned; an act of humiliation. His nose was pierced so that he could be led by a cord through city streets. He was accused of heresy. His enemies attempted his murder. He was placed in chains. He was put in the Síyáh-Chál. He was attacked and denounced.

Following a pilgrimage in which he attained the presence of Bahá'u'lláh and forgot all his troubles, he made his way to Hamadán. For twelve days he tarried. On the last day he adorned himself with his finest raiment, and perfumed himself. For an hour he asked to be alone. Then, as he was being assisted to undress, he said:

> "'That is enough'; the next moment he was gone - gone from this world. Thus, calmly and serenely, death brought release to Mullá Ṣádiq, Ismu'lláhu'l-Aṣdaq, from untold tribulations which would have broken a lesser man, but were endured by him with radiant acquiescence in the path of his Lord. His death occurred in the year 1889." [379]

Of him 'Abdu'l-Bahá wrote:

> "Ismu'lláh did not slacken under fire. . . . He was like a surging sea, a falcon that soared high. His visage shone, his tongue was eloquent, his strength and steadfastness astounding." [380]

* * *

Twenty years before her tragic death at sea, Dorothy Baker said to her family: 'I hope people don't make a shrine of my grave after I'm buried!' Her husband asked: 'And how can you make sure they won't?' She replied: 'If I could really have my choice, I would be buried at sea. . . . And if I could choose the sea, then it would be the Mediterranean, whose waves will lap eternally on the shores of 'Akká.'[381]

In 1954 Dorothy died when the plane she was on exploded over the Mediterranean Sea, near the island of Elba.

* * *

Counsellor Edith Senoga said that when the Faith was banned in Uganda, she was the first to arrive at the home of Enoch Olinga. There she knelt beside his bed as he was resting and told him about the ban. Upon receiving this news, he wept and said: 'Go into the sitting room. I will come and talk with you and we will decide what to do.'[382] In the sitting room they decided to go out. They went to the Temple where they saw everything was quiet.

Sometime before his death, he called Edith by name three times: 'Edith, Edith, Edith. As you knelt beside my bed about the ban on the Faith, this is how you will kneel beside my dead body.' She was horrified and replied: 'Mr Olinga, why do you say that? Maybe I'll die before you.'[383]

Later it happened like that. When he had been killed in 1979, Edith Senoga rushed to his home and knelt next to his dead body weeping. It was then she remembered what he had told her. She always wondered how he knew, how it was going to be.

* * *

Dr Muhájir had a strange dream of Enoch Olinga in which Enoch and Raḥmat were looking down on a tormented earth beneath them. Enoch remarked to Raḥmat how they had been spared the carnage.

Raḥmat believed this dream portended his own imminent departure from this world for the Abhá Kingdom where he would join his friend, Enoch. He was right because a few months after this dream Raḥmatu'lláh Muhájir unexpectedly died of heart failure in Ecuador in December, 1979; four months after dear Enoch had lost his life.[384]

* * *

In 1908 Sydney Sprague was appointed principal of the Tarbíyat School in Ṭihrán. Before his departure in 1910, he had the opportunity to familiarize himself with the Persian economic and educational conditions as well as become acquainted with the believers.

In a letter dated 19 March 1910, he wrote about the passing of Ḥájí Á<u>kh</u>únd:

> "The passing out of Haji Akhoun was very beautiful. He had returned one day from the bath, and complaining of feeling tired, he called for a glass of water, drank it and without a word the spirit left the body. About thirty years ago BAHA'O'LLAH had foretold, in a Tablet, that Haji Akhoun would die in this way, peacefully and calmly. He revealed this Tablet when Haji Akhoun was in prison and all were expecting that he would meet with some violent end. What a wonderful life to have lived and served and suffered for the Cause of God during fifty years! Before his conversion, too, he was a very important Mullah and he sacrificed position, wealth, name, everything for the sake of BAHA'O'LLAH. It was a great privilege to have met and known such a man." [385]

* * *

> ***. . . when the true lover findeth his Beloved, he yieldeth up his soul.*** [386]

At Desert Rose in 1998, Marguerite Sears wanted to convey the significance of her husband's last tour of the American Bahá'í community. In 1991 Mr Sears was concerned that the American Bahá'ís were behind in their goal of realizing a large increase in the number of new believers – an important goal of the community leading up to the Holy Year of 1992. Asking the National Assembly to select nine cities to which he could travel in order to rouse the friends to raise up 9,000 new believers by Riḍván 1992, he set out. In spite of suffering debility, diabetes, restricted vision, limited mobility and airport travel delays, he visited those cities and he urged the believers to arise. Returning home he was exhausted. Nevertheless, when he felt the friends were still not responding, he asked the National Assembly to provide him with another nine cities to visit.

These tours literally killed him, Mrs Sears said. But he so loved the Faith that he willingly sacrificed the last ounces of his ebbing strength in what would later be regarded as the final service of a warrior. Beginning in February 1992, he set out on the second tour of six weeks duration, visiting New York City, Cleveland, Washington DC, Chicago, Atlanta and Minneapolis. His next scheduled stop was Denver. But he collapsed one morning, unable to will his tired old body to respond to his dynamic driving spirit.

Marguerite tried desperately to lift him but could not. He said to her: 'I don't have the strength.' 'Come on, Bill,' she pleaded. 'No, just bring me a pillow and a cover. That will be sufficient.'[387] Then did the noble soul of the Hand of the Cause of God William Sears abandon the steed of his earthly throne for a loftier sovereignty. In their eulogy to William Sears, the Supreme Body called him 'STOUT-HEARTED STANDARD-BEARER FAITH BAHÁ'U'LLÁH'.[388]

At a national memorial service held within a half-year of his passing, a very appropriate Tablet was read in his honour:

> "Great is thy blessedness, inasmuch as thou hast been journeying throughout the lands of God, and been the embodiment of joy and assurance for the people of Bahá who have renounced all else but Him, and set their hearts towards this Court which hath shed its radiance upon all realms, and sprinkled them with the surging waters of this Ocean wherewith thou thyself hast been sprinkled – an Ocean which hath encompassed all created things. . . . Indeed thou

didst grasp the significance of rendering assistance unto God and didst arise to achieve this through the power of wisdom and utterance." [389]

* * *

On 21 March 1957 (New Year's Day in the Bahá'í Faith) George Townshend lay in the Baggot Street Hospital. In his lifetime of distinguished service to the Guardian, he had received 150 letters from Shoghi Effendi. Brian Townshend entered his father's room and gently mentioned a cable from the Guardian. George raised himself up and strongly seized Brian's coat, begging to know the contents. 'LOVING THOUGHTS FERVENT PRAYERS SURROUND YOU BE HAPPY CONFIDENT.'[390] George became relaxed and joyful, lifting his hand and waving it in a triumphant gesture. Four days later he laid aside his worn out body for the invisible realm.

* * *

"... I remember during July 1986 ... You were complaining of a backache; otherwise, you appeared quite healthy. You told us that months ago you had had a dream of the beloved Guardian. In that dream he asked you to arrange for the pilgrims to attend his presence, as you used to do during his lifetime. You looked around but could find no one. Since there was no one, you asked permission to make the pilgrimage yourself. The Guardian granted your request. You interpreted the dream to mean that you were going to leave us. You were thankful to Bahá'u'lláh for having permitted you to serve His Cause and to leave the world having witnessed the physical and spiritual ascendancy and triumph of His Faith, a Faith that you loved with your entire being. You prayed that all of your children and grandchildren would serve this Faith and place it at the centre of their lives. We tried in vain to convince you that your dream could have other interpretations and that it did not necessarily mean that you were going to leave this world. But you, in your characteristic, uncompromising manner, were convinced that the remaining days of your life were, indeed, numbered." [391]

Zukrullah Khadem passed away in November, 1986, of a malignant tumour, the pain of which had started as a backache.

* * *

The end of World War II was a period of intense nationalism in Burma. A mob of three thousand people surrounded the village of Daidanaw, determined to purge it of foreign influence. When the mob discovered that Siyyid Muṣṭafá Rúmí was not Burmese, they beheaded and dismembered his body. Earlier the believers had urged him to make his escape. But he had replied:

> "I am old. I will not leave the place that I chose to serve." [392]

* * *

Amín Banání had this to say about the last wish of his distinguished father, Músá Banání, the Spiritual Conqueror of Africa:

> "He was, at the end of his earthly life, a truly inspiring example of the triumph of the spirit over every earthly limitation. He had made a fortune and raised a Bahá'í family earlier; now he had spent most of his material substance in the crowning nineteen years of his life opening a continent to the Faith and adding thousands to the Bahá'í family of the world. He was able to look back upon his life with a profound sense of humility and gratitude. He felt that God had been extremely generous to him. Bahá'u'lláh had given him everything in this life that he had ever wished for, and he was given the opportunity to give it back to Him. His death in Kampala on September 4, 1971, and his interment in his favorite spot in the soil of Africa, within the shadow of the Mother Temple of that continent, was the generous fulfilment of his last wish." [393]

* * *

Roy Wilhelm asked the Master whether a person who is suffering from an incurable disease may be put to sleep with a powder. 'Abdu'l-Bahá replied:

> "He who gives life, must take it away." [394]

> ***Set not your affections on mortal sovereignty and rejoice not therein. Ye are even as the unwary bird that with full confidence warbleth upon the bough; till of a sudden the fowler Death throws it upon the dust . .*** [395]

In a skit she wrote entitled *Heard on High*, Rúḥíyyih Khánum portrays her idea of the reception awaiting souls according to their merit as they pass into the next world. Performed at the Bahá'í World Centre and elsewhere, this skit contrasts the reception awaiting earth-bound souls with that which awaits a developed soul.

Upon entering the next world, a formerly influential soul is asked by an interviewer to identify himself. He responds that he is a very important man, a famous doctor, an inventor, wise and clever (and boastful). The interviewer says to this newly arrived soul that the standards of the heavenly realm are not those of the earth. What is required is assisting undeveloped souls. Although this doctor is in the spiritual world, he is unsure why he is there and he does not believe there is a soul. The interviewer decides to put him in Class One where he can be educated.

Next in line is a housewife who identifies herself as having had a very good house and been a very good housekeeper. After she had described the beauty of her house to the interviewer, he explains that the heavenly realm has different standards. The woman only wants to be shown her new house and begins to cry as she realizes her future will now be very different. The interviewer sends her to Class Eight where she will be assisted by spiritually developed souls from Southeast Asia.

Next comes a man who is all pumped up with himself. As a way of introducing himself to the interviewer, he looks around for his visiting cards and his personal secretary. Feeling disoriented he informs the interviewer that he was an Ambassador, a famous man, a Harvard graduate, etc., etc. The interviewer tells him that their values are different. This man becomes angry and demands to see the Director. But the interviewer says that the Director is very busy, that the man doesn't speak His language and that he would not understand the Director. Asked about what language He speaks, the interviewer replies:

'He speaks the language of wisdom; He speaks the language of mercy; He speaks the language of justice; He speaks the language of a good heart, of good deeds; and you would not be able to understand Him at all.'

The interviewer sends him *to* a beginners' class where he will be helped by Bolivian Indian souls whose suffering and impoverishment in the physical world gave them much patience.

Another recently-arrived soul rejoices in his arrival. 'You know I have been longing to come here for a long time . . . Do you think that here I will be allowed to see His Face?' The interviewer replies: 'Yes, He has been waiting for you and you can go and see His Face.' And so this soul, radiant with the love of God, enters the Presence of his Creator.[396]

* * *

In a letter to a believer who was concerned about the state of her father who had passed away, Mr Faizi wrote tenderly:

> "As to your question about the passing of your father before you accepted the Faith. Rest assured my dear friend that your father is forgiven by God and accepted in the worlds beyond as a true Bahá'í. The reason is very clear. There are trees which yield sweet fruits and are recognized and adored. There had surely been in your dear father's essence sweetness of faith. This is his inheritance to you and he cherishes the result of your efforts in investigating after the true Faith of God." [397]

* * *

On 18 October 1939, the Guardian sent a telegram to the National Spiritual Assembly of the Bahá'ís of Iran in which he unveiled the welcome and station of Martha Root among the Supreme Concourse following her passing:

> "The pure leaf and renowned teacher, sign of severance torch of love and tenderness, standard of courage and faithfulness, consolation of the eyes of the people of Bahá, Martha Root, has ascended to the highest summits of paradise. The people of the Supreme Concourse came forth to meet her with the shout, 'Welcome to thee, O pride of men and women teachers! Well done, well done, thou who hast spent thy whole being in devotion to the Kingdom of the Lord of signs and utterances! Blessed, a thousandfold blessed art thou within this shining, proud and lofty station!'" [398]

# # #

Grief And Sorrow

O God, my God! Thou seest me immersed in the depths of grief, drowned in my sorrow, my heart on fire with the agony of parting, my inmost self aflame with longing.[399]

"... as I looked at him all I could think of was – how beautiful he is, how beautiful! A celestial beauty seemed to be poured over him and to rest on him and stream from him like a mighty benediction from on high. And the wonderful hands, so like the hands of Bahá'u'lláh, lay softly by his side; it seemed impossible the life had gone from them – or from that radiant face." [400]

Rúḥíyyih Khánum's final moments with her beloved Guardian and husband, 7 November 1957.

* * *

HAVE YOU SEEN MY LOVE

She set out upon the ways
Of the weary world
And wandered far and near.
She sought in secret lanes,
By soft waters and solitary lakes,
The one she thirsted for –
But wide as the world's ways were
There was no reward for her wandering,
Her restless, aching wandering!

"She" was my soul, my own poor heart,
Condemned to death in life as one,
Fevered with grief grown great in love.
She wrung her hands and walked far, wide ways
And to each one on those distant roads
She sought, she asked and questioned
"Have you seen my love go by?"
My love is bright and brave and better
Than the sun himself which shines!
My love so dear, so kingly, kind and high,
My love so wise and well and strong –

Have you not seen my love pass by?
His foot is small and high, and firm his step,
His hand is quick and small and brown and strong,
His eyes are hazel and grey and oh so bright!
And his smile you will never see again . . .

His voice rings in a plaintive tone,
Full of command and secret tears and thoughts –
Oh, say have you not seen my love
Go over the world's rim, pass on just there?
Tell me, tell me which the road he took![401]

-Rúḥíyyih Khánum, 20 March 1958

* * *

On Monday, 4 November 1957, Ugo Giachery is at home in Italy. At 2:15 in the afternoon, he receives a long distance telephone call from Rúḥíyyih Khánum: 'The Guardian is dead!'[402] Dr Giachery later wrote:

> "Reeling under the impact of such crushing news, with little strength and reason left, I manage to book an air passage . . . and reach the airport in time to board a plane leaving Rome for London at 4:55 p.m. . . . The journey is uneventful until we reach Switzerland; after that the weather becomes bad and we land in London half an hour later than scheduled, with the elements raging all around us.
>
> One and a half hours later I join Rúḥíyyih Khánum, Ḥasan Balyuzi and John Ferraby, and together we go to the Ḥaẓíratu'l-Quds at 27 Rutland Gate. The wind and the rain lash London all night; it is impossible to rest or accept with one's reason the reality of such a catastrophic situation." [403]

* * *

Leroy Ioas received the news from Rúḥíyyih Khánum at seven in the evening on 4 November 1957 that Shoghi Effendi had died. He fell to the floor in a momentary faint, and then managed to continue the terrible conversation. Later that night he and Sylvia Ioas and Milly Collins said many prayers at the Shrine of the Báb. Then they sent a cablegram to Rúḥíyyih Khánum:

> "In Guardian's passing whole Bahá'í world grieved crushed but your personal loss insurmountable. Sylvia myself send deepfelt sympathy love admiration your strong determination assist his released spirit gain even greater victories beloved Faith." [404]

In later years when Leroy Ioas spoke of the Guardian, he felt such grief and love as to affect his damaged heart. Repeatedly he would cough from the strain of the emotion. 'Alí-Akbar Furútan remembered Leroy's talks about the beloved Guardian to the pilgrims during the Interregnum.

> "Leroy always spoke about the life of the Guardian, his exalted station, his divine knowledge, his arduous and painstaking work. He showed such love and devotion towards the beloved Shoghi Effendi that all who heard him, young and old, were deeply touched." [405]

* * *

Amelia Collins had just returned to Haifa from America and eagerly looked forward to greeting the Guardian upon his return from London. She remembered how the previous June when he was leaving Haifa Shoghi Effendi had taken her hands, looked into her eyes and said: 'Don't be sad, Milly.'[406] Leroy Ioas broke the news of Shoghi Effendi's passing as gently as possible. She was very frail and was crushed by the news. She put her head on Leroy's shoulder and wept and wept.

Somehow through the prayers at the Shrine of the Báb that night and her effort to obey her beloved Guardian to not be sad, she rallied, and in coming days brought much comfort to Rúḥíyyih K͟hánum.

* * *

Abu'l-Qásim Faizí was in Europe when he received the news that the Guardian had ascended. Grief-stricken with uncontrollable sorrow, he proceeded to London for the funeral. Afterward he had no desire to live in this world. That which kept him alive was service to the Cause which he performed indefatigably the rest of his life.[407]

* * *

On 4 November 1957 Zikrullah Khadem was taking delivery of a car at a factory in Germany when he encountered a Bahá'í who tactlessly blurted out to him that the Guardian had passed away. Mr Khadem felt all his strength drain away at this devastating news. He left for the Bahá'í

Centre where the news was confirmed by Abu'l-Qásim Faizi. Mr Khadem became ill and could neither eat nor sleep. Mr Faizi looked after him. On the journey to London for the funeral, he remained incapacitated. He was so ill that his colleagues did not believe him able to attend the funeral. At the Great Northern London Cemetery, he was barely able to fulfil his desire to pay homage to his beloved.

The wife of Mr Khadem – Javidukht Khadem – was in Iran at this time. In her book on the life of her beloved husband, she wrote:

> "For a long time I had no news. Then one day there was a knock at the door of our house in Tehran. I opened the door and saw a man with a severe, expressionless face, standing immovable, like a statue, with all the weight of the world on his shoulders. This was my husband. I could hardly recognize him. He was the picture of despair. Words cannot convey what a difficult time this was for us." [408]

How Mr Khadem longed for his departed beloved one. 'The passing of the beloved Guardian, Shoghi Effendi,' he recorded for posterity, 'grieved the hearts of the Bahá'ís in a manner that defies explanation. How many nights his faithful ones did not sleep because of their separation from their beloved. How many days they did not have any desire to continue to live in this world.'[409]

* * *

'Alí-Akbar Furútan received a cable the morning of 5 November 1957 from Amatu'l-Bahá Rúḥíyyih Khánum informing him of the passing of the Guardian. Mr Furútan was badly shaken and he madly rushed to the home of a believer to consult on ways to inform the members of the National and Local Spiritual Assemblies. After meeting with them and in other meetings which followed, Mr Furútan struggled to assuage the grief of the friends even though he himself needed consolation.

Mr Furútan wrote that in the Guardian's messages dated 4 June and October 1957 . . .

> ". . . the signs of the separation of the beloved Guardian, the Sign of God, from his devoted followers were visible. But no one could believe that after only a short period of time the sun of beauty of that kind and compassionate Guardian would set, and tears of grief and sorrow would flow from the eyes of those who, life in hand, had dedicated themselves to the Cause he so cherished." [410]

* * *

On Tuesday morning, 5 November 1957, Rúḥíyyih Khánum put in a telephone call to Dr Adelbert Mühlschlegel to request that he prepare the body of the Guardian for burial. A physician and a man known for his spirituality, he would be able to perform this task in an appropriate spirit of consecration while enduring the sorrow of this service. Dr Mühlschlegel accepted with gratitude the charge placed upon him by Rúḥíyyih Khánum.

Thursday afternoon Dr Mühlschlegel and Rúḥíyyih Khánum drove to where the Guardian's body was to be washed. Delivering into his capable hands a quantity of the finest white silk available as well as towels, cloths and soap, Rúḥíyyih Khánum waited in an anti-room while the doctor performed his duty. While washing, wrapping and anointing the precious remains, Dr Mühlschlegel underwent a profound spiritual experience. Later he wrote down for posterity a glimpse of that experience.

> "Something new happened to me in that hour that I cannot, even after a few days, speak of, but I can mention the wisdom and love that I felt pour over me. In that room . . . there was a tremendous spiritual force such as I have only felt in my life in the holy Shrines. My first impression was the contrast between the body left behind and the majestic, transfigured face, a soul-stirring picture of the joyous victory of the eternal over the transient. My second impression, as I prayed and thought and carefully did what I had to do, was that in this degree of consecration to the work of God I should work all my life, and mankind should work a thousand years, in order to construct 'the Kingdom' on earth; and my third thought was . . . that I thanked those beloved hands which had worked and written to establish the Covenant, those feet that had walked for us, that mouth that had spoken to us, that head that had thought for us, and I prayed and meditated and supplicated that in the short time left to me, the members of my body might hasten to follow in his path of service; and my last thought was of my own distress because I felt how unworthy my hands were to anoint that blessed brow with attar-of-rose as the Masters of old were wont to do to their pupils; and yet what privileges, what duties fall to us, the living, to watch over what is past and mortal, be it ever so exalted. A great deal of mercy, love, and wisdom were hidden in this hour." [411]

* * *

Four days after Corrine True's 96th birthday on 5 November 1957, Rúḥíyyih Khánum telephoned the news of the Guardian's passing to Edna True. It was 2:30 in the morning. Immediately Edna shared the distressing news with her sister Katherine. They decided to wait until after breakfast to break the news to their mother, whose health was very fragile. Corrine, who had lost many of her own children to death, had been very close to Shoghi Effendi, had known him as a child and had served the Cause under his guidance throughout his ministry.

Corrine was sitting up in her bed surrounded by Bahá'í books when her daughters brought her breakfast. After breakfast they broke the news to her.

> "Corrine lowered her head. There was silence for a moment, maybe longer. Suddenly, she looked up, her face pale, but her eyes ablaze with an assurance her daughters had never seen before. 'You must know that this is the will of God,' she declared." [412]

* * *

The passing of the Guardian changed Dr Muhájir. Gone were his *overflowing humour*, *exuberant optimism* and *joyful banter*,[413] replaced by *quiet gentleness* and *contemplative hope* (ibid). He received the news of Shoghi Effendi's passing at a hotel in Padang on 5 November 1957 by telephone. Agonized and disbelieving, he and his wife spent that tormented night in prayer. Iran Furútan Muhájir wrote:

> "We were paralysed. Our beloved Guardian, for whom we were willing to give our lives, was gone. The Sign of God on earth, our only refuge, whose love and care had sustained us through all the hardships of the past five years, was not with us any more. We felt lost and aimless." [414]

* * *

> "The passing of the Guardian in 1957 was an irremediable personal blow for (Músá Bánáni), but it made him doubly resolute in fulfilling Shoghi Effendi's plans." [415] – Amin Banání

* * *

Following the stunning news of the ascension of Shoghi Effendi to the Abhá Kingdom, William Sears's . . .

> "... warm and loving nature, his sense of humor, and the sparkle in his eyes were intact, but there was a new intensity, a singleness of purpose, and no matter what else it might appear that he was doing, he was really concentrating on what he could do, himself and through his friends, to advance the Faith, and fulfil the responsibilities entrusted to him by Shoghi Effendi." [416]

* * *

At 10:00 a.m. on 9 November at the London Ḥaẓíra, friends have gathered in such numbers from around the world for the funeral of the beloved Guardian that movement is difficult. Sorrow is etched on the faces of his despairing lovers who await the signal to join the funeral procession. At 10:40 over 60 automobiles carrying over 360 people leave 27 Rutland Gate for the Great Northern Cemetery. The procession makes its way through the great London metropolis and its population so unaware of the historic occasion unfolding in its midst.

The procession reaches the cemetery where more distraught believers heartbroken by the tragedy have waited restlessly for a chance to draw near the coffin. The casket is taken into the chapel and placed to rest on the catafalque which is covered with green velvet. The casket itself is blanketed by roses, gardenias and lilies. In the centre of this floral display is a simple card with an inscription:

> "From Rúḥíyyih and all your loved ones and lovers all over the world whose hearts are broken." [417]

Attending the funeral services of the beloved Guardian were Hands of the Cause Rúḥíyyih Khánum, Amelia Collins, Mason Remey, Ugo Giachery, Paul Haney, William Sears, Adelbert Mühlschlegel, Hermann Grossmann, John Ferraby, Ḥasan Balyuzi, Abu'l-Qásam Faizi, Shu'á'u'lláh 'Alá'í, Ṭarázu'lláh Samandarí, Zikrullah Khadem, Músá Banání, Leroy Ioas, Enoch Olinga, and Raḥmatu'lláh Muhájir. Horace Holley was in hospital and unable to travel. John Robarts was unable to attend when his seat on a flight to London was taken by another person. Corrine True could not travel owing to her advanced age. 'Alí-Akbar Furútan remained in Iran at the request of the National Spiritual Assembly to attend the memorial gatherings and comfort the believers. Jalál Kházeh was unable to obtain the necessary travel documents in time for the funeral.

> "At once the chant of Abu'l-Qásim Faizi, steady, but interwoven with deep emotion, is in the air. It is the Prayer

> for the Dead of Bahá'u'lláh. It becomes our cry, our imploring. I cannot stand it, my heart is pounding to the breaking-point. Will God have mercy on us? . . . The rhythm of the chant rises and falls. I cannot understand the Arabic words but keep on repeating the refrains in Italian; I want to feel very near to the departed spirit. I repeat prayer after prayer almost unaware of the place and the surroundings." [418]

Ṭarázu'lláh Samandarí could be heard weeping loudly; this Hand of the Cause who uniquely had served and attained the presences of Bahá'u'lláh, 'Abdu'l-Bahá and Shoghi Effendi.

Other prayers are said and then the coffin is taken out to the funeral car to be driven the few hundred yards to his final resting place. At the gravesite hardly anyone can move around; such is the press of friends anxious to delay this final separation. The inevitable moment arrives. The coffin . . .

> ". . . is placed at the head of the grave. There is a moment of hushed silence, and then moaning and sobbing are heard again, this time much louder and more widely spread. It is a struggle to remain standing erect, when the weight of sorrow bends us down, down to the soil, nearer to him whom we loved so much."[419]

Rúhíyyih Khánum senses the agony of hearts surrounding her at this moment of final separation. In the midst of her own personal grief, she withdrew that the friends might pass by the coffin and pay their respects.

> "One by one, with an unprecedented demonstration of supreme love, wanting to empty our hearts for the last time to the hidden, lifeless, beloved Guardian of God's Faith, the friends fall on their knees, sobbing in despair, at the head of the casket. Flowers, attar of roses, kisses, tears, prayers, supplications, promises, vows are the offerings made at such a parting. Women, children, men in the prime of life, old bent men, all believers, pass for well two hours under the drizzling rain to pay the last homage, the last tribute, to him who for thirty-six years gave to them his whole life, his love, his guidance and the inspiration to rise above human limitation. What a debt of gratitude we owe him; it is too late now, our conscience well tells us how much gratitude we placed silently in the balance to recompense him for his labours!" [420]

* * *

At the first Conclave of the Hands of the Cause in the Mansion of Bahá'u'lláh at Bahjí after the passing of Shoghi Effendi . . .

> "All were seated around a table at the head of which a chair was left empty in respect for the beloved departed one. Tears poured over their faces at intervals, causing one of the Hands of the Cause to observe that they 'would blind our eyes.' We supplicated to the Blessed Beauty that He would help us to find our way and that we would arise to show our loyalty and devotion and to serve the Cause befittingly . . ." [421]

# # #

Guidance

> ***I pray God to remove all the veils and to illumine your hearts with lights shining from the Supreme Horizon, in such a manner that the light of guidance shall move before you and that your hearts shall dilate in perceiving great signs.*** [422]

> "'Abdu'l-Bahá said guidance was when the doors opened. If a person wants to do a thing, prays about it, exerts every effort to do it, questions his own sincerity and desire to do it, and still, in spite of all this, the way does not open for him to do it, then he should accept that it was not the right thing for him to do. However, to be sure it was not the right thing, the prayers, the motive and the effort to accomplish it must have been sincere and sustained in the first place. If he makes a half-hearted attempt to do something and fails, he cannot very well excuse himself by saying, 'It is not the will of God!'" [423] – Rúḥíyyih Khánum

* * *

George Townshend well understood the reality of guidance, which for him came whether separately or in combination through prayer, meditation or consultation. He had seen statements from the Guardian indicating that we can never be certain whether our supplications and consequent inner promptings are guidance. Nevertheless he would not hesitate to go forward if the *doors appear to open*. Otherwise, given no light on the matter or removal of difficulties in the way of achieving his goal, he felt that *divine approval is withheld.*[424]

* * *

As a youth Zikrullah Khadem was once bitterly disappointed that a position he wanted was not forthcoming. His father, perceiving his son's disappointment, consoled him: 'O my dear, my heart! Why are you agonized with what happens in this world? Does not the Lord know our heart? He knows. And whatever is good, He plans for you!' Quoting from the Qur'án, he said:

> "It may happen that you will hate a thing which is better for you; and it may happen that you will love a thing which is worse for you; God knows, and you know not. . . . Be happy with whatever God has planned for you." [425]

Many years later at a Bahá'í conference in Fort Worth, Texas, the Hand of the Cause Mr Khadem spoke exuberantly about how the will of God may interfere with our plans. His manner of presentation so joyfully taught the audience that we should never feel disappointment when God intervenes. But in recalling elsewhere that incident in his youth, Mr Khadem confessed:

> ". . . at that moment, if the angels themselves came down to tell me that it was not good for me to join that office, I would not have believed it." [426]

***

Dorothy Baker felt that we should rely on divine guidance as God knows our destiny. Whatever course runs contrary to His will may bring about endless troubles. So we should forget our own wishes even if what we desire seems the best advantage.

So what did Dorothy have to say about our own desires versus guidance?

> "Three steps may be followed to achieve the desired results. First, be quiet; meditate on the problem from all angles, and turn to God with a sense of listening. If possible, use one of the beautiful prayers of Bahá'u'lláh for guidance. The second step is to take hold of a definite conclusion with the full help of reason, facts, and, above all, the sense of being assisted by God. Sometimes this step comes in a clear flash; sometimes not. I have often arisen from a prayer for guidance without a sense of having achieved the answer, only to find that every door opened for the right fulfilment. The third step is to proceed courageously, knowing that it is answered. Banish all fear or anxiety and walk confidently; act as if the desired results have already been accomplished. If you fail to do this, your prayer is perhaps like a beautiful child still-born, and therefore of no avail to this world." [427]

In 1927 Ruth Moffett made a pilgrimage to the Holy Land in which she attained the presence of the Guardian. Shoghi Effendi asked her to emphasize to the believers the importance of prayer. Accordingly she produced a book, *DU'Á: On Wings of Prayer*, where she wrote:

"While I was in Haifa, the beloved Guardian of the Cause outlined for the writer a most concise, complete, and effective approach for the Dynamics of Prayer. After encouraging me to stress the need of more prayer and meditation among the friends, he said to use these five steps if we have a problem of any kind for which we desire a solution or wish help." [428]

She listed those five steps: 1) pray and meditate; 2) arrive and hold to a decision; 3) determine to carry it through; 4) have faith and confidence in achievement; 5) act as though one's prayer has already been answered.

In a letter dated 29 October 1952 and written on behalf of the Guardian, his secretary explained:

"In principle what Mrs. Moffett has said about prayer is quite sound; but, as we are not all alike temperamentally, it may not work out as well for you as for some others. The Master said guidance was when the doors opened after we tried. We can pray, ask to do God's will only, try hard, and then if we find our plan is not working out, assume it is not the right one, at least for the moment." [429]

Elsewhere through his secretary he stated:

"Regarding the five steps of prayer outlined by the Guardian . . . these, he wishes me to explain, are merely personal suggestions and need not, therefore, be adopted strictly and universally by the believers."[430]

* * *

Martha Root felt confirmed in her teaching work. She wrote:

"When I once get started in a city I do not even stop to write a postcard to my relatives. Everything goes like the rushing sweep of the Holy Spirit. Then nothing material matters. 'Abdu'l-Bahá and Baha'u'llah help me . . . & the people of the city help, rather they do it all, I just pray, listen to the Guidance & act." [431]

Martha used to write frequently to Shoghi Effendi of her travels for the Faith. In October, 1926, she cabled him: 'Love do you approve that I continue original plan starting Portugal late November please wire.' Shoghi Effendi replied: 'Do as Divine guidance inspires you. Tenderest love.'[432]

* * *

John Robarts was especially keen on prayer and guidance. He wrote:

> ". . . Divine inspiration and assistance (are obtainable) by developing a greater intensity of devotion to God and a determination to arise to serve Him. This we do through intensive and loving prayer, through reading some of the teachings morning and evening, and through arising to teach."[433]

In his letter in 1960 to the Canadian believers, Mr Robarts cited two important verses concerning this subject:

> "Whoso openeth his lips in this Day and maketh mention of the name of his Lord, the hosts of Divine inspiration shall descend upon him from the heaven of My name, the All-Knowing, the All-Wise. On him shall also descend the Concourse on High, each bearing aloft a chalice of pure light.[434]

> "It is known and clear that today the unseen divine assistance encompasseth those who deliver the Message. And if the work of delivering the Message be neglected, the assistance shall be entirely cut off, for it is impossible that the friends of God could receive assistance unless they be engaged in delivering the Message."[435]

* * *

John Henry Hyde Dunn had been ill since he and his wife Clara arrived in Sydney, Australia in April, 1920. Almost six months later when he was preparing the table for dinner, he heard a mental voice – as he later described it – say to him: 'Now is the time for you to write to the firm in Melbourne, regarding a position.' Hyde Dunn sent a letter in the post that very night to a firm in Melbourne with whom he felt himself competent to give good service. He soon received reply in which he was given employment. Soon the firm replied: 'Your application is most opportune. . . . Call and see our Sydney manager.'[436] Hyde acquired the position, which enabled the Dunns to deliver the Bahá'í Message across the continent.

* * *

> "In a mysterious way God prepares souls for the work which He destines for them in His service."[437]– Agnes Alexander

* * *

Clara Dunn was observed as guided in responding to questions. A seeker attending two meetings in which Mother Dunn, as she was affectionately known by the believers in Australia, was present found her two questions intuitively answered by Clara. She '. . . was well known for her ability to heal the sick by calling on the Divine Power. . . . (and) among the ladies for massage and the healing touch of her hands.'[438] In 1924, when Martha Root was in Perth, Australia, she suffered nagging pain in her back perhaps from advancing cancer. Clara brought her relief by massaging her back.

* * *

The father of 'Alí-Akbar Furútan was a persecuted but steadfast Bahá'í. Karbilá'í Muḥammad-'Alíy-i-Sabzivárí had declared his faith in the Cause of Bahá'u'lláh, and become known in Sabzivár as Muḥammad-'Alíy-i-Bábí. Because Sabzivár was known as 'the City of Worship' and 'the City of Believers', he was harassed by fanatical residents of the community. He was wrongly accused. He was threatened. He was ruthlessly accosted.

Nor did he find peace at home from his immediate family. Both his wife and mother were fanatical Shí'ih Muslims. They opposed him. His mother even sought from the local mujtahid a death sentence upon her only son, for in her mind he was both a heretic and heathen. Failing to win her objective, she abused him at home for the disgrace she believed he had brought upon the family.

This situation continued for some years until one night in a dream his wife heard an Imám scold her for afflicting her husband in spite of his believing in the Promised Qá'im. This dream was the turning point for both women who thereafter sought to compensate Mr Furútan's father for past wrongs. They both became believers in the Cause and set about educating the children.

About four years after their conversion, the grandmother dreamed of 'Abdu'l-Bahá in which He guided the family to change their residence to 'Ishqábád. Accordingly, in 1914 during the time of the Riḍván festival, the family arrived in this principal Asiatic city.[439]

* * *

In January, 1954, Raḥmat and Iran Muhájir arrived in Jakarta as pioneers from their home country. They had sent a telegram to a Bahá'í the week before their departure. However, at the airport, no one came to greet them. Moreover, in their rush to leave Iran, they had neglected to bring the Bahá'í's address. After more than five hours in Jakarta, their clothes were soaked with rain and perspiration. They had been repeating the Remover of Difficulties prayer, feeling that surely Bahá'u'lláh would come to their rescue. At this time a clerk at the post office was able to telephone the Bahá'í and within a half hour the Muhájirs were rescued.[440]

* * *

Bahá'u'lláh revealed for the father of Ṭarázu'lláh Samandarí – Shaykh Kázim Samandar – a prayer for guidance. This prayer was to be recited 19 times, followed by meditation on the problem, the formulation of a solution, and the implementation of a conceived solution.

> "O my God! Thou seest me detached from everything save Thee and clinging to Thee. Guide me then, in my doings, in a manner which profiteth me for the glory of Thy Cause and the loftiness of the state of Thy servants." [441]

* * *

Agnes Alexander had been absent from Japan over a year when she returned in August, 1919. Arriving in Yokohama she wanted very much to find a Mrs Ernst, but had no idea where the woman had gone. Recognized by the hotel manager at the Station Hotel, she was offered a room in the otherwise fully-occupied premises if she would wait until the evening. The following morning as Agnes was leaving her room, she noticed the adjoining room's door was open and chanced to see Mrs Ernst. Agnes felt certain that divine guidance had made this possible.

In 1920 Agnes met a student from Korea who had come to Japan to study. One day his otherwise bright spirit seemed clouded to her and she prayed for divine assistance that she might dispel his gloom. She felt no guidance until all at once she felt that she would take the Message to Korea. One morning the following year, Agnes became aware that the time had come for her to introduce the Faith in Korea. At the time under strict police surveillance, Agnes managed to get herself introduced to an influential viscount who was a friend of her cousin and a great financier and philanthropist. Explaining the purpose of her visit to Korea, she presented him with a statement of 'Abdu'l-Bahá on the apolitical position of Bahá'ís, which He had sent to Fanny Knobloch who went to South Africa:

> "It may be that the government of those regions will check thee. Thou shouldst say, 'I am a Bahá'í and a friend with

> all religions and nations. I consider all to be of one race and count them as my relatives. I have divine love and not racial and sectarian love. According to the palpable written command of Bahá'u'lláh I do not pronounce a word pertaining to politics, because we are forbidden to interfere in political affairs. We are concerned with affairs which are heavenly. We are servants unto the world of morality. We consider that religious, racial, political and national prejudices are destructive to the world of humanity. I believe that the whole of the surface of the earth constitutes one home and all mankind form one family. With all we are in the utmost sincerity and kindness."[442]

Delighted with this teaching, the viscount gave Agnes introductions to the governor of Korea and heads of Daiichi Bank in Seoul and Pusan. She took these introductions to Korea and promptly called at the government offices in Seoul. There she made favourable impressions on both government officials and the Chief of Police with the result that she was granted permission to teach the Faith in Korea.

She won wide publicity for the Faith, made mention of the Cause at the American Embassy, called on the manager at the bank in Seoul, saw that 'Abdu'l-Bahá's picture was published, and kept speaking engagements at various gatherings. At the very first Bahá'í meeting in Seoul, Agnes found around 900 Korean men waiting to hear what she had to say. Some women were also present sitting separately.

She spent a month on this first visit to Korea and later conveyed something of her trip:

> "Was it not a sign of the times that a western woman and Christian by birth, should tell of the Message for a new day to Buddhist students in an old Buddhist temple in that far away land.[443] . . . During the month spent in Seoul, God's power had been triumphant. All doors had been opened. Japanese and Koreans, both Buddhist and Christians, had heard the Bahá'í Message and were now free to search themselves. It could not be said they had been forgotten in God's great plan for the New Day."[444]

* * *

Before Roy Wilhelm was a Bahá'í, he used to arrive home each evening for his usual relaxation. Accustomed to routine and comfortable financially, he customarily wore dark suits, bought his newspaper from the same stand, rode the same train, and purchased flowers for his mother. Evenings he donned a dinner jacket and slippers for another evening's relaxation.

One evening while he was relaxing on his bed, his room underwent a dramatic change. Transformed before his eyes, he found himself somewhere where the walls were whitewashed and where he saw a divan. A majestic figure with a long black beard and apparently dressed in oriental clothing stood next to him. Approaching Roy, the apparition exchanged rings with him. Unaccustomed to supernatural happenings, Roy was transfixed.

Some time later – the year was 1907 - Roy's mother, a Bahá'í, wanted to make her pilgrimage to see 'Abdu'l-Bahá. Although she had tried unsuccessfully for some years to convert her son, he had remained untouched by the Faith and her devotion. But he would not allow her to travel so far alone, and so determined to accompany her.

In the Holy Land, Roy was welcomed by 'Abdu'l-Bahá. Urged by Him to visit Bahjí, Roy was taken to a small white house in the Garden of Riḍván in which Bahá'u'lláh had stayed. As he entered the house, Roy found himself in the same room he had seen in his vision back in his New York City bedroom. Shaken he retreated to the garden, determined to share his secret with 'Abdu'l-Bahá.

Later 'Abdu'l-Bahá explained to Roy that his vision meant that he had been wedded to the Faith. On that day Roy Wilhelm became a Bahá'í.[445]

* * *

> "There is nothing in the teachings anywhere which confers omniscience on the Hands of the Cause." [446] – Paul Haney

# # #

Pilgrimage

> ***. . . whenever one of (the pilgrims) would seek to express his or her deep gratitude for the honour of meeting him, he (Shoghi Effendi) would instantly turn this aside, saying the purpose of the pilgrimage was to visit the Holy Shrines.***[447]

Following his pilgrimage in 1907, Roy Wilhelm prepared a booklet entitled *Knock and it shall be opened unto you.*[448] He wrote:

> "That which most impresses the pilgrim to the 'Most Great Prison' at 'Akká, is the spirit of sacrifice. Nowhere have I witnessed such love, such perfect harmony. The desire of those in that prison was to serve one another. In our Western liberty it is difficult to realize the bitter antagonism and hatred which exists in the East between the followers of the several great religious systems. For example, a Jew and a Muḥammadan would refuse to sit at meat together: a Hindu to draw water from the well of either. Yet, in the house of 'Abdu'l-Bahá we found Christians, Jews, Muḥammadans, Zoroastrians, Hindus, blending together as children of the one God, living in perfect love and harmony . . . During our last meal 'Abdu'l-Bahá broke a quantity of bread into His bowl; then asking for the plates of the pilgrims He gave to each of us a portion. When the meal was finished, He said: 'I have given you to eat from My bowl – now distribute My Bread among the people.'" [449]

* * *

When he was about seventeen years of age, Ṭarázu'lláh Samandarí journeyed as a pilgrim to the Holy Land where he spent six months in and near the presence of Bahá'u'lláh. It happened that he became unwell after Ramaḍán and was therefore unable to visit the Supreme Manifestation for a short time. When he had improved he went alone from 'Akká to Bahjí where he asked a child to intercede on his behalf for permission to see Bahá'u'lláh, complaining that he had not had this bounty for some days. When the child returned bidding him welcome, Samandarí's limbs began to tremble as he made his way up the 22 steps to the room of Bahá'u'lláh. There the Blessed Beauty asked Ṭaráz Effendi whether he had seen 'Abdu'l-Bahá. When he responded affirmatively, Bahá'u'lláh asked: 'Then why did you complain that you did not have the reward of pilgrimage?' The implication was that in meeting the Master, Samandarí was meeting the Manifestation.

In coming years Ṭarázu'lláh Samandarí would share the memorable experiences of his six months pilgrimage during which he gazed upon the face of his Lord and experienced His favours. He recalled one of these occasions:

> "Twice I had the honor of being present in His room during the revelation of the Holy Verses. No one was there except His secretary, Mírzá Áqá Ján – and another time, Mírzá Badí'u'lláh was there copying Tablets.
>
> On these two precious occasions, as the Essence of Glory and Dignity (Bahá'u'lláh) paced the room and chanted verses, I could gaze upon Him and contemplate His luminous face, and behold the vision of the majesty of God and His divine Kingdom. This was indeed a great blessing. As He revealed the verses of God, His face was radiant. Sometimes, He would gesture with His hands while He looked through the window onto the sea.
>
> It was His custom to drink water while revealing the verses when His lips became dry. Mírzá Áqá Ján was occupied in taking down the revealed words. The floor of the room was covered with papers from the dictation. One might guess that they amounted to about one-fifth of the Qur'án, revealed during those few hours.
>
> The verses were revealed sometimes in a melodious voice, and sometimes with majesty and power – depending on the content of the revealed words. For instance, when the subject was prayer, a heavenly melody was heard; while admonitions and words of warning were uttered with the power of the Lord of lords!" [450]

Mr Samandarí was the only Hand of the Cause to serve the Faith during the ministries of Bahá'u'lláh, 'Abdu'l-Bahá and Shoghi Effendi followed by the governance of the first five years of the Universal House of Justice.

* * *

In 1926 Keith Ransom-Kehler made her pilgrimage and met the Guardian. She was profoundly impressed by him, contrasting his sufferings with his yearning for the believers to unite and teach. From her diary she recorded

Shoghi Effendi as *unique* and *outstanding.*[451] He was unique because of his responsibility as Guardian of the Faith; outstanding because of his orientation of the Faith being spread throughout the world.

Tenderly she described the Guardian and left a challenge for her fellow believers:

> ". . . This youth under thirty, labouring day and night for us, sacrificing every human desire and tendency to further our efforts, deprived for our sake of all those natural satisfactions so significant to an alert and sensitive nature; with no more personal life than a graven image, no more thought of self than a breeze or a flower, just a hollow reed for the divine melody. Any one of us is ready to die for him, but can we consciously number ourselves among those who are willing to live for him?" [452]

* * *

Dorothy Baker made her pilgrimage in 1953. Afterward she wrote about her impression of the Guardian:

> "I would not attempt to write the real things, the things of the heart, but I can say this, that the Glory of the Cause, its grandeur, shines like the sun; and as for our beloved Guardian; he is at times a servant, and again a king; and he is at once the point of all joy and again the nerve centre of suffering. One does not accept part of him and refuse part. He is, alas, a ransom; we are his beneficiaries. He suffers the grief of the Prophets, and yet is the 'true brother.' And as he casts himself into the sea of sacrifice, he is willing to cast us, one and all, into that shining sea also. America is the lead horse. He drives a chariot that must win over the combined forces of the world. He cracks the whip over the lead horse, not the others. Do the friends not realize this? The pilgrimage begins when you take his hand, and ends when you last look upon his dear face, and in between you kneel at the Shrines and ask for divine direction to serve him. And when your prayer is answered, there is no doubt about it at all; a thousand mercies circle around such an answer, and the Guardian is in the centre of them all." [453]

* * *

In his pilgrim's notes, William Sears shared his impression of Shoghi Effendi on his pilgrimage in 1954:

> "I watched the Guardian with rapt attention and ever increasing devotion. This was as close, in our day, as man could come to the direct source of the power of God, His Majesty, His Justice, His Mercy, His Love. I felt them all flowing from the Guardian.
>
> When he asked me about my journey I answered him and my words shamed me. I had made my living by words, but could think of nothing to say in his presence. My words were feeble, clumsy and uncertain. It was as though a glib tongue had been made fearful that it might try to say something witty or clever. This Guardian could be impressed by only one thing, service to the Faith. Nothing could ever influence his judgement, not wealth, position, power or friendship. . . .
>
> One thing was apparent to me at once. My life was changing. My concept of the Faith, of teaching, of service, none of these would ever be the same again. It changed from that moment when he had said, 'We are happy that you are here with us at last.'
>
> I knew the terror of the words of Bahá'u'lláh. 'I fear lest bereft of the melody of the dove of heaven, ye will sink back to the shades (of) utter loss.' I had gazed upon 'the beauty of the rose' and could never again be content to return to 'water and clay.'
>
> One thing is certain: the being changes while at Haifa. Though one may fail to live up to the promises of this great blessing, though one may fail to serve as God requires, the price will be paid. Having seen the light, darkness is abhorrent. Only an unending sorrow can be the reward for those who, having tasted of the pure crystal stream, turn aside and drink from another.
>
> The Guardian calls you to a higher service. He lifts you up to heights of limitless joy, then sets you gently down. Having revealed the treasure, he requests the payment, which is service to the Faith of God." [454]

***

By Benjamin Levy
1 May 2002

"I was twenty-six years of age when I first met dear Ugo Giachery and his endearing wife, Angeline, in Rome. I was an army sergeant arriving by bus from my pioneering post in Germany and a Bahá'í just two and one half years when I was welcomed into the Giachery's exquisite apartment. That very night - 8 March 1953 - it was my added good fortune to attend a banquet held by the Bahá'ís in honour of Hand of the Cause Dorothy Baker. She was passing through Rome at a time when official meetings of the Bahá'ís were prohibited throughout Italy.[455] Excitement filled the air as the friends listened to that wonderful soul. Then, upon learning from Ugo that I was departing the next day for my pilgrimage, Mrs Baker showered me with affectionate remarks and asked that I convey her abiding love to the Guardian.

Prior to my departure, Ugo took me on a brief tour of the Vatican. He was an imposing and aristocratic figure. While standing in St Peters Square, he swept his arm in a semi-circular movement and, speaking with a deep grasp of the subject, enlightened me on the Vatican, the Church of Rome as well as its current relationship to the Faith, and the history of the precipitous downfall of Pope Pius IX; a subject with which the Hand of the Cause was intimately familiar.

He and his wife served the Cause with intense fervour and were members of the first Italian Spiritual Assembly, that of Rome. Shoghi Effendi had told him 'nothing had pleased him more than the establishment of a Bahá'í administrative institution in the Christian capital of the world.' On one occasion, writing to Angeline from Haifa on 9 March 1952, Ugo said the Guardian had told him that he '. . . attaches great importance to Rome, as Rome will take the leading place in all of Europe.'[456] Once, when Dr Giachery was permitted to enter the bedroom of the beloved Guardian at Bahjí, he was amazed '. . . that, on the wall by the head of his bed, Shoghi Effendi had placed the photograph of the first Italian Local Assembly, that of Rome, to which both my wife Angeline and I belonged.'[457]

Dr Giachery was born and educated in Palermo, Sicily where he earned his doctorate in chemistry. His name was already legend in the worldwide Bahá'í community. He had been appointed by Shoghi Effendi as the Guardian's personal representative for all the work in Italy associated with the erection of the superstructure of the Shrine of the Báb. So outstanding were his services in this connection that the Guardian would announce in a cable to the New Delhi Intercontinental Conference later that year that he was naming one of the doors of the original Shrine as 'Báb-i-Giachery'.[458] He was already serving as a Hand of the Cause and Member-at-Large of the International Bahá'í Council (1952-1961).[459]

Reading his book, *Shoghi Effendi - Recollections* by Ugo Giachery, testifies to the mark of complete devotion stamped upon his brow. In his presence, one would become spellbound listening to his erudite commentaries, enunciated with a distinctive and delicious Italian accent. Although our paths would cross in coming years in such uncommon places as Stockholm, Frankfurt, Palermo, Haifa, Brussels and Miami Beach, this first encounter with Dr Giachery in 1953 when I was en route to Haifa was the most memorable for me. Now, for a brief moment in history, I was to become a direct link between our beloved Guardian and the Hand of the Cause.

The Giacherys bade me well and sent me off to Haifa on 9 March 1953 with the same unrestrained affection for the beloved Guardian as that of Dorothy Baker. Knowing that I would again pass through Rome on my return, they invited me again to stay with them.

Now at the dinner table during the six nights that we pilgrims dined with the beloved Guardian, Shoghi Effendi was alight with joy with the soon-to-be-launched Ten Year Spiritual Crusade the following month. Seated across from him and intimating the many wonders which would be witnessed during the Crusade, he promised for the following evening to bring the famous map he had drawn, many details which he elaborated on throughout those six evenings that we dined with him and members of the International Bahá'í Council. As the dinner drew to an end, he handed the map to me so I could study it that night. I was astounded at the map's sweeping scope and the enormity of the tasks which the Bahá'í world was being called upon to achieve.

The final evening of my pilgrimage on 16 March 1953, the beloved Guardian, knowing that I would pass through Rome on my way home, entrusted me with a large brown envelope to hand over to 'dear Ugo'. Exhilarated by the glorious honour of being a humble courier for Shoghi Effendi, I held tightly to that envelope as if my life depended upon it. On arriving in Rome, I immediately handed it over to Dr Giachery, which he accepted with submissiveness and then said nothing to me about the contents.

In her usual bubbling and excitable manner, Angeline provided us with delicious food that evening and we talked of my pilgrimage experience. She and Ugo were intensely in love with each other, and their devotion to one another was evident. In passing, anyone who knew both of them recognized their mutual adoration. Suffice it to read the article written by Dr Giachery about her life in the *In Memoriam* section of *The Bahá'í World* 1979-1983 Volume XVIII where he signed: 'Her inconsolable Ugo'.[460]

All during those passing years I often wondered what was in that envelope and thought perhaps it was the long Message to the East written by our Guardian to the Persian believers regarding the launching of the Crusade. Dr Giachery was living in the Europe Residence, Place des Moulins in Monte Carlo, Monaco when I decided to write him on 7 December 1987 – over thirty-four years later – to enquire as to the contents of that precious envelope I had carried on behalf of Shoghi Effendi.

In a two page handwritten letter in his kind, firm and unmistakable style, he explained: 'Yes, the map of the goals of the 10 years (year) crusade was the one you brought to Rome, it was made by the Guardian and reprocuded (reproduced) in the Eternal City.' It was the very map[461] that was printed and made available for the attendees participating in the 1953 Intercontinental Conferences of Kampala, Chicago, Stockholm and New Delhi, and distributed throughout the Bahá'í world." [462]

* * *

In 1925 Zikrullah Khadem yearned to make his first pilgrimage and attain the presence of the Guardian. He prayed ardently for this favour and waited in anguish. One night he dreamed he had realized his burning desire, weeping tears of joy such that his pillow was wet the next morning. So eager was he that he embarked without the necessary permission from Shoghi Effendi. It happened that he encountered Ḥájí Amín, the Trustee of the Ḥuqúqu'lláh, who assisted the young disciple in writing a letter requesting permission. Several times Zikrullah insisted the letter be more strongly worded.

Ḥájí Amín, who was sure that permission would be granted according to the Guardian's approval, insisted: 'If not (granted), so much the better because the paradise of good pleasure is preferable to the paradise of pilgrimage.'[463]

# # #

Prayer

> ***Whatsoever question thou hast in thy heart, turn thou thy heart toward the Kingdom of ABHÁ and entreat in the Threshold of the Almighty and reflect upon that problem, then unquestionably the light of truth shall dawn and the reality of that problem will become evident and clear to thee.***[464]

Dorothy Baker once told John Robarts that when she said the *Long Obligatory Prayer* her personal affairs went well, and when she said the *Tablet of Aḥmad* her Bahá'í work went well. In an informal talk she said:

> "The power of prayer is dammed up at the channel, never at the source. Spirituality is a measurable force, like electricity or light . . . Prayer is not conquering God's reluctance, but taking hold of God's willingness."[465]

And cited from the Bahá'í Writings: 'I swear by the Bounty of the Blessed Perfection that nothing will produce results save intense sincerity.'[466]

At a Bahá'í lecture in 1942, Dorothy challenged the group to read from a Bahá'í prayer book fifteen minutes a day for two weeks. Thereafter they would find themselves unable to live without the prayer book.

* * *

Martha Root reportedly stated: 'Whenever I enter a city . . . I pray nine times, the *Tablet of Aḥmad*, praying that doors will open to teach the Faith.'[467] Near miracles resulted from that formula. 'We must never forget that, with God, all things are possible.'[468]

When Dorothy Baker asked Martha how she overcame difficulties, Martha answered:

> "Dorothy, when I am faced with a difficulty, I use the Tablet of Aḥmad every day for nine days, asking God, in the name of that Holy Tablet, to remove the difficulty. If I am faced with an extremely difficult problem, I recite the Tablet of Aḥmad three times a day for nine days. And when I am faced with a problem that is completely impossible, and there is and can be no solution, I use the Tablet of Aḥmad nine times a day for nine days, and the problem is *always* solved."[469]

* * *

An American pioneering couple in the 1930s had had no results in their community for over three years in spite of diligent efforts. When they told Dorothy Baker, she recommended they pray *Yá Alláh El Mustagáth.* The wife of the couple was alarmed and exclaimed that this particular invocation was reserved for life or death situations. Dorothy responded: 'What greater calamity than for (you) to have spent three years in this town with no result?' This invocation was uttered 95 times. It marked the beginning of that city's Assembly.[470]

* * *

Zikrullah Khadem, his wife and a friend had been driving all night. They were entering Tabríz when Mr Khadem hit something. When they got out of the car, they discovered that the object struck was a man. He was lying motionless on the road, dead.

Certain that he would be arrested, tried and possibly imprisoned, Mr Khadem nevertheless determined to turn his self over to the authorities. A crowd had gathered and was agitated. There was no time to lose. Still they decided to pray: 'He is the prayer-hearing, prayer-answering God!'[471] Their praying became intense. Mr Khadem reported that he had never prayed so ardently in his life. He said: 'It was as if I were kneeling and taking the hem of the robe of the Blessed Beauty and begging for His assistance.'[472] Finally they had to stop their prayers; Mr Khadem would submit himself to the authorities.

However the victim was discovered to be alive; the crowd shouting, *Alláh-u-Akbar!* Their prayers had been answered.

* * *

On pilgrimage one of the believers thought he should pray for tests at the Shrine of the Báb. After prostrating himself in the Shrine and asking for tests, he realized that he really didn't want more tests in his life. Returning to the Pilgrim House, he found Mr Furútan and poured out his heart to him. In reply the Hand of the Cause said:

> "My son-in-law (Dr Muhájir) used to say 'Never tell God what to do!' No, we don't say to God, 'O God! Bring me tests.' We say, 'O God, when tests come to me, please give me the strength to overcome them in the best possible way.' In this way we are the humble servants and we never tell Him His business!"[473]

* * *

'Abu'l-Qásim Faizi said that according to the Báb, every living thing passes through seven stages from birth to death. As an example of the *problem of prayers*, he gave an example concerning the point at which prayer is no longer useful.

> ". . . you think about your life, your requirements, and whatever you need for your life, and so on. Suppose suddenly you think that you need a table. (step 1) He (the Báb) says as long as you are sitting here, it is in the stage of desire. . . . But the moment you decide and you get up to do something about it, the desire is changed into will. (step 2) Now the third thing is matter. (step 3) You need some material for it. You go and choose the best planks of wood that are available . . . After that you need someone to make it for you. (step 4) You need a carpenter. . . . (Y)ou take your material to the carpenter and tell him you want a table . . . He asks, "What kind of table?"[474]

After providing the carpenter with all the details for the table (step 5), Faizi said: 'From here on your freedom is stopped. Why? Because when you go home, the planks of wood you gave to the carpenter have been cut according to your measurements. But now you say you wanted a desk really five by nine, and you told him three by four. When you go back, he says that he has already cut the wood.'[475]

According to the Báb, Faizi said that once the wood is cut prayers will have no effect. The sixth step is *completion* which came about through our final decision and the seventh is *death*. So one must attract the assistance of God, praying that He will guide us in the first five steps over which we still have control.

***

> ***For the core of religious faith is that mystic feeling which unites man with God. This state of spiritual communion can be brought about and maintained by means of meditation and prayer. And this is the reason why Bahá'u'lláh has so much stressed the importance of worship. It is not sufficient for a believer merely to accept and observe the teachings. He should, in addition, cultivate the sense of spirituality which he can acquire chiefly by means of prayer . . .***[476]

In his *Letter to Bahá'ís* written in 1960, John Robarts expressed a conviction fundamental to his faith: 'Divine inspiration and assistance (are obtainable) . . . by developing a greater intensity of devotion to God and a determination to arise to serve Him.'[477] He wrote that we achieve this devotion '. . . through intensive and loving prayer, through reading some of the teachings morning and evening, and through arising to teach.'[478] He repeatedly stressed the power of the *Long Obligatory Prayer*, the *Tablet of Aḥmad*, the *Remover of Difficulties*, a teaching prayer and the repetition of the *Greatest Name* 95 times a day. He said that many individuals and communities experienced miraculous results when they recited these prayers often and sought guidance from God to increase their service to the Cause.

This letter followed a teaching trip John made to Canada where he spoke to the believers about prayer, '. . . and how we cannot live without it. It is the breath for our spiritual life, and that we should pray every day as Bahá'u'lláh has asked us, and to say the obligatory prayer, to learn the Tablet of Aḥmad, to learn Hidden Words by heart.'[479]

On pilgrimage in 1955, John asked the Guardian how much time should be spent in prayer. The Guardian replied that the American businessman was too busy to pray. The Indian meditated too much. There should be some praying, some studying every day. He told John that the service of his family in Bechuanaland was a continuous prayer.

***

In a talk entitled 'Mysterious Power in the Cause', Mr Khadem recalled something concerning response to prayer which Shoghi Effendi told him on one of his visits to the Holy Land:

> "The beloved Shoghi Effendi said: 'Let one be anywhere in the world. The moment you turn your heart to Bahá'u'lláh and His Shrine your prayers are answered.' This I tell you word for word what I heard from the Guardian. Anything you have in your heart concerning anything, any problem, Bahá'u'lláh is so powerful. He has all the world in His hands. . . . He answers our prayers. Anything you have in your heart just with great sincerity, absolute sincerity present it to Bahá'u'lláh. And He'll answer you."[480]

Javidukht Khadem wrote in her book on the life of her husband that mornings in the household of Zikrullah Khadem began with Mr Khadem chanting the *Long Obligatory Prayer*. Afterward he might chant some Tablets of 'Abdu'l-Bahá. His beautiful chanting transformed the atmosphere of the Khadem home. During the Fast he would chant the long fasting prayer, remarking that this prayer had a special potency. Such were the traces of absolute sincerity in which this beloved Hand of the Cause prayed.

* * *

Clara Dunn never hurried her prayers as every word was important to her. She cherished a particular prayer of 'Abdu'l-Bahá. In her old age, she could be seen with hands upraised, beseeching:

> "O Lord, my God and my Haven in my distress! My Shield and my Shelter in my woes! . . . Loose my tongue to laud Thy name amidst Thy people, that my voice may be raised in great assemblies and from my lips may stream the flood of Thy praise."[481]

When Rúḥíyyih Khánum was asked the secret of her speaking ability, she referred to this same prayer, a prayer which Shoghi Effendi had recommended she memorize.

* * *

Louis Gregory served the Cause for many years in the southern United States, travelling extensively and reaching thousands of people of the white and black races with the Message of Bahá'u'lláh. He used to utter the following prayer:

> "O Lord, confirm me with Thy penetrating potency so that I may speak out Thy promises and glorifications among Thy creatures and my heart become overflowed with the wine of Thy love and knowledge.
>
> Verily, Thou art powerful to do what Thou willest and thou art mighty over all things."[482]

# # #

Reflections

Every single manifestation of the myriad forms of creation is a reflection of the divine emanations, therefore the divine emanations are infinite, unlimited and illimitable.[483]

Marguerite Sears, esteemed wife of William Sears, wrote that the beloved Guardian said during her pilgrimage:

> "NSAs, LSAs, committees and individuals did not take advantage of the Supreme Concourse that it was filled with experts in every field – all we had to do was ask."[484]

* * *

In 1844: The Báb declared his mission to Mullá Ḥusayn. 'Abdu'l-Bahá was born in Ṭihrán. Shaykh Kázim-i-Samandar, father of Ṭarázu'lláh Samandarí and an Apostle of Bahá'u'lláh, was born. Mírzá Abu'l-Faḍl-i-Gulpáygání, another Apostle of Bahá'u'lláh, was born in Gulpáygán.[485] In 1844 the Russian composer Rimsky-Korsakov, the German philosopher Friedrich Wilhelm Nietzsche, the American outlaw Cole Younger, the French writer Anatole France, the British poet Andrew Lang, the Austrian physicist Ludwig Boltzmann, the French painter Henri Rousseau and America's best known sailor Joshua Slocum were born. Hans Christian Anderson completed *The Nightingale* and Edgar Allen Poe *Dreamland.*

* * *

Three people very dear to Louis Gregory were struck and killed by cars. Joseph Hannen who, together with his wife Pauline, nurtured Louis in the Faith was struck down in 1920 at about 48 years of age. He was carrying mail from the post office in Washington DC when an automobile took his life away; the letters he carried found afterward spattered with his blood. George Gregory, Louis's step-father who had provided him with a stable home in his youth and helped to educate him, was killed by an automobile in 1929 at the age of 87. Agnes Parsons, a co-worker in his race amity work, died in 1934 from a car at 73 years of age.[486]

* * *

In an email letter to the Research Department of the Bahá'í World Centre, the writer asked to know about the qualities of the Guardian reflected in the Hands of the Cause. They replied on 25 November 2002:

"The Research Department has studied the queries raised by . . . in his email message to the Bahá'í World Centre on 30 October 2002. Mr Harper asks whether there is information regarding 'the "rumour" that each of the Hands of the Cause of God possessed some outstanding quality of the Guardian'. He states that Shirley Macias mentions this in her unpublished book, "Conqueror of Hearts"....

The Research Department has not found any specific authoritative statement that refers to each Hand of the Cause possessing 'some outstanding quality of the Guardian'. Mr Harper undoubtedly is aware that the Hands of the Cause of God were assigned specific functions as required by the Guardian. We bring to his attention the following statement from a cablegram by Shoghi Effendi dated 24 December 1951 in which he announces the appointment of the first contingent of the Hands of the Cause of God, making reference to their duties and the assignment of specific functions, as the need arises:

'NINE ELEVATED RANK HAND THREE CONTINENTS OUTSIDE HOLY LAND ADVISED REMAIN PRESENT POSTS CONTINUE DISCHARGE VITAL ADMINISTRATIVE TEACHING DUTIES PENDING ASSIGNMENT SPECIFIC FUNCTIONS AS NEED ARISES.'

Note 183 of the "Kitab-i-Aqdas" provides further elucidation on the duties of the Hands of the Cause of God. The note reads:

> 'The Hands of the Cause of God were individuals appointed by Bahá'u'lláh and charged with various duties, especially those of protecting and propagating His Faith. In "*Memorials of the Faithful*" 'Abdu'l-Bahá referred to other outstanding believers as Hands of the Cause, and in His Will and Testament He included a provision calling upon the Guardian of the Faith to appoint Hands of the Cause at his discretion.'" [487]

***

From an Article by Ross Woodman
(Provided the author by Audrey Robarts)
10 February 1995

"Until he left with his family to pioneer in South Africa, John Robarts was the manager of the most successful sales office of the London Life in Canada. When in 1948 he became the first chairman of the NSA of Canada many of its meetings were held in his office. The way in which he conducted Monday morning meetings of his sales staff and the meetings of the NSA mirrored each other in such a way that the one reinforced the other. What they shared in common was two ways of relating to the soul's immortality. One way, the Bahá'í way, was through the soul's submission to the divine order of Bahá'u'lláh. The other way, the London Life way, was through the purchase of a policy that provided for the living after one had died. The two worlds, one relating directly to the spirit, the other directly to the flesh, were not in opposition. On the contrary, they together were a way of walking the spiritual path with practical feet. Like 'Abdu'l-Bahá, John knew how to do that. And in his own way, he showed his salesmen, some of whom became devoted Bahá'ís, how they also could do it. To understand John's early earthly success one had to understand its spiritual dimension. One had to understand that his astonishing commitment to life lay in his larger, spiritual vision of it. The real meaning of a life insurance policy lay in the recognition that the earth was now "the footstool of God," that what we inhabited was the Kingdom of God.

John was by nature grounded in the actual. The world which his five senses represented to him was a world that he continuously affirmed. 'Abdu'l-Bahá called this state of continuous affirmation "subjective faith." The Manifestation of God, he explained, is the root of the tree of life upon which the branches, leaves and fruits are dependent for their existence. "Subjective faith," which need not be conscious (or what 'Abdu'l-Bahá calls "objective"), is the faith that the fruit of the tree has in its root, a faith so fathomless that it remains at all times at one with the root. The world represented to John by his five senses was the tree of life upon the root of which he, like the whole of nature, was dependent for his life.

When John discovered that Bahá'u'lláh was the root, his "subjective faith" in the life unveiled to him by his senses became what 'Abdu'l-Bahá called "objective faith." What he instinctively knew at the level of his senses burst into a conscious knowledge of God. What in the realm of his senses bore a beautiful flower now became a glorious fruit. "He that abideth in me and I in him," declared Christ, "the same bringeth forth much fruit; for without me ye can do nothing." John's conscious knowledge of Bahá'u'lláh was the natural fruition of his "subjective faith". What as "objective faith" bore fruit was there in the root from the beginning awaiting in John its promised hour. John's surrender, like every other surrender to the Manifestation, is, Bahá'u'lláh explained, the crowning act of creation in which God's eternal act of creation finds in our conscious knowledge of Him that which alone can mirror it back, bringing creation itself to its predestined goal. . .

From a very early age John had what 'Abdu'l-Bahá called a "common sense" conviction that the gift of his senses was the Kingdom of God, that what his senses offered to him was to be celebrated rather than rejected. Life insurance, the selling of life insurance, was, for John, a celebration of an on-going life, a continuum that joined in one community the living and the dead. In the most immediate and practical way an insurance policy was a covenant between the dead and the living insuring an on-going life.

A far greater covenant, however, was the World Order of Bahá'u'lláh as an insurance policy protecting the living for at least the next thousand years. In charge of that policy was Shoghi Effendi. John's recognition of his role was instantaneous. The insurance policy that Shoghi Effendi, in the name of Bahá'u'lláh, was offering all the peoples of the world was a divine confirmation of everything John as a man of practical common sense had himself stood for and had sought to achieve. John in the work of the Guardian found at last the true meaning of his own business career, of what it had prepared him for. In rising to serve the Guardian he arrived at a conscious knowledge of himself, a knowledge which, Bahá'u'lláh declared, was identical with his knowledge of Him.

John embraced as his very life the work of the Guardian. In embracing it as his own, the work bestowed upon him

> a revelatory consciousness of what God from the start had predestined him to be. Inherent in that embrace was his station as a Hand of the Cause."[488]

* * *

William Sears wrote that the Guardian greatly prized hearing about *firsts* in the Cause of God. The '. . . first Navajo Indian believer, the first African tribe, the first new island, the first translation of one of Bahá'u'lláh's books, or the first Bahá'í prayer translated into a new language . . .'[489] In the sure knowledge that the opportunities to perform these *firsts* would eventually expire even as the '. . . knowledge of the glory of the Lord' (Bahá'u'lláh) was beginning to cover the earth 'as the waters cover the sea' *(ibid)*, he knew that the Bahá'ís must hurry.

He wrote:

> "Whenever some grave new problem arose to afflict our troubled world, such as drug abuse, excessive use of alcohol, dissolving marriages, divorce, the shattering of family life; whatever it was, we would share what Bahá'u'lláh and the Writings of His Faith had to say on the subject. . . . the Teachings of Bahá'u'lláh . . . (are) the material of which "firsts" (are) made in every area of human life."[490]

The following are some *firsts* from our Standard-bearers (by no means exhaustive!):

Ḥájí Amín:
First (posthumously) Hand of the Cause appointed Trustee of Ḥuqúqu'lláh (1880).[491]

Ibn-i-Aṣdaq:
First Hand of Cause to attain station of martyrdom without sacrificing his life (1882)[492]

Mírzá 'Alí-Muḥammad Varqá:
First (and only) Hand of the Cause to suffer and attain the station of physical martyrdom (1896).[493]

Ibn-i-Abhar:
Helped to establish Tarbíyat Bahá'í School for boys.[494]

Ḥasan-i-Adíb:
Significant part in establishing Tarbíyat Bahá'í School for boys.[495]

Agnes Alexander:
First Bahá'í in Hawaiian Islands (1901).[496]; Introduced Faith to Korea (1921).[497]

Corinne True:
First Financial Secretary of Bahá'í Temple Unity (1909-1922).[498]

Mason Remey:
First round-the-world Bahá'í teaching trip (1909-1910).[499]

Louis Gregory:
First marriage between a black (himself) and a white (Louisa Mathew) Bahá'í (1912);[500] first Bahá'í to make regular circuits to speak on Faith at Negro colleges in South.[501]

Hyde and Clara Dunn:
First to establish Faith in Australia (1920).[502]

Horace Holley:
Conceived idea for *The Bahá'í World* (c. 1925).[503]

Leroy Ioas:
Conceived and arranged first World Unity Conference held in San Francisco, California (1925).[504]

Martha Root:
Taught Queen Maria of Rumania, first ruler to accept Faith (1926);[505] First translations (arranged or encouraged) of *Bahá'u'lláh and the New Era* into Esperanto, [506]Chinese,[507] Hungarian,[508] Serbian,[509] Swedish,[510] Norwegian,[511] Greek,[512] Rumanian.[513]

Keith Ransom-Kehler:
First American martyr (1933).[514]

Amelia Collins:
First to contribute toward construction of Superstructure of Shrine of the Báb (1944);[515] first living Hand named by Guardian (1946).[516]

William Sears:
First Bahá'í radio series entitled *Mr Justice* (1945-46).[517]

Dorothy Baker:
First female chairperson of the NSA of the United States and Canada (1940s).[518]

Rúḥíyyih Khánum:

Donated first Bahá'í Canadian home (her parents) to NSA of Canada (1953).[519]

Enoch Olinga:

First to establish Faith in British Cameroons, being named a Knight of Bahá'u'lláh (1953).[520]

Raḥmatu'lláh Muhájir:

First with wife Iran to establish Faith in Mentawai Islands, winning accolade Knights of Bahá'u'lláh (1954).[521]

John Robarts:

First to establish Faith with wife Audrey and son Patrick in Bechuanaland; Knights of Bahá'u'lláh (1954).[522]

* * *

In 1908 Charles Mason Remey (CMR) together with Sydney Sprague embarked for Iran and Russia on an international teaching trip. Along their route the two men travelled to 'Ishqábád where they received a stupendous welcome from the believers of that community. An architect, CMR spent some time examining the nearly completed Bahá'í House of Worship. As Remey was an enthusiastic and active supporter of the American believers building their own House of Worship, he wrote:

> "The rearing of this temple in the East has been a great source of strength to the people there, for through thus expressing their unity the Bahais have become stronger and more united than ever before. Now in America the Bahais are arising to build a Mashrak-el-Azcar. Who can estimate the effect which will be produced by this building? It will be the cause of great strength and unity among the believers of the Occident . . . The erection of a temple in the West will strengthen the Holy Cause in the East more than anything which could happen in this country . . . Throughout the Bahai world the eyes of all are expectantly turned toward this country."[523]

At the American Bahá'í Convention in 1920, Mason Remey, Louis Bourgeois, and Sutherland Maxwell displayed their Temple designs. Each architect was allowed 20 minutes to explain his concept to the delegates in attendance. At Remey's urging the delegates selected the Bourgeois model. This action on Mason Remey's part drew praise from 'Abdu'l-Bahá.

CMR had actually influenced certain aspects of the Bourgeois design: first floor architectural problems as well as modifications to render the design less expensive and more durable.

'Abdu'l-Bahá, Who loved CMR very much, showered His favours on him in a 1921 Tablet:

> "Some time ago I wrote thee a letter the content of which was that, praise be to God, thou hast become confirmed in drawing a plan for the pilgrim (house) in Haifa. It is my hope that this pilgrim house may be built under your supervision. Also in the future a Mashreq'ul Azkar will be established on Mount Carmel. Thou wilt be its architect and founder. I give thee this glad tidings."[524]

About 1947 Shoghi Effendi charged Mason Remey with designing the Mt Carmel Temple. Working under the direction of the Guardian, CMR's design was eventually approved by Shoghi Effendi and a model thereof made. This model was unveiled at the 1953 Intercontinental Conference in Chicago with CMR on hand to explain the background of houses of worship in religious history and the character of his design in Bahá'í history.[525]

In coming years he would design the International Archives Building under the direction of Shoghi Effendi as well as the Bahá'í Temples in Kampala and Sydney.

Concerning the contributions of Charles Mason Remey who broke the Covenant and was expelled in 1960, the Universal House of Justice in a letter dated 19 November 1996 to the National Spiritual Assembly of the Bahá'ís of the United Kingdom wrote:

> "The part that certain Covenant-breakers played in the progress of the Cause while they were faithful believers should certainly not be obscured, nor the fact that they later broke the Covenant, although care must be taken not to give them undue prominence." [526]

###

Spiritual Birth

> ***Be thankful to God for having enabled you to recognize His Cause. Whoever has received this blessing must, prior to his acceptance, have performed some deed which, though he himself was unaware of its character, was ordained by God as a means whereby he has been guided to find and embrace the Truth.***[527]

Soon after the Declaration of the Báb in 1844, Mullá Ḥusayn passed through Iṣfáhán where he spoke to his old friend Mullá Ṣádiq about the advent of the Báb but without disclosing His identity. Upon being asked to divulge His name, Mullá Ḥusayn replied that to do so was forbidden. Mullá Ṣádiq asked whether he might therefore seek the identity of the Promised One independently through prayer, to which his friend replied: 'The door of His grace . . . is never closed before the face of him who seeks to find Him.'[528] Mullá Ṣádiq then retired to the privacy of a room in the house where he could commune with God. He later recorded:

> "In the midst of my contemplation, I suddenly remembered the face of a Youth whom I had often observed while in Karbilá, standing in an attitude of prayer, with His face bathed in tears . . . That same countenance now reappeared before my eyes. . . . He smiled as He gazed at me. I went towards Him, ready to throw myself at His feet. I was bending towards the ground, when, lo! that radiant figure vanished from before me. Overpowered with joy and gladness, I ran out to meet Mullá Ḥusayn, who with transport received me and assured me that I had, at last, attained the object of my desire."[529]

* * *

Over a ten year period, John and Audrey Robarts were exposed to the Bahá'í Faith. Harlan and Grace (Robarts) Ober often came to Toronto to further the Cause. Occasionally the Robartses attended Grace's meetings; otherwise shuttling them to and from firesides. One evening in November 1937, after dining with the Obers, John realized that he had accepted the station of Bahá'u'lláh. However his beloved aunt, 'who first inflamed his heart with her contagious love for this Cause,' died unexpectedly at the 1938 annual Bahá'í convention before he and Audrey had the chance to inform her of their conversion.[530]

* * *

Hermann Grossmann arrived late at a meeting of the Theosophical Society in Leipzig. Harlan and Grace Ober had been invited to speak on the Faith, having come to Germany at the behest of 'Abdu'l-Bahá following their pilgrimage in 1920. At the moment of his arrival, Hermann saw a radiant-looking woman at the speaker's table proclaiming Bahá'u'lláh's well-known utterance that all people are the leaves of one tree and the flowers of one garden. That woman was Grace Ober. After her talk, Grace approached Hermann, having perceived his receptivity. After they spoke together, Hermann wholeheartedly accepted the new Revelation.[531]

* * *

John Henry Hyde Dunn happened to be passing by a tinsmith shop in Seattle, Washington when he overheard someone sharing with the shop's owner Bahá'u'lláh's statement: 'Let not a man glory in this, that he loves his country; let him rather glory in this, that he loves his kind.'[532]

Hyde Dunn later said that these words reached him with dynamic force, its truth and power crystallizing in his heart. His being was magnetized by that one glorious utterance, and he found the salve for his *hungry, searching heart*.[533] 'Surely these words are a message from God,'[534] he interrupted the speaker, who then proceeded to confirm Hyde Dunn in the Faith.

* * *

Clara Davis was in her late thirties, working at a medical centre as a nurse in Walla Walla, Washington when Hyde Dunn showed up and engaged her in a conversation. Asking her if she was interested in spiritual things, she replied affirmatively if she knew of any. Hyde introduced her to the Bahá'í Faith and invited her to hear a lecture at a hotel that evening. There she accepted the Faith as her outlook was universal. Ten years later she married Hyde Dunn.[535]

* * *

Nabíl-i-Akbar was known as a man of great knowledge, profound in his erudition and a respected Shí'ih mujtahid. In 1852 Nabíl was on his way to the Holy Shrines of Najaf and Karbilá when he was arrested in Ṭihrán as a Bábí. Protesting that he was not a follower, he won his freedom. Nevertheless the event compelled him to study the writings of the Báb, resulting in his conversion.[536]

In 1911 Músá Banání was mistaken by the authorities as a Bahá'í, arrested and imprisoned. Mr Banání obtained his release by denying his allegiance to and reviling the faith of the Bahá'ís. Finding himself *seized by a profound spiritual convulsion*, he determined to investigate this Faith about which he knew so little. His investigation resulted in his becoming a believer.[537]

* * *

Young Dorothy Beecher struggled to understand whether man was the centre of his universe or God was the ruling force. Her father believed in the power of man as the arbiter of his destiny, and at times Dorothy could appreciate his point of view. Dorothy's grandmother Ellen Beecher believed on the other hand that the purpose of the intellect was to discern and follow the will of God.

Dorothy's parents Henry and Luella often had intellectual discussions at the dinner table. But they were not happy together and seemed unable to resolve their differences. Their unhappiness and irreconcilability convinced Dorothy that all strength does not come from within. Then an event occurred a few days before Ellen Beecher was to take her 13 year old granddaughter to see 'Abdu'l-Bahá in New York City that was to show Dorothy that some unknowable force was working both in the universe and in herself. Resting in bed one night, she felt herself suspended on an earth that turned in an endless unknown void. Her sudden awareness of a vast universe at the mercy of an *all-encompassing* yet incomprehensible God paralyzed her with fear.

On the day of meeting 'Abdu'l-Bahá, Dorothy felt the same fear. When the carriage pulled up in front of the meeting house, she remained seated. 'What if he looks at me?' she anxiously thought. Inside the house people were already being affected by 'Abdu'l-Bahá's loving presence. Once the meeting got underway, Dorothy was seated near 'Abdu'l-Bahá. Determined to avoid looking at Him, she focused her attention on the floor. Inevitably, in the presence of the Master Whose talk she would later be unable to recall, Dorothy's fear changed into a *passion for all people*.[538] She found herself yearning '. . . for her own soul to be lost in the immensity of His love . . .'[539] Unintentionally she turned and faced Him, focusing on His loving face and losing once for all her fear of the unknown.

Unable in the days to come to calm the stirrings in her heart, Dorothy wrote to 'Abdu'l-Bahá, begging to serve Him and His Father's Cause.

* * *

When Enoch Olinga volunteered to pioneer to West Africa, 'Alí and Violette Nakhjavání offered to take him across the continent to the British Cameroons. Setting off on 27 August 1953 in a small Peugeot station-wagon provided by Músá Banání, the journey of some 3,000 kilometres was full of adventure and danger. The group would have to pass through unfamiliar countries and over terrible roads.

Passing through Gabon the car became constantly stuck in mud with the result that 'Alí or Enoch would have to seek help from villagers who might live a long distance away. Progress could be especially slow: 100 kilometres in 16 hours and 25 kilometres in 14 hours. The area was plagued by disease and dreaded tsetse flies.

When the car broke down due to failure of the clutch, the Nakhjavánís and Enoch prayed and consulted. Enoch would go for help. He set out with a local guide toward a town 80 kilometres away. Braving strange African tribes, dangerous jungle animals and deadly snakes, Enoch became feverishly ill with dysentery and exhausted. While 'Alí and Violette were anxious for Enoch's safety, Enoch feared that his friends had been robbed or killed. Frightened and depressed, he asked himself what he was doing in the middle of a jungle with unfamiliar people far from home and family. If these people kill me he thought, no one will know.

Enoch fell asleep and then had a dream of the beloved Guardian. In the dream, he had fallen in the mud and Shoghi Effendi came to him, lifted him up, took him in his arms and said: 'I am well pleased with you.' Enoch awoke and felt refreshed, revived, calmed and determined. His immediate thought was his readiness to make such sacrifice for his beloved every day of his life.

In an interview years later, Violette Nakhjavání said that Enoch's rebirth in the Faith was on that trip, on that night when he had that very wonderful dream. Afterward he was not the same Enoch. He had much more energy, joy and hope. When he arrived in British Cameroons, he sent his cable on the last day of the Holy Year (15 October 1953), informing Shoghi Effendi of his arrival.[540]

***

George Townshend, as a student, had considered the Church as a career, but on graduation decided to assist his father by earning money. When that need was over he left his native Ireland in 1904 for the Rocky Mountains where he passed his time roaming about the grandeur of that majestic region. At the end of nearly two years, he came across the Bhagavadgita and, through perusing it, decided to devote his life to the search for the knowledge of God.[541]

***

Before the birth of Mary Sutherland Maxwell (Rúḥíyyih Khánum), her father William Sutherland Maxwell felt that he and his wife May were drifting apart. One day he pointed out to her that her devotion to serving the Faith of Bahá'u'lláh and his dedication to his architectural work meant that they were drifting apart. Mrs Maxwell loved her husband dearly and was terrified of losing him. But she told him: 'You remember when we were going to get married, I told you that my devotion and service to my Faith comes first; if you cannot go along with me, then I have to go alone.'[542] Mr Maxwell considered this and replied: 'I will go with you all the way.'[543] According to Rúḥíyyih Khánum, the spiritual strength of May Maxwell was the probable cause of her husband being guided to the Faith later on.

On their pilgrimage in 1909, Mr Maxwell said to 'Abdu'l-Bahá: 'The Christians worship God through Christ; my wife worships God through You; but I worship Him direct.' 'Where is He?' 'Abdu'l-Bahá replied. 'Why, God is everywhere,' said Sutherland. 'Everywhere is nowhere,'[544] answered his Host.

'Abdu'l-Bahá explained that worshipping God without something tangible as represented by the Manifestation is merely a *figment of the imagination*[545] without reality. This lesson received in the Prison City of 'Akká marked the germination of the seed of Sutherland Maxwell's faith.

* * *

Bertha Dobbins and Katherine Harcus were returning from Port Adelaide to Adelaide where they had gone on a teaching trip. Covering the 14-kilometre distance on foot, they stopped to rest at a park and called upon the Greatest Name that a home might be opened to the Faith.

When Madge Featherstone first heard of the Faith in 1944, she shared with Collis the knowledge and information she had received. Her teacher had said that the Faith was for everyone on earth. Attracted, Collis insisted on something suitable to read. Madge brought him *The Dawn-breakers*, which he proceeded to study that very night. When he reached page 92 and read the Báb's address to the Letters of the Living, he realized that the Bahá'í Faith was from God.

After Collis and Madge Featherstone accepted Bahá'u'lláh, they opened their home for evening Bahá'í meetings. Their home was the nearest one facing Bertha and her friend on that weary afternoon when they had leaned exhausted against a post and uttered the Greatest Name.[546]

* * *

For many years William Sears was mystified by dreams of a *shiny man*[547] who first appeared to him when he was but a year and a half old. After he had married Marguerite Reimer and they returned home from their honeymoon, Bill had another astonishing dream of the shiny man. White beard flowing in the breeze, he rushed by on a pair of skis and beckoned Bill to follow. Eventually they came to a point where Bill could see a city nestled in a valley. 'This is the city,'[548] the shiny man pointed and vanished.

After the couple with Bill's children had moved to Salt Lake City, the family were driving through the mountains nearby when they stopped near a ledge overlooking the city. As Bill stepped to the ledge, he exclaimed: 'This is the city.'[549] It was the same city he had seen so clearly in his dream.

At home Marguerite showed him a picture of 'Abdu'l-Bahá. Bill recognized his shiny man, and began to earnestly investigate the Faith. He became convinced of the truth of the Cause when he read *The Dawn-breakers.*

* * *

> ***It is better to guide one soul than to possess all that is on earth, for as long as that guided soul is under the shadow of the Tree of Divine Unity, he and the one who hath guided him will both be recipients of God's tender mercy . . .***[550]

In 1997 the writer and his family made a pilgrimage to the Bahá'í Holy Shrines. For nine days they basked in the unearthly radiance of those sacred environs. Each day was a new adventure in which they visited, absorbed, and prayed in the Pilgrim House on Mt Carmel, the Seat of the Universal House of Justice, the Monument Gardens, the Shrine of the Báb, the Shrine of 'Abdu'l-Bahá, the Prison-fortress at 'Akká, the House of 'Abbúd (which was joined after 1873 with the House of 'Údí Khammár), the House of 'Abdu'lláh Páshá, Mazra'ih, the Riḍván Garden, Bahjí, the Ḥaram-i-Aqdas, the Shrine of Bahá'u'lláh, the House of 'Abdu'l-Bahá, the International Archives Building, the obelisk on Mount Carmel which marks the site of the future Mashriqu'l-Adhkár, the Bahá'í Cemetery, and much more. Evenings were spent in the Pilgrim House where pilgrims were treated to a talk either by a distinguished member of the Universal House of Justice or the International Teaching Centre. Most evenings the Hand of the Cause of God, Mr 'Alí-Akbar Furútan, was present to meet with the pilgrims. The Hand of the Cause of God, Dr 'Alí Muḥammad Varqá, also was present at a few of those heavenly gatherings.

During sessions with Mr Furútan, whose profession was education and child psychology, he would ask questions of the pilgrims on the history of the Faith. 'Name the Intercontinental Conferences held in 1958. Who was the greatest Bahá'í scholar of the West? When were the Hands of the Cause appointed?' These were the kinds of questions which he asked and which found everyone anxious to attain his good pleasure by their responses. Having recently struggled through *Lights of Fortitude*, this writer was somewhat better postured to offer responses to Mr Furútan's questions, which soon prompted the Hand to teasingly discourage him from participating!

One evening when both Hands of the Cause were present, Mr Furútan began the meeting by asking participants who had become Bahá'í to tell their stories. Those who were born Bahá'í would have to sit quietly and listen. Following a show of hands, the writer's wife immediately volunteered him to tell his story first. Had she not drawn attention to him, he would have been content to sit and listen. He was then ushered to the front of the meeting room and made to sit between the two Hands, where he momentarily lost the power of utterance. During the telling of his early Bahá'í experience, Mr Furútan, according to his wife, periodically shook his head as the tale unfolded.

> "In 1961 my father Ross Avery Harper married Margaret Rowena Letbetter. They had been introduced to each other that summer by the pastor of a small Christian church they frequented in Odessa, Texas. At the time of their being introduced, I had been visiting relatives in Missouri and east Texas. Upon returning home six weeks later and meeting Margaret, I found her to be an evolved soul who, having endured long years of hardship, combined patience with firmness and loving-kindness. Until she died just ten years later and broke the hearts of her devoted family, she became as my own mother. Today she reigns supreme in my heart.
>
> Margaret had three children all senior to me: Donja, age 23; Don, age 21; and Barbara, age 17. I was 15 in 1961. Donja was married to Gilbert Murray whose career in the Navy meant that the couple and their three children would occasionally be uprooted. In 1964 Don would marry in Hawaii and then lose his wife in child-birth the following year. The unbearable sorrow that descended upon him became the catalyst that forever changed the lives of our family. Barbara was a secretary who would marry a medical student from Texas in 1962. Dr Randy and Mrs Barbara Taylor would eventually settle in Alaska.

Through the last quarter-century of his life, Dad was not well. Suffering multiple surgeries, painful recoveries and an uncertain future, he possessed an indomitable spirit, strong faith and will to survive. A WWII veteran, Dad was entitled to health care at the veteran's hospital in Houston, and so in 1966 he and Mother moved into an apartment in La Porte, Texas; by then a Houston suburb. As the year neared its end, Donja, now separated from her husband, was temporarily sharing their modest flat.

Meanwhile Don, who had left his son in the care of Mother and Dad, had re-enlisted in the Navy and been assigned, as an excellent jazz trumpeter, to the Boston Naval base band. During those days, he was sorely tried by his life. One night he came home and in the course of the evening dropped to his knees at the side of his bed and began praying to God: 'If you really exist, if there really is a God, just show me the light and I will take it from there. Point the way and I'll do the rest. Just let me know that you are really there.' Don said this over and over and really meant it. The next morning when he woke up on the floor, he felt as if he had been reborn. He never felt better in his life; as if the world had been lifted from his shoulders.

Don acquired a Bahá'í roommate. His curiosity was piqued when he noticed his new roommate had some strange looking Bahá'í books. Don listened as his questions were satisfactorily answered. He enlisted in the Faith in February, 1966. Excitedly he called home and tried to share his Bahá'í news. Mother responded by asking him: 'Well, honey, do you believe in God?' Don credits Mother for the way she raised him that enabled him to recognize Bahá'u'lláh.

During Christmas holidays, Don was finally able to set out for La Porte to host the Glad Tidings. He armed himself with a bag of clothes and a bag of Bahá'í books. After sharing the Message with the family, Mother and Donja accepted the Faith spontaneously on 4 January 1967. Dad, who was fundamentalist in his view of the Bible and prophecy, was immediately defensive. Don slipped him William Sears's *Thief in the Night.* Dad retired to his room determined to lead this son back to the shores of righteousness. Later when he emerged, he was waving *Thief in the Night* and shouting, 'This is it! This is it!' Dad had a way of grinning ear to ear like the Cheshire cat in *Alice in Wonderland* when something really pleased him and at that moment he was wearing his famous grin. In coming years as a Biblical Bahá'í scholar, Dad would amaze friends and antagonists with his recitation of Bible proofs.

Don, who had returned to Boston after putting them in contact with a Bahá'í couple in La Porte, received a telephone call from Dad in which he said they had all joined the Faith. Don is still unable to recall that phone call without weeping tears of joy.

In January 1967, I received a letter from Dad in which he informed me of the Bahá'í Faith. At the time feeling overwhelmed by personal crises, I reacted to Dad's news convinced that Bahá'u'lláh had something to do with Cassius Clay's conversion to the Muslim Religion and his name change to Muḥammad Ali. Several months would pass before the unhappiness in my life prompted me to phone the Bahá'ís. Then – it was the month of May – at my first fireside and much to my astonishment, I encountered a CEO and an African American relating to each other in complete harmony.

As a child growing up in the 1950s in Odessa and Dallas, Texas, I had not been able to understand the separation of the races. In both cities, blacks, Mexicans and whites lived, worked, ate and worshipped within clearly defined areas and rules. As an inquisitive six year old roaming the concrete citadels of Big D commerce, I had entered a black church, drank from a black water fountain, gone into a black restroom and sat in the back of a public bus among blacks. My curiosity never quite satisfied, I could not find any justification for blacks and whites existing in a parallel world. So the fireside in 1967 followed by other firesides exposed me to the true meaning of religion and to Christ's words uttered so many centuries ago: 'A new commandment I have given you that ye love one another.' Now in Bahá'í meetings I was being exposed to believers from the races of mankind associating together in perfect love and harmony. Before the year was finished, I embraced the Faith. Ironically Don had been initially attracted to the Faith on the principle of elimination of all prejudice.

Around the time Dad was writing me about Bahá'u'lláh, Donja was sending her estranged husband information on the Faith. In coming months Gilbert studied and pondered the Bahá'í teachings while attending firesides in San Diego, California. Dr Ugo Giachery was present at one of these firesides. Gil recalled in later years how the Hand of the Cause was excitedly sharing news at the meeting about an entire family who had embraced the Cause of Bahá'u'lláh. As Gil sat listening, he realized that this was his family and eagerly shared this news. Dr Giachery was beside himself and showered his love and congratulations on Gilbert, who had recently accepted the Faith on 3 March 1967. Naturally Gil was not at the time able to appreciate the station of Dr Giachery and the bounty of being in his presence until years later.

In 1969 I met my future companion throughout all the worlds of God - Nancy Lee. She had just declared her belief in Bahá'u'lláh when we were introduced to each another by a Bahá'í couple in Austin, Texas. Two and a half years later we were married.

On a visit to the Air Force Academy in Colorado Springs where the Taylors were then residing in 1969, Mother conveniently left behind her prayer book as well as brochure of Bahá'í publications when she returned home. When Barbara expressed interest to acquire a few books from the list, Mother immediately sent her own books, being delayed only by the time required to reach the post office. Barbara, a thoughtful take-her-time kind of person, took her time pondering the truths contained in *The Divine Art of Living* before writing a declaration of faith remarkable in content and cherished by her mother. But she continued to ponder another 18 months before eventually signing her declaration card late in 1970.

Before leaving this world to join Mother and Dad, Donja and Gil in their senior years were home-front pioneers in Livingston, Texas near the Alabama-Coushatta Indian Reservation. Don, a Florida resident, lost his second wife to cancer. Indomitable as a facilitator in the Institute Process, he remarried. Barbara, after years of serving Bahá'í institutions, continued her meritorious services at the Bahá'í World Centre. Nancy and Barron left their native land to be pioneers abroad.

> All of us would all like to think that Dad and Mother look down from the eternal realm on their children and extended family with certain pride; truth is, they would more likely have urged us to 'Be not content with the ease of a passing day . . . '[551] and give honour to our host." [552]

* * *

As a young man, Louis Gregory supported the social activist ideas of W.E.B. DuBois and the Niagara Movement (later the N.A.A.C.P.). The Movement stood for '. . . manhood suffrage, equal civil rights, equal economic opportunity, free compulsory elementary education and access to high schools and colleges, legal and penal reform to end racial discrimination, fair treatment by both management and labour unions, and abolition of Jim Crow accommodations.'[553] In his support for ideas considered radical at the time, Louis favoured agitation to remove the wrongs suffered by his people. In its "Declaration of Principles", the Movement aired grievances which Louis may have supported:

> "We repudiate the monstrous doctrine that the oppressor should be the sole authority as to the rights of the oppressed. The Negro race in America stolen, ravished and degraded, struggling up through difficulties and oppression, needs sympathy and receives criticism; needs help and is given hindrance, needs protection and is given mob-violence, needs justice and is given charity, needs leadership and is given cowardice and apology, needs bread and is given a stone. This nation will never stand justified before God until these things are changed."[554]

At the Treasury Department where he worked in Washington, DC, Louis argued the cause of black activism with two older white colleagues. Surprisingly open-minded, these men befriended rather than offended Louis, patiently indulging his drastic ideas and intentions. One of these men became the cause of Louis's guidance. Thomas H Gibbs had attended a few Bahá'í meetings where he gained some limited but attractive ideas. He insisted that Louis attend a meeting. And Louis, who could not have otherwise been diverted from his program of agitation and who did not want to investigate religion, bowed to his friend's insistence.

On a cold and dismal night late in 1907, he heard Lua Getsinger recount the early history of the Faith. Intrigued Louis continued attending meetings under the loving tutelage of Joseph and Pauline Hannen over an 18-month period. 'The light they unfolded was so wonderful,' Louis later wrote, 'that for about a year we sat in dumb amazement, listening to their patient, loving talks, not knowing whether to advance or retreat, yet held by supernal power.'[555] In June 1909, Louis Gregory became a Bahá'í.

In coming years, Louis Gregory never set aside his platform for racial justice. But, through the influence of the Faith, he realized that the solution to racial issues exists in the establishment of the new world Faith, which he had espoused and which he would promote as a race amity worker.

* * *

May Maxwell confirmed Charles Mason Remey, Thomas Breakwell and her daughter Mary (Rúḥíyyih Khánum) in the Faith. Keith Ransom-Kehler turned to May for prayers. May was instrumental in Leonora Holsapple pioneering to Brazil. Paul Haney was blessed by May's loving encouragement. She nurtured Agnes Alexander in the Faith. She taught the Faith at Green Acre to Lorol Schopflocher who in turn brought her husband Siegfried Schopflocher into the Faith. Future Universal House of Justice member, Mr David Hofman, learned of the Faith through May Maxwell and her husband.[556]

* * *

Mírzá Abu'l-Faḍl, the greatest Bahá'í scholar of the East, taught the Faith to 'Abdu'l-Jalíl Bey Sa'ad. [557]

* * *

Marguerite Reimer introduced her future husband William Sears to the Faith. According to Marguerite, Mary Sutherland Maxwell (Rúḥíyyih Khánum) '. . . was greatly instrumental in confirming me. She called me her Spiritual Child.'[558]

* * *

Mullá Ṣádiq helped to confirm Ḥájí Ákhúnd in the Faith of the Báb in 1861.[559]

* * *

After long discussions, Nabíl-i-Akbar confirmed Ḥájí Mírzá Ḥasan-i-Adíb in the Faith. The year was about 1889. Soon after, Bahá'u'lláh named him a Hand of the Cause. Adíb never attained the presence of the Manifestation.[560]

* * *

Hyde Dunn became a Bahá'í in 1905 through Ward Fitz-Gerald who was confirmed in the Faith in Washington D.C. where he attended meetings held in Charles Mason Remey's office.[561]

* * *

Bertha Dobbins, who brought the knowledge of the Faith to Madge and Collis Featherstone in 1944, regularly spent Saturday evenings in the home of Hyde and Clara Dunn where she became acquainted with the Faith in 1929. At the beginning of the World Crusade, Collis and Madge offered to support Bertha in a pioneering effort to the New Hebrides, where she won the accolade Knight of Bahá'u'lláh.[562]

* * *

Martha Root was society editor and religion editor for the *Pittsburgh Post*. In 1908 she was covering an interdenominational missionary convention. Martha was seated with her friends in the crowded dining room of Child's Restaurant. Roy Wilhelm was seated next to her table. He had been to the Holy Land in 1907 where he had met 'Abdu'l-Bahá. When he overheard a young woman at Martha's table say that '. . . it seemed a pity that all of the heathen must be lost,' and another reply '. . . that there was one Creator whom she believed was interested in all human beings,'[563] Roy asked permission to speak. He told them how he and his mother . . .

> ". . . had just returned from a visit to the East during which we met those born into other Systems of Religion, and observing that they also said their prayers, and led kind, helpful lives, we now believed that all humanity were being educated to the recognition of One God and real 'brotherhood of man' . . ."[564]

His comments appealed to Martha, who gave him her card. In the course of the coming year, Roy sent Bahá'í literature to Martha. Rather than read the literature, she gave it out to those she felt interested in *queer religious notions*.[565] Eventually she began to read and ask intelligent questions of Roy. Later she spoke with Thornton Chase for several hours. Martha considered the Faith methodically through research and reflection, becoming a Bahá'í in 1909.

Years later Roy would pay this tribute to Martha Root:

> "Martha was unique. She seemed to have been born for her special work. I doubt if there is another who has brought

attention to the Faith to so many tens of thousands over so many corners of the earth. I sometimes think my chief reason for being born was to get Martha started."[566]

* * *

"Beloved Mother Dunn,

My heart was gladdened to know of your being made a Hand of the Cause, and I am grateful from my heart for the wonderful way you taught me the Cause of Bahá'u'lláh, not to put in my own interpretations but to rely on the Direct Word. Tests and tribulations have kept me firmer in the Cause and I hope that the balance of my life may be spent only in service to the Faith.

I pray for you and hope you will pray for me that I may be faithful to the end, in serving Bahá'u'lláh . . ."

With deepest love,
Your spiritual daughter
23 April 1952[567]

# # #

Supreme Concourse

The Lord of Hosts, the King of Kings has pledged unfailing support to every crusader battling for His Cause. Invisible battalions are mustered, rank upon rank, ready to pour forth reinforcements from on high . . .[568]

"Death does not separate the soul of the believer from his scene of previous activity, but only increases his powers. All those who work for this Great Cause will continue to do so whether they are in the body or out of it. If martyred, they will attach to those who can best secure their influence, and the power of these will be doubled or quadrupled by the dynamic assistance of those who have already left the scenes of outward action." – copied from Amelia Collins's prayer book by the mother of Dorothy Baker [569]

* * *

In her pilgrim's notes, Dorothy Baker wrote:

"There is a very close connection between the souls beyond and souls here. This connection depends upon certain difficult conditions – concentration, purity of heart, purity of motive. It will be possible to communicate, but do not attempt to experiment now. . . . The Supreme Concourse are beings of whom we have no conception, but it includes souls of people who have been very devoted and other beings as well of whom we are not aware. The higher the position, the greater the influence. They rush to the assistance of the sincere servants who arise now. . . . God assures each one that every act is a magnet for the Supreme Concourse."[570]

* * *

Following his wife's passing in 1940, Sutherland Maxwell always felt her closeness to him.[571]

* * *

In Swaziland where she was travelling in 1972 on her 'Great African Safari', Rúḥíyyih Khánum said that . . .

"... (A)fter the passing of the beloved Guardian, at the time of the completion of the Bahá'í Temples or the building of the grave of Shoghi Effendi, she had called on her own father for help. She explained that in our prayers to our loved ones for help we should remember that we are not praying to them, but are asking them to intercede on our behalf."[572]

Facing dangers and difficulties in her travels through Africa, she and her travelling companion Violette Nakhjavání were covering a distance of 50 kilometres between towns when the Land-rover started losing power. Every time the engine sputtered, Rúḥíyyih Khánum would call out: 'Someone up there, help me!'[573] Somehow they managed to climb each hill and reach their destination.

* * *

In the aftermath of the sudden death of the Guardian, Mr Khadem was sustained through the very difficult period of the Interregnum by his conviction of the assistance of Shoghi Effendi from the other world. He often remarked that the feeling of nearness of the Guardian in his heart prevented his perishing.[574]

* * *

"One of the last holidays we had with Papa Olinga and Mama Elizabeth was in Kampala home. One day he shared with us a mystical dream he had had the night before. We were in the sitting room. He said he dreamed he had ascended to the next world. He was surprised to see Bach, Beethoven and Brahms working hard composing music. He asked them: 'What are you doing?' They replied: 'The same thing we have been doing in the earth.' He was surprised, and said: 'I thought when we come to the next world we will rest, and there will be no more work.' Beethoven laughed and said: 'In fact you need to work harder in the next world and there is no rest.' Papa Olinga asked: 'But why, why is it like that?' They replied: 'Because we are supposed to inspire the people on the earth. So be ready to work harder.'

Papa Olinga was beautifully telling the story. He said: 'Children, do you understand what this means?' He looked and said: 'I thought I am going to be resting. You know children I am very tired. I have been travelling. I have been

> teaching the Faith. I am tired. And I thought I will go and rest.' Then he broke into laughter and said: 'It seems there is no rest. Well, if that is the wish of Bahá'u'lláh, then let's work harder.' (Pause) 'Pray for me'" [575]

* * *

The seventh child born to Corinne and Moses True was Nathanael. He was an especial joy to the family with his sweet giggling and witty perception. A few months past his second birthday, Nathanael, along with several of the True children, contracted diphtheria. In late 19th century, there were no reliable cures for this dreaded disease, which can cause suffocating, severe coughing, high fever and heart damage.

One night Corinne was holding Nathanael on her lap. He was listless when suddenly he extended his hands and pleaded: 'Oh, play with me.'[576] The next moment he died, two weeks short of two-and-one-half years of age. The date of his passing was 31 May 1899.

When 'Abdu'l-Bahá was in Chicago in 1912, He spoke to Corinne about the after-life. She had lost her husband and five of her children, and yearned for the Master's reassurance of eternal reunion. Letting her know that she would indeed be reunited with her loved ones, He told her that the spiritual world is quite near to us and that each of us without our being aware is assisted by souls from the next world.[577]

* * *

Mr Faizi referred to something from Bahá'u'lláh: 'Those who rise to serve Me, they will be aided by hosts of angels.'[578] 'Because of this statement,' Mr Faizi explained, 'they (hosts of angels) will come, they will circumambulate you, they will guide your steps, they will even guide your words.'[579]

In perhaps a lighter moment, Faizi encouraged the friends to show some appreciation for those angels. He said that those souls . . .

> ". . . can know everything about us . . . 'Abdu'l-Bahá says there is only one complaint that they make, and that is their relatives do not do anything good in their names. For instance, my mother has this sorrow in her heart that, 'He's not doing anything in my name.' Therefore, whoever you have of your dear ones in the next world, do something in their names. It's very important."[580]

* * *

> ***He will come to your aid with invisible hosts, and support you with armies of inspiration from the Concourse above; He will send unto you sweet perfumes from the highest Paradise, and waft over you the pure breathings that blow from the rose gardens of the Company on high.***[581]

Enoch Olinga spoke of the assistance available to every believer. Citing the Guardian, he said that the Holy Spirit is hovering, ready to enter the hearts. Meetings are always encompassed by this Spirit, which is why the Bahá'ís must have conferences and gatherings to enjoy fellowship, love and unity. These gatherings will attract divine confirmations so that when people leave they will be guided and helped in their work. He said that the difference between the Faith and other ideologies is that Bahá'u'lláh has released enormous amounts of divine love. This is why it is possible to unite the world. This unity will lead to peace. This is the power that is assisting the Bahá'ís to teach. It is a divine power. If one could see the inner world, he would see that this power is luminous and dynamic. Mortals cannot stop it. No one can extinguish it.[582]

* * *

William Sears used to remind the believers of the divine assistance available to any believer who arises to teach. Quoting from a little booklet entitled *Victory Promises*, he occasionally inspired his listeners:

> "Say, verily any one follower of this Faith can, by the leave of God, prevail over all who dwell in heaven and earth . . ."[583]
>
> "Should anyone arise for the triumph of our Cause, him will God render victorious though tens of thousands of enemies be leagued against him."[584]
>
> "These few have been endued with the Divine Elixir that can, alone, transmute into purest gold the dross of the world, and have been empowered to administer the infallible remedy for all the ills that afflict the children of men."[585]

* * *

> ***A seeing eye beholdeth the splendors of the sun and a hearing ear listeneth to the melody of the Supreme Concourse.***[586]

William Sears used to urge the believers to rely on the assistance of the Supreme Concourse, a resource so under-used that the accumulation of power waiting to come to their aid was awesome. Marguerite Sears in a letter to the writer wrote how her husband drew on this power:

> "Firstly, earnest daily prayer. Not only morning and night – but frequently during the day.
>
> His complete reliance on the creative word and his "pondering" to get more and more answers from every word.
>
> His work, whatever he was doing at the time, was always in the forefront of his mind. He carried a very small notebook always in case an idea came when (he was) away from his desk so he could write it down to transfer where needed later.
>
> His concentration was complete when he was working. Nothing else existed – there were not half-way measures. . . . It was like an acetylene torch in its intensity – and as a result of this, I'm sure attracted help constantly from the Supreme Concourse."[587]

* * *

Leroy Ioas's power of concentration was intense. He became oblivious of unrelated matters and surroundings. Nothing interfered with his services to the Faith.[588]

* * *

According to his wife Audrey, John Robarts '. . . possessed the ability to concentrate for long and unbroken periods of time, such as when preparing talks for writing reports or letters.'[589] He always carried with him a *little black notebook* (ibid) into which . . .

> ". . . he recorded inspiration and ideas as they occurred to him, often during the night or while travelling. His mind was continually active in the service of the Faith."[590]
> ". . . John was not easily deflected from his purpose."[591]

* * *

The work which Horace Holley accomplished was superhuman. When asked about how he accomplished so much work, he replied that he sometimes operated in a *zone of energy*, providing him with more than normal strength for his prodigious tasks.[592]

Unity

> ***So powerful is the light of unity that it can illuminate the whole earth.***[593]

In the opening programme of a radio series called *Mr Justice* developed by William Sears and Robert Quigley in the years immediately following the Second World War, the absurdity of prejudice was exposed to American audiences. Entitled 'Send them back where they came from,' the programme focused on a New York City apartment house.

The setting is mid-winter in Manhattan where a blizzard rages outside. The apartment is cold because the Norwegian janitor has gone back to his country. The Italian milkman has not delivered the morning milk because he has returned to Milan. The Dutch baker has delivered no bread, having departed for Amsterdam. The Irish electrician now back in Dublin cannot fix the fuse box in order to restore electricity to the apartment.

Naturally the disaster worsens. Soon there are no utilities, no taxis, no buses, no trains, no subways. Everyone has gone back to his or her home country because the poor apartment owner could not tolerate all the foreigners ruining the ethnic purity of the neighbourhood.[594]

The writer remembers watching the comedian Bill Cosby perform a very funny skit on this same theme, probably in the 1970s, in which he acted out this drama.

* * *

In 1969 at a public meeting at the Bahá'í Centre in Asmara, Eritrea, Rúḥíyyih <u>Kh</u>ánum, in addressing her audience, proposed the idea of unity as providing the solution to world problems. Because the world lacks unity, she felt that benefiting from modern inventions and education does not appear possible. She wondered:

> ". . . if a great many of our troubles in the world today are not due to . . . the passionate state of inharmony that the world is in today. It is really a disease, the degree to which people disagree with each other all over the world."[595]

* * *

Amatu'l-Bahá pointed out that a symptom of inharmony is seen in the trend of peoples within countries to want to fracture themselves into smaller and smaller units, whereas unity in a spirit of equality and brotherhood represents the only hope for humanity. She said:

> "It doesn't seem possible that men can be so insane as to spend money . . . on ways of fighting, ways of developing ever smaller units instead of co-operating to create ever larger units; and that we would spend money that way instead of spending it on the needs of humanity, when all of us are so very conscious of the fact that two-thirds of humanity still needs education, is for the most part illiterate or very ill-informed, and still needs in many places the necessities of life such as enough to eat and a little bit of clothing and a little bit of comfort, and also medical care. All these things are needed and yet we, in some kind of insanity, are spending our money still on arms and on what we call resisting aggression and what we say will prevent another war. Well, everybody hopes that it will, but nobody knows if it will or not. So if you really analyse it, the greatest need in the whole world today is for people to create bonds of unity and understanding amongst themselves, and through doing that to be able to create a world peace."[596]

* * *

Near the end of Mr Furútan's pilgrimage, the Guardian told him that '. . . everyone should be accorded absolute freedom to choose whether to join the Bahá'í community or not. However, since Bahá'ís should not participate in politics even in conversation, it is very important not to accept into the Faith under any circumstances those who do participate in politics.'[597]

* * *

Mírzá 'Alí-Muḥammad Varqá once asked Bahá'u'lláh how mankind will adopt the Cause of God. Bahá'u'lláh replied:

> "(F)irst, the nations of the world would arm themselves with infernal engines of war, and when fully armed would attack each other like bloodthirsty beasts. As a result, there would be enormous bloodshed throughout the world. Then the wise from all nations would gather together to investigate the cause of such bloodshed. They would come to the conclusion that prejudices were the cause, a major form being religious prejudice. They would therefore try to eliminate

religion so as to eliminate prejudice. Later they would realize that man cannot live without religion. Then they would study the teachings of all religions to see which of the religions conformed to the prevailing conditions of the time. It is then that the Cause of God would become universal." [598]

* * *

Hermann Grossmann
by Hartmut Grossmann
2002

"Hermann Grossmann was born 1899 in Rosario, Argentina, died 1968 in Heidelberg, Germany, became a Bahá'í in 1920 and was appointed a Hand of the Cause of God in 1951 by Shoghi Effendi. After his appointment he used to travel even more and especially in countries all over Europe. Hermann Grossmann was a great orator and a blessed teacher, well able to share his deep knowledge with others. At the same time he was constantly concerned about what and how he conveyed the Faith to his audience. For many years I was accompanying him when he travelled in Germany and met with Bahá'ís and non-Bahá'ís alike.

On our way to a meeting he would again and again ask me to drive faster to make sure we would be on time, saying that Shoghi Effendi had told him, to be on time was a courtesy to the audience, and 'Courtesy is a virtue of the kings' as he put it. On the way home, late at night, he relaxed and we took our time. Then he would very carefully analyse what he had said that evening. Why had he addressed the audience of scientists about the need to adhere to religious truth; the people of the press to report truthfully and with a deep sense of responsibility; a Jesuit about the working of Bahá'í Administration where Spirit became Form; and a mother who had lost a child with a vision of bliss in the next life? He liked to appeal to the good in everyone, to call on one's sense of responsibility or simply to challenge people; he wanted his audience to think for themselves. I remember an incident, which proved his fluency of speech and sentiment, as well as, his discipline. In a rural area he spoke once to a somewhat sceptical Catholic audience and compared the suffering of Christ with that of Bahá'u'lláh's, which made the statement of the Blessed Beauty, having been wronged by this world as no Manifestation before Him, so susceptible that, had he gone a little further, some sensitive people might have lost control and fainted. He warned of misusing speech to lead one's listener astray and deprive them of their willpower and control. Only much later did I realize that in these analyses he had taught me how to address people for the sake of Bahá'u'lláh and to rely entirely on His guidance and confirmation.

Hermann Grossmann was always young at heart and had a heart for the young. The way he spoke to the youth was different: direct, enthusiastic and simple. He was with them in camps and youth hostels; sharing what was available in those years after the war. One summer day we went to a youth camp on a truck from my father's company. We sat on top of tents, kitchen equipment and sacks with potatoes, tins and army rations that our Bahá'í friends, American Bahá'í army personnel stationed in Germany, had provided for this camp. Food was scarce at the time. On the way to the camp we drove on a country road under trees and had to duck deep not to be thrown off the truck. Suddenly the truck stopped, reversed and parked right under a tree with beautiful apples. My father climbed up to where we were and helped us pick the apples, but only after having explained to us that we could do so because the fruit trees were general property and the apples could be picked by anyone. Then we continued the journey, he sitting with us on top of the load and teaching us songs. Little wonder we all loved him."[599]

* * *

"The future of the African continent, of the African people, is very great. . . . Africa is witnessing a very great change, a spiritual revolution. In Uganda, where I come from, there are thousands and thousands of believers in Bahá'u'lláh and many many Local Spiritual Assemblies. And we have the Bahá'í Temple there. I can say that in a short while from now there will be a real explosion, spiritually speaking, when thousands upon thousands will rush to the Cause and embrace the Faith, and will become identified with the Name of the greatest Manifestation, Bahá'u'lláh. We are living in wonderful days, the days of the Lord of mankind. And I believe very fervently Bahá'u'lláh is the King of Glory, the King of Kings, the Lord of Hosts. Aren't you proud to be a Bahá'í?"[600] - Enoch Olinga

# # #

YOUTH

Blessed is he who in the prime of his youth and the heyday of his life will arise to serve the Cause of the Lord of the beginning and of the end, and adorn his heart with His love. The manifestation of such a grace is greater than the creation of the heavens and of the earth.[601]

When Raḥmatu'lláh Muhájir was barely twenty years of age, he was already encouraging his friends in a Bahá'í year of service. He believed that such a service brought significance into the life of an 18 year old and actually helped a young person attain a clearer understanding of his schooling. Although he was admitted to the school of medicine at the University of Ṭihrán the next year, he left his studies to serve the Cause in the northern province of Á<u>dh</u>irbáyján for two years.[602]

The Báb was almost 25 years old when He declared His mission. Mullá Ḥusayn was barely in his 30s when he recognized and embraced the Cause of the Báb, and, after five years of daring exploits, laid down his life. The immortal Quddús was but 22 years old when he embraced the Faith of the Báb. Shoghi Effendi was 24 when he assumed the reigns of the Guardianship.

Youth can indeed move the world. However in his 42nd year William Sears left a nationally televised CBS program and a lucrative salary to pioneer with his wife Marguerite to South Africa.[603] Martha Root was several weeks shy of her 47th birthday when she spontaneously arose to the challenge of the *Tablets of the Divine Plan* unveiled at the annual Bahá'í convention in New York City.[604] John Robarts was 52 when he and his wife Audrey left behind a prosperous career and settled life to be pioneers to Bechuanaland in southern Africa.[605] Rúḥíyyih <u>Kh</u>ánum began her world travels in 1964 at the age of 54[606] after which she would visit 154 countries in the next 34 years. Keith Ransom-Kehler was 56 when she entered Iran on a mission entrusted her by the Guardian for which she would lay down her life.[607] John Henry Hyde Dunn was 62 when he set out with his wife Clara to spiritually conquer the continent of Australia in 1920.[608] And Amelia Collins was 77 years of age when she was called by the beloved Guardian to Haifa to serve on the International Bahá'í Council as its vice-president. [609]

Dr Adelbert Mühlschlegel once described the difference between an old and a young person as one who no longer has any goals in life. In his 79th year, Dr Mühlschlegel, a linguist, set out to learn another language.[610]

Serving the Cause of God

Administrative Order

> ***The Bahá'í Administrative Order . . . will come to be regarded not only as the nucleus but as the very pattern of the New World Order, destined to embrace, in the fullness of time, the whole of mankind.***[611]

On 5 November 1961 the Hands of the Cause in a message to the Bahá'í world called for the election of the first Universal House of Justice. The election would take place on the first day of Riḍván 1963 at the World Centre, which was the first day of a three day Convention. Those eligible to vote would be the members of all National and Regional Spiritual Assemblies elected by the Bahá'ís at Riḍván 1962. The Chief Stewards wrote:

> "All male voting members throughout the Bahá'í world are eligible for election to the Universal House of Justice. The Hands of the Cause do not limit the freedom of the electors. However, as they have been given the explicit duties of guarding over the security and ensuring the propagation of the Faith, they ask the electors to leave them free at this time to discharge their duties."[612]

Five hundred and four delegates representing the 56 National and Regional Assemblies then in existence would be eligible to cast their ballots. In anticipation of this great event, Rúḥíyyih Khánum with approval of her colleagues arranged to hold the election in the House of 'Abdu'l-Bahá, so historic in terms of the enfoldment of the Administrative Order of Bahá'u'lláh. 'Abdu'l-Bahá Himself had once said: 'This very hall will witness the election of the House of Justice.'[613] Twelve doors leading to the reception area were removed in order to seat 288 members representing 51 Assemblies (five Assemblies were unable to send delegates owing to travel restrictions). Eighteen tellers from as many countries and representing National Assemblies would count the votes.

Owing to the supreme sacredness of the occasion, the Hands of the Cause arranged for the delegates to visit holy places on Mt Carmel and in 'Akká in what would later be described as the '. . . greatest mass pilgrimage ever to have been made to the World Centre of our Faith.'[614] The Shrines of the Báb and Bahá'u'lláh were also closed to the public and the Archives Building was made available at specific times to accommodate the delegates who had been invited to arrive on 18 April to prepare themselves spiritually.

On the morning of 21 April 1963, the delegates arrived and seated themselves in the central salon in anticipation of this most historic of events. The Hands of the Cause attending as observers were inside alcoves. At 9:30 a.m. the Convention opened with prayers in various languages being read or chanted. Acting as chairperson of the Convention, Rúḥíyyih Khánum addressed the delegates and explained how the election would proceed. The voting commenced in an atmosphere of utter silence, after which the roll of the Assemblies was called in alphabetical order. As each Assembly's name was called, the members present submitted their ballots. Chief tellers made sure that absentee ballots were submitted. In all, 504 ballots were received.

The work of counting the ballots kept the tellers busy through the night. At the close of the morning session of the Convention's second day, 22 April, the results of the election were announced and the nine members of the Supreme Institution were introduced. One of the delegates observed their sense of wonderment, awe and humility as their names were called, while a Hand of the Cause saw that they were *stunned by the news* with the participants at the peak of joy. A few days later at the Most Great Jubilee celebration in London attended by 12 Hands of the Cause, the nine newly elected members of the Universal House of Justice and some 7,000 believers, Paul Haney commented on the historic significance of the election:

> ". . . (We) were privileged to witness one of the great events of history taking place before our eyes . . . When the balloting was completed, every one felt that Bahá'u'lláh had indeed been present in that gathering and that a unique and wonderful pattern had been established for the world to marvel at and, in the fullness of time, to follow."[615]

Following the election, the Hands of the Cause sent the following announcement to the Bahá'í world:

> "OCCASION WORLDWIDE CELEBRATIONS MOST GREAT JUBILEE COMMEMORATING CENTENARY ASCENSION BAHA'U'LLAH THRONE HIS SOVEREIGNTY WITH HEARTS OVERFLOWING GRATITUDE HIS UNFAILING PROTECTION OVERFLOWING BOUNTIES JOYOUSLY ANNOUNCE FRIENDS EAST WEST ELECTION SUPREME LEGISLATIVE BODY ORDAINED BY HIM IN HIS MOST

> HOLY BOOK PROMISED BY HIM RECEIVE HIS INFALLIBLE GUIDANCE STOP MEMBERS FIRST HISTORIC HOUSE JUSTICE DULY ELECTED BY DELEGATES COMPRISING MEMBERS FIFTYSIX NATIONAL ASSEMBLIES ARE CHARLES WOLCOTT ALI NAKHJAVANI BORRAH KAVELIN IAN SEMPLE LOTFULLAH HAKIM DAVID HOFMAN HUGH CHANCE AMOZ GIBSON HUSHMAND FATHEAZAM STOP TO JUBILATION ENTIRE BAHA'I WORLD VICTORIOUS COMPLETION BELOVED GUARDIAN'S UNIQUE CRUSADE NOW ADDED HUMBLE GRATITUDE PROFOUND THANKSGIVING FOLLOWERS BAHA'U'LLAH FOR ERECTION UNIVERSAL HOUSE JUSTICE AUGUST BODY TO WHOM ALL BELIEVERS MUST TURN WHOSE DESTINY IS TO GUIDE UNFOLDMENT HIS EMBRYONIC WORLD ORDER THROUGH ADMINISTRATIVE INSTITUTIONS PRESCRIBED BY BAHA'U'LLAH ELABORATED BY ABDU'L-BAHA LABORIOUSLY ERECTED BY SHOGHI EFFENDI AND ENSURE EARLY DAWN GOLDEN AGE FAITH WHEN THE WORD OF THE LORD WILL COVER THE EARTH AS THE WATERS COVER THE SEA STOP . . ."[616]

* * *

John Robarts was a man of integrity who deviated not from spiritual principles. Perhaps because Shoghi Effendi had said that one should seek the principle and act upon it, John was able to focus the attention of deliberations within committees and Assemblies on the basic principle involved in greater and lesser situations. Under his leadership as chairman on administrative bodies, consulting members were inspired by his love and confidence to embrace their divine mission.

His wife remembered:

> "John had some sort of inner compass by which he was able to find the true north, the basic principle involved in situations, large or small. The fluctuation of the needle of other ideas, opinions and fancies did not distract his heart or mind to side issues. He listened well and could change his mind because he had faith in the power of consultation. He was a doer from childhood. He was noted for this, combined with trust and a perception of what was or was not honest. He was a hard worker, accepting and carrying out responsibilities, sometimes very heavy ones."[617]

* * *

Coincidental to this important matter was Rúḥíyyih Khánum's talk in 1953 at the Chicago Intercontinental Conference. There she '... spoke of the absolute necessity for us to learn to think in terms of principle and not in terms of personality':

> "It seems to be a terrible disease that we all have, of constantly thinking of everything in terms of personality. We never seem to get to terms of principle. You see, the Guardian doesn't care anything about personality. It doesn't exist as far as he is concerned. He cares only for principle. There are no exceptions to this rule. It doesn't matter who you are or what you have done, how much you have given, how prominent you are, anything to do with you that you might feel entitles you to some special consideration.... It is only principle.... We are never, never going to get this administrative order swinging until we forget all individuals, however much they get into our hair, and devote ourselves to the application of the principles involved.... You will be astonished what you can do if you ever get over the question of personalities."[618]

At the Most Great Jubilee in 1963, she again brought out this characteristic of the Guardian. She said: 'Nothing could interfere with what he considered right. Nothing swayed him at all, neither love, nor hate, nor danger.'[619] One of the examples she gave was that of Valíyu'lláh Varqá. When he had applied for his pilgrimage, he had to wait his turn in spite of his standing as a Hand of the Cause and Trustee of Ḥuqúqu'lláh. She said:

> "It made no difference to Shoghi Effendi who anyone was, if there was a matter of principle involved. . . . (W)here a matter of principle in the Faith was involved, Shoghi Effendi was "absolutely impervious". It is these things we must learn from him. This kind of integrity will keep this Cause spotless for a thousand years. The example of the integrity of Shoghi Effendi must be followed by the Bahá'ís and the Assemblies, because it is the standard of God."[620]

* * *

The relationship of Horace Holley to the Administrative Order cannot be underestimated. A rugged individualist, Horace was able to grasp Shoghi Effendi's instructions and play a supreme and historic role in the enfoldment of the Bahá'í Administrative Order. He was both a master of correct Bahá'í procedure and a scholar of the Bahá'í teachings.

Paul Vreeland had this to say about Mr Holley and the Bahá'í Administrative Order:

> "Horace Holley may be among the first western administrators to come to terms with the Bahá'í distinction between power and authority. And if Shoghi Effendi used (him) as the anvil upon which to hammer out the administrative order, Horace's inner life may have represented an early sacrifice of western individualism. Power, authority and individualism are concepts that continue to test the evolution of the order." [621]

* * *

Who was Horace Holley?
By Sophie Loeding
1974

> "Those associated with Mr Holley at the National Centre during his tenure as secretary . . . knew him as a highly intellectual man, greatly gifted in the literary field, the author of many articles and books about the Faith, and the compiler of many of the writings of Bahá'u'lláh, 'Abdu'l-Bahá, and the Guardian for the deepening and guidance of the friends. He was also a poet and among his works was a published book of verse which unfortunately is no longer available.
>
> Those who worked with him knew him as a kind man, generous and thoughtful of others, never showing impatience, never demanding but always getting from us the utmost in cooperation and service. He was a great reader and student, had a phenomenal memory and a keenly analytical mind. As secretary of the National Spiritual Assembly for a period of many years he was called upon, as the Cause spread, to deal with an ever-increasing correspondence ranging over a wide spectrum of topics.
>
> His letters were well reasoned, concise, and always conveyed the exact meaning he had in mind. He had a voluminous correspondence with the beloved Guardian, who expressed admiration and appreciation for his services and gave him many literary tasks to perform. Perhaps the most outstanding was that of arranging in legally acceptable

form Shoghi Effendi's instructions regarding the structure and organization of the Administrative Order of Bahá'u'lláh: The American Declaration of Trust of the National Spiritual Assembly and the By-laws of a Local Spiritual Assembly.

After Mr Holley – in conjunction with Mountfort Mills, a Bahá'í lawyer – completed this important task, the material was submitted to the Guardian who approved it and designated it the pattern to be followed by all national Bahá'í communities in the world. The achievement of this immensely important task assigned to him by the Guardian will no doubt stand over the years as the crowning point of a distinguishing career.

The range of information stored in Horace Holley's memory was wide indeed, and factual. He knew the literature of the Faith and of related subjects as few others did, and could call upon this knowledge at will when necessary. He was a fluent and scholarly speaker, both in extemporaneous discourses and with carefully prepared material. He never used a written text to give presentations. Once when asked if in preparing his addresses he wrote out the text, he said: 'I make myself a skeleton and dress the skeleton as I go along.' The "dressed skeleton" was always a thorough presentation of the topic, the "dress" being taken from the vast fund of information stored in his remarkable memory.

His many gifts made Horace Holley a natural channel for furthering the work of the Cause, not only in the United States, but abroad as well; the clarity of his thinking, his broad vision and ability to convey, through both the written and the spoken word, the fundamental teachings of the Faith and their application to our daily lives, made him an unforgettable figure in the annals of the Faith.

Contemporary, friend, and co-worker of well-remembered believers like May Maxwell and Siegfried Schopflocher of Canada, Mountfort Mills, Roy Wilhelm, John Bosch, George Latimer, Nellie French, Corinne True, Amelia Collins, Helen S. Goodall, Ella Cooper and many other great souls who responded to the call of Bahá'u'lláh, Mr. Holley was one of those who did the "spade work" for the magnificent edifice the young Bahá'ís of today and tomorrow will ultimately erect.

> To have had the opportunity to serve as his secretary was a great privilege and a great learning opportunity. He had a keen sense of humor, was wise, unselfish, clear thinking; a ready tool forged for use by the beloved Guardian, to whom he was always faithful, loyal and obedient." [622]

* * *

In 1942 Ḥasan Balyuzi was elected chairman of the British NSA, a post he would be elected to for 17 years. He was described as bringing *loving patience*, *deep sympathy*, *profound wisdom* and *lovable hilarity* to the meetings. One member remembered the joy, eagerness and excitement of the meetings. Another remembered him as gentle and influential, and still another recalled his anecdotes, light-hearted stories and perfect chairmanship.[623]

# # #

Contributions And The Right Of God

Our contributions to the Faith are the surest way of lifting once for all time the burden of hunger and misery from mankind.[624]

The Guardian referred to Amelia Collins as the *outstanding benefactress of the Faith.*[625] Through her generous contributions, Shoghi Effendi was able to develop properties at the World Centre in 1926. A large meeting hall was erected at Geyserville in 1936, and a fully equipped dormitory for 50 people built there in 1937. She was the first to contribute to the Bahíyyih Khánum Fund for the erection of the Mother Temple of the West. She made substantial contributions to the Persia Temple Fund. She made possible the purchase of 19 Temple sites in Latin America, Europe and Asia. She donated entire sums to buy many national Ḥaẓíratu'l-Quds and establish endowments on five continents. She paid for the first publication of Bahá'í literature in Amharic. She defrayed the cost of publishing four volumes of the Bahá'í World. And she made many other generous contributions.[626]

***

During the years when the Wilmette Temple was under construction, Fred Schopflocher's generosity helped to build this holiest House of Worship, inspire others to contribute and cheer the heart of the Guardian. In 1928 he contributed $25,000; 1929, $100,000; and 1937, another $100,000 – sizeable sums in an age when $5,000 could purchase a home. He also took an interest in the maintenance of Green Acre and donated several important properties to the school.

Zikrullah Khadem said that once when Mr Schopflocher was in the presence of the Guardian and the Temple construction was stopped for want of money, Fred offered $100,000 for the renewal of the construction. His spontaneous offer brought tears to the eyes of Shoghi Effendi. When Mr Khadem recalled this act in the presence of Mr Schopflocher, the latter just pressed the former's hand and changed the subject.

Fred understood early in his Bahá'í career the importance of the Temple to the growth of the Faith through visits to the Guardian. When his wife Loral – herself a world traveller for the Faith – was on pilgrimage in 1929, the Guardian handed her a cable from her husband, which she recalled three decades later: 'Are you willing to contribute $50,000 to the Temple which may mean you do not get a new Cadillac this year?'

Laughing in the presence of the Guardian, she sent her reply through Fugeta (Fujita) to the telegraph office: 'Why not $100,000?' Fred replied: 'You win, love to Shoghi Effendi, love, Fred.'[627] No wonder Shoghi Effendi designated Siegfried (Fred) the *Chief Temple Builder.*[628]

* * *

> "(I am reminded) of a Chicago Bahá'í, now dead, and perhaps many will recall to whom I refer in this story. She lived alone in a very poor part of the city and earned her living by giving piano lessons. All she could do on her slim earnings was to exist, frail, and I suspect, undernourished. When we had our great drive to build the Temple's (Wilmette) exterior crust of ornamentation, she had no way of getting any money to give to it, but, she told my Mother, she found a way: she walked to her lessons instead of taking a street car. Such self-sacrifice, on the part of a delicate, often ailing, middle-aged woman, must seem far out of proportion to the tiny sum she was able to save, over a long period, and send in to the Temple Fund. The work was completed, but she had never seen it. One day, though, she said she just could not wait any longer, so she blew herself . . . to Wilmette, and, as she said, when her eyes lighted on the erected Temple, all she could find to say was: 'Oh you darling!' Can anyone doubt how that believer's contribution has added to the spiritual blessing our Temple confers? We often say: 'it's not what you do, but how you do it;' or 'it's not what you say but how you say it.'" It is also true: 'not what you give, but how you give it.'[629]

At the Intercontinental Conference held in Chicago in 1953, Rúḥíyyih K͟hánum told the story of how Shoghi Effendi returned a £34 000 contribution to a donor '. . . with whom (he) was displeased. He considered that the man's spirit was not right, that his motives were not pure, and Shoghi Effendi could not accept money from him. He said, "How can I take his money and not reinstate him in my good graces? And he can't buy me."'[630]

She concluded this story, saying:

> "You see, it is these things that set the standard of Bahá'ís in the world. When our integrity is as shining and as clear cut as Shoghi Effendi's, we will not have much trouble bringing people into the Faith."[631]

***

During his second imprisonment in Ṭihrán around 1896, Mullá Muḥammad-Riḍá saw that a certain prisoner had no shirt. He turned to his fellow-prisoner Áqá Mírzá Ḥusayn and proposed they provide him with their spare shirt. The latter countered that as he had just washed the shirt, Mullá Riḍá should wear it and give the man the shirt he was wearing. Losing his temper at such a suggestion, the mullá retorted:

> "Do you mean to say that I put on the clean shirt and place my used one in the hands of the Blessed Beauty? How dare you make such a cruel suggestion? Aren't you a Bahá'í? Bahá'u'lláh says it is not charity unless you give away the things you hold dear."[632]

***

Mr Faizi reminded an audience that they should have the courage to give generously to the Cause of God. Hearts should not be attached to worldly things. The joy of one's heart should not depend on worldly things. In this way will the Cause not be in need of funds.

He likened our reluctance to contribute to giving our affections to worldly things. Bahá'u'lláh asks only for our hearts but we attach ourselves to the *ashtray of the world* where there is neither light nor joy. The result is broken families, shattered communities and a miserable world. Few people accept the Faith and fewer obey Bahá'u'lláh. How therefore can we expect the world to ever be happy?[633]

***

When Roy Wilhelm passed away, he bequeathed to the Faith an estate which enabled the Guardian after 30 years' effort to acquire 23,000 square meters of land and a building in the precincts of the Shrine of the Báb.[634]

***

> ***It is clear and evident that the payment of the Right of God (Ḥuqúqu'lláh) is conducive to prosperity, to blessing, and to honour and divine protection. . . . And this is on condition that the individual should observe the injunctions prescribed in the Book with the utmost radiance, gladness and willing acquiescence.***[635]

Shortly before His ascension, Bahá'u'lláh in the *Lawḥ-i-Dunyá* (Tablet for the Advancement of the World) described the loftiness of the station of the Hands of the Cause. Revealed in honour of Áqá Mírzá Áqáy-i-Afnán, surnamed Núr'u'd-Dín - nephew of Khadíjih Bagum, the wife of the Báb - Bahá'u'lláh revealed counsels for His followers for the betterment of the world. He begins this Tablet by bestowing His bounties on Hand of the Cause Mullá 'Alí-Akbar-i-Shahmírzádí (Ḥájí Ákhúnd) and Trustee of Ḥuqúq Ḥájí Abu'l-Ḥasan-i-Ardikání (Ḥájí Amín):

> "Praise and thanksgiving beseem the Lord of manifest dominion Who hath adorned this mighty prison with the presence of their honours 'Alí Akbar and Amín, and hath illumined it with the light of certitude, constancy and assurance. The glory of God and the glory of all that are in the heavens and on the earth be upon them."[636]

At the time of the revelation of this Tablet, these two distinguished men were incarcerated in the mighty prison of Qazvín. When 'Abdu'l-Bahá saw a photograph of them which had been taken for the Sháh, He rejoiced at their resignation and calm. He placed this photograph in the hallway opposite His room where He gazed upon it many times.

Ḥájí Abu'l-Ḥasan-i-Ardakání was the second Trustee of Ḥuqúqu'lláh. His unusual qualities of nobility and detachment attracted the attention of the first Trustee, Ḥájí Sháh Muḥammad. Inevitably the two men became the closest of companions, with the former choosing the latter to be his assistant. When on a journey together in 1881 Ḥájí Sháh Muḥammad was killed during a Kurdish revolt, Bahá'u'lláh conferred the office of Trusteeship on Jináb-i-Ḥájí Abu'l-Ḥasan or Ḥájí Amín (the Trusted One).

For 47 years he served as Trustee of Ḥuqúqu'lláh with courage and steadfastness. As Trustee he offered up whatever he possessed to the Cause of God and strived to convey to the believers this same attitude. Ḥájí Amín was frugal and felt that extravagance reduced the friends' ability to support the Cause. Through his example the believers gave of their substance to promote the Cause even though many were poor and some were needy. The Research Department of the Universal House of Justice has written this moving account of this much beloved Trustee:

> "He was a symbol of magnanimity and detachment. He had no worldly possessions, no home or shelter of his own. His habitation was in the hearts and souls of the Bahá'í friends who would receive and entertain him with warmth and love. Each one would impatiently await his arrival, to enjoy the sweet melody of his prayers and chanting of the Tablets, and the glad-tidings and encouragement he would bring. Every day he would bid goodbye to one family to spend the night in another household, illumining another gathering with his presence. He was continually on the move, travelling to most Iranian cities and being the trusted advisor of many Bahá'í friends in their personal affairs."[637]

* * *

Ḥájí Mullá Mihdí was both a simple and learned man. He was familiar with Muslim sacred traditions, able to penetrate mysteries and a fount of sacred traditions. A native of Yazd, he incurred the wrath of the 'ulamás when he fearlessly declared his allegiance to the Faith. They decreed that he must die, forcing him to quit his home.

He set out for 'Akká with his two sons in a quest for his Beloved. Along the way Ḥájí Mullá Mihdí was imprisoned, passed through difficult terrain, and suffered many hardships. Though he became increasingly ill, he continued on. Eventually, as he approached the house of Bahá'u'lláh at the village of Mazra'ih, he fell, having '. . . gambled away his life in his yearning after the Light of the World.'[638]

So exalted was his station that Bahá'u'lláh occasionally stopped at his gravesite on His way to 'Akká or Mazra'ih and revealed exalted verses and a Tablet of Visitation in his honour, investing his soul with indescribable glory. This was the illustrious progenitor of three generations of Hands of the Cause called Varqá.

Of Ḥájí Mullá Mihdí's three sons Mírzá 'Alí-Muḥammad Varqá attained the presence of His Lord at about 22 years of age when he lost his father in 1878-9. He became a new creation on this pilgrimage. On another pilgrimage circa 1891, he begged Bahá'u'lláh for martyrdom. Bahá'u'lláh accepted his plea. In 1896 he was martyred together with his 12 year old son Rúḥu'lláh. Bahá'u'lláh revealed many Tablets for Varqá and 'Abdu'l-Bahá referred to him as a Hand of the Cause: 'Among the Hands of the

Cause of God who have departed this life and ascended to the Supreme Horizon . . . was the revered martyr, Áqá Mírzá Varqá.'[639]

Mírzá 'Alí-Muḥammad Varqá had four sons: 'Azízu'lláh, Rúḥu'lláh, Valíyu'lláh and Badí'u'lláh. Valíyu'lláh Varqá was raised by his grandmother. A fanatical Muslim, she managed to poison young Valíyu'lláh's heart against his father and the Faith such that he wept at the apparent deviation of his father. Fortuitously, when he was 16, an uncle removed him from that noxious atmosphere and schooled him in the Bahá'í Faith. Sometime before he was turned 20, Valíyu'lláh became a believer. Later, as a student at the American University in Beirut, he was able to deepen his knowledge in the Faith under 'Abdu'l-Bahá's guidance during summer vacations. Still later he was honoured to join 'Abdu'l-Bahá's entourage in Europe and the United States as His interpreter.

Upon the birth of Valíyu'lláh Varqá's son in 1912, 'Azízu'lláh took the infant's picture and sent it to the father in America. A believer took the picture to 'Abdu'l-Bahá Who wrote on the arms of the child, 'Yad', which means Hand, and 'Mu'ayyad', which means Assisted or Confirmed one, and named him 'Alí-Muḥammad after his martyred grandfather. Thus, while in his infancy, the future Hand of the Cause Dr 'Alí-Muḥammad Varqá was appointed by the beloved Master to this high station (Confirmed Hand).

In 1939 Valíyu'lláh Varqá was appointed the fourth Trustee of Ḥuqúqu'lláh by the beloved Guardian. During his custodianship, the law of Ḥuqúqu'lláh became universal in Iran. As Trustee he resigned his employment to devote his full time energies to the work of Ḥuqúqu'lláh. In 1951 the Guardian appointed him a Hand of the Cause in the first contingent and thereafter Valíyu'lláh Varqá's services expanded in the form of new opportunities outside Iran to meet and cheer the hearts of the friends.

In 1955 he experienced severe pain following a pilgrimage and his return to Iran. He went to Europe for treatment, eventually entering a hospital in Germany. On 30 September 1955 the Guardian wrote:

> "This precious Hand of the Cause of God was always an honoured and favoured servant of the Faith during the days of the Master, and very close to His heart; and has always been a completely trusted and truly dedicated helper of the Guardian, who loves him very deeply. To know of his present condition does grieve the heart, and distresses and saddens the Guardian greatly."[640]

When Valíyu'lláh Varqá passed away on 12 November 1955 following a failed operation, Shoghi Effendi sent a cable to the Bahá'í world that . . .

> ". . . His mantle as Trustee of funds of Ḥuqúq now falls on 'Alí Muḥammad his son. . . . Newly appointed Trustee of Ḥuqúq is now elevated to rank of Hand of Cause."[641]

Following the appointment of Dr Varqá as a Hand of the Cause, the family of Valíyu'lláh Varqá realized in a mysterious way that what 'Abdu'l-Bahá had inscribed on the photo of 'Alí-Muḥammad in 1912 was literally fulfilled. Thus the unerring pen of the Master and the infallible wish of the beloved Guardian were one and the same. The Guardian was not aware of this photo and inscription until after he had made the appointment.

In following years, Dr 'Alí-Muḥammad Varqá, who earned his doctorate in the faculty of literature and human sciences from the Sorbonne in 1950, had to contend with problems relating to the safeguarding and sale of properties donated to Ḥuqúq from the persecuted friends in Iran. An outflow of pioneers from his native land resulted in his appointing Deputies and Representative in countries outside of Iran.

When the law of Ḥuqúq became universally applicable, the Universal House of Justice announced:

> "With humility before our sovereign Lord, we now announce that as of Riḍván 1992, the beginning of the Holy Year, the Law of Ḥuqúqu'lláh, the Right of God, will become universally applicable. All are lovingly called to observe it."[642]

The same year the Supreme Body announced:

> "The Office of Ḥuqúqu'lláh has been established in the Holy Land under the direction of the Chief Trustee of Ḥuqúqu'lláh, the Hand of the Cause of God 'Alí-Muḥammad Varqá, in anticipation of the worldwide application of the Law of Ḥuqúqu'lláh next Riḍván."[643]

In 1995 and 2001 Ḥuqúqu'lláh videos were produced. Educational materials in various languages were also published. On the Day of the Covenant, November 2001, an Ḥuqúqu'lláh website was launched for use of members of the institution. Meanwhile Boards of Trustees as well as Deputies and Representatives of Ḥuqúqu'lláh have developed around the world. The Universal House of Justice has stated that the . . .

> "... institution of Ḥuqúqu'lláh ... will expand and flourish in the centuries to come, and will provide material resources for the advancement of the human race."[644]

Concerning this great Law, Dr 'Alí-Muḥammad Varqá stated during the Sixth International Convention in 1988:

> ". . . Payment of the Right of God is like a magnet, which attracts divine blessings and confirmation. It is the mainspring of God's mercy and compassion. Bahá'u'lláh, in His Writings, showers His limitless benediction upon those who observe this law. . Withholding the payment of Ḥuq'uqu'lláh or spending it on other concerns, no matter how charitable their nature, would be interpreted as misappropriation of the funds belonging to God, and an act of dishonesty. . God Almighty has decreed that the payment of the Right of God is conducive to prosperity, and assists the progress of the human soul in the spiritual realms of the everlasting world.
>
> . . . we cannot expect to comprehend the essence and the wisdom hidden in this sacred law. They are kept in the treasury of God's knowledge and are related to the evolution and progress of the human soul in the world of God. What we can conceive by our human understanding is that the payment of Ḥuqúqu'lláh is the sign of our love and obedience, a proof of our firmness and steadfastness and a symbol of our trustworthiness in the Covenant of Bahá'u'lláh."[645]

***

At Riḍván 2005, the Universal House of Justice brought into being an International Board of Trustees of Ḥuqúqu'lláh. The role of the Board is to guide and supervise the work of Regional and National Boards of Ḥuqúqu'lláh Trustees throughout the world. This decision was taken just two and one half years prior to the passing of Dr 'Alí-Muḥammad Varqá, historically the final Chief Trustee of the Institution of Ḥuqúqu'lláh. The members of the newly created Board would perform their services at the Bahá'í World Centre.

***

Zikrullah Khadem was a strong believer in paying Ḥuqúq. In an interview, his wife said to the writer that they never had financial problems because of his strict observance of this great law. Mrs Khadem said that they never had to rely on the Bahá'í Fund through Mr Khadem's years of service for the Cause in the west, and in her senior years she found her financial needs satisfied.

In 1984, at the 75th National Convention of the Bahá'ís of the United States, Mr Khadem was unexpectedly inspired to address the delegates as the meeting was about to close. Exhilarated and transformed, he turned the attention of the friends to the great Law of Ḥuqúqu'lláh. The application of and obedience to this Law by the friends would, he was convinced, '. . . purify their financial affairs, ensure recompense by God and resolve all the material needs of the Cause.'[646] Quoting from the Will and Testament of 'Abdu'l-Bahá, Mr Khadem recalled that He states that Ḥuqúqu'lláh 'causeth the people to become firm and steadfast and draweth Divine increase upon them.'[647]

The audience was so inspired that they scrambled to sign their names to a scroll, asking the Universal House of Justice to confer the blessing of Ḥuqúq on the Western believers.

* * *

Músá Banání had concluded and received cash in a business transaction. The evening was already late. Nevertheless he went straight to the home of the Trustee of Ḥuqúqu'lláh Valíyu'lláh Varqá who was asleep. His sleep disturbed, Mr Varqá enquired of Mr Banání the purpose of his visit. Mr Banání replied that he had come to pay his Ḥuqúq. Couldn't he wait until the next day, Mr Varqá inquired. Mr Banání's rejoinder was to ask whether Mr Varqá could guarantee his (Mr Banání) being alive tomorrow? Mr Varqá graciously received Mr Banání's payment which the latter had already calculated.[648] – 'Alí Nakhjavání

# # #

Education

It grieves our hearts to realize that in so many parts of the world children are employed as soldiers, exploited as labourers, sold into virtual slavery, forced into prostitution, made the objects of pornography, abandoned by parents centred on their own desires, and subjected to other forms of victimization too numerous to mention. Many such horrors are inflicted by the parents themselves upon their own children. The spiritual and psychological damage defies estimation.[649]

George Townshend in his book *The Heart of the Gospel* points out . . .

> ". . . that the history of the world needs an entirely new interpretation. It has dwelt almost exclusively on a catalogue of wars and disasters, overlooking the true underlying interpretation, a spiritual interpretation, as mankind struggles on the planet to develop those virtues and attributes that make him or her 'in the image' and 'likeness' of God. That struggle . . . is the real interpretation of history."[650]

* * *

In the environs of the Mashriqu'l-Adhkár in 'Ishqábád, nine-year-old 'Alí-Akbar Furútan found beauty and spirituality unknown in oppressive Sabzivár where the family had formerly resided. There he entered school in the vicinity of the Temple and studied for four years. Afterward he taught first-graders until 1922 and then acquired his secondary education graduating in 1925.

Mr Furútan, whose field was education and child psychology, was attracted by a Tablet revealed by 'Abdu'l-Bahá, which reads in part:

> "Instruction in schools must begin with instruction in religion. Following religious training, and the binding of the child's heart to the love of God, proceed with his education in the other branches of knowledge."[651]

During his 12 years in 'Ishqábád, he was very active in the Faith. In his 15th year Mr Furútan was appointed to the National Youth Committee and elected its secretary. On the committee he wrote articles and humorous stories, which were well received by youth and adults. At a youth meeting he demonstrated knowledge of the Writings by silencing criticism. The Local Assembly sent him to teach the Faith in Baku since he was known to be familiar with Turkish and Russian as well as versed in modern sciences. He became principal of several schools in 1925. He was both custodian and manager of the Bahá'í library in the vicinity of the Temple. And he spoke at many Bahá'í gatherings.

In 1926 he left for Moscow where he continued his education. At the time, only one out of 50 students was admitted to the university. Mr Furútan passed his examination, gained admittance, and then even received a scholarship. He studied diligently in that city of 1,600 churches.

Next year he spent his winter recess with his parents in 'Is͟hqábád. There he found his father ill and approaching death. The older man said to his son: 'I wish to dedicate one of my sons to the Cause so that after me, detached from all material concerns, he will spend his life in service to the Faith. I have chosen you, my second son, for this purpose, and my wish for you is that after you have completed your education you will engage in nothing else but Bahá'í activities. You must give me a Bahá'í promise at this moment, and pledge that you will carry out my wishes.'[652] The son replied that he also desired this service and therefore he would obey his father. Mr Furútan had already acquired a burning desire to immerse himself in the Writings and avoid materialistic ideologies.

Only a year before, he had received a lengthy letter in which the Guardian through his secretary helped Mr Furútan resolve the conflict he had felt between continuing his education versus teaching the Faith. Encouraging him to *cling to the cord of consultation* and consult with the Spiritual Assembly, the Guardian conveyed, in part:

> "Teaching the Cause of God is possible under all circumstances, even through trade and commerce and through right conduct, as it is said that goodly deeds and a praiseworthy character are in themselves the teachers of the Cause. Therefore, any individual, in whatever profession he may be engaged, if he conducts himself in a praiseworthy manner and exemplifies human perfections, will himself become the sign of the propagation of the Word of God and will hoist the banner of the glory of the Cause."[653]

After the Assembly decided that he should continue his education, Mr Furútan eventually completed his studies in Psychology and Education. His thesis on education was accepted, praised and published. A certificate was awarded: "Alí-Akbar-i-Furútan has proved himself to be a very active, serious, and conscientious student during his years of study in the University . . .'[654]

In coming years Mr Furútan fondly remembered the literary, scientific and artistic centres as well as fine theatres and opera houses of Moscow. While he served on the Local Spiritual Assembly of Moscow and held Bahá'í classes for children and youth, Mr Furútan visited the beautiful city of St Petersburg (Leningrad) with its lovely houses, wide streets, and fine buildings. He visited the Kremlin whose beauty he praised. And he made a pilgrimage to the resting place of Tolstoy. He also wrote about his travels in various parts of that vast country.

Upon finishing his education, Mr Furútan was expelled to his native land by the Government for his Bahá'í activities. He received from the Guardian a letter dated 11 May 1930 which brought him consolation after the stresses he suffered in being forcibly evicted from a country which had become his home and which held his affections for 16 years:

> "O spiritual friend,
>
> Be not disturbed and saddened by the current difficulties . . . What will remain and persist will be the institutions which the friends have established in that land. Patience and endurance are needed. He will indeed aid the weak through the power of His might, and help His loved ones with the exalted angels of His most glorious Kingdom.
>
> For the present you should remain in Persia, and engage in the activities of the Cause in that country. It is my hope that in the days to come you will also be enabled to render great and outstanding services in the countries of Russia." [655]

Continuing his steadfast services for the Faith in Iran, Mr Furútan, following his marriage in 1931, established a school in Saysán for the education of Bahá'í children there where he served for two years. In 1933 he was appointed principal of the Tarbíyat School in Ṭihrán until its forced closure by the Government at the end of 1934. At the first National Convention of the Bahá'ís of Iran the same year as his appointment, Mr Furútan was elected to the National Spiritual Assembly on which he served as Secretary for 24 years. Mr Furútan was among the first contingent of Hands of the Cause appointed in 1951, a contingent the beloved Guardian distinguished in his eulogy to William Sutherland Maxwell as the *front ranks of the Hands of the Cause of God.*[656] In 1957 he was nominated by his colleagues as one of the Custodians to serve at the World Centre, from where he continued his devoted services both locally and internationally through the remaining 46 years of his long and productive life.

The remarkable promise of the Guardian in that 1930 letter was realized 60 years later when Mr Furútan revisited the land of his childhood and youth in 1990. Lasting 45 days, the Hand of the Cause set out on 15 March 1990, travelling to Moscow, 'Ishqábád, Mary, Tashkent, Dushanbe, Samarqand, Leningrad and Murmansk. His daughter, Iran Furútan Muhájir, wrote that this trip was *full of miraculous events.*[657] He gave many talks, attended many meetings, received wide publicity, inspired declarations of faith, lectured on child psychology, stood on the grounds of the 'Ishqábád Temple site, prayed at an old Bahá'í cemetery near the site, visited the Moscow university where he graduated, spoke at the College of Marxism on the Faith and participated in the election and re-establishment of the Moscow Local Spiritual Assembly after a 60 year lapse.

As thrilling and emotional as must have been the experiences of visiting Russia after so many years, Mr Furútan must also have been thrilled by the request of the editor of *Progress*, a Soviet publishing house. The editor had read *Mothers, Fathers and Children.* So impressed was he by that gem of a book which provides guidance on the education of children that he asked permission of Mr Furútan to print 250,000 copies in Russian and in four Asiatic languages.

Back in 1946 Mr Furútan in response to an invitation from the Iranian Radio and Broadcasting Service gave a series of lectures over a six month period on children's education. These lectures became quite popular and were eventually merged with other articles into a book entitled *Essays on Education (Maghálát-i-Tarbíyatí).* Reprinted many times, the substance of this book became *Mothers, Fathers and Children.*[658]

Concerning the training and education of children, Mr Furútan imparted these jewels of wisdom in this book:

> "There is great wisdom in the long duration of childhood, and every educator should be aware of it. If parents do not give this subject the attention it deserves, they may forgo an extremely precious opportunity, and out of some lack of knowledge, unwittingly make their little sweethearts bitter and dismal throughout their lives.[659] . . . There is no doubt that children are truly blessed if, through the care and attention of those entrusted with their upbringing, they learn praiseworthy conduct and shun blameworthy

behaviour, and their childhood is spent in pursuing knowledge and human perfections, so that, when older, they may become fruitful trees – useful and progressive elements of society.[660] . . . Experts are all united in the opinion that it is the parents who establish the morals and manners of their children, with the characteristics and virtues of the mother exerting a greater influence. Whatever the parents may do and whatever they may say (be it good or ill), will become a pattern for the child's conduct...[661] 'Knowledge received in childhood is like an engraving made on stone.'"[662]

The House of Justice in its eulogy of Mr Furútan dated 27 November 2003 recalled the impact of his amazing life:

"'Alí Akbar Furútan's single-minded devotion to the Faith and its Guardian, the vital role he played in the establishment of the Administrative Order in Iran, his contribution to the spiritual and material education of children, his services as a Hand of the Cause of God, and his unswerving support of the Universal House of Justice together constitute an imperishable record of service in the annals of the Cause. His penetrating mind, his loving concern and his sparkling humour are ineffaceable memories in the hearts of the thousands of believers with whom he spoke."[663]

* * *

The children must, from their infancy, be raised to be spiritual and godly Bahá'ís. If such be their training, they will remain safe from every test.[664]

Circa 1934 Abu'l-Qásim Faizi accepted a position with the Anglo-Iranian Oil Company in Ṭihrán. Although he would have had material advantages of a good salary and rapid advancement, he left the oil company to teach the Bahá'í children of the village of Najafábád, near Iṣfahán for five years.

When Shoghi Effendi read of Faizi's remarkable decision in an NSA report, he wrote:

"This spontaneous decision will attract divine confirmation and is a clear proof of the high endeavour, the pure motive, and the self-sacrifice of that favoured servant of the divine Threshold. I am extremely pleased and grateful to him and I pray from the depths of my heart for the success of that active, radiant youth . . ."[665]

* * *

George Townshend's attitude toward parenthood was highly spiritual. From his acclaimed book *The Altar on the Hearth* published in 1927, he had this to say about children:

"While they are at your side, love these little ones to the utmost. Forget yourself. Serve them; care for them; lavish all your tenderness on them. Value your good fortune while it is with you, and let nothing of the sweetness of their babyhood go unprized. Not for long will you keep the happiness that now lies within your reach. You will not always walk in the sunshine with a little warm, soft hand nestling in each of yours, nor hear little feet pattering beside you, and eager baby voices questioning and prattling of a thousand things with ceaseless excitement. Not always will you see that trusting face upturned to yours, feel those little arms about your neck, and those tender lips pressed upon your cheek, nor will you have that tiny form to kneel beside you, and murmur baby prayers into your ear.

Love them and win their love, and shower on them all the treasures of your heart. Fill up their days with happiness, and share with them their mirth and innocent delights. Childhood is but for a day. Ere you are aware it will be gone with all its gifts for ever."[666]

* * *

"Our children learned at a very young age that reverence and love for the Faith are essential to one's existence. They all tried to emulate their father, who nurtured so effectively their love for 'Abdu'l-Bahá and the Guardian. We learned from his example that all of our affairs – whether they concerned marriage, family life, finances, or career – would be successful when we put the love of God at the centre of our lives.

. . . When our children were very young, he would carefully instruct them. However, once they were of age, he never monitored their spiritual activity, never chastened them, never coerced them or interfered in their right to conduct their own spiritual lives.

He stood behind them financially until they finished their education, supporting them just enough for them to continue, but was never lavish with them. The moment they were able to work on their own, he no longer supported them. He felt they should find their own destiny, experience their own successes and setbacks, and become mature through becoming accustomed to hardship, as 'Abdu'l-Bahá taught. He thought parents should not give children whatever they want, nor should they cushion their falls financially. Otherwise, they will lack determination and ambition to acquire excellence. Mr Khadem wanted our children to be victorious in life through their own efforts and accomplishments." [667] – Javidukht Khadem

* * *

Observe carefully how education and the arts of civilization bring honor, prosperity, independence and freedom to a government and its people.[668]

Among the popular themes catching the attention of readers are books relating to self-help. How to improve your marriage, children, relationships, job, wealth, success, or odds are among the great variety of subjects included in self-help literature. Ultimately it is the hunger of people for happier circumstances which compels people to search through this literature for keys to inward change. Occasionally one may be challenged in the course of investigating self-help that to change one's expectations is the key to winning a desired set of circumstances.

In reply to a question as to whether one's circumstances are the outcome of one's expectations, Mr Furútan wrote:

"According to the rules of psychology, a person's beliefs and thoughts form the principal foundation of his behaviour and conduct – meaning that his outward actions are the manifestations of his beliefs. Therefore, it is incumbent upon every believer to learn that which the Manifestation of God has urged him to do, and that which He has forbidden."[669]

* * *

Ibn-i-Abhar helped to promote the education of women. He not only encouraged his wife to found the first Bahá'í school for girls in Ṭihrán but he also worked with her on a special committee for the liberation of women in Persia.[670]

Martyrdom

> ***Seek a martyr's death in My path, content with My pleasure and thankful for that which I ordain, that thou mayest repose with Me beneath the canopy of majesty behind the tabernacle of glory.***[671]

In about 1891, Mírzá Alí-Muḥammad Varqá made his second pilgrimage to 'Akká where he attained the presence of Bahá'u'lláh. One evening Bahá'u'lláh said to Varqá: 'At stated periods souls are sent to earth by the Mighty God with what we call the Power of the Great Ether. And they who possess this power can do anything; they have all power . . . Jesus Christ had this power. People thought of Him as a poor young man Whom they had crucified; but He possessed the Power of the Great Ether. Therefore He could not remain underground. This ethereal Power arose and quickened the world. And now look to the Master, for this power is His.'[672] Upon hearing these words from the Father of 'Abdu'l-Bahá, Varqá begged to lay down his life and the life of one of his sons for the Master. His desire was granted and some five years later he won his heart's desire.

Varqá, an Apostle of Bahá'u'lláh and youngest son of Ḥájí Mullá Mihdí, was an outstanding poet, familiar with the science of ancient medicine, versed in religious subjects and history, and an eloquent teacher of the Cause. It was Bahá'u'lláh Himself who bestowed the name 'Varqá' (Dove) on Mírzá 'Alí-Muḥammad. He treated the Manifestation with a remedy, prescribed medicine which enabled his future mother-in-law to bear a child, and helped others coming to him with cures. He engaged learned men at the Court of the Crown Prince Muẓaffari'd-Dín Mírzá in stimulating discussions, and later as a captive of the governor of Zanján, 'Alá'u'd-Dawlih, he refuted daily arguments of the divines. He travelled extensively through the province of Á<u>dh</u>arbáyján to promote the Faith.

On Varqá's third pilgrimage following the passing of Bahá'u'lláh in which he was accompanied by his sons 'Azízu'lláh and Rúḥu'lláh, 'Abdu'l-Bahá advised him to remove his Tablets and Bahá'í archives from Zanján. Following this pilgrimage, Varqá set out from Zanján for Ṭihrán with some pack animals loaded with his goods in two trunks in the company of his father-in-law and Ruḥu'lláh. However they were intercepted by order of the imperious governor and brought back to the gaol in Zanján. The pack animals made their way to Qazvín where the trunks were rescued. After some weeks, 'Alá'u'd-Dawlih had had enough of the divines' tedious attempts to win over Varqá to their doctrine. He ordered that Varqá and Rúḥu'lláh be escorted to the capital.

Suffering abuse on their trip, Varqá and his son were placed in the dungeon in Ṭihrán where the poet was sure neither would survive. Soon there occurred that which precipitated their martyrdom: the assassination of Náṣiri'd-Dín Sháh on the eve of his jubilee celebration. In his history of the first hundred years of the Faith, Shoghi Effendi recalled Varqá's and Rúḥu'lláh's martyrdoms:

> "Even the Sháh's assassination had at first been laid at the door of that community, as evidenced by the cruel death suffered, immediately after the murder of the sovereign, by the renowned teacher and poet, Mírzá 'Alí-Muḥammad, surnamed "Varqá" (Dove) by Bahá'u'lláh, who, together with his twelve-year-old son, Rúḥu'lláh, was inhumanly put to death in the prison of Ṭihrán, by the brutal Ḥájibu'd-Dawlih, who, after thrusting his dagger into the belly of the father and cutting him into pieces, before the eyes of his son, adjured the boy to recant, and, meeting with a blunt refusal, strangled him with a rope."[673]

Ṭaherzadeh has written that those who have not become utterly devoted to Bahá'u'lláh and *intoxicated with the wine of His Revelation,*[674] cannot, referring to Varqá

> ". . . understand the motive of a high-minded person, talented and well-balanced, in seeking to give his life for the Cause. These people who sought martyrdom must have attained the pinnacle of faith and assurance. They must have seen with their spiritual eyes a glimpse of the inner reality of their Lord, and have become magnetized by His glory. These souls, the moth-like lovers of His beauty, were so dazzled by the splendours of the light of His countenance that they wished to sacrifice themselves in His path."[675]

When He was in New York City, 'Abdu'l-Bahá recounted the story of the martyrdom of Varqá and Rúḥu'lláh. He asked Valíyu'lláh Varqá, one of Mírzá 'Alí-Muḥammad Varqá's other sons who had accompanied Him to America in 1912 at His invitation, to sit near Him during the telling. Upon finishing the tale, 'Abdu'l-Bahá retired to his room from where He was heard weeping.

Martha Root was also present in that gathering. She was profoundly affected. Twenty years later this living martyr for the Cause of God wrote an account of these martyrs under the title, *White Roses of Persia.* [676]

* * *

In his closing remarks at the 1953 Intercontinental Conference in Stockholm, Mr Furútan in referring to the heroic deeds of the Dawn-Breakers mentioned a saying of 'Abdu'l-Bahá:

> "A small piece of cotton can prevent the ear from hearing sweet melodies. A very thin veil can cover the eyes and make it impossible for them to see. A very small headache can cause our mind to stop functioning . . . a small drop of mortal poison can kill the person who takes it. The veils of selfishness are like the piece of cotton, the thin veil, the small headache and the drop, but those heroic souls, the Dawn-Breakers, did not let any veils come in between them and their true responsibility."[677]

* * *

George Townshend closed his talk on the sufferings of Bahá'u'lláh with this comment:

> "Love is a priceless thing, only to be won at the cost of death . . . Those heroic souls who are rapt in the love of the Lord, they are the true lovers." [678]

* * *

Ibn-i-Aṣdaq had a passionate love for Bahá'u'lláh. When he was around 30 years old, he sent a plea to Bahá'u'lláh in which he yearned for the station of absolute nothingness or martyrdom. The Manifestation replied that one could live and yet '. . . be counted as a martyr in the sight of God.'[679] Two years later, after he had asked Bahá'u'lláh once again for martyrdom, the Blessed Beauty revealed a Tablet in which in He stated that in the sight of God both Ibn-i-Aṣdaq and his father, who taught His Cause with heroism and wisdom, had attained the station of martyrdom without sacrifice of physical life. Bahá'u'lláh preferred that the friends protect their lives in order to teach His Cause. The reward of martyrdom has been replaced with teaching the Faith.[680]

* * *

In a letter Ibn-i-Abhar asked Bahá'u'lláh which was more meritorious: '. . . to lay down one's life for the love of God or to teach the Cause with wisdom and the power of utterance.'[681] Bahá'u'lláh confirmed the latter. Although He has '. . . ordained teaching the Cause to be as meritorious as giving one's life . . .'[682], '(m)artyrdom in the path of God is undoubtedly the greatest bounty provided it takes place through circumstances beyond one's control.'[683]

* * *

Following the passing of Bahá'u'lláh, Ṭarázu'lláh Samandarí '. . . begged 'Abdu'l-Bahá for martyrdom, but the Master told him he must live to serve the Faith with the spirit of martyrdom . . .'[684]

* * *

Marzieh Gail has written that Martha Root would not have sought martyrdom. Though she sacrificed her life with heroic fortitude as a living martyr for the Faith in order not to leave any work undone, Martha, when she first visited Iran in 1930, commented in the midst of risky circumstances that she was *sometimes afraid*.[685] In her immortal book *Ṭáhirih, the Pure* she pondered:

> "Was Ṭáhirih great enough instantly to say, 'O God, I give my life to establish this Faith among mankind,' or did she too, need to be trained by the Infinite God to long to give her life as a martyr to serve this new universal Revelation?"[686]

* * *

Concerning martyrdom Keith Ransom-Kehler, whom Shoghi Effendi eulogized as the first American martyr, wrote:

> "Impartial Europeans, acquainted with the history of Persia, or writing it . . . are agreed that a most challenging aspect of her modern development has been the army of glorious martyrs who have laid down their lives for a great religious principle. Lord Curzon says that Europe's faith in the power of Persia to revive and advance from her decadence, derives from the spiritual vitality shown in Bábí and Bahá'í martyrdoms.
>
> The conclusion of the morbid peasantry who went out to witness the burning of John Huss was that martyrdoms

> make poor spectacles. Certainly from the viewpoint of agony and writhings they do, for it is evident, from the testimony of eye-witnesses throughout the course of history, that the psychology of martyrdom lifts the victim 'above all earthly conditions'; but from the viewpoint of the convincing superiority of a dedicated human spirit to that remorseless and indifferent fate, which urges a tragic incident to its inevitable conclusion, the martyrs of history have, by an irresistible contagion, convinced those about them of the reality of their faith, impervious to human corruption. . . .
>
> To investigate Bahá'í Martyrdoms is to behold in the face of life's terrors a bliss that only the fire of the love of God could enkindle in the human breast; a rapture incomparably greater than any earthly happiness. To have engendered in man and woman this supreme devotion is one of the great proofs of the station of Bahá'u'lláh, for we do not idly toss away our lives for base and ignoble purposes, and none save God can awaken in us this mighty love that counts life itself a very little thing to bestow in proof of it.
>
> In paying His tribute to these magnificent souls, specialized by God for the unique service of watering with the essence of their hearts those seeds for the unprecedented harvest of peace and good-will on earth, 'Abdu'l-Bahá says: 'they hastened, wrapt in holy ecstasy, to the glorious field of martyrdom and writ with their life-blood upon the Tablet of the world the verses of God's divine unity."[687]

* * *

Both Mr Faizi and Mr Balyuzi in their published works have mentioned Ḥají Muḥammad-Isma'il-i-Dhabíh-i-Káshání. He was one of the early believers who converted to the Faith when in the presence of The Báb as he witnessed the rapidity and power with which He penned a lengthy epistle and uttered some of its verses.

Over ten years later in Baghdád, Dhabíh attained to the Presence of Bahá'u'lláh. Dhabíh was transformed by the Manifestation's words of indescribable power. Consequently over time his love for Bahá'u'lláh intensified beyond his capacity to sustain his life. Balyuzi has recorded Siyyid Ismá'il's dilemma which he gave in response to Nabíl's query to share his experience:

> "What I have seen cannot be described. After I asked Him for spiritual sustenance . . . door after door opened upon my heart, and my soul became acquainted with thoughts not of this world. One night, in His biruni, His Blessed Person asked for a candle to peruse a paper, and I, as usual lost in wonderment at my own condition, suddenly thought: 'Is it possible that that visage, the sight of which the Chosen Ones and the Messengers of God had longed to behold, could be unveiled in a human temple?' and as soon as this thought passed through my mind, His blessed voice called out to me: 'Aqa Siyyid Ismá'il, look!' and when I gazed at His blessed face, I saw that which no word can ever describe. . . . My last word to you is this: never ask for anything like this and be contented with what is given unto you . . ."[688]

A learned man of noble descent, Dhabíh set himself the task of sweeping the approaches of Bahá'u'lláh's house. At the hour of dawn, he would unwind his green turban and patiently gather the rubble which his Beloved had trodden under foot and cast it into the banks of the river. Eventually he was unable to contain the love bursting within his soul. Betaking himself to the banks of the river (Tigris), he, after performing his ablutions, took his own life by severing his throat with a razor.

Bahá'u'lláh extolled Dhabíh (Sacrifice) as the 'King and Beloved of Martyrs.' He reportedly revealed:

> "No blood has, till now, been poured upon the earth as pure as the blood he shed."[689]

# # #

Perseverance

> ***To try, to persevere, is to insure ultimate and complete victory.***[690]

Over a nine-year period, Dr Ugo Giachery worked under the guidance of the Guardian in securing material for the outer structure of the Shrine of the Báb and the International Archives Building. Dr Giachery's role in acting as the Guardian's personal representative was to select material, supervise artistic carving, pack and ship finished work, secure insurance and handle voluminous mail and technical data.

He faced formidable difficulties carrying out his tasks. In Italy at the time, public services due to the war were virtually non-existent; railroads were severely damaged; rolling-stock had been destroyed or confiscated; shipping was at a standstill; millions of the male population were still prisoners of war; Rome was occupied by Allied Forces; reparation indemnities being paid to the Allies were staggering; food, electricity and water were rationed or unavailable; waters were still mined; shipping space was practically unavailable; and shipping itself was often confiscated off the shores of Israel by hostile warships.

In the shattered economy, Dr Giachery searched out an appropriate quarry whose approaches had not been blown up by the retreating enemy. He meticulously translated the discussions held in English and Italian; and transcribed technical details and terms to the World Centre at a time when the means of communications with the Holy Land were uncertain. He was regularly harassed as a Bahá'í.

Meanwhile the nation's industrial power was geared to reconstruction and not to foreign projects. Such was the demand for building materials that they were practically impossible to obtain. Every item – cement, steel, lumber, nails, wire, pipe, paint, switches, mouldings, etc. – required a licence from the Ministry of Industry and Commerce. Lengthy procedure was needed to obtain these licences as well as the approval of the Ministries of Foreign Trade and Finance for export and customs. At Ministries, in committees and with officials scattered in various offices all over Rome, Dr Giachery had to occupy himself many hours, filling out forms and paying application fees in order to move the work forward.

Dr Giachery faced other crises too. A drought in 1949 limited industrial electrical power to three working days a week, which curtailed workers' use of the great pneumatic drills, chisels and cutting saws. A partner in a key contracting firm died suddenly. Steamers did not arrive as scheduled, keeping cargo destined for Israel on a wharf for days and days. An earthquake forced the evacuation of a seaside town, leaving no one to load a ship. The captain of another ship became alarmed by an airplane as cargo was being unloaded in Haifa and hastily returned to Italy with half the ship unloaded. A fire broke out on another steamer. On still another steamer a full load of stone went to the bottom of the sea at the port of Haifa. In 1952 the architect William S Maxwell died.

In spite of these difficulties Dr Giachery oversaw the work of scores of men who quarried tons of marble and granite and who carved columns, pilasters, capitals, star panels, arcade arches and walls, monumental corners, cornices and parapet panels. Seventeen steamers shipped nearly 800 tons of finished materials in 1,800 wooden cases. In all, 4,587 finished pieces were sent from Italy to Mt Carmel for the Shrine of the Báb in a 19 month period.

Summarizing this remarkable effort, the president of the International Bahá'í Council in a report to the National Spiritual Assembly of the Bahá'ís of the United States wrote:

> ". . . when the Shrine is completed, not the least interesting of the facts associated with it and the romance of its construction will be that about sixteen hundred tons of granite was quarried, cut and carved in Italy and imported to Israel during undoubtedly one of the most disturbed periods in the world's history, and more particularly, in the history of the Holy Land."[691]

Later the International Archives project required 17 ships to carry 1,000 tons of carved marble. Other ships transported structural steel, cement, floor and roof tiles, lumber, stained and clear glass, small and large iron window frames, varnish and paint, chandeliers, wire, bronze doors, balustrades, lamp posts, chain lifts, nails, and drain pipes. 1/3 section of every column weighed two tons. The roof tiles, some 12,000, weighed 40 tons and were packed in 7,200 cardboard boxes using 25,000 meters of gummed paper in strips.

Of Dr Giachery's work, the Guardian said:

> "The service you have rendered is not sufficiently appreciated today, but it will be fully appreciated in the future. . . . Single-handed, you have rendered an historic service to the Cause."[692]

Dr Giachery offered the following observation on the power of perseverance:

> "Perseverance was one of Shoghi Effendi's most noble qualities, and taught me many a lesson. I learned much from him in pursuing and accomplishing any given task. It is part of human nature to give up when attempts fail at the beginning; only a few persist in an endeavour when beset with obstacles of all sorts. His instructions to me, always to go or appeal to the highest authorities, to seek always the best, to accomplish things in the shortest time possible, and to persevere under all circumstances, became my second nature while I was privileged to work for the Cause under his personal guidance. In nearly every letter I received from him over a period of many years, the word *persevere* is repeated. It had the power of a talisman for me . . . Were I to relate all the difficulties, some nearly insurmountable, that I met during the years of supervising production of the carved marble and other material needed to construct the Báb's Shrine and the International Archives, I should have to write at much greater length. In nearly every case I did not trouble the Guardian with these obstacles. Clad with the armour of perseverance . . . I knew that the impossible could be accomplished."[693]

* * *

As Secretary-general of the International Bahá'í Council and the Guardian's assistant secretary, Leroy Ioas shouldered enormous responsibilities in the Holy Land from 1952 to 1957. He worked to strengthen ties between the Council and the civil authorities of Israel; negotiated the purchase of properties on Mt Carmel and near the Shrine of Bahá'u'lláh; established branches of four National Spiritual Assemblies in Israel to hold title to these properties; vigorously defended the Faith against Covenant-breakers who sought to oppose the Guardian's plans; supervised the building of the drum and dome of the Shrine of the Báb; oversaw the construction of the International Archives Building; and secured for the Faith the properties around the Shrine of Bahá'u'lláh, which had been for 60 years in the hands of the Covenant-breakers. He accomplished his manifold tasks in spite of the '. . . austerities of a new State, the conditions of labour, the interminable procedures of officialdom, the excessive burdens which they strove to carry, and even their own inexperience for the tasks assigned . . .'[694]

When the Guardian named the Octagon door of the Shrine of the Báb for Leroy as a reward for his sterling services on that Holy Sepulchre, Ugo Giachery wrote to him:

> "The news of the Door, Báb-i-Ioas as it shall be called, has brought me great happiness, because it rewards you in all eternity for all your labors, sacrifices, sufferings and the hundreds of obstacles and difficulties you have met in carrying on the completion of the Shrine. The generosity and recognition of the Guardian, on your behalf, is more than touching and I wish I could be there to thank him from the depth of my heart . . ."[695]

Leroy Ioas was known as the Guardian's Hercules.[696]

* * *

Dr Muhájir said that the characteristic he most admired in the Guardian was the latter's determination to see his tasks through to the end. He said that the Guardian never let obstacles get in the way of his plans.[697]

* * *

> ***The harder you strive to attain your goal, the greater will be the confirmations of Bahá'u'lláh, and the more certain you can feel to attain success.***[698]

One of the early administrative groups formed in the United States was the Chicago House of Justice in 1901. Consisting of nine elected men, the governing body became the House of Spirituality the following year at 'Abdu'l-Bahá's behest. Even though women were still disfranchised in the early 20th century, Corinne True was not pleased that this elected body excluded women. Certain that Bahá'u'lláh had intended women to have equal status with men, she would work to change the all-male status. Meanwhile the Chicago Bahá'í women went ahead and formed a body which soon became known as the Women's Assembly of Teaching (WAT). WAT became an unwitting parallel institution, organizing meetings and reporting to the House of Spirituality.

Not surprisingly the two groups would conflict. The women were assertive and as such unsettled the men who preferred submissive females consistent with the Victorian era's male chauvinist thinking and a more cautious approach to teaching. In 1902 WAT wanted to promote teaching, favouring a downtown hall, weekly meetings and a soup kitchen. Since their ideas were regarded as extravagant by the men, the House of Spirituality would not lend its support. At a general meeting of the two groups, the women used the occasion to challenge the all-male character of the House. Later the women would go ahead and hold Sunday meetings in a rented room following inaction by the men. For their part the men resolved to pray for guidance and sponsor community meetings. Parallel activities continued in 1902 but gradually the two groups realized they must work together, which drew praise from 'Abdu'l-Bahá.

From 1902 to 1909, the Chicago House of Spirituality became the coordinating body for the North American believers. In 1903 it petitioned 'Abdu'l-Bahá for permission to erect a House of Worship, the members having been inspired by news of the 'Ishqábád Temple. While He approved the idea in two Tablets, 'Abdu'l-Bahá also sent a Tablet to Corinne True, the contents of which startled her and which read in part:

> "Whosoever arises for the service of this building shall be assisted with a great power from His Supreme Kingdom and upon him spiritual and heavenly blessings shall descend . . ."[699]

Although she was not specifically mentioned as being charged with building the Temple, Corinne felt that He wanted her to become involved. When 'Abdu'l-Bahá wrote instructions about the Temple to her, she was nonplussed. After all, her higher education was limited to a southern finishing school and her occupation was that of housewife! Nevertheless she arose and with remarkable perseverance became the mainspring for the building of this holy House of Worship.

As founder and president of WAT, she shared the Master's Tablet and presented the problem to her colleagues. They raised some money and opened an account. However, because resources were scarce and both sexes were preoccupied with teaching and community development, excitement for the project waned. Nothing much would be done for the next three and one half years. Still Corinne was not idle; she thought about the project almost daily.

In 1906 following the death of another son from a boating accident, Corinne decided to see the Master. In February 1907, she arrived in Palestine with a petition signed by nearly 800 believers, calling for a start to the Temple construction. On the morning of her second day in 'Akká, Corinne had an audience with 'Abdu'l-Bahá. Concealing the precious scroll behind her on a divan, she proceeded to present him with gifts from the friends. Soon He came over to her, picked up the scroll and exclaimed: 'Mashriqu'l-Adhkár! This . . . this is what gives me great joy.

Go back . . . go back and work for the Temple; it is a great work, the best thing you could do, Mrs True.'[700]

'Abdu'l-Bahá described how the Temple should be located and appear. He emphasized that Corinne should stay in Chicago, devote herself to the project and expect difficulties. When Thornton Chase, who was a dominant force on the House of Spirituality, who favoured male only membership and who was not happy with Corinne's interference, made his pilgrimage as Corinne was making her way home from 'Akká, he asked 'Abdu'l-Bahá for guidance in building the Temple. He was given a shock when the Master replied: 'When you return consult with Mrs True – I have given her complete instructions.'[701]

Having received a divine mandate, Corinne became vigorous in her devotion to the Temple project. Endorsed by WAT she set out to ask every North American believer to contribute. Soon the House of Spirituality named her the Temple Fund secretary. She conveyed 'Abdu'l-Bahá's desire for the Temple to the American believers through her *Notes Taken at Akka*, and later rallied support in *Star of the West*.

Meanwhile, even though one of the members of the House of Spirituality had in 1904 located land for the Temple near the site of the Columbian Exposition, Corinne set out in search of land which, according to 'Abdu'l-Bahá, should be isolated from commercial sites and could be near the lake's shore (Lake Michigan). Exhausting herself after many efforts that took her beyond city limits through fields, over fences and across streams in heavy work shoes, she eventually located a wooded tract at Grosse Pointe in the village of Wilmette.

Following a period of recuperation, Corinne encouraged the House of Spirituality to sponsor a national Temple project. As a result and at the invitation of the House of Spirituality, the first American national conference was held on 26 November 1907. Attendees visited proposed Temple sites and then debated their merits. But no decision was taken on which site to purchase. But less than six months later and in response to Corinne's urging, WAT persuaded the House of Spirituality to purchase two lots at Grosse Pointe with an option held by Corinne on 12 adjoining lots.

Thornton Chase, who had resisted making any commitment to purchasing land until the Faith had sufficient funds, felt that Corinne was manipulative. He understood that 'Abdu'l-Bahá did not want the Temple project to incur debt. Nevertheless, when 'Abdu'l-Bahá received a map of the site, He expressed His pleasure and recommended the site be enlarged. Corinne felt that the remaining acreage should be secured but doubted the House of Spirituality and the Chicago Bahá'í community capable of advancing the Temple work.

Accordingly she shared with 'Abdu'l-Bahá her plan for a national organization of American Bahá'í communities to assume responsibility for the Temple. The Master gave His approval and stated that women should also be members. In 1909 Bahá'í Temple Unity (BTU) was formed at a convention in Chicago in which 35 cities were represented. There the delegates unanimously decided to build the Temple at Grosse Pointe. A nine member Executive Board was chosen on which Corinne was financial secretary, a work which would come to occupy her full-time. Two months after the convention, the Bahá'ís purchased the remaining 12 lots.

As financial secretary Corinne would work for financial support of the Temple project for many years, monitor the Temple's financial needs, prepare monthly financial reports, and painstakingly thank contributors in hundreds of hand-written letters. Receiving Tablets from 'Abdu'l-Bahá in which He emphasized the importance of the Temple work, Corinne was convinced that this work would play a major part in bringing the American Bahá'í community together. She believed that the Temple project marked *the beginning of our nationality.*[702]

When the prospect of 'Abdu'l-Bahá visiting America became evident, Corinne wrote probably to Helen Goodall: 'I feel like mounting the housetops . . . (and) shouting to the people to Arise for the Temple – because if you do this Abdul Baha will bless the Land of America with His Holy Presence.'[703] Her personal goal was to complete the Temple within the Master's lifetime.

'Abdu'l-Bahá did reach America and Chicago where He spoke to over a 1,000 people about the Temple at the closing public session of the Bahá'í Temple Unity convention on 30 April 1912; a day also marked by the death of Corinne's son Davis of tuberculosis. Next day He arrived at Grosse Pointe to dedicate the Temple site. On His way He asked Corinne to accompany Him. No one is sure what transpired between the Master and His disciple.

Between 1912 and 1920 raising money to pay off the property and to fund construction preoccupied the believers. When a mortgage payment could not be met, Corinne recalled: 'We were beside ourselves. We opened our purses and counted up our net capital, trying to find a way to somehow meet the emergency. All seemed lost. . . .'[704] At the last moment, the

Executive Board was able thanks to a gift to make the mortgage payment, causing Corinne to exclaim: 'At every turn in the road, we were protected in this way and the Temple is another of the miracles that prove the power in the Cause.'[705] On another occasion when BTU decided to borrow $6,000 from the Temple Fund to support a teaching campaign, Corinne wired the Master: 'SHOULD ANY OF TEMPLE FUND BE USED FOR TEACHING FRIENDS?'[706] To which 'Abdu'l-Bahá replied: '. . . USE TEMPLE FUNDS FOR TEMPLE ONLY.'[707] But in 1913 the land was finally paid off; $63,716 having been raised over a six year period.

Determined to keep the project moving forward, Corinne asked 'Abdu'l-Bahá in 1913 to send specifications for the dome. Given some specifications she felt that the foundation could then be constructed. A design would come later. She continued to energetically pursue fund-raising and appealed in *Star of the West*: 'Where can you show a tract of land bought by voluntary contributions sent in from nearly every country of the globe – from the former adherents of all the seven great religions? Literally "from Greenland's icy mountains to India's coral strand" have the contributions been sent.' [708]

From the outset of World War I, contributions declined significantly. So did Tablets from 'Abdu'l-Bahá. In 1916 the Executive Board appealed to the American believers in *Star of the West* for contributions. Then, in a letter to every Bahá'í, the Board proposed a plan to raise $200,000 in two years for the foundation. The goal would not be met until 1920. However Corinne did receive a Tablet from the Master in 1916, encouraging her work for the Temple:

> "O thou my daughter of the Kingdom:
>
> Praise be to God, that thou art assisted and confirmed in the service of the Mashrak-el-Azkar and art spending thy effort in the erection of this edifice. The construction of this great building is the first divine foundation of the people of Unity in America and it will be like unto (a) Mother unto the temples of God. All the temples which will be built in the future are born from this great Temple."[709]

At the Bahá'í Congress in 1919, Corinne spoke on the relationship of the Temple to teaching:

> "The great Mashrekol-Azkar stands for that sacrifice of self, that sacrifice of the personal, so that we may come into this knowledge of the oneness of humanity . . . . . . In a temple of the Lord, in the house of God, man must be submissive to God. He must enter into a covenant with his Lord in order

> that he shall obey his commands and become unified with his fellow man . . . he must recognize all as one family, one race, one nativity, all the servants of one God, dwelling beneath the shelter of the mercy of one God."[710]

Some months before the 1920 Convention, Corinne received a Tablet from 'Abdu'l-Bahá concerning a question she had addressed to him about the Temple. He replied:

> ". . . In every respect all the affairs relative to the Mashreq'ul-Azkar are to be referred to the annual Convention. Whatever the Convention, with a majority of opinions, decides, must be accepted and executed."[711]

For 17 years Corinne had been the liaison between 'Abdu'l-Bahá and the American Bahá'í community in most matters relating to the Temple. This new arrangement was difficult for her but it reflected the consolidation of the Bahá'í community of North America. And perhaps a reflection as well of the Master's pending departure for the Abhá Kingdom.

Even so she continued as financial secretary. After the National Spiritual Assembly was formally elected in 1925, she kept on the post even though she was never elected to that national governing body. Three years later the NSA changed her title to assistant to the treasurer. The same year - her 66th - she became chairman of the Temple Program Committee. And for the first time, the annual convention was held in the Temple's Foundation Hall.

Although by 1930 she was no longer directly involved in the Temple project, Corinne never lost her enthusiasm and support. Moreover, at her advancing age, the Guardian asked her to regard the Temple as her *most sacred obligation*.[712] To be nearer to the Temple, she moved the same year to a stucco house just five blocks from the Temple. Having set in motion the goal of building the Temple, she continued promoting the project in talks and letters. Living within sight of the Temple, she was able to watch the progress of its construction. She was among noted Bahá'ís who spoke before large audiences in the Temple's Foundation Hall. In 1944, at the request of the National Secretary, she wrote a history of the development of the Ma<u>sh</u>riqu'l-A<u>dh</u>kár from 1903 to 1915.

In 1953, Hand of the Cause of God Corinne Knight True attended the dedication of the House of Worship. 'I have never seen her so affected by anything as she was by the fact that she was going to the dedication,' a daughter recalled. 'As she approached the Temple everyone stopped her wanting to speak to her, but she couldn't. She did not weep, but she could not speak. She could hardly raise her head. It was a tremendously moving moment.'[713]

A few years later, William Sears wrote the following touching letter to her:

> "This is a letter of love, to send to you the deepest, heartfelt appreciation for all your great services to our precious Faith. Your devotion and sacrifice in helping to raise up that most Holy House of Worship in Wilmette, is an immortal achievement. The beloved Master said that when the Temple was completed, from that point of light, the Faith of Bahá'u'lláh would be carried to all parts of the world. This prophecy came true in 1953, with the launching of the great World Crusade, and all the victories I have seen and thrilled to can be directly traced back to the building and raising up of that great edifice, with whose name, your own name, will be forever linked."[714]

# # #

Pioneering

They that have forsaken their country for the purpose of teaching Our Cause – these shall the Faithful Spirit strengthen through its power. . . By My life! No act, however great can compare with it . . . Such a service is, indeed, the prince of all goodly deeds . .[715]

FAREWELL pussy-footers!

I can no longer wait,
The time grows short, the world moves on,
The sun goes down and the hour is late.

Far off I hear His onward marching legions
Drawing nearer
With me, unmoved,
Still standing here.

The trumpet sounds, the sweet beat
Of the distant drums
Rings clear.

I see them now.
With banners flying
And in my heart I fear
They'll pass me by.
My torch unlit
This winter, spring
This fall, this year.

O God Forbid!
This crisis finds me
Still waiting here.

Some chances, we are told
Come once in life.
Some, every hundred years
And, some like this, of ours
Comes only once
Then never re-appears.

Which chance is this
Today, for us
Dear Friends?
We must decide our fate.
Arise and mount our steeds?
Or tarry at the gate?

It can be built this better world
It's all God-planned.
Perhaps, before we die,
If we have heart.

So take my hand
Together in another land. . . . [716]

- At The Gathering by William Sears

* * *

At The Gathering, Batterwood, Ontario in Canada, 1980, John Robarts had this to say about pioneering:

> "Pioneering is the greatest bounty that can come to one – one steps into a new arena of service . . . one stands on the threshold of this arena and knows that there is only one weapon that will permit victory . . . complete reliance on Bahá'u'lláh. One prays every step of the way. One feels within one's self a new connection with God, a sense of nearness is born because one soon becomes aware of answers – the path being marked for one; the needs of self that seemed so important at home, that took up so much time and energy fall away or find a new level. One knows, eventually, that one is never alone . . . There are tests – one cannot step into the arena and have focussed on one the spiritual spotlight of service without exposing weakness. This, too, is part of the bounty. One begins to know himself. So I would say to anyone – grab the chance before it's too late. Embrace this bounty. Have no fear. Step into the arena. Above all things, pray that one will succeed, will not falter halfway across the arena. What a great bounty to have been born now, in the early days, when pioneering IS possible . . . when you offer to pioneer, you don't need to know where you're going, you don't need to care where you're going. Because you're going out you will be guided by Bahá'u'lláh. We are blessed that

> God will assist all those who will arise to serve Him. We know that we are accompanied by a band of chosen angels who will open the doors and prepare the way for us."[717]

* * *

Raḥmatu'lláh Muhájir was not yet 31 years of age when he and his young wife Iran, 10 years his junior, pioneered to Indonesia. As young people in those days were still unaccustomed to leaving Iran for strange lands, the Muhájir's relatives were convinced that their departure represented a final farewell. Indeed the International Goals Committee in Ṭihrán had tried to discourage the couple from pioneering, pointing to their youth, the brevity of their marriage, Raḥmat's good job, and the uncertainty of job prospects in their proposed pioneering post.

Raḥmat, who knew that pioneering meant isolation, uncertainty and home-sickness, believed in the rewards of perseverance and patience. He felt that the living conditions of a country were irrelevant to one's decision to pioneer there. What mattered was whether one wanted to spread the Faith and to this end Raḥmat devoted many hours in prayer, supplicating for the bounty of serving the Plan of God.

So keen was he to serve the Faith outside his home turf that at 16 years of age he had initiated extensive trips around Iran. To sites made sacred by the Báb, Bahá'u'lláh and the martyrs, he preferred to travel, sometimes accompanied by friends. Following an exhausting day of travelling on foot with his companions, he would sit up far into the night reading *The Dawn-breakers* while others slept.

When he was 19 in 1943, Raḥmat initiated the concept of a Bahá'í year of service in which a young person interrupted his studies to visit and inspire believers around the country. Later in his travels as a Hand of the Cause, he would encourage others to embrace this much-cherished idea. He believed that this service actually brought about a greater appreciation for education rather than the interruption diminishing its importance. When he was 21 and had been admitted to the school of medicine at the University of Ṭihrán, Raḥmat left his studies for two years in order to serve the Cause in the province of Á<u>dh</u>irbáyján.

In 1948 he began serving on the National Pioneering Committee in Iran where he enthusiastically worked to send out pioneers on the home-front and foreign-front. When the 45 Month Plan called for foreign pioneers, Raḥmat, as secretary of the committee, busied himself with encouraging and sacrificing for the friends in order to help them fulfil the goals. He himself longed for the time when he too could join them abroad in this joyous service. At one point he again left his studies in order to spend all of his time in fulfilling the Plan's pioneering goals.

Five years later, writing to the Continental Pioneer Committee holding sessions at the 1953 New Delhi Intercontinental Conference, Raḥmat offered to fill any goal of the Ten Year Crusade regardless of living conditions. It was Collis Featherstone who suggested the Mentawai Islands, territories of Indonesia where there were no Bahá'ís. Only a physician could obtain a visa there. Although neither Raḥmat nor his wife knew the location, the culture or the climate of the islands, Dr Muhájir accepted the recommendation of the Committee immediately.

In spite of lack of finances and experience, Dr Muhájir resigned a position coveted by many doctors at the hospital in Iṣfahán where he had been earning four times the salary paid in other clinics. Leaving Iran on a bitterly cold afternoon for Indonesia in January 1954, the couple encountered unbearable heat and torrential rains upon their arrival in Jakarta.

Greeted and provided hospitality by a Bahá'í couple, Raḥmat was restless to find a job and open the Mentawaii Islands to the Faith. Promptly applying at the Ministry of Health, he was offered a position by the Deputy Minister in Bukittinggi, a city of 500,000 inhabitants, on the island of Sumatra where the climate and living conditions were comfortable. However Dr Muhájir astonished the minister by requesting to work in the Mentawaii Islands, which had been used as a Dutch penal colony where malaria, skin diseases, tropical heat, snakes, centipedes, rats and other inhospitable conditions threatened an early death. Reluctantly acquiescing to Raḥmat's insistence, the minister expressed the conviction that his wife would not survive the conditions on the islands.

Temporarily housed in a local schoolhouse at Muarasiberut on one of the four Mentawaii islands, their 'house' consisted of two small rooms and a shed. They began the process of acquiring some basic furnishings and adjusting to primitive living conditions as well as contending with severe tropical malaria, which caused chills, fever, fatigue and weakness. Soon Dr Muhájir began to visit natives upriver and would be away for days and weeks on these trips. Occasionally, to reach these remote hamlets, he would trek through thick jungles and marshes for days with Mentawaii guides, emerging after weeks of absence with his clothes bloody from leeches.

As a physician whose training was preventive medicine, Dr Muhájir was able to introduce a system for eradicating malaria and other diseases. He taught the Mentawais the use of soap for bathing and washing clothes, the proper burial of their dead, dental hygiene, valuing their goods for profit, and the preference for not smoking. He established schools, translated and published a Bahá'í leaflet into Mentawai, until then a uniquely spoken language, and taught them the Faith.

He loved these people and they loved him. They were like his children and they responded to him and to the Faith. In spite of many physical hardships and even though both of these Knights of Bahá'u'lláh nearly lost their lives in separate incidents, Raḥmat longed to remain at their pioneering post for the rest of his life. However, following the passing of the Guardian, he was needed to assume broader responsibilities as a Hand of the Cause. Sadly and reluctantly he left, but only after his fellow Hands had urged him for some months to do so. Into the care of Bahá'í teachers, Dr Muhájir committed nearly 9,000 believers and eight schools.

'In his talks with the pilgrims,' according to his wife, '(the Guardian) often mentioned the Mentawai Islands and Raḥmat's services to the Faith. Once he had likened Raḥmat to Hand of the Cause Banání, and called him a true pioneer.'[718]

* * *

William Sears gave up an extremely lucrative and highly successful professional career which could read like a Who's Who in public broadcasting to pioneer to South Africa in 1953. He directed a Little Theatre Group for five years, won the University of Wisconsin Playwriting Award in 1933, and published nine One-Act plays; two of which became Award-winners and one of which appeared in the Year-Book of best plays. In 1938 he began his radio career as a News Editor and Newscaster for WOMT in Manitowoc, Wisconsin, in which he handled 15 minutes of news every hour on the hour for 12 hours a day. Later in Salt Lake City, he served as Assistant Manager of KUTA and Radio Director for an advertising agency. Next he continued as Radio Director in San Francisco. For two years he was Narrator on an NBC daytime Soap Strip. In Sacramento he did a daily 15 minute show called 'Today at the Legislature'. At the peak of his career, he helped write and star in a half-hour coast-to-coast television comedy drama for CBS called *In the Park.*

An avid sports fan, Bill Sears broadcast the play-by-play for the Philadelphia Eagles of the National Football League, the television games of the University of Pennsylvania and radio for Villanova University, the play-by-play of Penn Basketball and Utah Basketball of the university, and their football, track and field. He worked the CBS-Football Roundup from WCAU-Philadelphia, covered running description of professional and amateur tennis, U.S. open golf tournament, and play-by-play baseball for General Mills in which he won an award for both accuracy and colour.

As to professional accolades in his career, William Sears won the first TV-Guide Magazine Award for the most popular 15-minute television sports program (WCAU-Philadelphia) and another award from BBC for INTERNATIONAL QUIZ as the Master of Ceremonies. He had the highest rated two hour night time music-humour program on Philadelphia radio (WCAU-CBS Affiliate). When he switched to a two hour morning program, the morning show became the most popularly rated (WCAU-Radio). He did a two and a half hour morning television program five days a week in which he took audience honours in the rating field (WCAU-TV, CBS Affiliate). He was also a member of the National Radio-Television Committee of the United States.

In 1953 Bill and family abandoned this enviable life in order to respond to the Guardian's appeal for pioneers at the outset of the World Crusade. They established themselves on a farm some 25 kilometres from Johannesburg, and cultivated fruits, vegetables, peacocks, firesides and study classes.

When the family could not sustain itself, Mr Sears launched a three-times-a-week radio show with the South African Broadcasting Corporation, called 'That Man Sears'. The show became the most popular of its kind, heard from coast to coast (Atlantic to Indian oceans). Later, in order to support the family, he carved hand-puppets, toured Africa and appeared as guest artist on radio and television.

In spite of financial as well as physical difficulties, Mr Sears fell in love with pioneering. One has only to peruse his book *All Flags Flying* to appreciate his strongly felt views of this lofty service. He repeatedly quoted from the writings of the Faith to reinforce his views:

> "To the band of pioneers, . . . who have forsaken their homes, who have scattered far and wide, who have willingly sacrificed their comfort, their health and even their lives . . . future generations . . . will no doubt pay adequate tribute."[719]

> "They that have forsaken their country in the path of God and subsequently ascended unto His presence, such souls shall be blessed by the Concourse on High and their

names recorded by the Pen of Glory among such as have laid down their lives as martyrs in the path of God . . ."[720]

"Whoso hath attained their presence will glory in their meeting, and all that dwell in every land will be illumined by their memory."[721]

"The inscrutable wisdom of God has so decreed that we, who are the chosen bearers of the world's greatest Message to suffering humanity, should toil and promote our work under the most trying conditions of life, amidst unhelpful surroundings, and in the face of unprecedented trials, and without means, influence or support, achieve, steadily and surely, the conquest and regeneration of human hearts."[722]

Concerning this great bounty which he felt was vital to the future well-being of mankind, he said:

". . . every teaching victory in the Faith can be traced in the beginning to a pioneer . . . Nothing can enrich a human life and give it meaning and satisfaction as the act of arising to pioneer . . . It is a blessing, a bounty, given to those of us, in this day, through the mercy and kindness of Bahá'u'lláh."[723]

And, in his 1954 pilgrim's notes, he recorded his impressions from the mind of the Guardian on the spiritual significance of pioneering:

"The (G)uardian said that the friends feel that it is difficult to leave their homes and pioneer, even to move to the goals inside their own countries. They do not see that he is not asking them to make a sacrifice. What he is doing is protecting them not only from the calamity that is rushing toward them outwardly, but he is protecting them from the calamity that is rushing toward them inwardly."[724]

***

To remain at one's post, to undergo sacrifice and hardship, loneliness and, if necessary, persecution, in order to hold aloft the torch of Bahá'u'lláh, is the true function of every pioneer.[725]

Abu'l-Qásim Faizi was self-sacrificing as a pioneer. Baḥrayn where Faizi was a long-time pioneer can be hot and humid. When Zikrullah Khadem and his wife visited Mr Faizi in 1955, the weather was uncomfortable and Mr Khadem asked him for a glass of water. The water was hot because Faizi did not own a refrigerator. Later Mrs Khadem learned that Mr Faizi could have purchased a refrigerator from his income teaching English but could not accept owning such a luxury as the other pioneers were unable to afford one.

When Mr Faizi asked the Khadems to accompany him on a visit to a family, the Khadems welcomed the opportunity. To reach the home of this family, they had to pass through many streets until they reached an impoverished and unsightly part of town. Entering through a big garage door, they found themselves in a room devoid of furniture except for a wooden bed. Upon the bed lay a sick woman. Two poorly clad children in need of a wash were also present.

'Uncle Faizi! Uncle Faizi!' The children joyfully exclaimed upon seeing Faizi. Gently Mr Faizi embraced them, washed their faces and gave them sweets. Then he turned his attention to the mother, feeding her a bowl of soup that he had brought. 'I cannot describe the emotions that surged within us,' Mrs Khadem wrote years later, 'as we observed that family's devastating poverty and the overpowering love and care that Faizí showered on them.'[726]

At the New Delhi Intercontinental Teaching Conference in October, 1953, Gloria Faizi spoke about the pioneering experiences of herself and Mr Faizi in Arabia:

> "The pioneers to Arabia are poor, very poor. The people belong to the Sunní sect of Islám and whenever you openly speak about the Faith, you are advised to keep quiet if you wish to stay in Arabia. After the Guardian asked the Persians to volunteer for Arabia many wanted to go, but only two families out of forty were able to get there.
>
> We at Baḥrayn are in a position to see all the pioneers who are on the way to Arabia. We see young men who have finished their studies in colleges and have obtained their degrees, leaving their education behind to take jobs as carpenters, tailors, barbers. After completing their studies, they take a short course in some manual work so that they can earn a livelihood. . . . A large family lives in only one room in the winter and during the summer months of intense heat and moisture, they live on the roof of the house, which is merely a covering of palm branches and leaves. They have no water

> in the house, nor electricity. Their food consists of bread, rice, dates and tea, and in the winter a few vegetables. But do not think they are less happy than people in other parts of the world. . . ."[727]

* * *

John Robarts was a successful businessman. As District Manager of the London Life Insurance Company's Toronto King Street Agency, John had developed the agency into the most productive in Canada over a 15 year period from 1938 to 1953. An outstanding model branch, the production of his men was likely the highest in Canada with every one being a member of the prestigious Million Dollar Round Table.

In 1953 Fred Schopflocher was planning to attend the Intercontinental Teaching Conference in New Delhi as representative from Canada. He held much affection for the Indian friends and looked forward to attending this conference in October. When he unexpectedly passed away after a few days illness on 27 July, John cabled Shoghi Effendi on 16 September:

> 'IF IMPERATIVE HAVE CANADIAN REPRESENTATIVE NEW DELHI I WILL ATTEND AT PROBABLE SACRIFICE CORDIAL EMPLOYER RELATIONS. DEEPEST DEVOTION, JOHN ROBARTS.'[728]
>
> Shoghi Effendi replied on 19 September: 'PRESENCE CANADIAN REPRESENTATIVE IMPERATIVE. LOVE, SHOGHI'[729]

John attended that inspiring conference held 7-15 October during which he heard the stirring appeal of Shoghi Effendi's message relating to the launching of the Ten Year Crusade. Many races attended the meetings as well as Hands of the Cause Horace Holley, Dorothy Baker, Ugo Giachery, Valíyu'lláh Varqá, Ṭarázu'lláh Samandarí, 'Alí-Akbar Furútan, Shu'á'u'lláh 'Alá'í, Dhikru'lláh Khádem, Músá Banání, Clara Dunn, and Mason Remey, as well as future Hands Agnes Alexander, Collis Featherstone, Abu'l Qásim Faizi and of course John Robarts himself. John was among the speakers at the Town Hall meeting. Shoghi Effendi set out 13 goals which included opening 'forty-one virgin territories and islands'[730] to the Faith and urging the assembled believers to consecrate themselves to sending out pioneers.

At one of the sessions a succession of distinguished believers who had pioneered in previous years addressed the gathering with tales of their experiences: Clara Dunn, Agnes Alexander, Músá Banání, Gloria Faizi,

Artemus Lamb, Jamshíd Fozdár, C.P.M. Anver Cadir, Shirin Fozdár and others recalled inspiring experiences fraught with unexpected challenges and emerging confirmations.

John was undoubtedly inspired to offer his services as a foreign pioneer during this Conference. Cabling his wife Audrey to meet him in New York as he made his way homeward, John, together with Audrey, cabled the Guardian on 19 October, offering their pioneering services anywhere in the world. Shoghi Effendi replied by cable on 22 October: 'BECHUANALAND HIGHLY MERITORIOUS. LOVE, SHOGHI.'[731]

Neither one knew the location of Bechuanaland. After looking it up in the encyclopaedia, they discovered a landlocked country situated in southern Africa, '. . . the size of France, without tarred roads, mostly Kalahari Desert . . .'[732] Together with two of their four children, Patrick and Nina, they abandoned John's successful career and comfortable life-style for a very different if not dangerous way of life under Apartheid.

In 1948 the Nationalist party in South Africa was victorious in elections. They had campaigned on a theme of the black danger (swart gevaar), proclaiming twin slogans of 'The nigger in his place' and 'The coolies out of the country'; coolies being Indians. The Nationalists were embittered by perceptions of English domination and African disloyalty. Led by a former minister of the Dutch Reform Church whose platform was apartheid (or apartness), the new government set out to pass laws designed to oppress blacks and uphold white supremacy. Soon the government of South Africa . . .

> ". . . announced their intention to curb the trade union movement and do away with the limited franchises of the Indian, Coloured, and African peoples. The Separate Representation of Voters Act eventually robbed the Coloureds of their representation in Parliament. The Prohibition of Mixed Marriages Act was introduced in 1949 and was followed in rapid succession by the Immorality Act, making sexual relations between white and nonwhite illegal. The Population Registration Act labelled all South Africans by race, making color the single most important arbiter of individuals. . . introduced the Group Areas Act – which he described as "the very essence of apartheid" – requiring separate urban areas for each racial group. In the past, whites took land by force; now they secured it by legislation."[733]

Strikes on the part of Africans became criminal offences under Apartheid. The rights of free speech and movement were curtailed. By 1952 it was a crime for Africans to . . .

> ". . . walk through a Whites Only door, a crime to ride a Whites Only bus, a crime to use a Whites Only drinking fountain, a crime to walk on a Whites Only beach, a crime to be on the streets past eleven, a crime not to have a pass book and a crime to have the wrong signature in that book, a crime to be unemployed and a crime to be employed in the wrong place, a crime to live in certain places and a crime to have no place to live."[734]

Compelled to settle in Mafeking, the capital of Bechuanaland which happened to be located within the boundaries of South Africa, the Robartses were subject to the laws of Apartheid. According to Audrey Robarts, around the time of their arrival:

> "These laws were becoming quite strict, and very much stricter in the three years that we were there teaching in the south end of Bechuanaland, and finally it would have been very dangerous for the African friends and very bad if we should be thrown out of the country before completing our mission. . . . We were living among white people, yet our mission was to teach black people. Shoghi Effendi's instructions were to teach one African thoroughly, deepen and encourage him or her to teach their own people. We should remain in the background and never let them lose confidence in us. It would be very difficult to regain – if ever. The whites in the past had gone to Africa to take something. We were going there to bring them something, he said."[735]

They were to teach the Africans. The authorities could not object to the formation of all African Assemblies; only to mixed Assemblies. Whites were to be avoided except for business purposes as they could cause trouble. After two years, the Robartses were able to begin cautiously winning African recruits to the Faith, some of whom were under surveillance. Naturally, due to security reasons, the Faith could not be mentioned boldly. When the couple held weekly firesides, Audrey made 125 yards of curtains to cover the windows so no one could see what they were doing. Seekers crept in the dark to receive the Message of Bahá'u'lláh. Audrey recalled the uncertainty of those days:

> "The pioneers read in the newspaper every day of raids by the Anti-Subversive police squads – and we all felt we were watched and thus had that feeling very often. We were obeying laws – but bending customs! The Greys Building in Johannesburg hinted at chains rattling. Truth to tell I had a small folder with family photos, a prayer book and some favourite quotes and small things on what I laughed about and called my "Jail Kit"! And indeed we were informed later that they had a dossier on each one of us!!"[736]

The Greys Building had a fearful reputation as the centre for activity of the security police. No one wanted to go there. The author of the report on South and West Africa for the *Bahá'í World,* years 1954-1963, stirringly introduced his theme:

> "The pioneers who opened this area to the Faith were, as the Guardian testified, 'a singularly distinguished and devoted group of pioneers' and more than most, they needed heroic qualities and wisdom to deal with the manifold problems confronting them in this part of the world. One day their story will be told freely, and their glorious deeds will be cherished by generations to come."[737]

Indicative of their influence and the times in which they served is the following letter written to John and Audrey in 1987:

> "I recall back in the fifties (1950s) when the Prophet Bahá'u'lláh was first mentioned in Mafikeng on Botswana land in the late Dr. Molema's home by you (Audrey and John). It was not mentioned boldly as it is said today but was whispered because of security reasons.... I remember getting to your house creeping in the dark to be taught the teachings of Bahá'u'lláh. I recollect those spiritual moments we enjoyed – the spiritual love, harmony to hear of the good tidings of Bahá'u'lláh which were said to us. We had lost hope – I was very desperate, did not have the future and your pioneering changed our attitudes to the white man and humanity at large. We are a balanced people today because of the Teachings of Bahá'u'lláh."[738]

The Robartses served in Bechuanaland and Rhodesia from 1953 to 1966 before the Universal House of Justice called John back to Canada. By 1995 the foundation so heroically laid in Bechuanaland

(Bophuthatswana and Botswana) had yielded 67 Local Spiritual Assemblies, 81 groups and over 7,000 believers.

* * *

> ***The fleeting hours of man's life on earth pass swiftly by and the little that still remaineth shall come to an end, but that which endureth and lasteth for evermore is the fruit that man reapeth from his servitude at the Divine Threshold.***[739]

In 1937 Dorothy Baker wrote to a friend on the eve of her departure as a pioneer:

> "Make a joyous thing of the *little* services, because you can never tell which is little and which is big in God's sight. Bahá'u'lláh said: A single deed done in My Name is equal to the deeds of a hundred thousand years; nay, I ask pardon of God for this limitation, for such a deed is without limited reward. So when you speak His Holy Name, rejoice, be quiet in your heart, and know that this is a Very Great Occasion, an occasion of pure joy. He verily is the Lord of Hosts, and will assist you at all times."[740]

Four years later in a talk she gave at Rice Lake, Dorothy said:

> "Never again will there be a time when souls can arise to be pioneers. The pioneers are taking the seed of heroic martyrs, and putting it together with bricks. . . . Every act will be remembered. The people of the ages will be those who give all. The intimates of the Guardian are those who packed up their houses and walked."[741]

She often quoted the following words of Bahá'u'lláh to her audiences:

> "This is a matchless Day. Matchless must, likewise, be the tongue that celebrateth the praise of the Desire of all nations, and matchless the deed that aspireth to be acceptable in His sight."[742]

* * *

As a Hand of the Cause, Raḥmatu'lláh Muhájir was observed to possess a sense of urgency in hastening from country to country. Whether he realized that his life might be cut short or that the opportunity to bring about the spiritual conquest of the planet was fleeting, he visited over

140 countries and islands of the world as well as 29 American states during which he sought primarily to promote mass teaching.

Between 1958 and 1979 when he passed away in Quito, Ecuador, he made an astonishing 600 teaching trips: 19 to India, 17 to Malasia, 17 to the Philippines, 16 to Japan, 15 to Hong Kong, 12 to Thailand, 11 to Indonesia, and multiple visits to many other places.

He always encouraged the pioneers to be courageous and daring. It was possible that they would encounter hardships of all kinds, but the Faith of Bahá'u'lláh always progressed through the sacrifice of His followers. He believed that pioneering is a great bounty, but that not everyone was worthy. Through prayer and supplication to God, one might attain unto this bounty. [743]

* * *

Abu'l-Qásim Faizi always prayed that the pioneers would have the means to remain at their posts. There they learn about the ways of the people and their language, and they form friendships. The pioneers should remain long enough to establish the Faith. Such an endeavour requires patience so that the seeds sown will sprout. Otherwise to seek out another pioneering post dissipates one's energies, resources and time. Later, as aging pioneers in a new post, they will not have the same level of enthusiasm and patience as before.

At the first World Congress in 1963, he said:

> "Patience is a quality which is described in the Qur'án as having rewards unlimited. Please have patience. God will work through you and, even if it is not in your lifetime, in the lifetime of generations after you, all services will be rewarded."[744]

* * *

Hyde Dunn described the role of pioneers:

> "Pioneers must be strong and ready to face all the hardships that may appear on their path. These are as naught compared with the delights of loving response and the confirmation that follow. The readiness to accept any vicissitudes is an essential of service to God. The service awakens the consciousness within us of our real rank and station in the world of humanity – the rank and station ordained for the

> release of perfections and virtues. Thus does God become visible in this world of creation – this is the station of the human soul."[745]

The Guardian referred to Hyde and Clara Dunn as '. . . true conquerors because they stayed where they pioneered.'[746]

* * *

During the years of the Interregnum, Leroy Ioas spoke about the goals of a pioneer at a gathering of Assembly members in Switzerland:

> "The purpose of the teacher is not to perfect an administrative structure but to reach the hearts of the local inhabitants. The pioneers should concentrate on making friends among the people, winning their confidence, and then offering them Bahá'u'lláh's teachings. You have come to teach, not to build the administrative order and worry over details and issues which stifle activity; throw out seventy-five percent of your committees and *teach*. The whole purpose of Bahá'í institutions today and in the foreseeable future is to facilitate the teaching work and what is needed is concentration on the task at hand. The purpose, the Guardian has said, is not the maintenance of Assemblies composed of pioneers, but the emergence of Assemblies formed of native believers."[747]

* * *

Ṭarázu'lláh Samandarí told a group of believers that steadfastness is found in the endurance of men, women and children who remained at their pioneering posts regardless of the difficulties. At the European Intercontinental Teaching Conference in 1953, he said:

> "Pioneering is the equivalent of martyrdom and suffering. They will reap the same fruits as the early believers for their sacrifice." [748]

* * *

Shoghi Effendi hoped that the pioneers would remain at their posts. When he was very ill in Ṭihrán, Músá Banání wept, saying:

> "Get me back to Africa, quickly. I don't want to die in Ṭihrán. I want to go back and die at my pioneer post. I want to go back where the Guardian sent me, I want to go back to Africa."[749]

Músá Banání did return to Africa where he died and was laid to rest in the precincts of the African Temple. His grave is very important to the African believers there.

***

Ugo Giachery and his wife, Angeline, were living in New York City in 1946 when the Guardian launched the Second Seven Year Plan. A major goal of this plan was the expansion of the Faith in Europe. The Giacherys sold their home and settled in Rome as pioneers. While Angeline was particularly distressed at the living conditions in the Italian capital following the Second World War, the Guardian cheered them in a cable:

> 'SUPPLICATING ABUNDANT BLESSINGS NOBLE MISSION.'[750]

A few years later at the Stockholm Intercontinental Conference in 1953, Dr Giachery made this observation about pioneering:

> ". . . by pioneering we can accomplish something that will last for all eternity."[751]

***

And Dr 'Alí Muḥammad Varqá had this to say about the role of pioneers:

> "I believe . . . the pioneers have a very special place, a very, very appreciated rank, because it is them that carry the divine torch for the plans. The expansion does not come with people who are settled in one place. It is for this reason that Bahá'ís are asked to go all over the world. The whole world needs the Bahá'í Faith."[752]

***

Corinne True gave the following advice to a dear friend who was on her way as a pioneer to Africa in 1954:

> "Rely on Bahá'u'lláh. Study the teachings hard. Know your subject when you speak. But don't lecture to people and tell them what they should be. Give them love. And be simple."[753]

***

From 1929 to 1933 when she died, Keith Ransom-Kehler travelled to Barbados, the American mid- and north-west, Japan, China, Australia, New Zealand, Burma, India and Persia, meeting many pioneers in her travels. She wrote of these intrepid voyagers in an article appropriately titled, "In the Footsteps of the Pioneers".

Some of her reminiscences included:

> "(Hyde) Dunn has the rarest and most charming disposition: loving, forgiving, genial, his spiritual attributes fit him peculiarly to teach the Bahá'í Cause."[754]

> "(Clara) Dunn has a quality of faith that I have seldom met. She lives in the Presence of God with a kind of awe and candor that assure men of His Power and Benignity; while her service is like the service of the earth to the sun, of the magnet to the pole, of the lover to his beloved. When so ill, with a dangerous illness, that any other woman would have been in a hospital, she was still ministering and serving and helping and soothing, until her very persistence in doing carried its own great message."[755]

> "The youthful exuberance of the venerable Siyyid Muṣṭafá (Rúmí) was a constant surprise. Though now advanced in years he never seemed to show weariness or ennui or delation (if there be such a word - the normal swing from elation). His was a peace and a joy that the world can neither give nor take away."[756]

> "The traces of a world pioneer I have found in many places where his foot has never trod; our "ambassador without portfolio" as it were, Mr. Roy C. Wilhelm. Carrying on a world-wide correspondence, his cordial and cheerful letters, his gifts of reading matter and Bahá'í books, his continuous encouragement and helpfulness to those scattered beyond the confines of ordinary Bahá'í association, have made him, though personally unseen, one of the most popular and beloved of the Bahá'í teachers."[757]

Keith was so enamoured of Bahá'í pioneers labouring throughout the world that she concluded her tale:

> "Amidst the perplexities, hardships and problems that often beset my path I think that my abiding protection

is a sense of deep and reverent gratitude; gratitude that I have been privileged, not to hear about, but to witness, in a thousand gleaming camp fires round the world the marshalling of the army of the Lord of Hosts; to behold in every land the unsheathing of His terrible, swift sword; to see, with mine own eyes, the Glory of the Coming of the Lord. Men and women from every tribe and kindred of the earth, forgetting their age-old tutelage of hatred and antagonism, abandoning their prejudices and racial inhibitions, rejecting the animosities of ancient creed and dogma, learning new and shining lessons of forbearance, love and forgiveness; pressing forward in deadly, deadly earnest against man's eternal foes: ignorance, oppression, superstition, greed, crime, war, poverty, injustice; putting aside every personal consideration to serve the mighty ends of peace and righteousness. Surely gratitude is the only appropriate emotion with which to regard the spectacle of life at the flood tide of its spiritual ardor."[758]

# # #

Proclamation

> ***Rest assured that the breathings of the Holy Spirit will loosen thy tongue. Speak, therefore; speak out with great courage at every meeting. When thou art about to begin thine address, turn first to Bahá'u'lláh, and ask for the confirmations of the Holy Spirit, then open thy lips and say whatever is suggested to thy heart; this however, with the utmost courage, dignity and conviction.***[759]

In His summons to the world's religious leaders, Bahá'u'lláh called upon Pope Pius IX (1846 - 1878) to recognize in the coming of the Father the promise of the Son. It was in 1869 that Bahá'u'lláh called upon the pope to abandon his kingdom and minister among the people. Unwittingly Pope John XXIII (1958 - 1963) was the first Pontiff to respond to Bahá'u'lláh's summons when he issued an Encyclical - "***Pacem in Terris***" - in the same month and year of the one hundredth anniversary of Bahá'u'lláh's Declaration in the Garden of Riḍván outside Baghdád. Addressed to "All Men of Goodwill" in addition to 'the officials and the faithful of the church'[760], the Encyclical dealt with world problems, won world-wide acclaim and echoed the principles of the Bahá'í Faith. So astonishing was the parallel between the Pope's and Bahá'u'lláh's principles that Dr Ugo Giachery in an article entitled *One God, One Truth, One People* drew a comparison between the two:

A world community
Search after truth
Universal education
Equality between men and women
Oneness of mankind
Oneness of God
Science and religion
Disarmament
Atomic energy
Spiritual solution to the economic problem
Obedience to rulers
The common good

Pope John's successor, Pope Paul VI (1963 - 1978), was the first Pontiff to visit continents and countries outside the Vatican in 20 centuries. Pope John Paul II(1978 - 2005) after more than a quarter-century in office was widely acknowledged as the most travelled pope in the history of the

Catholic Church. Even though a century of silence followed Bahá'u'lláh's Tablet to Pope Pius IX, the bidding of the Supreme Manifestation does not go unheeded!

Back in 1869 Pope Pius IX was both temporal and spiritual ruler. In 1870 ten centuries of temporal authority ended when King Victor Emmanuel I declared war with the Papal States and imposed new leadership on the Eternal City. The Pope shut himself away, declaring himself "the Prisoner of the Vatican"[761]. Thus did Rome become '. . . the seat of the new kingdom, and the scene of that humiliation which Bahá'u'lláh had anticipated and which the Prisoner of the Vatican had imposed upon himself.'[762]

On 9 April 1968 at the behest of the Universal House of Justice, Dr Giachery presented *The Proclamation of Bahá'u'lláh* to the Vatican. In 1968 when in Portugal he also presented the same book to the exiled Italian king, Umberto II.

* * *

Corinne True's faith was tested in 1912 when 'Abdu'l-Bahá charged her with speaking of the Faith in public. She did not believe she could speak in public and found herself in quite a dilemma. Only the Master understanding her capacity and therefore imposing this duty compelled her to make a try. Sensing her quandary, 'Abdu'l-Bahá said to her: 'Forget what you can't do. Stand up and turn your heart wholly toward me. Look over the heads of the audience and I'll never fail you.'[763]

Trusting in Him she became in coming years an outstanding speaker. In 1950 at the European Teaching Conference in Copenhagen, the friends who heard her speak were amazed at her gem-like utterances. She was asked from where she drew upon such wisdom. She replied:

> "It was 'Abdu'l-Bahá speaking, not I. He told me when I said I could not speak, 'Get yourself out of the way and I will come through,' so I did just that."[764]

* * *

By Audrey Robarts
1995

> "One of the wonderful stories John (Robarts) used to tell concerned Harlan Ober and Hooper Harris when they went to visit 'Abdu'l-Bahá on pilgrimage. What happened was that they went and they met 'Abdu'l-Bahá, and He said He wanted them to go to India to teach. So when they got in their room that night, Hooper said to Harlan: 'Oh dear, isn't this awful. What are we going to do?' Harlan said: 'Abdu'l-Bahá will tell us.'
>
> Well, one day went by of the pilgrimage and then another went by and still another day went by. They had still not heard from 'Abdu'l-Bahá. He had not sent for them. It was the last day, and they were packing up; ready to go, according to Harlan. Somebody came to their room and said that 'Abdu'l-Bahá wanted to see Hooper Harris. So he went. When he came back, Harlan said to Hooper Harris: 'What did 'Abdu'l-Bahá tell you?' 'Oh, He didn't tell me a thing.' Harlan said: 'Oh yes, He surely must have told you something. Of course He told you something.' 'No,' Hooper said. 'He really didn't tell me a thing.' Harlan said: 'Well, alright. Tell me exactly what happened.'
>
> 'Well 'Abdu'l-Bahá said that you look at the people. Look at their faces. And then you love them. You turn your heart to 'Abdu'l-Bahá and then you start to speak.' 'What good would that do?' Then Harlan realized that that was in essence a very remarkable way to teach, and people would have confidence and that they would succeed in communicating."[765]

In the In Memoriam article about Harlan Ober, 'Abdu'l-Bahá according to the writers said: 'Whenever difficult questions or problems come to you, turn your hearts to the heart of 'Abdu'l-Bahá and you will receive help.'[766] Subsequently in India, Hooper and Harlan found every question answered with both questioner and answerer often astonished at the outcome.

***

In a Tablet to Hermann Grossmann, the Master wrote: 'When you speak, do not think.'[767]

***

Dorothy Baker wished to kindle feelings and touch hearts when she gave the Message. She advised that when addressing an audience:

> "Pretend that you are speaking to just one person and you will never be nervous."[768]

* * *

Rúḥíyyih Khánum never underrated interviews with the media. Praying beforehand for God's guidance, she agonized about what she would say.

> "She used to tell the friends that when they met the representatives of the media, their principal aim should be to create a good impression of the Faith. . . . (They should) have enough printed information about the teachings and concepts of the Faith always available in advance as hand-outs, because the media representatives never remembered verbal information correctly."[769]

* * *

Trade journals which contained Roy Wilhelm's business advertisements also included a brief Bahá'í text. Due to the paucity of Bahá'í literature during the early days of the Faith in America, he made available compilations from the sacred texts for use at firesides and public meetings. During his lifetime, he saw to the printing of hundreds of thousands of Bahá'í pamphlets. Curtis Kelsey remembered seeing him in his office after midnight, making hundreds of copies of the Master's latest Tablets on a typewriter.

When Roy was 16 years of age, he had injured his back jumping from a barn onto a hay wagon which concealed a pitchfork. As a result he often suffered severe pain and sometimes worked standing up to ease the pain.[770]

* * *

> "Father (Dunn) used to sit up late at night after a hard day's work and type out these precious Tablets (from 'Abdu'l-Bahá) then he would distribute them to the friends at the meetings. . . . Late in his life when Father was going blind, he would still type out the Holy Words, with Mother (Dunn) dictating to him, because by that time he had learnt where the keys were. He apologised for his errors, though of course sense could still be made of what he had typed."[771]

* * *

When Ṭarázu'lláh Samandarí was in the Holy Land a question was raised of 'Abdu'l-Bahá concerning the promotion of the Cause by certain leaders of Persia. The Master replied that such would-be champions have inevitably been cut off by death from fulfilling their intentions. Such enamoured prominent souls included Manú<u>ch</u>ihr <u>Kh</u>án and Amínu'd-Dawlih. The first was the governor of Iṣfáhán who concealed the Báb and offered his fortune to further the Cause. The second was the Prime Minister who offered to proclaim the Faith of Bahá'u'lláh. Both lives were cut short.

'Abdu'l-Bahá said:

> "It is certain that the Manifestations are fully able to raise up important personages, leaders of men, to promulgate their Cause. But God has willed otherwise, so that invariably the Holy Manifestations have (prevailed) through the helpless, the lowly, the poor – like the disciples of Jesus, Son of Mary; like the companions of the noble Prophet (Muḥammad). It is the same in the days of the Supreme Manifestation. He has desired that the Law of God should be spread abroad through us, helpless as we are, and weak."[772]

# # #

Scholarship

The man of consummate learning and the sage endowed with penetrating wisdom are the two eyes to the body of mankind.[773]

Horace Holley was largely responsible for drafting the *Declaration of Trust and By-laws of the National Spiritual Assembly*, which was adopted by the American NSA and became the pattern for all such legal instruments of other national Bahá'í communities. He served on the editorial board of *The Bahá'í World*. He wrote the statement *Aims and Purposes of the Bahá'í Faith*, which appear at the beginning of ten volumes of *The Bahá'í World*. He wrote every *International Survey of Current Bahá'í Activities* – an historical record of the growth of the Cause in nine volumes of *The Bahá'í World*. He prepared study guides to the *Kitáb-i-Íqán* and *God Passes By*. He wrote the introductions to *Bahá'í World Faith, World Order of Bahá'u'lláh, The Secret of Divine Civilization, Foundations of World Unity, The Reality of Man, Messages to the Bahá'í World* and *Bahá'í Administration*.

Mr Holley wrote "In Memoriam" articles on the lives of Mountfort Mills, George Latimer and Roy Wilhelm. He sent letters to Reza Sháh Pahlaví and President Harry Truman. He wrote articles entitled "The World Economy of Bahá'u'lláh", "The Spiritual Basis of World Peace", "Religion and World Order", "The Bahá'í Principle of Civilization", "The Human Situation", "The Bahá'í Faith and Labour", "The Root of Struggle", "Challenge to Chaos", "Communion with the Infinite" and "Our Covenant with 'Abdu'l-Bahá". He gave the titles and subtitles found on and in *The Promised Day is Come, The Goal of a New World Order* and *The Dispensation of Bahá'u'lláh*. It was his initiative that created the American *Bahá'í News*. He wrote several introductory works on the Faith, and his compilation of *Bahá'í Scriptures* was later revised by him as *Bahá'í World Faith*.

Several examples of his exalted and penetrating style of writing follow:

> "The world about us is terrifying, people become more and more abandoned to pleasure as a flight from the solitude which we know too well is the emptiness where God has not brought His compassion, His understanding, His strength and His healing. It is within this emptiness at the centre of being, that our anxieties are distilled."[774]

> "True independent investigation of reality leads to the investigation of our inmost being, and makes us realize that severance from the self of passion and desire is the supreme independence."[775]

> "The individual has become engulfed in struggles of competitive groups employing different weapons to attain irreconcilable ends."[776]

> "Public policy is the graveyard in which the claim to perfect personal guidance lies interred."[777]

> "As long as social sovereignty remains partly national and partly international in character and influence, the problem of the existing inequitable distribution of wealth will continue to provoke conflicting theories and methods of solution."[778]

> "At present, education is limited to the aim of assuring personal survival in a competitive society, and the effect of this mental and moral strangulation is to leave the essential core of personality . . . to the overwhelming influence of an already perverted society."[779]

Back in 1913 when Horace sent 'Abdu'l-Bahá his first introductory book on the Faith – *Bahaism: The Modern Social Religion*, the Master made this remarkable statement:

> ". . . thy aim is to render service to the Kingdom of Abhá and to promote the teachings of Bahá'u'lláh. Although the glory and greatness of this service is not known at present, in future ages it will assume the greatest importance and will attract the attention of learned men."[780]

* * *

Described by the Universal House of Justice as one of the Faith's most resourceful historians, Ḥasan Balyúzí was an outstanding scholar whose books were described by Ugo Giachery as being *gem-like* and which '. . . will remain among the most outstanding writings to enlighten the paths of seekers for centuries to come.'[781] Between 1960 and 1980, he worked on and completed first the task Shoghi Effendi had set him so many years before, writing the trilogy on the Central Figures of the Faith: *Bahá'u'lláh: The Word Made Flesh*;

'Abdu'l-Bahá: The Centre of the Covenant of Bahá'u'lláh; and *The Báb: The Herald of the Day of Days.* He also completed *Edward Granville Browne and the Bahá'í Faith, Muḥammad and the Course of Islam* and *Bahá'u'lláh: the King of Glory.*

Marion Hofman, herself a great scholar, wrote of Mr. Balyuzi's writing. She stated that he would:

> "... work on two or three books at the same time, thereby relieving the fatigue of long hours of concentration on a single manuscript. Often it was his habit to continue far into the night, and so he would turn for refreshment from writing, to research, to reading for background. It is probable that his mind dwelt on the work in hand almost constantly. He was meticulous in assembling his materials, was known to spend three days in the determination of a single date, and gave most careful thought to the transliteration of Persian, Arabic and Turkish names whose pronunciation could vary according to region. All his books were submitted in his own handwriting, and even quotations were copied by hand to ensure that his choice of deletions would be followed."[782]

Dr Moojan Momen, who worked as Mr Balyuzi's research assistant, described his work as ...

> ". . . imbued with two qualities which will cause it to be remembered long after much other material written to such standards has been forgotten. First, was his assiduous pursuit of truth. He would take endless trouble to track down even the most minor fact or date. He would write several letters in pursuit of just one piece of information which might take up only one line in his book. He did not hesitate to discard large sections of his manuscript if his researches left any doubt as to the truth of what he had written. . . .
>
> Second, was his integrity. There are no hidden motives in his writings. He wrote nothing for fame or self-advancement. He wrote only what he thought correct after due consideration. . . .
>
> Another characteristic that marked him out was his generosity with the materials in his possession. Not for him to jealously guard his sources to prevent others

> from using them before he could get into print. He lent whatever he had freely and without hesitation."[783]

In 1973 when it had received signed copies of *'Abdu'l-Bahá* and *The Báb*, the Universal House of Justice wrote to him:

> "We sincerely hope that nothing will prevent you from continuing your invaluable and devoted labours, whose results are of such infinite value in increasing the knowledge and deepening the understanding of the believers." [784]

When he passed away in 1980, the Supreme Body commented on his 'OUTSTANDING SCHOLARLY PURSUITS' [785] and resourcefulness as a historian.

* * *

In his old age, Ḥájí Mírzá Ḥaydar-'Alí was known as the *Angel of Mount Carmel* for his *dignity, serenity and vivacity.*[786] Many years before, after he had accepted the advent of the Qá'im, the Ḥájí was oppressed, exiled and imprisoned. In spite of the misery which descended upon him, he did not retaliate or seek retribution. He was a veteran warrior of the Faith who was invited by the Master to spend the remaining days of his life close to the Centre of the Covenant.

Ḥájí Mírzá Ḥaydar-'Alí wrote down the story of his life. He had become accustomed during long years of imprisonment to shaving his head, and he continued doing so after his release. After he had moved his residence to Haifa and complained of eye trouble, 'Abdu'l-Bahá advised him to stop shaving his head and to write a few pages each day. His resulting work - *Stories from the Delight of Hearts* - was published in 1913. This book was translated by the beloved Abu'l-Qásim Faizi for the delight of the friends in the year of his passing.

Mr Faizi's other best-known works include *Payám-i-Dúst va Bahár-i-Ṣad-u-Bíst* - 120 BE (1963-1964); *Dástán-i-Dústán* - 121 BE (1964-1965); *The Priceless Pearl* translated into Persian – 1969; *Three Meditations on the Eve of November the Fourth* – 1970; *Explanation of the Emblem of the Greatest Name* – 1970-1971; *Our Precious Trusts* – 1973; and *The Wonder Lamp* – 1975.[787]

* * *

In *The Priceless Pearl* Rúḥíyyih Khánum wrote that Martha Root and Sutherland Maxwell '. . . brought (the Guardian) more deep personal satisfaction than any other believers. They were very much alike in some ways, saintly and modest souls who adored Shoghi Effendi and gladly gave him the best they had in service and loyalty.'[788] During the lifetime of 'Abdu'l-Bahá and the early years of the Guardianship, Dr John E Esslemont was another saintly soul who endeared himself to Shoghi Effendi. Receiving from the pen of Shoghi Effendi the lengthiest eulogy in English of any Hand of the Cause, the Guardian praised his *noble qualities, high spiritual standing, beautiful character and his knowledge of the Cause.*[789] He touchingly wrote:

> "To me personally, he was the warmest of friends, a trusted counsellor, an indefatigable collaborator, a lovable companion. . . . by the conspicuous achievements of his book, he has immortalised his name . . ."[790]

Just 51 years of age at the time of his passing from the debilitating effects of tuberculosis, Dr John Esslemont was an energetic man who excelled in the field of medicine, the study of languages, a devotion to the Faith, and his scholarship. Following his introduction to the Faith in December 1914, Dr Esslemont began an intense study of the Faith from all the books he could find in English. Due to the difficulty he experienced in obtaining desired literature, he decided to put together a book for others to study what he had learned.

On 24 October 1916 in a letter to Dr Luṭfu'lláh Ḥakím he first mentioned that he had begun a book on the Faith. Progress was slow owing to his professional duties. However, when his name came to the attention of Shoghi Effendi, the future Guardian on 19 November 1918 initiated a correspondence with Dr Esslemont:

> "My dear spiritual brother,
>
> . . . (Captain Tudor Pole) mentioned your name to the Beloved and mentioned your untiring services in the Cause. How gratified the Beloved was to hear that. He prayed for you and asked His Heavenly Father for confirmation and help.
>
> I secured your address from Capt. Tudor Pole and I now hasten, altho late at night, to open a correspondence with you which shall be continuous, inspiring and regular. . . ."[791]

In early January 1919, Dr Esslemont received a Tablet from 'Abdu'l-Bahá asking him to send Him a copy of the book he was editing. Esslemont immediately forwarded the first nine chapters to Him. At 'Abdu'l-Bahá's cordial invitation, Dr Esslemont then journeyed to Haifa, arriving on 5 November 1919. He later wrote:

> ". . . I had the privilege of spending two and a half months as the guest of 'Abdu'l-Bahá during the winter of 1919-20. During this visit, 'Abdu'l-Bahá discussed the book with me on various occasions. He gave several valuable suggestions for its improvement . . . 'Abdu'l-Bahá found time, amid His busy life, to correct some three and a half chapters (Chapters I, II, V and part of III) before He passed away. It is a matter of profound regret to me that 'Abdu'l-Bahá was not able to complete the correction of the manuscript, as the value of the book would thereby have been greatly enhanced."[792]

During his visit to Haifa that winter, a close friendship developed between John Esslemont and Shoghi Effendi. The two men spent much time together. Shoghi Effendi gave him a drop of Bahá'u'lláh's sacred blood and ringlets of the Manifestation's hair.

By 10 August 1920 Dr Esslemont had finished his book and sent the manuscript to 'Abdu'l-Bahá. The following month Shoghi Effendi visited him for a few days at the Sanatorium in Bournemouth where he worked. In July 1921 Shoghi Effendi spent a fortnight with him. Not many months later upon the passing of 'Abdu'l-Bahá, Dr Esslemont was able to bring some comfort to Shoghi Effendi and assist the stricken youth in his journey to Haifa.

Time passed as Shoghi Effendi took over the helm of the Guardianship. Near the beginning of 1923 he had reviewed Dr Esslemont's book and made several suggestions. The book was finally published in September with the American edition being brought out 13 months later. 'Your book,' the Guardian had written him, '. . . is the finest presentation that has so far been given of the Cause and I am confident that it will arouse immense interest.'[793]

At Shoghi Effendi's invitation, John Esslemont transferred his residence to Haifa on 21 November 1924. The Sanatorium had been sold in 1923 and John required a warmer climate for his deteriorating health. After his arrival, he became concerned for Shoghi Effendi's overwork and determined to serve him. Soon he was acting as the Guardian's English language secretary and as a translator. However his health ebbed and flowed such that he was hindered in doing his work. Finally, on 22 November 1925, he succumbed to consumption. Shoghi Effendi, who had stayed at the bedside of his friend and collaborator throughout Dr Esslemont's final night, placed on the doctor's finger his own Bahá'í ring. His touching eulogy begins:

> "It is with feelings of overwhelming sorrow that I communicate to you the news of yet another loss which the Almighty, in His inscrutable wisdom, has chosen to inflict upon our beloved Cause."[794]

The author of *Dr John E Esslemont Hand of the Cause of God* which was approved for publication by the National Spiritual Assembly of the Bahá'ís of the United Kingdom in 1975, had this to say about Esslemont's scholarship:

> "Dr Esslemont's greatest achievement was of course his book, *Bahá'u'lláh and the New Era.* Shoghi Effendi regarded it as "the textbook of the Faith", actively promoted its translation and publication into various languages and supervised its revision in 1937. The importance of Esslemont's book at the time of its publication was monumental. For four decades the Faith had been spreading in the West, being taught by eminent Bahá'ís, each of whom had placed their personal interpretations and understandings upon it. The result was the spread of mystical ideas, factual distortions and a great uncertainty, even among the Bahá'ís themselves, as to exactly what the Faith did teach. Esslemont's book, so much more accurate, clearly written and easy to read, was a spark of light coinciding with the commencement of one of the most important periods of Bahá'í history. The book's importance to us today lies, in Shoghi Effendi's words, in the "pure intention" of the author. The purity of Esslemont's soul allowed him to distil the essence of the Bahá'í Faith, unsullied by personal prejudices and bias, while his literary ability enabled him to convey it to the pages of a well-written and readable book."[795]

When the Hand of the Cause George Townshend passed away just over 31 years after John Esslemont's death, Shoghi Effendi made the following remarkable statement:

> "HIS (George Townshend's) STERLING QUALITIES HIS SCHOLARSHIP HIS CHALLENGING WRITINGS HIS HIGH ECCLESIASTICAL POSITION UNRIVALLED ANY BAHÁ'Í WESTERN WORLD ENTITLE HIM RANK WITH THOMAS BREAKWELL DR. ESSLEMONT ONE OF THREE LUMINARIES SHEDDING BRILLIANT LUSTRE ANNALS IRISH ENGLISH SCOTTISH BAHÁ'Í COMMUNITIES."[796]

***

George Townshend was known to be shy, absent-minded, and unimpressive outwardly. He was known to accept a luncheon engagement during the Bahá'í Fast and then excuse himself upon arrival. Or he might completely forget an appointment. Yet, if he was not always successful in fostering relationships in person, he was highly successful doing so with his pen. Indeed, described by the Guardian as the *pre-eminent Bahá'í writer*,[797] George Townshend wrote more than sixty books, pamphlets, poems and commentaries. At Shoghi Effendi's request, he contributed essays and poems to successive volumes of *The Bahá'í World* and presented a paper on *Bahá'u'lláh's Groundplan for World Fellowship* to the first conference of the World Congress of Faiths in London in 1936. His best-known works are his trilogy on the Bible and the Bahá'í Faith: *The Promise of All Ages, The Heart of the Gospel* and *Christ and Bahá'u'lláh.*

During an 18-year period, George collaborated with the Guardian by reviewing and editing most of the latter's English-language translations of the Holy Writings as well as *God Passes By*. George gave the titles to and wrote the Introductions to *The Dawn-Breakers* and *God Passes By*, but declined to have his name printed as the author of the former. Such was the excellence of George's exalted style of writing that Hasan Balyuzi attributed a paragraph from George's Introduction (to *The Dawn-Breakers)* in the dedication of his greatest work *Bahá'u'lláh: the King of Glory* to Shoghi Effendi. Martha Root in her historic account of the life of Ṭáhirih also attributed this same Introduction to Shoghi Effendi. In 1980 the House of Justice clarified George's authorship.[798]

At the Ninth Annual Conference of the Association for Bahá'í Studies held in Ottawa in 1984, Zikrullah Khadem had this to say about George Townshend's scholarship:

> "George Townshend . . . The Cause of God has not yet produced another like him. The beloved Shoghi Effendi once said, 'The best scholar we have in Persia is Abu'l-Faḍl, and the best in the West is George Townshend.' To my mind, he had the greatest honor showered upon him by the beloved Guardian, who asked him to write the preface for *God Passes By* and for *The Hidden Words*. Nobody else has been given that kind of task. Just imagine! 'Abdu'l-Bahá said that His writings and the writings of Bahá'u'lláh should not be compiled in one volume. Who are we to write a preface to be compiled with the words of the beloved Guardian? Who is it that the beloved Shoghi Effendi chose from among the Bahá'ís to do that job?"[799]

***

In its eulogy to William Sears, the Universal House of Justice referred to his '. . .

CREATIVE AND ENERGETIC CAPACITIES AS WRITER, EDITOR, LECTURER, (and) RADIO AND TELEVISION PROGRAMME DIRECTOR . . .' from which he generously applied his '. . . UNFLINCHING DEVOTION TO BELOVED GUARDIAN, INFECTIOUS ENTHUSIASM FOR TEACHING, GALVANIZING SENSE DRAMA, DISARMING HUMOUR (and) SPECIAL LOVE FOR CHILDREN . . .'[800] Although the creative output of Mr Sears in his more than half-century of service must await the attention of some future researcher, his scholarship as a writer could be distinguished between religious, historical, autobiographical and entertaining.

He wrote 14 books of which the Bahá'í world is familiar and possibly others which remain unpublished. His scholarly legacy includes four works from the point of view of prophecy and the Bible. In *Thief in the Night* (1961) Mr Sears created a mystery novel in which he leads the reader along the path he took in search of the missing millennium. Inspired by his unorthodox protestant grandfather in his youth to search for truth and read the Bible, young Bill began a furtive study under the watchful eyes of his father who was determined he would not. Bill won out and the result was not only his own discovery of the fulfilment of prophecy in the coming of Bahá'u'lláh but this gem of a book that has helped countless seekers find the Promised One from a biblical perspective. *Prince of Peace* (1986) was written to show how Bahá'u'lláh fulfils the prophecy in the 9th chapter of Isaiah: 'For unto us a child is born, unto us a son is given: and the government shall be upon his shoulder: and his name shall be called Wonderful, Counsellor, The mighty God, The everlasting Father, The Prince of Peace.'[801] And how Bahá'u'lláh, the Prince of Peace, brings teachings which are destined to establish peace on earth. *The Half Inch Prophecy* (2000) concerns the *amazing Micah*[802] in which the prophet foretells where Bahá'u'lláh would appear: 'In that day also he shall come even to thee from Assyria, and from the fortified cities, and from the fortress even to the river, and from sea to sea, and from mountain to mountain.'[803] After Mr Sears introduces the prophecy as just a half inch in his Bible, he shows how Bahá'u'lláh exactly fulfils each part of this prophecy.

William Sears historical works begin with *Release the Sun* (1960) in which he presents the early history of the Faith in highly readable terms. As Mr Sears unfolds the epic of the Báb and the Dawn-Breakers, he draws the reader into the wondrous happenings and stirring events associated with the birth of a new world religion. In *Wine of Astonishment* (1963) he explains from a Bahá'í perspective the significance of such age-old Christian themes as Baptism, Son of God, confession, the Trinity, miracles, heaven and hell, and stars falling from heaven. Some of Mr Sears's finest scholarly presentation can be found in his historical elucidations contained in this little book.

The Prisoner and the Kings (1971) is Mr Sears's exciting account of Bahá'u'lláh's addresses to the 19th century rulers of the world: Napoleon III, Emperor of France; Emperor Kaiser Wilhelm I of Germany; Alexander II, Czar of Russia; Franz-Josef, king-emperor of the Austro-Hungarian monarchy; Queen Victoria of Great Britain; Náṣiri'd-Dín Sháh, king of Persia; Sultan 'Abdu'l-'Azíz, Sulṭán of Turkey; Pope Pius IX, head of Catholic Church and Papal states; the reactions of these rulers to His addresses and the consequences to their kingdoms of their rejection.

The Flame (1972) is an account of the life of Lua Getsinger which Mr Sears wrote with his good friend, Robert Quigley. Lua was passionately devoted to 'Abdu'l-Bahá and nominated by Him as the Herald of the Covenant. *Cry from the Heart* (1982) was written to protest the atrocities being committed against Bahá'ís in Iran. Mr Sears had travelled extensively in Iran and was acquainted with believers there. A '. . . refutation of the false and contradictory charges levelled against them (believers), and an exposé of the genocidal purpose of the present outbreak',[804] the book brought pressure on the government of Iran to end the persecutions at that time.

God Loves Laughter (1960), *All Flags Flying* (1985) and *Tokoloshe* (1990) are humorous accounts of Mr Sears's life from his childhood in Minnesota to his world-wide services as a Hand of the Cause. These accounts are so well done that one cannot help but fall in love with Mr Sears and with service to the Faith. When he wrote *In Grandfather's Barn* and *Run to Glory* (1989), he brought back the principle characters from *God Loves Laughter* and in so doing also brought his audience back to the kind of wholesome entertainment which characterized his earlier work.

* * *

The works of Charles Mason Remey's consist of 119 volumes entitled *Reminiscences and letters* and 56 volumes of *Bahá'í reminiscences, diary, letters and other documents*. The Bahá'í World Centre Library wrote the writer that . . .

> "These records include the contents by volume number in the "abstract" sections . . . The records also show the

publisher as Mason Remey himself since, in fact, these multi-volumed works were not published per se although they were reproduced in numerous copies in typewritten (or carbon) form and bound at the instruction of, and at the expense of, Mason Remey between the years 1938-1940.

At some point Mason Remey sent these works to various libraries, mostly in the United States, and restricted access to these and other papers of his life and works "published" in the same fashion. The Bahá'í World Centre Library holds in its collections the vast majority of the works of Charles Mason Remey . . . The restriction he placed on these repositories was for a certain number of years, with permission to open the box or boxes given for 1995 A.D."[805]

* * *

If any man were to arise to defend, in his writings, the Cause of God against its assailants, such a man, however inconsiderable his share, shall be so honoured in the world to come that the Concourse on high would envy his glory. No pen can depict the loftiness of his station, neither can any tongue describe its splendour.[806]

In the 1920s Egypt being a Muslim country had no civil code. Consequently the Bahá'ís tended to be adversely affected in matters of marriage, divorce and inheritance. Subject to Muslim jurisprudence, rulings could be handed down by antagonistic courts. In 1925 the highest ecclesiastical court pronounced the Bahá'í Faith an independent religion.

The decision came about when the Bahá'ís in a small village in Upper Egypt formed their Spiritual Assembly. The fanatical headman demanded that the Muḥammadan wives of husbands who had become believers file for divorce on grounds their spouses were now heretics. The court debated that as Muḥammad was the last of the prophets and messengers from God, therefore Islám is the religion of God and Muḥammadans are the chosen people. Therefore he who accepts another religion beside Islám is not acceptable in the sight of God. Anyone who departs from Islám and its unalterable laws and duties is a heretic. In concluding that the Bahá'í religion was independent of Islám due to differences and contradictions between the two religions, the court could be seen as supporting the headman's view that the Bahá'ís were heretical.

The Guardian saw the ecclesiastical court's judgement of the Faith as an independent religion an emancipation for the Bahá'í religion from the fetters of the Islámic religion. Under his guidance the Bahá'ís in the East overcame the charge that the Faith was a heresy inside Islám. The National Spiritual Assembly of the Bahá'ís of Egypt published a compilation of important laws and ordinances from the Aqdás which it then presented to the Egyptian government. This step and some other ones aroused the enmity of leading Egyptian divines with the result that a well-known Shaykh attacked some of the Faith's *social, spiritual and religious Teachings*[807] in a prominent Cairo newspaper. Criticising the principles, institutions, inheritance and equality teachings of the Faith, the author published a series of articles under the title "Bahaism, a Delightful Fancy".

'Abdu'l-Jalíl Bey Sa'ad made a scholarly refutation of the Shaykh's arguments in the same newspaper. A judge in the Civil Courts of the country, he aroused considerable interest in the Faith in his series of four articles: 'Baha'ism Is an Eternal Truth, and Not a Delightful Fancy'; 'Baha'ism and Universal Peace'; 'Baha'ism is an Everlasting Truth – It Is a Blessing and a Bounty for Islam, Not a Calamity and a Requital'; 'Baha'ism and the Freedom of Women.'

His first article proved the authenticity, perfection and universality of the Faith as well as the Bahá'í point of view that divine attributes are a manifestation and not incarnation of the divine spirit. Bey Sa'ad's second article expatiated on the Most Great Peace and the New World Order from Bahá'u'lláh's writings and on Universal Peace and Unity from 'Abdu'l-Bahá's talks. His third article referred to the Faith as confirming rather than repudiating Islám. He quoted from the Hadith and the Qur'án: 'By Him (the Divine Messenger) Islam will be glorified after its humiliation,' and 'At the beginning of every age, God shall send unto this nation (the Muslim) Him who will renew (for them) the status of His (God's) religion'.[808] His final article focused on the Bahá'í elevation of the status of women. He drew attention to the wisdom and justice of Bahá'í laws and to women in Islam, Christianity and the Bahá'í Faith '. . . who by their physical prowess, intellectual abilities and spiritual loftiness surpassed many a man supposedly their superior.'[809] He also referred to the advancement of women in modern times.

Concerning Bey Sa'ad's scholarship, the Spiritual Assembly of Haifa in a circular letter wrote:

> "This valiant upholder of the Faith of Bahá'u'lláh has shown remarkable assiduity and courage in proclaiming and supporting the Cause publicly and without any veil

or disguise in a Muslim land where only recently the believers had to face most formidable obstacles in their struggle to enfranchise the Faith from the fetters of Muslim orthodoxy."[810]

'Abdu'l-Jalíl Bey Sa'ad was again defending the Faith in his writings in 1934 when a certain learned Shaykh published a series of articles entitled 'The Bahá'í Faith Is a Pleasing Illusion'. Responding in a series of 14 articles under the title 'The Bahá'í Faith Is an Everlasting Truth', Bey Sa'ad successfully refuted the arguments of the opposition through his '. . . graphic presentation of the teachings (and) ample . . . proofs in support of them . . .'[811] Bey Sa'ad was disciplined for his efforts, being transferred to Upper Egypt. In that isolated locale, he busied himself translating *The Dawn-Breakers* into Arabic for study by the believers in Arabic-speaking countries.

* * *

It is the concern of the True One to reveal, and the concern of men to spread what hath been revealed. . . . Spiritual souls will assuredly emerge from behind the veil of divine protection who will gather together the tokens and verses of God and put them into the most excellent order.[812]

Collis Featherstone was very conscious of the importance of every moment. He used to tell the believers with whom he met that they were making history now. He collected and bound copies of early Bahá'í magazines. He kept detailed records of correspondence, programmes, itineraries and reports of all his travels. He collected photographs and became a photographer. He made a tape of Mother Dunn relating her experience in meeting 'Abdu'l-Bahá in San Francisco in 1912. He made a 16 mm colour film at the November 1958 Conclave showing the 25 Hands of the Cause in attendance, the only such record of this period.[813]

* * *

On a pilgrimage in 1939, Shoghi Effendi told Zikrullah Khadem: 'I will send you to the West, to America, to witness with your own eyes, the secret, the mystery, the light of the Cause in those lands.'[814] Following his appointment as a Hand of the Cause, Zikrullah Khadem's services really began in the West. Under the guidance of the Guardian from 1952 to 1957, he travelled extensively throughout Europe, Africa, the Caribbean, the Far East, and the Americas.

From the outset of these travels, Mr Khadem kept a detailed journal in which he '. . . documented his times of arrival and departure, names and addresses of everyone he met, hotels he stayed at, planes he boarded, etc. He believed that every act under the direction of the Guardian of the Cause of God had historical significance.' [815]

Teaching

It has often happened that one blessed soul has become the cause of the guidance of a nation. [816]

Hyde and Clara Dunn were inspired in 1919 by the *Tablets of the Divine Plan* to embark for far-off Australia as pioneers. 'It was all very simple,' Hyde later wrote. '(A) wave that came into our lives possessing and satisfying every desire to serve our Beloved Cause of Bahá'u'lláh and His Glorious Covenant. Mother (Clara) was reading ('Abdu'l-Bahá's) seventh call to the Western States and His appeal for Australia was so penetrating and thrilling it pierced our hearts.'[817] 'Oh how I long that it could be made possible for me to travel through these parts,' 'Abdu'l-Bahá yearningly appealed, 'even if necessary on foot and with the utmost poverty, and while passing through the cities, villages, mountains, deserts and oceans, cry at the top of my voice, "Yá-Bahá'u'l-Abhá!" and promote the divine teachings. But now this is not feasible for me; therefore I live in great regret; perchance, God willing, ye may become assisted therein.'[818]

They arose in their senior years at ages when people think of settling into a quieter life in a retirement community or small town. They left their home and their livelihood with no outward assurances of security or earnings. They embarked upon a very long journey to a new continent. They could have remained in California and perhaps home-front pioneered. After all, Hyde was a travelling salesman already familiar with his turf, employed and employable. Even Clara was unsure that their decision was prudent, and so in the midst of their preparations she wrote to 'Abdu'l-Bahá. But His reply, when it finally arrived, reassured her. Hyde too. 'Highly advisable,'[819] He had cabled.

They settled in Sydney where Hyde became ill and Clara took a job for about half a year. Then he acquired a job as a travelling salesman, enabling him to eventually venture into the whole of Australia, Tasmania and New Zealand. Meanwhile they were to persevere in New South Wales for about two and a half years before they found someone to accept the Faith. Establishing a study group in Sydney, they travelled from place to place. Clara would set up housekeeping and organize meetings there while Hyde did business and also taught the Faith in various towns. He seized opportunities to teach the Faith: 'On trains. At railway stations. Hotel lounges. Dining rooms, Cafes. In the street. At work etc.'[820] Weekends Hyde would speak to the seekers Clara had invited during the week. Many people showed up at their regular meetings thanks to their persistence. They repeated this pattern as they moved from city to city.

Both Hyde and Clara possessed a dignity which attracted others to them. This dignity was born out of their love for and dedication to the spread of the Message of Bahá'u'lláh throughout Australia and New Zealand. Hyde was described as being '. . . courteous, sincere, his manner . . . at all times kind and gentle, he was patient and radiated joy and love.'[821] Clara was a very '. . . warm, loving, gentle but determined person (who) could relate to anybody of any age or circumstance – a truly amazing ability to talk unaffectedly and humanly with anybody.'[822]

The Guardian sent many letters praising their services. Whether written on his behalf or by him personally, Shoghi Effendi conveyed his joy, gratitude and praise as the years passed. 'The fruits of your work are too glorious and abundant to escape the notice of the Bahá'í world.'[823] 'Your names, your services, your high endeavours are graven upon my heart & your example is truly inspiring.'[824] 'You cannot imagine what a comfort it is to him to be assured of your sustained efforts and pioneer work in that vast continent . . .'[825] 'I truly admire your unwavering constancy & unflinching determination to carry on the sacred work entrusted to your charge.'[826] 'May Bahá'u'lláh, Whose Cause you have served & are still serving with such exemplary faith & fidelity, fulfil your wishes, & enable you to enrich the noble record of your unforgettable achievements.'[827] 'The tribute so abundantly and yet so deservedly paid by the Guardian in this unique epistle (*Advent of Divine Justice*) to your magnificent teaching services is assuredly destined to transmit to the future Bahá'í generations, and in particular to the Bahá'í teachers and pioneers of succeeding centuries, such measure of inspiration and such example of true pioneer service as cannot but inspire and guide them to follow in your footsteps and emulate your noble example.'[828]

Named Australia's spiritual conqueror by the Guardian in a letter to the National Spiritual Assembly of the Bahá'ís of Australia and New Zealand shortly after the passing of Hyde Dunn,[829] the Guardian, in his immortal history of the first hundred years of the Faith completed three years later, wrote of John Henry Hyde Dunn:

> "A new continent was opened to the Cause when, in response to the Tablets of the Divine Plan unveiled at the first Convention after the war, the great-hearted and heroic Hyde Dunn, at the advanced age of sixty-two, promptly forsook his home in California, and, seconded and accompanied by his wife, settled as a pioneer in Australia, where he was able

> to carry the Message to no less than seven hundred towns throughout that Commonwealth."[830]

Eight years later and soon after he had appointed Clara a Hand of the Cause, Shoghi Effendi in a letter written on his behalf on 7 May 1952 wrote to her: 'It was not without conviction that the beloved Guardian appointed you a Hand of the Cause. He feels that your long and steadfast pioneer service in Australia certainly entitles you to this distinction. . .'[831] In his own words appended to the letter, Shoghi Effendi added: 'May the Almighty guide & sustain you always, aid you to enrich the record of your splendid services to His Faith, & win still greater victories.'[832]

* * *

> ***The role of the individual is of unique importance in the work of the Cause. It is the individual who manifests the vitality of faith upon which the success of the teaching work and the development of the community depend. . . . The individual alone can exercise those capacities which include the ability to take the initiative, to seize opportunities, to form friendships, to interact personally with others, to build relationships, to win the cooperation of others in common service to the Faith and society . . .***[833]

John Robarts was an achiever who inspired confidence in those who chanced to observe his dedication or work under his leadership. Throughout his career he never had to seek employment, every position being offered to him. From 1927 to 1934, he presided over the Overhead Door Company. The firm maintained high quality standards and filled many large orders. When the company was sold owing to the Depression, John did not accept the offer of another job until he could find employment for every one of the 20 factory employees.

Later, as district manager of the Toronto King Street Agency of London Life Insurance Company from 1938 to 1953, John ran the agency in such a way that it became the most productive in Canada. He was able to inspire his agents in achieving goals such that every single one became a member of the prestigious Million Dollar Round Table. When he resigned this position to pioneer to Africa, his reputation resulted in his being offered two managerial positions before he could disembark the boat at Cape Town!

Becoming a Bahá'í in 1938 John immediately set out to contribute his share to fulfilling the goals set by Shoghi Effendi. To establish local assemblies during the first Seven Year Plan, he travelled to various localities in the Maritime provinces. For a year he went by train to Hamilton one night each week. There he would dine with someone, attend a fireside and, afterwards, meet over coffee at a restaurant with ten or more people. He would stay the night in a hotel and return to Toronto early the next morning in time for work. After the Assembly was formed, he made the same sacrifice for Ottawa.

His talent for organizing and following up teaching activity brought excellent results. John created teaching opportunities. Conscious of the value of time, he hired a private dining room near his office and began weekly lunchtime firesides in Toronto. Business associates would gather, invite their friends and hear different speakers. He constantly arranged other meetings including firesides in his home, brought people together, involved individuals in teaching, widened the field of friendships, generated exciting news and encouraged people to give talks.

According to his daughter, one of John's favourite passages which he had memorized and often quoted was from *The Advent of Divine Justice*:

> "The field is indeed so immense, the period so critical, the Cause so great, the workers so few, the time so short, the privilege so priceless, that no follower of the Faith of Bahá'u'lláh, worthy to bear His name, can afford a moment's hesitation . . . "[834]

According to his wife:

> "John was . . . a 'do-er'. After serving the Faith for over 55 of our 63 years of marriage, teaching became our first priority."[835]

* * *

by Donald Witzel
20 April 2002

> "My wife Mignon and I had several experiences with Hand of the Cause Dr Muhájir in critical moments in our lives. One was after Riḍván 1961 following the establishment of 21 National Spiritual Assemblies in Latin America when this Hand of the Faith visited the capital city of Panama and recommended that we accept the challenge of teaching the Guaymi Indians in the mountains of the Province of Chiriqui

in Panama. In fact he told me that if I didn't accept this task I would never become a pioneer to the Indian peoples. We moved to David, the provincial capital, and accepted the challenge.

On another occasion in 1965, when we had transferred our residence to Bucaramanga, Colombia, at the request of the Hands of the Faith in the Western Hemisphere, Dr Muhájir once again came into our lives. We were both teachers at the Colegio Panamericano (a primary and high school). I received a cablegram from Dr Muhájir a few days before our annual summer vacation, requesting that I meet him at a pension in the city of Valledupar with a jeep in order to make a trip of several weeks duration throughout the Colombian Guajira Indian area. During this trip we taught the Faith together. Sometimes I would interpret into Spanish and other times he would ask me to teach the Guajiros. I learned a great deal from him.

At the beginning of this trip we visited a small town of Adventists in South Guajira that had never been previously visited by Bahá'ís. He told me not to speak either about the Bible or prophecies – only about the coming of Bahá'u'lláh and His history. When they asked me about prophecies, he told me to tell them that Bahá'u'lláh was the Promised One of all religions and to return to the theme of His life and sacrifice for humanity. Thus six or seven of them became Bahá'ís, and the majority of them requested our prompt return.

I remember when we were completely lost in the desert somewhere between Manaure (the coastal salt mines) and the frontier with Venezuela. I had no idea where we were. We stopped the jeep in front of a windmill (for water) where a young Guajiro man was standing in front of the water trough. I wanted to ask him for directions to follow one of the several trails as we were completely lost. Dr Muhájir told me to teach him the Faith. I responded that I didn't know where we were and probably wouldn't ever see the man again. He told me to teach him the Faith and that I would find him again. This young man spoke Spanish fluently, accepted the Faith, and I found him again at two different times in other places.

Dr Muhájir did not wish to continue on into Venezuela, but to visit other parts of Colombia. Before leaving me in Riohacha, he requested that I leave the school and dedicate myself full time once again to teaching the Indian peoples, specially the Colombian Guajiros for one year. He sent a cablegram to the Universal House of Justice to this effect and recommended that the Hand of the Cause Jalál Kházeh visit us in Bucaramanga in order to convince Mignon of this need. She accepted this challenge after we received a cablegram from the Supreme Body and the visit of the Hand of the Cause. In this way Dr Muhájir changed the lives of many Bahá'ís in the service of the Cause of God throughout the world. He had a very special gift in inspiring others to service and in his own life exemplified and consecrated himself to teaching the Faith and raising up others to do the same."[836]

* * *

"Teaching was always the dearest thing in the world to the heart of dear Leroy (Ioas). It was his life. He was perhaps the most gifted of all teachers I have known at answering the questions of seekers at fireside meetings."[837] – William Sears

* * *

In his lifetime Ṭarázu'lláh Samandarí travelled extensively for the Faith. Around 1895 he married Ṭarázíyyih, a second cousin. On an occasion when Ṭaráz Effendi had been away on a lengthy journey, she received a Tablet from 'Abdu'l-Bahá in which He offered:

". . . consolation in their separation and (prayed) that this temporary separation would be the cause of eternal reunion; whereas other unions end in separation, unity of spiritual aspiration and service elevated a marriage to the station of a real union, a meeting that has no end."[838]

The effect of this Tablet on the couple must have been profound. In 1947 when Ṭarázíyyih died at her pioneering post in Zanján, Persia without having seen her husband for three years while he remained in Shíráz as a result of having been asked to protect the Faith there, the Guardian wrote:

"...that dear handmaiden of the Ancient Beauty (had been engaged in) spreading the Word of God . . . with absolute detachment and

> steadfastness. (She now resides) in the loftiest mansions of heaven."[839]

Samandarí joined her 21 years later when he passed away in the Holy Land. The Universal House of Justice referred to him:

> "FAITHFUL TO LAST BREATH INSTRUCTIONS HIS LORD HIS MASTER HIS GUARDIAN HE CONTINUED SELFLESS DEVOTED SERVICE UNABATED UNTIL FALLING ILL DURING RECENT TEACHING MISSION."[840]

* * *

On 27 September 1912 Louis Gregory and Louisa Mathew were married by 'Abdu'l-Bahá in New York. They had been introduced to each other by the Master Who wished them to marry. Their union was the first between a black and a white Bahá'í. In coming years owing to the colour barrier then so pervasive in the United States, Louis and Louisa would suffer hostility and discrimination. In some American states, intermarriage was illegal between the two races. They were not always able to travel together. They were denied living accommodations. Believers felt awkward around them. And they were apart for months and years.

They were, however, very much in love with each other and enjoyed one another's company on those occasions when they were able to do so. Louis was overjoyed when he learned from Mrs. True that 'Abdu'l-Bahá had said of him and Louisa: 'Those two souls found each other.'[841] And Louisa received these beautiful words from Him in 1920:

> "O thou revered wife of his honor, Gregory. Do thou consider what a bounty God hath bestowed upon thee in giving thee a husband like Mr. Gregory who is the essence of the love of God and is a symbol of guidance. . ." [842]

Still, in confidence to a friend in the early 1930s and reflective of their loneliness in being so much apart, Louis said:

> "It is our hope that our enforced separation along the line of service to the Divine Cause will mercifully bring to us eternal reunion in the worlds of God." [843]

* * *

> ***. . . let us arise to teach His Cause with righteousness, conviction, understanding and vigor . . . Let us make it the dominating passion in our life. Let us scatter to the uttermost corners of the earth; sacrifice our personal interests, comforts, tastes and pleasures; mingle with the divers kindreds and peoples of the world . . .***[844]

One day while Rúḥíyyih Kh̲ánum was at her desk, Shoghi Effendi stopped by and said to her: 'What will become of you after I die?'[845] She was shattered and driven to tears by his remark: 'Oh Shoghi Effendi, don't say such terrible things. I don't want to live without you.'[846] Upon his passing in 1957, she would resist the urge to take her own life, knowing he would not be pleased with her. Paying no attention to her outburst, he continued: 'I suppose you will travel and encourage the friends'.[847] Such was Shoghi Effendi's only comment to his beloved consort concerning the life he hoped she would lead after he left behind the cares of the Guardianship.

Following the election of the first Universal House of Justice in 1963, this most highly esteemed Hand of the Cause set out at the age of 53 on a series of journeys which over the next 30 years would take her more than 100,000 miles overland and some half million miles by air in a mighty effort to fulfil his hope. In her lifetime she would visit 185 countries, dependencies and major islands of the globe – some countries like India as many as nine times!

In 1964 she spent nine months in the Indian subcontinent, travelling almost 55,000 miles by air, rail, car and cart to visit Bahá'ís in villages and towns. Between August 1969 and February 1973, she undertook her *Great African Safari* in which she and Violette Nak̲h̲javání drove a Land-rover some 36,000 miles through 34 African countries. In 1975 she embarked on the seven month *Green Light Expedition*, travelling mostly by boat over 8,000 miles through the Amazon basin.

As Ambassadress for the Faith, she met with Heads of State and high-ranking authorities at national, local and village levels where she explained she had come from the World Centre of the Bahá'í Faith and was visiting the Bahá'ís who were well-wishers of and obedient to government and apolitical. She felt that her role should be to gain the trust of officials and dignitaries so that in future Bahá'í institutions could more easily approach the government with requests. She had hundreds of interviews with representatives of the media. She attended international Bahá'í conferences, dedicated Bahá'í Temples, and wrote and produced outstanding literary and visual works.

Concerning her travels, Amatu'l-Bahá Rúḥíyyih Khánum said:

> "After Shoghi Effendi passed away, I did not know any way that I could say to the Bahá'ís, 'Please go out and do his work and fulfil his hopes and obey his commands.' So I said the best thing is I will go myself. Maybe this is the loudest voice with which one can speak."[848]

* * *

Shoghi Effendi noted in *God Passes By* that Martha Root was 'The first to arise, in the very year the Tablets of the Divine Plan were unveiled in the United States of America . . . embarking, with unswerving resolve and a spirit of sublime detachment, on her world journeys . . .'[849] She travelled to South America (Brazil, Argentina, Chile, Peru, Cuba, and Panama), the United States and Canada, Mexico and Central America from 1919 to 1921; the Far East (Japan, China, Hong Kong, Viet Nam and Cambodia), Australia, New Zealand and Tasmania, and South Africa from 1923 to 1925; the Holy Land, Europe (Switzerland, the Balkans, Hungary, Austria, Rumania, British Isles, Spain, Portugal, Germany, Poland, Czechoslovakia, Denmark, Netherlands, Belgium, Turkey, Greece, Yugoslavia and Bulgaria and the Baltic and Scandinavian countries, Egypt and Palestine between 1925 and 1929; the Holy Land, Syria, Iraq, Iran, India and Burma, the Far East (China and Japan), and Hawaii from 1929 to 1931; the United States and Canada, Europe (Switzerland, Czechoslovakia, Poland, Austria, Hungary, Yugoslavia, Albania, Bulgaria, Rumania, Greece, Turkey, Lithuania, Sweden and Norway) and Iceland from 1931 to 1936; and the United States, Hawaii, the Far East (Japan, China and the Philippines), Ceylon, Burma, India, Australia, Tasmania, New Zealand, Fiji and Hawaii from 1936 to 1939.

In her four round-the-world trips, Martha passed through numbers of these countries more than once where she fearlessly took the Message of Bahá'u'lláh '. . . to kings, queens, princes and princesses, presidents of republics, ministers and statesmen, publicists, professors, clergymen and poets, as well as a vast number of people in various walks of life . . .'[850] She attended '. . . religious congresses, peace societies, Esperanto associations, socialist congresses, Theosophical societies, women's clubs and other kindred organizations.'[851]

Martha wrote prolifically about her travels for the Faith. In the early *Bahá'í World* volumes, one can read her essays about the Bahá'í presence at Esperanto congresses and universities in North America, Germany and India. She wrote about some of the personalities she met on her travels: King Faisel, Prince Paul and Princess Olga, King Haakon, President Eduard Benes and Queen Marie. She wrote about the greatness of the Bahá'í movement, Leo Tolstoy and the Bahá'í Faith, Ṭáhirih's message to the modern world, Russia's cultural contribution to the Faith and her visit to Adrianople. And she produced a beautiful book about the life of Ṭáhirih.

The beloved Guardian in paying tribute to Martha's exploits records her successive interviews with Queen Marie of Rumania as well as Princess Ileana and the prince and princess of Yugoslavia, and then continues:

> ". . . The lectures which she delivered in over four hundred universities and colleges in both the East and the West; her twice repeated visits to all German universities with the exception of two, as well as to nearly a hundred universities, colleges and schools in China; the innumerable articles which she published in newspapers and magazines in practically every country she visited; the numerous broadcasts which she delivered and the unnumbered books she placed in private and state libraries; her personal meetings with the statesmen of more than fifty countries, during her three-months stay in Geneva, in 1932, at the time of the Disarmament Conference; the painstaking efforts she exerted, while on her arduous journeys, in supervising the translation and production of a large number of versions of Dr. Esslemont's "*Bahá'u'lláh and the New Era*"; the correspondence exchanged with, and the presentation of Bahá'í books to, men of eminence and learning; her pilgrimage to Persia, and the touching homage paid by her to the memory of the heroes of the Faith when visiting the Bahá'í historic sites in that country; her visit to Adrianople, where, in her overflowing love for Bahá'u'lláh, she searched out the houses where He had dwelt and the people whom He had met during His exile to that city, and where she was entertained by its governor and mayor; the ready and unfailing assistance extended by her to the administrators of the Faith in all countries where its institutions had been erected or were being established – these may be regarded as the highlights of a service which, in many of its aspects, is without parallel in the entire history of the first Bahá'í century."[852]

* * *

Louis Gregory believed that the world is in transition and that building a new world order was more important than trying to salvage temporary security from the old one. Graduating with his LL.B. degree in 1902, Louis was one of only 2,000 African Americans out of some nine million to have a college education. Yet, at the age of 35, he abandoned a promising law career and set out over the next 40 years to travel, write, lecture and teach in the cause of racial unity – obedient to 'Abdu'l-Bahá's address to him five months after he became a believer in 1909:

> "I hope that thou mayest become . . . the means whereby the white and coloured people shall close their eyes to racial differences and behold the reality of humanity . . ." [853]

Concerning his travels, Harlan Ober, one of the early American believers and husband of Grace Robarts, left this testimony:

> "It is probable that no individual teacher in the Faith has travelled more extensively throughout the United States than Mr Gregory. Living in the utmost simplicity, sacrificing at every turn, he spoke in schools, colleges, churches, forums, conferences and with individuals throughout the land. With a marvellous blending of humility and courage, of tenderness and adamantine firmness and steadfastness, he met high and low, rich and poor, educated and ignorant, and gave to them the cup of the Water of Life."[854]

Mariam Haney, who served on the National Teaching Committee, observed:

> "I do not think we have had anything that approached (his success as a teacher) in any way (since the Cause) first started in this country . . . because it is the first time that any teacher so marvellously illumined as Mr Gregory has been able to reach thousand(s) and thousands of people, colored and white. This is why we must consider it a very remarkable spiritual work."[855]

* * *

'Alí Nakhjavání and the dark-skinned races had been mentioned by the Guardian to Dorothy Baker on her pilgrimage in February, 1953. At the All-America Intercontinental Teaching Conference in Chicago, she shared her impressions with her audience. 'The Guardian . . .

> ". . . spoke of 'Alí Nakhjavání. He spoke of the fact that this intrepid youth had gone into the jungles of Africa . . . and assisted by Philip Hainsworth of Britain they lived with the Teso people. They ate the food of the Teso people. They slept

> on straw mats or leaves or whatever it is that you sleep on among the Teso people. The rain falls on your head and salamanders drop in your tea, if there is tea. And they stayed. And they did not say conditions do not warrant it because these people eat herbs and things that would just kill us. They stayed.
>
> . . . Now the dark-skinned people he said would have an upsurge that is both spiritual and social. The spiritual upsurge will rapidly bring them great gifts because this is an act of God. And it is so intended. And all the world's prejudiced forces will not hold it back one hair's breadth. . . . The social repercussions of race suppressions around the world will increase at the same time and, frightened, the world's forces will see that the dark-skinned peoples are really rising to the top; a cream that has latent gifts only to be brought out by divine bounties.
>
> Where do the Bahá'ís stand in this? Again and again he pointed out that the Bahá'ís must be in the vanguard of finding them and giving them the Faith. For the social repercussions will at times become dreadful if we do not. And we shall be judged by God." [856]

Challenging her listeners, Dorothy asked several times whether there was an 'Alí Nakhjavání in America to teach the African-American and Indian peoples.

At the same conference, Músá Banání also mentioned 'Alí Nakhjavání who . . .

> ". . . went and lived with the Africans in the heart of the jungle . . . and this was a new experience for the Africans, because at no time previously had any white man acted toward these Africans as he did. In the past the Africans had heard many promises and many beautiful words from white men, but in actions they had always seen the opposite. When they saw that words and deeds were one in the person of 'Alí Nakhjavání they immediately warmed up to the Faith and have received the Message of the Faith very eagerly and in exultation."[857]

* * *

After Enoch Olinga became a Bahá'í in Kampala, Uganda in February 1952, the transformation in his conduct was remarkable. Previously he had become disillusioned and drank heavily with the result that he was discharged from the good job he had as a government translator. When he joined the ranks of the few believers in Uganda at that time, he had already received a derogatory report on his impaired working capacity. Introduced to the Faith by 'Alí Nakhjavání, Enoch was among the first fruits of the Músá Banání family who had pioneered to Uganda the year before. 'Alí was the son-in-law of Mr and Mrs Banání, and Enoch Olinga had become a Bahá'í in their home.

Upon his declaration of faith, Enoch underwent an astonishing transformation in conduct and began to study the available literature of the Faith. When Enoch returned to his home in Tilling on a visit to acquaint the Teso tribe in the northeast of Uganda to which he belonged with the Message of Bahá'u'lláh, he aroused much interest. With the help of his spiritual parent and friend, 'Alí Nakhjavání, regular enrolment began. During a two week period in which Enoch sacrificed his vacation time to teach in the Teso and Mbale areas, 72 Africans immediately accepted the Faith. By January 1953, the growth of the Faith in that region was so heart-warming to the Guardian that he compared it to the propagation of the Faith by the Dawn-Breakers. He went on to announce to the Bahá'í world that the number of enrolments in 15 months in Kampala and outlying districts exceeded 200 men and women of 16 tribes. Nine localities would be eligible to elect their LSAs by Riḍván 1953. Meanwhile the Kampala Intercontinental Conference held in February, 1953 would be attended by 232 believers representing 30 ethnic groups and 19 countries; a remarkable representation in that at the outset of the Africa Campaign just two years before the African continent had remained largely untouched by the teachings of Bahá'u'lláh. So, with joyous heart, the Guardian addressed that conference:

> "I welcome with open arms the unexpectedly large number of the representatives of the pure-hearted and the spiritually receptive Negro race, so dearly loved by 'Abdu'l-Bahá, for whose conversion to His Father's Faith He so deeply yearned and whose interests He so ardently championed in the course of His memorable visit to the North American continent. . . . I feel particularly gratified by the substantial participation in this epoch-making Conference of the members of a race dwelling in a continent which for the most part has retained its primitive simplicity and remained uncontaminated by the evils of a gross, a rampant and cancerous materialism undermining the fabric of human society alike in the East and in the West, eating into the vitals of the conflicting peoples and

> races inhabiting the American, the European and the Asiatic continents, and alas threatening to engulf in one common catastrophic convulsion the generality of mankind."[858]

Little wonder, in view of the threat of dreadful social repercussions and contaminating materialism, the Guardian should in his same address call upon the National Spiritual Assemblies of the American, British, Persian, Egyptian, Indian and other Bahá'í Communities to introduce the Faith into the remaining territories and neighbouring islands of the African continent. The upcoming Ten Year Crusade should witness, he wrote, the erection of three National Spiritual Assemblies on the African continent, the purchase of land for three Mashriqu'l-Adhkárs, the opening of 33 virgin territories and islands, the translation and publication of Bahá'í literature into 31 African languages, the consolidation of 24 territories already opened to the Faith, the establishment of a National Bahá'í Court in Cairo, the incorporation of the three Regional National Spiritual Assemblies, the establishment of National Bahá'í Endowments and three Ḥazíratu'l-Quds, the formation of a National Bahá'í Publishing Trust in Cairo and an Israel Branch of the National Spiritual Assembly of the Bahá'ís of Egypt and Súdán, and the appointment of nine members to the newly constituted Auxiliary Board.

Enoch responded to the Guardian's appeal to open the 33 territories. In August of 1953, he left behind his job, family and home, and set out across the continent for British Cameroon. There he was the mainspring of astonishing growth in the Cause of God in the immediate years ahead. Summarized in a letter to Músá Banání written on 15 February 1957, the Guardian through his secretary highlighted his triumphs:

> "Enoch Olinga has achieved many victories for the Faith; first in his work in Uganda; then by pioneering in the British Cameroons, becoming a Knight of Bahá'u'lláh there. Five of his spiritual children went from the Cameroons, to virgin areas of the Ten Year Crusade, thus becoming themselves, Knights of Bahá'u'lláh. He himself has confirmed 300 souls, with five Assemblies. The Guardian considers this unique in the history of the Crusade, in both the East and West; and he has blessed the one who so selflessly served, and won these victories for the Cause of God, by naming him 'Abu'l-Futúḥ', the "Father of Victories". The Guardian felt you and Ali would be pleased to know this, as he was Ali's spiritual child."[859]

After the passing of the Guardian, Rúḥíyyih Khánum had erected over his resting-place 'A single marble column, crowned by a Corinthian capital . . . surmounted by a globe, the map of Africa facing forward . . .'[860] due to the victories won in Africa which had brought him such joy in the last year of his life.

* * *

In 1971 the writer chanced to accompany a group of believers from Dallas, Texas to Jackson, Mississippi to hear Mr Olinga. In the days immediately preceding their departure, he pondered on the significance of the Guardian's appointing this youngest Hand of the Cause the Father of Victories. At the opening of the conference, Mr Olinga, as a way of greeting the friends, asked to know from where the attendees had journeyed. When he discovered that the writer's group had journeyed 500 miles - farther than anyone else attending - he made a fuss by inviting us to approach his presence. Then he proceeded to greet each one of us with a hug and a kiss. The writer remembers the overwhelming effect of that embrace, which was like sending one's soul into paradise. Afterward he realized that the spiritual force Mr Olinga possessed was what "fathered" many victories. Years later when he was on pilgrimage in 1997, he was also embraced by Mr 'Alí Nakhjavání and experienced a similar paradisiacal condition.

When Enoch and his immediate family were killed by unknown assassins in September 1979, their deaths had a tremendous effect on the believers to arise and teach in the memory of the Hand of the Cause and his family. The genesis of this effect may be seen in the message from the Universal House of Justice read at the funeral:

> ". . . HIS RADIANT SPIRIT HIS UNWAVERING FAITH HIS ALL-EMBRACING LOVE HIS LEONINE AUDACITY IN THE TEACHING FIELD HIS TITLES KNIGHT BAHAULLAH FATHER VICTORIES CONFERRED BELOVED GUARDIAN ALL COMBINE DISTINGUISH HIM AS PREEMINENT MEMBER HIS RACE IN ANNALS FAITH AFRICAN CONTINENT. URGE FRIENDS EVERYWHERE HOLD MEMORIAL GATHERINGS BEFITTING TRIBUTE HIS IMPERISHABLE MEMORY."[861]

* * *

Iran Furútan Muhájir described her husband as '. . . the initiator of mass teaching projects.' In 1961 Dr Muhájir went to India where Bahá'ís numbered 850. Meeting with the NSA, he emphasized mass teaching. So profound was his influence that by 1963 the number of believers had increased to 65,000.[862]

* * *

Ibn-i-Aṣdaq travelled throughout many parts of Persia in service to the Cause of God. He was married to a princess who was also a devoted believer, and this marriage enabled him to teach influential people who could in turn alleviate the sufferings of the believers. Bahá'u'lláh revealed the following well-known Tablet in his honour:

> "The movement itself from place to place, when undertaken for the sake of God, hath always exerted, and can now exert, its influence in the world."[863]

* * *

'Abu'l-Qásim Faizi travelled with two small suitcases. In one he kept an extra shirt, underwear, socks and gifts of perfumes or colognes to give away. In the other he kept his stationery: coloured pencils, paper, envelopes, ink and special thin cane pens with which he would write down some Holy Writings and letters in his beautiful Persian calligraphy to the friends. The second suitcase was the most important to him. [864]

* * *

At the 1953 Intercontinental Conference in Chicago in which 12 Hands of the Cause were present, Valíyu'lláh Varqá told the audience how the Greatest Holy Leaf asked his brother, Rúḥu'lláh about his activity in Persia. The eight year old boy replied that he was teaching. When Bahíyyih Khánum asked him about his method of teaching, Rúḥu'lláh replied that he only taught perceptive persons.

As two sons of Bahá'u'lláh were present, she asked him whether these sons were perceptive. Approaching them Rúḥu'lláh, after looking closely into their eyes, replied: 'They are not worth looking into.' Interestingly these brothers later broke the Covenant.[865]

* * *

> ***Whoso ariseth among you to teach the Cause of his Lord, let him, before all else, teach his own self, that his speech may attract the hearts of them that hear him. Unless he teacheth his own self, the words of his mouth will not influence the heart of the seeker.*** [866]

Ellen Virginia Tuller was an outspoken advocate of women participating side by side with men in church and community service work. Her stance was not well received in a Victorian society or by those who understood the Apostle Paul to prefer silence in women. Energetically she involved herself in prison reform, showed interest in the advancement of women and participated in the Temperance League. After her marriage to a young newspaperman, Joseph Beecher, in 1866 who she met while working in the New York slums, she became disillusioned with her inability to make any real difference correcting injustices as well as her painful life with a husband whose passion for causes contributed to in-harmony in their home.

Unhappy she longed for release from her tormented world. One night, however, she fell asleep in the home of some friends where she often went for solace. She dreamed of . . .

> ". . . a Glorious Man, robed in white and wearing a white turban. I dare not attempt to describe the majesty of that Presence. The moment I saw him, he extended his hands to me. 'I know that you long to die,' he said with exceeding gentleness. 'You may go with me now if you wish.' The room seemed suddenly flooded with light. How I longed to arise and go with him! Then he spoke again, telling me that although I might make my choice as I willed, a great blessing lay in my remaining here of my own volition, and that all things would be made plain to me. My soul cried out to go, yet immediately my desire to be obedient to this Shining Person obliterated all other desire. Joy filled my being as I acquiesced to the things he had spoken."[867]

Decades of search would pass ere Ellen Beecher would at last find her Beloved. Through a Persian rug dealer around the turn of the century did she hear something of Bahá'u'lláh. She attended Bahá'í meetings and came across a picture of 'Abdu'l-Bahá Who she recognized as the Glorious Man in her dream so many years ago. All of her life she had believed that she was living in the time foretold in the Lord's Prayer. Now, in the Bahá'í Faith, Ellen was confirmed in her belief.

From 1897 Ellen would receive at least 10 Tablets from 'Abdu'l-Bahá. She was still not sure what the blessing predicted in her dream as a young woman meant, but supposed the meaning lay in service to the Cause of God. And so for the remaining 30 years of her life she would travel extensively, assist local Bahá'í communities and teach Bahá'u'lláh's message of unity. Through her influence she became affectionately known as *Mother Beecher* by the American believers.

In 1912 an incident occurred which would forever link her own spiritual destiny with that of her granddaughter, Dorothy Beecher: 'Abdu'l-Bahá charged her to train Dorothy and said she was His own daughter. In coming years Mother Beecher wrote to and fretted over her young charge. In 1917 she was writing about her teaching experiences in Canada, about the joy of closeness to God, about mingling with the people, about *shining from within*.[868] For her part Dorothy was intuitively rooted in living a spiritual life even though her Bahá'í life for some years to come would be tended as something apart from her regular one. She might appreciate her grandmother's admonishments. But school and profession followed by marriage and children required her fuller attention.

In 1928 Ellen Beecher came to Lima, Ohio for her annual visit with Dorothy and her growing family. Dorothy, who realized that her grandmother – now 88 – appeared too fragile to continue travelling, invited Mother Beecher with husband Frank's concurrence to settle in with the family. Delighted, this early itinerant teacher who had not had a real home for many years accepted the invitation. Now she would have first-hand opportunity to encourage her granddaughter into active Bahá'í service, and so together with Ruth Moffett began a prayer campaign to this end.

By 1929 grandmother and granddaughter were studying the writings every day. Occasionally they prayed the Tablet of Aḥmad for 19 days. Gradually Dorothy's Bahá'í life developed as the wings of her spirit unfolded. Her family noticed she studied more intensely, sitting on the floor with books which she marked, indexed and organized. In 1932 Ellen Beecher, age 92, broke her brittle hip bone. Ten days later she passed from this world, having succeeded in training her beloved granddaughter to be a steadfast Bahá'í.

Not long after her grandmother's passing in August, 1932, Dorothy was confronted by the challenge of preparing for a Bahá'í fireside. Frank had invited a group to their home to hear Dorothy speak on religion. Over the next four days, she spent some 30 hours preparing for the fireside. The meeting must have been successful. It led to two study groups and the formation by 2 February 1933 of a Bahá'í community in Lima consisting of 18 members. Dorothy was spending from 20 to 40 hours a week in order to prepare herself for these classes. By the following year the Lima community could account for 29 active believers.

From 1934 Dorothy was addressing groups outside Lima. Her star rose steadily until it literally embraced the whole of mankind. She became known as the most outstanding Bahá'í speaker of her generation. She often said that 'Nothing worth knowing is attained without labor, tremendous effort, and undivided attention.'[869] As a near perfect student of the Bahá'í teachings, she overflowed with the Revelation of Bahá'u'lláh such that she gave out *thoughts that breathe.*[870] Whether speaking before small or large groups, she was eloquent, persuasive, sincere and dedicated. An early believer recalled the impression Dorothy made in Foundation Hall in 1929:

> "Her first talk before the public was given in Foundation Hall of the Temple, probably about 1929, at a Riḍván Feast. I shall never forget how the friends rejoiced in her "arising," as they called it; in fact she was surrounded, both before and after this talk, and one could hear the comments about the attainment of Mother Beecher's granddaughter. It produced a profound sensation because most of the friends did not know that Dorothy had become (among all the young people) one of the best informed on the Bahá'í Teachings. From that time on, the evolution of this Bahá'í speaker was rapid, phenomenal. She was wanted everywhere."[871]

* * *

> ***There is no paradise more wondrous for any soul than to be exposed to God's Manifestation in His Day, to hear His verses and believe in them . . .*** [872]

Martha Root once said: 'If you want to give the Message to anyone, love them, and if you love them, they will listen . . .' She felt that 'we live in moments, not in years.' Every meeting was to her an occasion. 'Give something always,' she would say, 'if only a flower, some candy, or fruit. Pray that they will accept from you the Greater Gift.'[873]

* * *

In 1996 while in Portugal, Rúḥýyih Khánum said:

> "Everyone has opportunities in some way, however humbly or of any age, to share the Message of Bahá'u'lláh. I remember in the Writings to seize opportunity for it comes but once. Life is very precious and short, relatively speaking. My idea of hell is to look back on my life in this world and see what I didn't do."[874]

* * *

John Robarts, whose profession was the insurance business, had this to say about teaching: 'We have the world's most difficult product to sell. But we have what no other salesman or product has: the promised assistance of God!'[875] He continually encouraged the believers to attract confirmations by teaching. This way others will join in, even the disaffected. The one remedy for all our ills is teaching. Mr Robarts emphasized:

> "One thing is that wherever there are Bahá'ís there are people waiting, ready to accept Bahá'u'lláh, to give their love and life to Him. We are surrounded by these devoted seekers. God will guide us to them, or them to us, if we will turn to Him in that greater intensity of devotion."[876]

* * *

Enoch Olinga reportedly told some believers that there are many Bahá'ís in the world today who have not been informed of Bahá'u'lláh. When we are sincere, we will be led to them. Believe in Bahá'u'lláh, surrender yourself to the Divine Will, trust in Bahá'u'lláh and go out. He will lead you to those Bahá'ís.

* * *

Abu'l-Qásim Faizi wisely suggested that the friends in their firesides must first allow their contacts to empty themselves. Once this occurs the contact can be taught. Ask that person by what standard he/she accepted Moses, Jesus, Muḥammad, etc., as a Prophet of God. If a follower of Christ is faithful to the books, he will acknowledge that the only standard laid down by Christ was that you will know (the Prophets) by their fruits. The Prophets are all giving the same standard.

Moses was asked how we can distinguish a Prophet from a false prophet. He replied that you cannot have grapes from thistles. Muḥammad said that the word of God is like a tree which bears fruit. Bahá'u'lláh taught that the word of God grows and influences the world. When a Prophet of God says something, His word is creative. '. . . people will follow it whether they know it or not. Willingly, or unwillingly, the people will apply the rules of the Prophet.'[877]

Even if the contacts of the Bahá'í teachers do not reply to the question of standards for awhile, they must have patience. He continued:

> ". . . I have learned this from many of our old, old teachers of the Cause. You know, they would talk to someone about this

> problem, and after one month of talking, the person would go from one subject to another, and the teacher would patiently listen to him, and after all the weeks and days, he will say, 'All right, what you said is interesting. We will come back to it. But I want to know what are the standards by which you know the Prophet . . .?' He would return again and again to the same subject, until some sort of awakening appeared in the mind of the contact.'"[878]

* * *

Ugo Giachery once sent this letter relating to the brevity of life and the mission entrusted to the Bahá'ís:

> "There is yet no one, who has not reached my advanced age, that can justly evaluate the speed of time and the impelling necessity to hasten the propagation of the regenerating Teachings of Bahá'u'lláh's Revelation. Youth in general believe that there is a magnitude of time ahead of them . . . the grown ups . . . feel that the little efforts they can make are sufficient to appease the Creator and silence their conscience. Centuries are passing as fast as the twinkling of an eye, and very often human beings leave this contingent world suddenly, without having accomplished, in whole or in part, what was a divine mandate at the time of their birth . . ."[879]

* * *

William Sears sometimes called out in a thunderous voice which shook the room and the hearts of the believers when he felt the Bahá'ís not rising to their true potential:

> "Night hath succeeded day, and day hath succeeded night, and the hours and moments of your lives have come and gone, and yet none of you hath, for one instant, consented to detach himself from that which perisheth. Bestir yourselves, that the brief moments that are still yours may not be dissipated and lost. Even as the swiftness of lightening your days shall pass, and your bodies shall be laid to rest beneath a canopy of dust. What can ye then achieve? How can ye atone for your past failure?"[880]

# # #

Endnotes

[1] 'Abdu'l-Bahá, *Foundations of World Unity,* p. 101.
[2] 'Abdu'l-Bahá, *Will and Testament,* p. 10.
[3] Bahá'u'lláh, *Proclamation,* p. 91.
[4] Universal House of Justice, *Messages,* p. 197.
[5] Bahá'u'lláh, *Hidden Words,* Arabic #30.
[6] *Bahá'í World,* vol. 13, p. 333.
[7] Shoghi Effendi, *Messages to the Bahá'í World,* p. 122.
[8] ibid. p. 127.
[9] *Bahá'í World,* vol. 13, pp. 342, 346.
[10] *Bahá'í World,* vol. 18, p. 526.
[11] Universal House of Justice, *Messages,* p. 132.
[12] 'Abdu'l-Bahá, *Will and Testament,* p. 3.
[13] Universal House of Justice, *Eulogy to Hand of the Cause Dr 'Alí-Muḥammad Varqá,* 09.23.07.
[14] 'Abdu'l-Bahá, *Will and Testament,* p. 13.
[15] Ṭaherzadeh, *Revelation of Bahá'u'lláh,* vol. 4, pp. 278, 283.
[16] ibid. p. 296.
[17] 'Abdu'l-Bahá, quoted in Ṭaherzadeh, *Revelation of Bahá'u'lláh,* vol. 4, p. 285.
[18] 'Abdu'l-Bahá, quoted in Hornby, *Lights of Guidance,* #1079.
[19] Olinga, *Enoch Olinga,* a video presentation.
[20] Bahá'u'lláh, quoted in Hornby, *Lights of Guidance,* #1080.
[21] Shoghi Effendi, *Messages to the Bahá'í World,* p. 153.
[22] Bahá'u'lláh, *Gleanings,* p. 287.
[23] Bahá'u'lláh, *Hidden Words,* Persian #56.
[24] Bahá'u'lláh, *Gleanings,* p. 265.
[25] McKay, *Fires in Many Hearts,* p. 31.
[26] ibid. p. 32.
[27] Rabbani, *Pioneering, Challenge to Bahá'í Youth,* a recorded talk.
[28] Bahá'u'lláh, *Hidden Words,* Arabic # 27, 26.
[29] Macias, *Conqueror of Hearts,* Hawaii Seminar, p. 17.
[30] ibid. p. 45.
[31] 'Abdu'l-Bahá, *Selections,* pp. 230-1.
[32] Horace Holley, quoted in *Bahá'í News,* August 1963, p.1.
[33] Hornby, *Lights of Guidance,* #305.
[34] Furútan, *Mothers, Fathers and Children,* p. 195.
[35] ibid. p. 197.
[36] Bahá'u'lláh, *Gleanings,* p. 160.
[37] Rabbani, *Priceless Pearl,* p. 238.

[38] *Bahá'í World,* vol. 12, p. 658.
[39] ibid.
[40] Rabbani, *Priceless Pearl,* p. 154.
[41] Giachery, *Shoghi Effendi,* p. 64.
[42] Sura LXIX, v17 from the *Qur'án,* quoted in Giachery, *Shoghi Effendi,* p. 83.
[43] *Films of the Hand of the Cause of God A.Q. Faizi.*
[44] Giachery, *Shoghi Effendi,* Appendix IX, pp. 214-5.
[45] ibid. p. 83.
[46] Shoghi Effendi, *This Decisive Hour,* p. 96.
[47] Shoghi Effendi, *Messages of Shoghi Effendi to the Indian Subcontinent,* p. 357.
[48] ibid.
[49] *Bahá'í World,* vol. 12, p. 657.
[50] Giachery, *Shoghi Effendi,* p. 93.
[51] *The New Freewoman,* September 1913, #6.
[52] 'Abdu'l-Bahá, *Selections,* pp. 146-7.
[53] Khadem, *Zikrullah Khadem,* p. 26.
[54] Nakhjavání, *Tribute,* pp. 51-2.
[55] Roy Williams, quoted in Morrison, *To Move the World,* p. 94.
[56] Harper, *Lights of Fortitude,* p. 57.
[57] Notes of Harold and Florence Fitzner.
[58] The Universal House of Justice, quoted by Rúḥíyyih Khánum, in a letter to the author, 1989.
[59] Bahá'u'lláh, *Tablets,* p. 156.
[60] 'Abdu'l-Bahá, *Selections,* p. 206.
[61] Bahá'u'lláh, *Hidden Words,* Arabic #46, quoted by Faizi in Macias, *Conqueror of Hearts,* Hawaii Seminar, p. 19.
[62] Macias, ibid.
[63] ibid.
[64] 'Abdu'l-Bahá, quoted in Hofman, *George Townshend,* revised, p. 50.
[65] Hofman, *George Townshend,* revised, p. 98.
[66] From a letter written on behalf of Shoghi Effendi, 28 October 1925, quoted in Hofman, ibid.
[67] Shoghi Effendi, partially quoted in Hofman, ibid. p. 109.
[68] Hofman, ibid. pp. 151-2; also some editing of this quote by Mr Hofman for this book.
[69] ibid. p. 101.
[70] ibid. p. 100.
[71] ibid. p. 139.
[72] ibid. p. 151.
[73] ibid.
[74] From a letter written on behalf of Shoghi Effendi, 23 November 1928, quoted in Hofman, ibid. p. 103.
[75] Shoghi Effendi, quoted in Hofman, ibid. p. 152.
[76] Shoghi Effendi, quoted in Hofman, ibid. p. 132.

[77] Shoghi Effendi, quoted in Hofman, ibid. p. 131.
[78] From a letter written on behalf of Shoghi Effendi, 5 October 1946, quoted in Hofman, ibid. p. 101.
[79] Hofman, ibid. pp. 6- 7.
[80] Shoghi Effendi, quoted in Hofman, ibid. p. 187.
[81] *Act Now Newsletter,* #62.
[82] *Ministry of the Custodians,* p. 10.
[83] ibid.
[84] Butler, *An Illustrated History of the Gestapo,* p. 38.
[85] ibid. p. 9.
[86] Pfaff-Grossmann translated this paragraph for the author from her book, *Hand der Sache Gottes Hermann Grossmann - ein Leben für den Glauben.*
[87] *Bahá'í World,* vol. 10, p. 22.
[88] Hartmut Grossmann translated these paragraphs for the author from Susanne Pfaff-Grossmann's book, ibid.
[89] *Bahá'í World,* vol. 20, p. 789.
[90] Shoghi Effendi, quoted in Ruhe-Schoen, *Love Which Does Not Wait,* p. 156.
[91] *Bahá'í World,* vol. 16, p. 68.
[92] *Bahá'í World,* vol. 5, pp. 57 & 59.
[93] 'Alí-Akbar Furútan, quoted in *Tribute to Hand of the Cause Shua Alai,* a video presentation.
[94] 'Abdu'l-Bahá, Tablets, vol. 2, p. 303.
[95] Mullá Riḍa, quoted in Ṭaherzadeh, *Revelation of Bahá'u'lláh,* vol. 1, p. 87.
[96] Mullá Riḍa, quoted in ibid., p. 88.
[97] Mullá Ṣádiq, quoted in Balyuzi, *Eminent Bahá'ís,* pp. 14.
[98] Ibn-i-Abhar, quoted in Ṭaherzadeh, *Revelation of Bahá'u'lláh,* vol. 4, pp. 308.
[99] 'Abdu'l-Bahá, quoted in Ṭaherzadeh, ibid. p. 307.
[100] 'Abdu'l-Bahá, *Promulgation of Universal Peace,* p. 190.
[101] An interview with Hand of the Cause Dr 'Alí-Muḥammad Varqá, 1990.
[102] Dr 'Alí-Muḥammad Varqá, in a letter to the author, 2003.
[103] Shoghi Effendi, *Letters from the Guardian to Australia and New Zealand 1923-1957,* p. 17.
[104] Harper, *Lights of Fortitude,* p. 181.
[105] Nakhjavání, *Tribute,* p. 71.
[106] *Dr. John E. Esslemont,* pp. 2, 3, 6-7.
[107] Marguerite Sears, in a letter to the author, 1992.
[108] McKay, *Fires in Many Hearts,* p. 265.
[109] Notes of Harold and Florence Fitzner.
[110] *Bahá'í World,* vol. 12, p. 664.
[111] *Bahá'í World,* vol. 10, pp. 518-9.
[112] ibid. pp. 519-20.
[113] Tinnion, *John A.. Robarts Memorial Article,* pp. 2-3.
[114] *Bahá'í World,* vol. 18, p. 643.

[115] ibid. p. 644.
[116] *Bahá'í World,* vol. 11, p. 501.
[117] Bahá'u'lláh, *Gleanings,* p. 289.
[118] 'Alí Na<u>kh</u>javání, quoted in Freeman, *Copper to Gold,* p. 269.
[119] Morrison, *To Move the World,* pp. 115-6.
[120] Rabbani, *Priceless Pearl,* p. 118.
[121] ibid. p. 121.
[122] 'Abdu'l-Bahá, *Selections,* p. 214.
[123] Sears, *Significance of Covenant-breaking,* a taped recoding.
[124] Chapman, *Leroy Ioas,* pp. 67-8.
[125] 'Abdu'l-Bahá, quoted in Ṭaherzadeh, *Child of the Covenant,* p. 238.
[126] Rúḥíyyih <u>Kh</u>ánum, quoted by John Robarts in a talk at the 1958 Intercontinental Conference in Wilmette.
[127] 'Abdu'l-Bahá, *Will and Testament,* p. 13.
[128] Charles Mason Remey, quoted in Stockman, *Bahá'í Faith in America,* vol. 2, p. 152.
[129] *Bahá'í World,* vol. 3, pp. 168-9. Also in volumes 2 and 4.
[130] 'Abdu'l-Bahá, *Tablets,* vol. 2, p. 459.
[131] ibid.
[132] 'Abdu'l-Bahá, *Will and Testament,* p. 11.
[133] ibid. p. 12.
[134] *Ministry of the Custodians,* pp. 35-6.
[135] 'Abdu'l-Bahá, *Will and Testament,* p. 12.
[136] Universal House of Justice, *Wellspring of Guidance,* p. 11.
[137] Bahá'u'lláh, quoted by the Supreme Body in Ṭaherzadeh, *Child of the Covenant,* pp. 360-1. Also see Bahá'u'lláh, *The Kitáb-i-Aqdas,* pp. 34-5.
[138] Ṭaherzadeh, ibid. pp. 361.
[139] ibid. pp. 361-2.
[140] *Ministry of the Custodians,* p. 16.
[141] ibid. p. 197.
[142] 'Abdu'l-Bahá, *Will and Testament,* p. 14.
[143] *Ministry of the Custodians,* p. 210.
[144] Letter from the Universal House of Justice to an individual believer, *Covenant-Breaking and the Hands,* 4 June 1997.
[145] ibid.
[146] Shoghi Effendi, *Messages to America,* p. 51.
[147] Shoghi Effendi, *Principles of Bahá'í Administration,* p. 26.
[148] The Universal House of Justice, *Messages,* p. 271.
[149] The Universal House of Justice, *Mason Remey and Those Who Followed Him,* p. 2.
[150] 'Abdu'l-Bahá, *Will and Testament,* p. 20.
[151] Bahá'u'lláh, *Covenant of Bahá'u'lláh,* pp. 134, 137-8.
[152] Shoghi Effendi, *Messages to the Bahá'í World,* p. 123.
[153] 'Abdu'l-Bahá, quoted by the Universal House of Justice *Mason Remey and Those Who Followed Him,* p.1.
[154] ibid.

[155] ibid. Also found in *Bahá'í World Faith,* pp. 357-8.
[156] Macias, *Conqueror of Hearts,* Hawaii Seminar, p. 23.
[157] *Ministry of the Custodians,* pp. 235-6.
[158] Dr. Yúnis Khán quoting 'Abdu'l-Bahá in Ṭaherzadeh, *Child of the Covenant,* p. 242.
[159] Muhajir, *Dr. Muhajir,* p. 648.
[160] Bahá'u'lláh, *Hidden Words,* Arabic #36.
[161] Macias, *Conqueror of Hearts,* Hawaii Seminar, p. 18.
[162] ibid. p. 19.
[163] ibid.
[164] Harper, *Lights of Fortitude,* p. 469-70.
[165] *Bahá'í World,* vol. 9, p. 931.
[166] 'Abdu'l-Bahá, *Promulgation of Universal Peace,* p. 218.
[167] *Bahá'í World,* vol. 18, pp. 626-7.
[168] Robarts, *Audrey Robarts Speaking about John A. Robarts.*
[169] *Bahá'í World,* vol. 20, p. 807.
[170] Morrison, *To Move the World,* p. 70.
[171] ibid. p. 89.
[172] *Bahá'í World,* vol. 20, p. 800.
[173] Sears, *God Loves Laughter,* pp. 52-4.
[174] *Films of Hand of the Cause A.Q. Faizi*
[175] Muhájir, *Dr. Muhajir,* p. 659.
[176] Hofman, *George Townshend,* revised, p. 221.
[177] Ḥájí Ákhúnd, quoted in Balyuzi, *Eminent Bahá'ís,* p. 105.
[178] Mullá Riḍá, quoted in ibid, pp. 105-6.
[179] Leroy Ioas, quoted in McKay, *Fires in Many Hearts,* p. 135.
[180] Balyuzi, *'Abdu'l-Bahá,* pp. 347.
[181] Garis, *Martha Root,* p. 368.
[182] Rabbani, *Priceless Pearl,* p. 103.
[183] Shoghi Effendi, quoted in ibid. p. 102.
[184] Howard Gail, quoted in Root, *Ṭáhirih The Pure,* p. 14.
[185] Gail, *Other People, Other Places,* p. 36.
[186] *Bahá'í World,* vol. 13, p. 858.
[187] Featherstone and Waterman, *The Dunns - Keys to Their Success,* p. 5.
[188] Freeman, *Copper to Gold,* revised, pp. 303-4.
[189] Hornby, *Lights of Guidance,* #120.
[190] *Films of Hand of the Cause A.Q. Faizi.*
[191] Shomais Afnan, an article provided the author, 2003.
[192] A taped recording of Mr Kházeh speaking in Arlington, Texas, 1974.
[193] ibid.
[194] Shoghi Effendi, quoted in ibid.
[195] Louis Gregory, quoted in Freeman, *Copper to Gold,* p. 132.
[196] Louis Gregory, quoted in McKay, *Fires in Many Hearts,* p. 97.
[197] *Bahá'í World,* vol. 15, p. 423.
[198] Leroy Ioas, quoted in Freeman, *Copper to Gold,* p. 257.

[199] *Bahá'í World,* vol. 18, p. 626.
[200] *Bahá'í World,* vol. 12, p. 661.
[201] Shoghi Effendi, quoted in Khadem, *Zikrullah Khadem,* p. 47.
[202] Interview with Mrs Javidukht Khadem, 2000.
[203] ibid.
[204] ibid.
[205] ibid.
[206] ibid.
[207] Freeman, *Copper to Gold,* pp. 255, 257.
[208] *Ministry of the Custodians,* p. 4.
[209] Muhájir, *Dr Muhajir,* p. 80.
[210] *Ministry of the Custodians,* p. 4.
[211] Horace Holley, quoted in Whitehead, *Some Bahá'ís to Remember,* p. 241.
[212] Rutstein, *Corinne True,* p. 203.
[213] Mayberry, *Great Adventure,* p. 131.
[214] Featherstone and Waterman, *The Dunns - Keys to Their Success,* p. 5.
[215] *Bahá'í World,* vol. 20, p. 814.
[216] Shoghi Effendi, quoted in *The Vision of Shoghi Effendi,* p. 176.
[217] Músá Banání, quoted in Robarts, *Letter to Bahá'ís,* p. 9.
[218] Shoghi Effendi, *Unfolding Destiny,* p. 486.
[219] Nabíl-i-Akbar, quoted in Ṭaherzadeh, *Revelation of Bahá'u'lláh,* vol. 1, pp. 93-4.
[220] 'Abdu'l-Bahá, *Memorials of the Faithful,* pp. 4-5.
[221] 'Abdu'l-Bahá, *Paris Talks,* pp. 179-180.
[222] 'Alí-Muḥammad Varqá, the martyr, quoted in Balyuzi, *Eminent Bahá'ís,* p. 75.
[223] Faizi, *Milly,* pp. 21-2.
[224] Shoghi Effendi, quoted in Whitehead, *Portraits of Some Bahá'í Women,* pp. 87-8.
[225] Faizi, *Milly,* p. 18.
[226] Rabbani, *Priceless Pearl,* p. 149.
[227] Collins, *Tribute to Shoghi Effendi,* a transcribed talk, 1958.
[228] *Bahá'í World,* vol. 11, p. 501.
[229] John Robarts, quoted in *The Vision of Shoghi Effendi,* p. 171.
[230] Douglas Martin, quoted in ibid. p. 176.
[231] John Robarts, quoted in ibid. p. 177.
[232] Tinnion, *John A. Robarts Memorial Article,* p. 32.
[233] *Bahá'í World,* vol. 4, p. 522.
[234] Shirley Macias, an article written for the author, 2002.
[235] 'Abdu'l-Bahá, *Selections,* p. 3.
[236] Unknown, in a letter to the author about Emma Adams, 1988.
[237] *'Abdu'l-Bahá in London,* p. 68.
[238] Morrison, *To Move the World,* pp. 135-8, 140-1, 167-71.
[239] Zikrullah Khadem, quoted in *The Vision of Shoghi Effendi,* p. 122.
[240] Tinnion, *John A. Robarts Memorial Article,* p. 62.
[241] Nancy Coker, in an email to the author, 1998.
[242] 'Abdu'l-Bahá, *Paris Talks,* p. 80.

[243] Giachery, *Closing remarks at Intercontinental Conference in Wilmette*, a taped recording, 1958.
[244] *Bahá'í World*, vol. 18, pp. 641-2.
[245] ibid. p. 642.
[246] Brigitte Ferraby Beales, an article written for the author, 2003.
[247] *Bahá'í World*, vol. 16, p. 512.
[248] Shoghi Effendi, *Dawn of a New Day*, p. 61.
[249] Bahá'u'lláh, *Kitáb-i-Aqdas*, p. 35.
[250] Shoghi Effendi, *Messages to the Bahá'í World*, p. 127.
[251] *Ministry of the Custodians*, pp. 9, 11-21.
[252] The Universal House of Justice, *Wellspring of Guidance*, p. 45.
[253] Ṭaherzadeh, *Child of the Covenant*, pp. 368-9.
[254] Bahá'u'lláh, *Hidden Words*, Persian #40.
[255] Bahá'u'lláh, *Gleanings*, p. 289.
[256] Bahá'u'lláh, *Hidden Words*, Persian #62.
[257] ibid. #71.
[258] Macias, *Conqueror of Hearts*, Hawaii Seminar, p. 13.
[259] Bahá'u'lláh, *Gleanings*, p. 88.
[260] Rutstein, *He Loved and Served*, p. 27.
[261] Rabbani, *Priceless Pearl*, p. 160.
[262] See Bahá'u'lláh, *Gleanings*, p. 95.
[263] See *Lights of Guidance*, #541.
[264] See *Lights of Guidance*, #534.
[265] Rúḥíyyih Khánum, *Pioneering, Challenge to Bahá'í Youth*, a taped recording, 1970.
[266] Nakhjavání, *Great African Safari*, p. 537.
[267] Orval Minney, in a letter to the author, 1998.
[268] 'Abdu'l-Bahá, *Tablets*, vol. 3, p. 552.
[269] Khadem, *Sacrifice*, a taped talk provided the author by Roger Coe.
[270] Shoghi Effendi, *World Order of Bahá'u'lláh*, p. 108; cited by Khadem, ibid.
[271] McKay, *Fires in Many Hearts*, p. 147.
[272] Shoghi Effendi, *God Passes By*, p. 308.
[273] ibid. p. 344.
[274] Rabbani, *Priceless Pearl*, p. 101.
[275] ibid. p. 103.
[276] ibid. p. 106.
[277] ibid. p. 107.
[278] Shoghi Effendi, *God Passes By*, p. 388.
[279] Ruhe-Schoen, *Love Which Does Not Wait*, p. 150.
[280] ibid.
[281] Shoghi Effendi, quoted in ibid., p. 154.
[282] *Bahá'í World*, vol. 5, p. 91.
[283] ibid. p. 409.
[284] ibid. p. 26.
[285] Shoghi Effendi, *Advent of Divine Justice*, p. 71.

[286] Rutstein, *Corinne True*, p. 21.
[287] 'Abdu'l-Bahá, *Tablets of 'Abdu'l-Bahá Abbas*, vol. 1, pp. 85-6; quoted in Rutstein, ibid. p. 27.
[288] 'Abdu'l-Bahá, *Selections*, p. 164; quoted in Rutstein, ibid. p. 38.
[289] 'Abdu'l-Bahá, *Tablets*, vol. 1, p. 99; quoted in Rutstein, ibid. pp. 50-1.
[290] Rutstein, ibid. pp. 94-5.
[291] ibid. p. 109.
[292] Shoghi Effendi, quoted in Rutstein, ibid. p. 200.
[293] 'Abdu'l-Bahá, *Memorials of the Faithful*, pp. 3-4.
[294] Hofman, *George Townshend*, revised, p. 27.
[295] ibid. p. 39.
[296] ibid.
[297] 'Abdu'l-Bahá, quoted in ibid. p. 50.
[298] ibid. p. 94.
[299] Featherstone and Waterman, *The Dunns - Keys to Their Success*, p. 4.
[300] *Bahá'í World*, vol. 13, p. 859.
[301] Whitehead, *Some Bahá'ís to Remember*, p. 161.
[302] ibid.
[303] Featherstone and Waterman, *The Dunns - Keys to Their Success*, p.6.
[304] *Bahá'í World*, vol. 6, p. 96.
[305] ibid. pp. 100-1.
[306] ibid. p. 102.
[307] ibid.
[308] ibid.
[309] *Bahá'í World*, vol. 14, p. 248.
[310] Bahá'u'lláh, *Epistle to Son of the Wolf*, p. 114.
[311] 'Abdu'l-Bahá, *Memorials of the Faithful*, p. 11.
[312] Ḥájí Á<u>kh</u>únd, quoted in Ṭaherzadeh, *Revelation of Bahá'u'lláh*, vol. 4, pp. 322-3.
[313] Muhájir, *Dr. Muhajir*, p. 75.
[314] Alexander, *Personal Recollections*, p. 5.
[315] *Bahá'í World*, vol. 15, p. 425.
[316] ibid.
[317] Alexander, *Personal Recollections*, p. 4.
[318] ibid. p. 5.
[319] ibid. p. 7.
[320] ibid. p. 8.
[321] ibid. p. 10.
[322] ibid.
[323] ibid.
[324] ibid.
[325] ibid. p. 12.
[326] Alexander, *MY ONLY DESIRE*, a taped recording, 1980.
[327] Alexander, *Bahá'í Faith in Japan*, p. 8.
[328] ibid. p. 21.
[329] ibid. p. 23.

[330] *Bahá'í World,* vol. 15, p. 427.
[331] Alexander, *Personal Recollections,* p. 7.
[332] *Bahá'í World,* vol. 15, p. 424.
[333] *John 3:7.*
[334] 'Abdu'l-Bahá, quoted in Alexander, *Personal Recollections,* p. 9.
[335] 'Abdu'l-Bahá, *Tablets of the Divine Plan,* pp. 13-14.
[336] Alexander, *Personal Recollections,* p. 24.
[337] Alexander, *MY ONLY DESIRE,* a taped recording, 1980.
[338] 'Abdu'l-Bahá, quoted in Alexander, *Personal Recollections,* p. 24.
[339] Shoghi Effendi, quoted in Alexander, *Bahá'í Faith in Japan,* p. 8.
[340] 'Abdu'l-Bahá, quoted in Alexander, *Personal Recollections,* pp. 24-5.
[341] Alexander, *Bahá'í Faith in Japan,* p. 10.
[342] ibid. p. 14.
[343] ibid.
[344] 'Abdu'l-Bahá, quoted in *Japan Will Turn Ablaze,* p. 6.
[345] Shoghi Effendi, quoted in ibid. p. 51.
[346] Donald Witzel, an article written for the author, 2003.
[347] Ian Semple, in a letter to the author, 2003.
[348] *Bahá'í World,* vol. 15, p. 429.
[349] Bahá'u'lláh, *Tablets,* p. 37.
[350] Sharp, *Shu'á'u'lláh 'Alá'í, Hand of the Cause of God,* 1995, p. 9.
[351] *In Memoriam, Shu'á'u'lláh 'Alá'í - 1889-1984,* p.4.
[352] ibid.
[353] *Tribute to Hand of the Cause Shua Alai,* a video presentation.
[354] *Bahá'í World,* vol. 19, p. 595.
[355] Hornby, *Lights of Guidance,* #447.
[356] Macias, *Conqueror of Hearts,* Memories, p. 26.
[357] Macias, ibid., Hawaii Seminar, pp. 27-8.
[358] 'Abdu'l-Bahá, quoted in ibid.' p. 28.
[359] Macias, ibid.
[360] Chapman, *Leroy Ioas,* p. 89.
[361] Hofman, *George Townshend,* revised, p. 230.
[362] Townshend, *Christ and Bahá'u'lláh,* pp. 54-5.
[363] *John 8:35.*
[364] Townshend, *Christ and Bahá'u'lláh,* p. 55.
[365] Holley, *Annual Bahá'í Convention,* a taped recording, 1954.
[366] Bahá'u'lláh, *Prayers and Meditations,* p. 82.
[367] Haney, *Hand of the Cause of God Paul Haney at Falls Church, VA,* a taped recording, 1982.
[368] Louis Gregory, quoted in Alexander, *Bahá'í Faith in Japan,* p. 50.
[369] Sims, *Traces That Remain,* pp. 68-70.
[370] Alexander, *Bahá'í Faith in Japan,* p. 34.
[371] *Bahá'í World,* vol. 14, pp. 229-230.
[372] ibid. p. 230.
[373] ibid. p. 248.

[374] ibid. p. 232.
[375] Giachery, *Closing Talk at the Intercontinental Conference in Wilmette,* a taped recording, 1958.
[376] Keith Ransom-Kehler, quoted in McKay, *Fires in Many Hearts,* p. 52.
[377] Bahá'u'lláh, *Hidden Words,* Persian, #44.
[378] Rabbani, *Poems of the Passing,* p. 26.
[379] Balyuzi, *Eminent Bahá'ís,* p. 23.
[380] 'Abdu'l-Bahá, *Memorials of the Faithful,* pp. 7-8.
[381] Freeman, *Copper to Gold,* p. 311.
[382] Olinga, *Enoch Olinga,* a video presentation, 2000.
[383] ibid.
[384] Muhájir, *Dr. Muhajir,* p. 643.
[385] *Star of the West,* vol. 1, no. 3, pp. 5-6.
[386] 'Abdu'l-Bahá, *Selections,* p. 76.
[387] *El Ruisenor,* May 1992, p. 1.
[388] *Bahá'í World,* vol. 20, p. 800.
[389] Bahá'u'lláh, *Tablets,* p. 196.
[390] Shoghi Effendi, quoted in Hofman, *George Townshend,* revised, p. 92.
[391] Mozhan Khadem, quoted in Khadem, *Zikrullah Khadem,* pp. 175-6.
[392] Muṣṭafáy-i-Rúmí, quoted in Khadem, *Zikrullah Khadem,* p. 112.
[393] Amín Banání, quoted in *Vision of Shoghi Effendi,* p. 177.
[394] Roy Wilhelm, quoting 'Abdu'l-Bahá in Randall-Winckler, *William Henry Randall,* p. 214.
[395] Bahá'u'lláh, *Hidden Words,* Persian #75.
[396] Nakhjavání, *The Great African Safari,* pp. 534-7.
[397] From a letter written by Abu'l-Qásim Faizi dated 8 September 1978 in answer to some questions asked him by Mary Gregory and provided by her to the author, 1998.
[398] *Bahá'í World,* vol. 8, p. 183.
[399] Bahíyyih Khánum, p. 125.
[400] *Bahá'í World,* vol. 13, p. 220.
[401] Rabbani, *Poems of the Passing,* p. 76.
[402] Giachery, *Shoghi Effendi,* p. 175.
[403] ibid.
[404] Chapman, *Leroy Ioas,* p. 274.
[405] ibid. p. 285.
[406] *Bahá'í World,* vol. 13, p. 840.
[407] *Bahá'í World,* vol. 18, p. 664.
[408] Khadem, *Zikrullah Khadem,* pp. 118-9.
[409] ibid. p. 119.
[410] Furútan, *Story of My Heart,* p. 127.
[411] *Bahá'í World,* vol. 13, pp. 218, 220.
[412] Rutstein, *Corinne True,* p. 212.
[413] Muhájir, *Dr. Muhajir,* p. 81.

[414] ibid.
[415] *Bahá'í World*, vol. 15, p. 423.
[416] *Bahá'í World*, vol. 20, p. 797.
[417] *Bahá'í World*, vol. 13, p. 223.
[418] Giachery, *Shoghi Effendi*, pp. 180-1.
[419] ibid. p. 181.
[420] ibid. pp. 181-2.
[421] Khadem, *Zikrullah Khadem*, p. 119.
[422] 'Abdu'l-Bahá, *Tablets*, vol. 2, pp. 317-8.
[423] Rabbani, *Manual for Pioneers*, p. 5.
[424] Hofman, *George Townshend*, revised, p. 208.
[425] Khadem, *Zikrullah Khadem*, p. 7.
[426] ibid.
[427] Freeman, *Copper to Gold*, p. 147.
[428] Moffett, *Du'á: On Wings of Prayer*, p. 27.
[429] Shoghi Effendi, quoted in Moffett, ibid.
[430] ibid.
[431] Garis, *Martha Root*, p. 236.
[432] Rabbani, *Priceless Pearl*, p. 102.
[433] Robarts, *Letter to Bahá'ís*, p. 1.
[434] Bahá'u'lláh, quoted in Robarts, ibid. See *Gleanings*, p. 280.
[435] 'Abdu'l-Bahá, quoted in Robarts, ibid., See *Bahá'í World Faith*, p. 385.
[436] *Bahá'í World*, vol. 9, p. 595.
[437] Alexander, *Bahá'í Faith in Japan*, p. 8.
[438] Featherstone and Waterman, *The Dunns - Keys to Their Success*, p. 5.
[439] Furútan, *Story of My Heart.*
[440] Muhájir, *Dr. Muhajir*, pp. 36-7.
[441] Statement of Research Department of Universal House of Justice, 29 August 2001.
[442] 'Abdu'l-Bahá, quoted in Alexander, *Bahá'í Faith in Japan*, p. 65.
[443] Sims, *Traces That Remain*, p. 62.
[444] *Bahá'í World*, vol. 15, p. 427.
[445] Rutstein, *He Loved and Served*, pp. 24-6.
[446] Haney, *Hand of the Cause of God Paul Haney at Falls Church, VA.*, a taped recording, 1982.
[447] Rabbani, *The Guardian*, p. 58.
[448] *Matthew 7:7.*
[449] *Bahá'í World*, vol. 12, p. 663.
[450] Samandarí, *Moments with Bahá'u'lláh*, pp. 60-1.
[451] *Bahá'í World*, vol. 2, p. 132.
[452] Ruhe-Schoen, *Love Which Does Not Wait*, p. 132.
[453] *Bahá'í World*, vol. 12, p. 674.
[454] Sears, *Reminiscences*, pp. 11-13.
[455] Levy, referring to Freeman, *Copper to Gold*, p. 301.

[456] Levy, quoting Giachery, *Shoghi Effendi,* p. 198.
[457] ibid.
[458] Levy, citing Giachery, ibid. cover.
[459] Levy, citing *Bahá'í World,* vol. 13, p. 385.
[460] *Bahá'í World,* vol. 18, p. 719.
[461] Levy, see article on p. 155 of this book, citing *Bahá'í World*, vol. 12, Levy: 'Original map printed by Casetti in Rome. Annexed in pocket cover . . .' 'See "CONTENTS – PART ONE", page vii, paragraph VII, Inside Front Cover . . .' for Maps of the Ten Year Plan, one of three of which was the original one conceived and drawn by the beloved Guardian and entrusted to Ben Levy for delivery to Ugo Giachery (But see inside cover *Bahá'í World*, vol. 13).
[462] Ben Levy, an article written for the author, 2002.
[463] Ḥájí Amín, quoted in Khadem, *Zikrullah Khadem,* p. 9.
[464] 'Abdu'l-Bahá, *Tablets,* vol. 3, p. 692.
[465] Freeman, *Copper to Gold,* p. 264.
[466] ibid.
[467] Martha Root, quoted in McKay, *Fires in Many Hearts,* p. 178.
[468] ibid.
[469] Freeman, *Copper to Gold,* revised, pp. 251-2.
[470] Dorothy Baker, quoted in this paragraph by McKay, *Fires in Many Hearts,* pp. 265, 267.
[471] Khadem, *Zikrullah Khadem,* p. 32.
[472] ibid.
[473] A general email from Cyril Tirandaz, forwarded to the writer by Eric Harper, 1998.
[474] Macias, *Conqueror of Hearts,* Australia, p. 5.
[475] ibid.
[476] Hornby, *Lights of Guidance,* #1845.
[477] Robarts, *Letter to Bahá'ís,* p. 1.
[478] ibid.
[479] Robarts, *Audrey Robarts Speaking about John A. Robarts.*
[480] Khadem, *A Myserious Power in This Cause,* a taped recording.
[481] *To Follow a Dreamtime,* p. 18.
[482] A prayer of Bahá'u'lláh used by Louis Gregory, quoted in McKay, *Fires in Many Hearts,* p. 182.
[483] 'Abdu'l-Bahá, *Divine Philosophy,* p. 168.
[484] Marguerite Sears, in a letter to the author, 2000.
[485] See *Basic Bahá'í Chronology.*
[486] Garis, *To Move the World,* pp. 4, 110, 186, 198.
[487] Research Department of the Universal House of Justice in a letter to the author, 2002.
[488] Ross Woodman, from an article provided the author by Audrey Robarts, 1995.

[489] Sears, *All Flags Flying,* p. 285.
[490] ibid. p. 289.
[491] Balyuzi, *Eminent Bahá'ís,* p. 263.
[492] ibid. p. 173.
[493] ibid. p. 96.
[494] ibid. p. 268.
[495] Ṭaherzadeh, *Revelation of Bahá'u'lláh,* vol. 4, p. 314.
[496] *Bahá'í World,* vol. 15, p. 426.
[497] ibid. p. 582.
[498] *Bahá'í World,* vol. 13, p. 849.
[499] Harper, *Lights of Fortitude,* pp. 293-4.
[500] Morrison, *To Move the World,* p. 72.
[501] *Bahá'í World,* vol. 16, p. 75.
[502] *To Follow a Dreamtime,* p. 4.
[503] *Bahá'í World,* vol. 13, p. 854.
[504] *Bahá'í World,* vol. 14, p. 292.
[505] *Bahá'í World,* vol. 6, p. 580.
[506] Garis, *Martha Root,* p. 312.
[507] ibid. p. 362.
[508] ibid. p. 390.
[509] ibid.
[510] ibid. p. 407.
[511] ibid. p. 406.
[512] ibid. p. 392.
[513] ibid. p. 400.
[514] Shoghi Effendi, *Messages to America,* p. 3.
[515] *Bahá'í World,* vol. 13, p. 837.
[516] Rabbani, *Priceless Pearl,* pp. 258-9.
[517] Sears, *All Flags Flying,* p. 286.
[518] Freeman, *Copper to Gold,* revised, p. 303.
[519] *Bahá'í World,* vol. 12, p. 67.
[520] *Bahá'í World,* vol. 18, pp. 621-2.
[521] Muhájir, *Dr. Muhajir,* p. 51.
[522] *Bahá'í World,* vol. 13, p. 449.
[523] Stockman, *Bahá'í Faith in America,* vol. 2, p. 291.
[524] *Star of the West,* vol. 13, p. 221.
[525] Charles Mason Remey's model of Mt Carmel Temple can be seen in *Bahá'í World,* vol. 12, p. 548. On his pilgrimage in 1997, the writer asked Leslie Ṭaherzadeh, wife of Adib Ṭaherzadeh, whether CMR's design, in view of his having broken the Covenant, would still be used as the model from which to build the Temple on Mt Carmel. She did not know.
[526] The Universal House of Justice in a letter to the National Spiritual Assembly of the Bahá'ís of the United Kingdom, 19 November 1996.

[527] Nabíl-i-A'ẓam, *Dawn-Breakers,* p. 586.
[528] Mullá Ḥusayn, quoted in Nabíl-i-A'ẓam, *Dawn-Breakers,* p. 100.
[529] Mullá Ṣádiq, quoted in ibid. pp. 100-1.
[530] Tinnion, *John A. Robarts Memorial Article,* p. 5.
[531] *Bahá'í World,* vol. 15, p. 417.
[532] *Bahá'í World,* vol. 9, p. 593.
[533] *To Follow a Dreamtime,* p. 1.
[534] ibid.
[535] *Bahá'í World,* vol. 13, p. 859; *To Follow a Dreamtime,* pp. 1-2.
[536] Balyuzi, *Eminent Bahá'ís,* p. 113.
[537] *Bahá'í World,* vol. 15, pp. 421-2.
[538] Freeman, *Copper to Gold,* p. 313.
[539] ibid. p. 10.
[540] *Bahá'í World,* vol. 18, pp. 621-2; Olinga, *Enoch Olinga,* a video presentation.
[541] Hofman, *George Townshend,* revised, p. 19.
[542] May Maxwell, quoted in Nakhjavání, *The Great African Safari,* p. 294.
[543] William Sutherland Maxwell, quoted in ibid.
[544] *Bahá'í World,* vol. 12, p. 658.
[545] ibid.
[546] *Bahá'í World,* vol. 20, pp. 809-10.
[547] Sears, *God Loves Laughter,* pp. 23, 25.
[548] ibid. p. 127.
[549] ibid. p. 141.
[550] The Báb, *Selections,* p. 77.
[551] Bahá'u'lláh, *Hidden Words,* Persian #39.
[552] Contributors to this article among Margaret's and Ross's children: Don Letbetter, Gilbert and Donja Murray, Barbara Taylor, and Barron Harper.
[553] Morrison, *To Move the World,* p. 23.
[554] Niagara Movement's "Declaration of Principles", quoted in Morrison, ibid.
[555] Morrison, ibid. p. 4.
[556] Harper, *Lights of Fortitude,* pp. 100, 147, 158, 169, 287-8; *Bahá'í World News Service,* 9 May 2003.
[557] *Bahá'í World,* vol. 9, p. 597.
[558] Marguerite Sears, in a letter to the author, 2000.
[559] Harper, *Lights of Fortitude,* p. 3.
[560] Balyuzi, *Eminent Bahá'ís,* p. 272; Harper, ibid. p. 17.
[561] *To Follow a Dreamtime,* p. 1; Stockman, *Bahá'í Faith in America,* vol. 2, p. 195.
[562] *Bahá'í World,* vol. 20, p. 849; Harper, *Lights of Fortitude,* p. 441.
[563] Garis, *Martha Root,* p. 40.
[564] Roy Wilhelm, cited in Garis, ibid. pp. 40-1.
[565] Garis, ibid. p. 41.
[566] Roy Wilhelm, quoted in ibid. p. 494.

[567] Madge Feathertone, in a letter to Mother Dunn, 1952.
[568] National Spiritual Assembly of Hawaii, *Victory Promises,* p. 5.
[569] Freeman, *Copper to Gold,* revised, p. 146.
[570] Freeman, *Copper to Gold,* p. 263.
[571] *Bahá'í World,* vol. 12, p. 661.
[572] Nakhjavání, *The Great African Safari,* pp. 387-8.
[573] ibid. p. 208.
[574] *Bahá'í World,* vol. 20, p. 787.
[575] Olinga, *Enoch Olinga,* a video presentation, 2000.
[576] Rutstein, *Corinne True,* p. 22.
[577] ibid. p. 103.
[578] Bahá'u'lláh, paraphrased by Faizi in Macias, *Conqueror of Hearts,* Hawaii Seminar, p. 64.
[579] ibid.
[580] ibid. pp. 50-1.
[581] 'Abdu'l-Bahá, *Selections,* p. 186.
[582] Enoch Olinga, *Are You Happy?,* a recorded talk, 1980.
[583] The Báb, quoted in National Spiritual Assembly of Hawaii, *Victory Promises,* p. 7.
[584] Bahá'u'lláh, quoted in ibid. p. 9.
[585] ibid. p. 10.
[586] 'Abdu'l-Bahá, *Tablets,* vol. 2, p. 387.
[587] Marguerite Sears, in a letter to the author, 1992.
[588] Chapman, *Leroy Ioas,* p. 64.
[589] Robarts, *Audrey Robarts Speaking about John A. Robarts.*
[590] Tinnion, *John A. Robarts Memorial Article,* p. 30.
[591] ibid. p. 10.
[592] McKay, *Fires in Many Hearts,* p. 58.
[593] Bahá'u'lláh, *Epistle to Son of the Wolf,* p. 14.
[594] Sears, *All Flags Flying,* pp. 287-8.
[595] Rúḥíyyih Khánum, quoted in Nakhjavání, *The Great African Safari,* p. 481.
[596] ibid. p. 482.
[597] Furútan, *Story of My Heart,* p. 75.
[598] Varqá, the martyr, recalling the words of Bahá'u'lláh in Ṭaherzadeh, *Revelation of Bahá'u'lláh,* vol. 4, p. 56.
[599] Hartmut Grossmann, an article written for the author, 2002.
[600] Olinga, *Enoch Olinga, a video presentation,* 2000.
[601] Hornby, *Lights of Guidance,* #2139.
[602] Muhájir, *Dr. Muhajir,* p. 15.
[603] *Bahá'í World,* vol. 20, p. 796.
[604] Garis, *Martha Root,* p. 88.
[605] *Bahá'í World,* vol. 20, p. 804.
[606] Nakhjavání, *Tribute,* p. 67.
[607] Ruhe-Schoen, *Love Which Does Not Wait,* p. 157.

[608] Shoghi Effendi, *God Passes By*, p. 308.
[609] *Bahá'í World*, vol. 13, p. 839.
[610] Bijan Khadem-Missagh, as told to the author, 2003.
[611] Shoghi Effendi, *Principles of Bahá'í Administration*, p. 1.
[612] *Ministry of the Custodians*, p. 321.
[613] 'Abdu'l-Bahá, quoted in Chapman, *Leroy Ioas*, p. 330.
[614] *Bahá'í World*, vol. 14, p. 427.
[615] ibid. p. 429.
[616] *Ministry of the Custodians*, pp. 425-6.
[617] Robarts, *Audrey Robarts Speaking about John A. Robarts.*
[618] *Bahá'í World*, vol. 12, pp. 146-7.
[619] *Bahá'í World*, vol. 14, p. 76.
[620] ibid.
[621] Paul Vreeland, in response to questions addressed to his mother, Claire Vreeland, 2002.
[622] Sophie Loeding, *Bahá'í News* #645, December 1984, p. 8. Article was first published in *Bahá'í News*, December 1974 issue, according to Bud Humphrey, editor at *American Bahá'í.*
[623] *Bahá'í World*, vol. 18, p 641.
[624] *Developing Distinctive Bahá'í Communities*, 10.3.
[625] *Bahá'í World*, vol. 13, p. 837.
[626] Harper, *Lights of Fortitude*, p. 205.
[627] Whitmore, *Dawning Place*, p. 132.
[628] *Bahá'í World*, vol. 12, p. 664.
[629] *Bahá'í News* #226, December 1949, p. 11; cited in *For the Celebration of My Praise*, p. 26.
[630] *Bahá'í World*, vol. 12, p. 146.
[631] ibid.
[632] Mullá Riḍá, quoted in Ṭaherzadeh, *Revelation of Bahá'u'lláh*, vol. 1, p. 90.
[633] Macias, *Conqueror of Hearts, Hawaii Seminar*, p. 21.
[634] Shoghi Effendi, *Messages to the Bahá'í World*, p. 48.
[635] *Ḥuqúqu'lláh Compilation*, p. 2.
[636] Bahá'u'lláh, quoted in Ṭaherzadeh, *Revelation of Bahá'u'lláh*, vol. 3, pp. 85-6.
[637] Research Department of the Universal House of Justice, *The Development of the Institution of Ḥuqúqu'lláh*, p. 2.
[638] 'Abdu'l-Bahá, *Memorials of the Faithful*, p. 86.
[639] ibid. p. 5.
[640] Shoghi Effendi, *The Light of Divine Guidance*, vol. 2, p. 114.
[641] Shoghi Effendi, *Messages to the Bahá'í World*, p. 174.
[642] Universal House of Justice, *Wider Horizon*, p. 92.
[643] Research Department of the Universal House of Justice, *The Development of the Institution of Ḥuqúqu'lláh*, p.5.
[644] ibid.

[645] Varqá, *Fundamentals,* pp. 2-5.
[646] Khadem, *Implementation of Ḥuqúqu'lláh in the West,* a transcribed talk, p. 2.
[647] 'Abdu'l-Bahá, quoted in Khadem, ibid.
[648] 'Alí Nakhjavání, in a letter to the author confirming this story, 2002.
[649] Universal House of Justice, *Riḍván Message 2000.*
[650] George Townshend, quoted in Sears, *All Flags Flying,* p. 219.
[651] Furútan, *Story of My Heart,* p. 9.
[652] ibid. p. 25.
[653] ibid. p. 22.
[654] ibid. p. 35.
[655] Muhájir, *The Beloved Guardian's Promise,* a video presentation, 1990.
[656] *Bahá'í World,* vol. 12, p. 657.
[657] Muhájir, *The Beloved Guardian's Promise,* ibid.
[658] Furútan, *Story of My Heart,* p. 81.
[659] Furútan, *Mothers, Fathers and Children,* p. 8.
[660] ibid. p. 12.
[661] ibid. p. 13.
[662] Unknown author quoted in Furútan, ibid. p. 12.
[663] Universal House of Justice, *In Memoriam,* 2003.11.27.
[664] Hornby, *Lights of Guidance,* #489.
[665] *Bahá'í World,* vol. 18, p. 661.
[666] Hofman, *George Townshend,* revised, p. 223.
[667] Khadem, *Zikrullah Khadem,* pp. 21-2.
[668] 'Abdu'l-Bahá, *Secret of Divine Civilization,* p. 111.
[669] 'Alí-Akbar Furútan, in a letter to the author, 1993.
[670] Ṭaherzadeh, *Revelation of Bahá'u'lláh,* vol. 4, p. 312.
[671] Bahá'u'lláh, *Hidden Words,* Arabic #45.
[672] Baha'u'lláh, quoted in Balyuzi, *Eminent Bahá'ís,* pp. 81-2.
[673] Shoghi Effendi, *God Passes By,* p. 296.
[674] Ṭaherzadeh, *Revelation of Bahá'u'lláh,* vol. 4, p. 57.
[675] ibid.
[676] Garis, *Martha Root,* p. 54.
[677] 'Abdu'l-Bahá, quoted in a talk by 'Ali-Akbar Furútan, *Bahá'í World,* vol. 12, p. 175.
[678] *Bahá'í World,* vol. 12, p. 173.
[679] Bahá'u'lláh, quoted in Ṭaherzadeh, *Revelation of Bahá'u'lláh,* vol. 4, p. 303.
[680] Ṭaherzadeh, *Revelation of Bahá'u'lláh,* pp. 302-3; *Child of the Covenant,* p. 248.
[681] Ibn-i-Abhar, quoted in Ṭaherzadeh, ibid. p. 305.
[682] Ṭaherzadeh, ibid.
[683] ibid.
[684] *Bahá'í World,* vol. 15, p. 412.
[685] Garis, *Martha Root,* p. 350.
[686] Root, *Ṭáhirih The Pure,* p. 44.
[687] *Bahá'í World,* vol. 4, pp. 400, 403-4.

688 Balyuzi, *King of Glory*, pp. 131-3.
689 Shoghi Effendi, *God Passes By*, pp. 136-7.
690 Shoghi Effendi, *Messages to America*, p. 17.
691 *Bahá'í World*, vol. 12, p. 381.
692 Shoghi Effendi, quoted in Giachery, *Shoghi Effendi*, p. 79.
693 Giachery, ibid. p. 25.
694 *Bahá'í World*, vol. 14, p. 296.
695 Ugo Giachery, quoted in Chapman, *Leroy Ioas*, p. 232.
696 *Bahá'í World*, vol. 14, p. 291.
697 Muhájir, *Dr. Muhajir*, p. 662.
698 Shoghi Effendi, *Unfolding Destiny*, p. 436.
699 'Abdu'l-Bahá, quoted in Rutstein, *Corinne True*, p. 41.
700 ibid. p. 60.
701 Whitmore, *Dawning Place*, p. 36.
702 Corinne True, quoted in Whitmore, *Dawning Place*, p. 237.
703 ibid. p. 57.
704 ibid. p. 67.
705 ibid.
706 Rutstein, *Corinne True*, p. 111.
707 'Abdu'l-Bahá, quoted in ibid. p. 111.
708 Corinne True, quoted in Whitmore, *Dawning Place*, p. 69.
709 'Abdu'l-Bahá, quoted in Rutstein, *Corinne True*, p. 126.
710 Rutstein, ibid. p. 139.
711 'Abdu'l-Bahá, quoted in Rutstein, *Corinne True*, p. 149.
712 Shoghi Effendi, quoted in ibid. p. 177.
713 Edna True, quoted in Whitmore, *Dawning Place*, p. 231.
714 William Sears, quoted in Rutstein, *Corinne True*, p. 213.
715 Bahá'u'lláh, *Gleanings*, p. 334.
716 William Sears, quoted in *Quickeners of Mankind*, pp. 103-4.
717 John Robarts, quoted in ibid. pp. 102-3.
718 Muhájir, *Dr. Muhajir*, p. 73.
719 Bahá'u'lláh, quoted in Sears, *All Flags Flying*, p. 226.
720 Bahá'u'lláh, quoted in ibid. p 227.
721 Bahá'u'lláh, quoted in ibid. p. 228.
722 Bahá'u'lláh, quoted in ibid. pp. 228-9.
723 William Sears, quoted in *Quickeners of Mankind*, p. 103.
724 Sears, *Reminiscences*, p. 26.
725 *Bahá'í World*, vol. 12, p. 676.
726 Khadem, *Zikrullah Khadem*, p. 39.
727 *Bahá'í World*, vol. 12, pp. 184, 186.
728 Tinnion, *John A. Robarts Memorial Article*, p. 16.
729 Shoghi Effendi, quoted in ibid.
730 *Bahá'í World*, vol. 12, p. 182.
731 Shoghi Effendi, quoted in Tinnion, *John A. Robarts Memorial Article*, p. 17.

[732] Tinnion, ibid.
[733] Mandela, *Long Walk to Freedom,* p. 113.
[734] ibid. p. 149.
[735] Robarts, *Audrey Robarts Speaking about John A. Robarts,* 1995.
[736] Audrey Robarts, in a letter to the author, c. 1996.
[737] *Bahá'í World,* vol. 13, p. 289.
[738] Stanlake and Ditshane Kukama, quoted in Tinnion, *John A. Robarts Memorial Article,* p. 52.
[739] 'Abdu'l-Bahá, *Selections,* p. 234.
[740] Freeman, *Copper to Gold,* p. 313.
[741] ibid. p. 193.
[742] *Bahá'í World,* vol. 12, p. 673.
[743] *Bahá'í World,* vol. 18, p. 652.
[744] *Bahá'í World,* vol. 14, p. 78.
[745] *To Follow a Dreamtime,* p. 12.
[746] *Bahá'í World,* vol. 13, p. 862.
[747] Chapman, *Leroy Ioas,* p. 317.
[748] *Bahá'í World,* vol. 12, p. 175.
[749] Músá Banání, quoted in *Quickeners of Mankind,* p. 101.
[750] *Bahá'í World,* vol. 18, p. 718.
[751] Ugo Giachery, quoted in *Quickeners of Mankind,* p. 106.
[752] 'Alí-Muḥammad Varqá, quoted in *Quickeners of Mankind,* pp. 108-9.
[753] Rutstein, *Corinne True,* p. 166.
[754] *Bahá'í World,* vol. 5, p. 520.
[755] ibid.
[756] ibid p. 522.
[757] ibid. p. 520.
[758] ibid. p. 525.
[759] 'Abdu'l-Bahá, *Selections,* p. 269.
[760] *Bahá'í World,* vol. 14, p. 614.
[761] Sears, *The Prisoner and the Kings,* p. 189.
[762] ibid.
[763] 'Abdu'l-Bahá, quoted in Rutstein, *Corinne True,* p. 108.
[764] *Bahá'í World,* vol. 13, p. 848.
[765] Robarts, *Audrey Robarts Speaking about John A. Robarts,* 1995.
[766] *Bahá'í World,* vol. 13, p. 869.
[767] 'Abdu'l-Bahá, quoted in Gail, *Summon Up Remembrance,* p. 120.
[768] Dorothy Baker, quoted in McKay, *Fires in Many Hearts,* p. 39.
[769] Nakhjavání, *Tribute,* pp. 70-1.
[770] Rutstein, *He Loved and Served,* pp. 27-8; *Bahá'í World,* vol. 12, p. 662; Whitehead, *Some Early Bahá'ís of the West,* p. 87.
[771] Featherstone and Waterman, *The Dunns - Keys to Their Success,* p. 8.
[772] 'Abdu'l-Bahá, quoted in Samandarí, *Moments with Bahá'u'lláh,* p. 74.
[773] Bahá'u'lláh, *Tablets,* p.171.

[774] *Bahá'í World,* vol. 12, pp. 868-9.
[775] *Bahá'í World,* vol. 2, p. 232.
[776] *Bahá'í World,* vol. 11, p. 654.
[777] ibid. p. 656.
[778] Holley, *Religion for Mankind,* p. 169.
[779] ibid. p. 151.
[780] *Bahá'í World,* vol. 12, pp. 851-2.
[781] *Bahá'í World,* vol. 18, p. 651.
[782] Ibid. pp. 649-50.
[783] Momen, *Ḥasan M. Balyuzi,* pp. xvii-xviii.
[784] *Bahá'í World,* vol. 18, p. 649.
[785] ibid. p. 635.
[786] Balyuzi, *Eminent Bahá'ís,* p. 237.
[787] *Bahá'í World,* vol. 18, p. 665.
[788] Rabbani, *Priceless Pearl,* pp. 237-8.
[789] Shoghi Effendi, *Bahá'í Administration,* p. 98.
[790] ibid.
[791] Shoghi Effendi, quoted in Momen, *Dr. John E. Esslemont,* p. 10.
[792] *Bahá'í World,* vol. 8, p. 932.
[793] Shoghi Effendi, quoted in Momen, *Dr. John E Esslemont,* p. 27.
[794] *Bahá'í World,* vol. 9, p. 934.
[795] Momen, *Dr. John E. Esslemont,* pp. 37-8.
[796] Shoghi Effendi, *Unfolding Destiny,* p. 377.
[797] Hofman, *George Townshend,* revised, p. 241.
[798] ibid. p. 254.
[799] Khadem, *Zikrullah Khadem,* p. 61.
[800] *Bahá'í World,* vol. 20, p. 800.
[801] *Isaiah 9:6.*
[802] Sears, *Thief in the Night,* p. 123.
[803] *Micah 7:12.*
[804] Sears, *Cry From the Heart,* p. 2.
[805] Bahá'í World Centre Library, *Bahá'í reminiscences,* p. 1.
[806] Bahá'u'lláh, *Gleanings,* p. 330.
[807] *Bahá'í World,* vol. 5, p. 51.
[808] ibid. p. 52.
[809] ibid.
[810] ibid. p. 51.
[811] *Bahá'í World,* vol. 9, p. 598.
[812] Hornby, *Lights of Guidance,* #327.
[813] *Bahá'í World,* vol. 20, pp. 815-6.
[814] *Bahá'í World,* vol. 20, p. 786.
[815] ibid. p. 787.
[816] Shoghi Effendi, *Advent of Divine Justice,* p. 48.

[817] *To Follow a Dreamtime,* p. 3.
[818] 'Abdu'l-Bahá, *Tablets of the Divine Plan,* p. 13.
[819] 'Abdu'l-Bahá, quoted in *To Follow a Dreamtime,* p. 3.
[820] Harold and Florence Fitzner, quoted in Featherstone and Waterman, *The Dunns Keys to Their Success,* p. 7.
[821] ibid. p. 3.
[822] ibid. pp. 4-5.
[823] Shoghi Effendi, *Messages to the Antipodes,* p. 47.
[824] ibid. p. 51.
[825] ibid. p. 53.
[826] ibid. p. 54.
[827] ibid. p. 125.
[828] ibid. p. 152.
[829] ibid. p. 168.
[830] Shoghi Effendi, *God Passes By,* p. 308.
[831] Shoghi Effendi, *Messages to the Antipodes,* p. 323.
[832] ibid.
[833] Universal House of Justice, *Riḍván 153.*
[834] Shoghi Effendi, *Advent of Divine Justice,* p. 39.
[835] Robarts, *Audrey Robarts Speaking about John A. Robarts,* 1995.
[836] Former Counselor Donald Witzel, an article written for the author, 2002.
[837] William Sears, quoted in Chapman, *Leroy Ioas,* p. 81.
[838] *Bahá'í World,* vol. 15, p. 413.
[839] ibid. p. 414.
[840] ibid. p. 416.
[841] *Bahá'í World,* vol. 13, p. 877.
[842] ibid.
[843] Garis, *To Move the World,* p. 89.
[844] Shoghi Effendi, *Bahá'í Administration,* p. 69.
[845] Shoghi Effendi, quoted in Nakhjavání, *Tribute,* p. 67.
[846] Nakhjavání, ibid.
[847] Shoghi Effendi, quoted in Nakhjavání, ibid.
[848] *Bahá'í World,* vol. 15, p. 589.
[849] Shoghi Effendi, *God Passes By,* p. 386.
[850] ibid.
[851] ibid.
[852] ibid. pp. 387-8.
[853] Morrison, *To Move the World,* p. 7.
[854] *Bahá'í World,* vol. 12, p. 669.
[855] Marian Haney, quoted in Morrison, *To Move the World,* p. 117.
[856] Baker and Collins, *Because We Love the Faith,* a taped recording.
[857] *Bahá'í World,* vol. 12, p. 144.
[858] ibid. p. 121.

[859] *Baha'í World,* vol. 18, pp. 625-6.
[860] Rabbani, *Priceless Pearl,* p. 451.
[861] *Bahá'í World,* vol. 18, p. 634.
[862] Harper, *Lights of Fortitude,* p. 459 (article by Iran Furútan Muhájir).
[863] Shoghi Effendi, *Advent of Divine Justice,* p. 70; quoted in Ṭaherzadeh, *Revelation of Bahá'u'lláh,* vol. 4, p. 303.
[864] Fuad Izadinia, in an email to the author, 1998.
[865] Ṭaherzadeh, *Revelation of Bahá'u'lláh,* vol. 4, pp. 59-60.
[866] Bahá'u'lláh, *Gleanings,* p. 277.
[867] Freeman, *Copper to Gold, revised,* p. 19.
[868] ibid. p. 37.
[869] *Bahá'í World,* vol. 12, p. 671.
[870] ibid.
[871] ibid. p. 672.
[872] The Báb, *Selections,* p. 77.
[873] *Bahá'í News,* April 1976, p. 4.
[874] Author's notes.
[875] Robarts, *Letter to Bahá'ís.*
[876] ibid.
[877] Macias, *Conqueror of Hearts,* Australia Talk, p. 3.
[878] ibid.
[879] *Bahá'í World,* vol. 20, p. 782.
[880] Bahá'u'lláh, *Gleanings,* p. 321.

BIBLIOGRAPHY

'Abdu'l-Bahá. *Foundations of World Unity.* Wilmette, IL: Bahá'í Publishing Trust, 1945.
--- *Memorials of the Faithful.* Wilmette, IL.: Bahá'í Publishing Trust, 1971.
--- *Paris Talks.* London: Bahá'í Publishing Trust, 1969.
— *Promulgation of Universal Peace, The.* Wilmette, IL.: Bahá'í Publishing Trust, 1982.
--- *Secret of Divine Civilization, The.* Wilmette, IL.: Bahá'í Publishing Trust, 1970.
--- *Selections from the Writings of 'Abdu'l-Bahá.* Haifa: Bahá'í World Centre, 1978.
— *Tablets of Abdul-Baha Abbas.* New York: Bahá'í Publishing Committee, vol. 1, 1930.
— *Tablets of Abdul-Baha Abbas.* New York: Bahá'í Publishing Committee, vol. 2, 1940.
— *Tablets of Abdul-Baha Abbas,* New York: Bahá'í Publishing Committee, vol. 3, 1940.
---*Tablets of The Divine Plan.* Wilmette, IL.: Bahá'í Publishing Trust, 1959.
— *Will and Testament of 'Abdu'l-Bahá, The.* Wilmette, IL.: Bahá'í Publishing Trust, 1971.
'Abdu'l-Bahá in London - Addresses & Notes of Conversations. London: Bahá'í Publishing Trust, 1987.
Act Now Newsletter. European Bahá'í Youth Council, #62.
Alexander, Agnes. *History of the Bahá'í Faith in Japan 1914-1938.* Osaka: Bahá'í Publishing Trust, 1977.
--- *MY ONLY DESIRE . . . WAS TO SERVE HIS CAUSE, HAND OF THE CAUSE OF GOD AGNES ALEXANDER.* Wilmette, IL.: Bahá'í Publishing Trust, 1980.
--- *Personal Recollections of a Bahá'í Life in the Hawaiian Islands.* Honolulu: The National Spiritual Assembly of the Bahá'ís of the Hawaiian Islands, 1974.
Ayman, Iraj. *Significance of Sacrifice.* Setapak, Malaysia: Bahá'í Publishing Trust, 1985.
Báb, The. *Selections from the Writings of the Báb.* Haifa: Bahá'í World Centre, 1976.
Bahá'í News, The. National Spiritual Assembly of the United States. December 1949, August 1963, April 1976.
Bahá'í reminiscences. Washington, D.C., 1938. See Bahá'í World Centre Library.
Bahá'í World, The. vol. 2, 1925-54. reprint. Wilmette, IL.: Bahá'í Publishing Trust, 1980.
Bahá'í World, The. vol. 3, 1925-54. reprint. Wilmette, IL.: Bahá'í Publishing Trust,1980.
Bahá'í World, The. vol. 4, 1925-54. reprint. Wilmette, IL.: Bahá'í Publishing Trust, 1980.
Bahá'í World, The. vol. 5, 1925-54. reprint. Wilmette, IL.: Bahá'í Publishing Trust, 1980.
Bahá'í World, The. vol. 6, 1925-54. reprint. Wilmette, IL.: Bahá'í Publishing Trust, 1980.
Bahá'í World, The. vol. 8, 1925-54. reprint. Wilmette, IL.: Bahá'í Publishing Trust, 1980.
Bahá'í World, The. vol. 9, 1925-54. reprint. Wilmette, IL.: Bahá'í Publishing Trust, 1980.
Bahá'í World, The. vol. 10, 1925-54. reprint. Wilmette, IL.: Bahá'í Publishing Trust, 1980.
Bahá'í World, The. vol. 11, 1925-54. reprint. Wilmette, IL.: Bahá'í Publishing Trust, 1980.
Bahá'í World, The. vol. 12, 1925-54. reprint. Wilmette, IL.: Bahá'í Publishing Trust,1980.
Bahá'í World, The. vol. 13. Haifa: The Universal House of Justice, 1970.
Bahá'í World, The. vol. 14. Haifa: The Universal House of Justice, 1974.

Bahá'í World, The. vol. 15. Haifa: Bahá'í World Centre, 1976.
Bahá'í World, The. vol. 16. Haifa: Bahá'í World Centre, 1978.
Bahá'í World, The. vol. 18. Haifa: Bahá'í World Centre, 1986.
Bahá'í World, The. vol. 19. Haifa: Bahá'í World Centre, 1997.
Bahá'í World, The. vol. 20. Haifa: Bahá'í World Centre, 1998.
Bahá'í World Faith. Selected Writings of Bahá'u'lláh and 'Abdu'l-Bahá. Wilmette, IL.: Bahá'í Publishing Trust, 1956.
Bahá'u'lláh. *Covenant of Bahá'u'lláh, a compilation.* London: Bahá'í Publishing Trust, 1963.
--- *Epistle to the Son of the Wolf.* Wilmette, IL.: Bahá'í Publishing Trust, 1988.
--- *Gleanings from the Writings of Bahá'u'lláh.* Wilmette, IL.: Bahá'í Publishing Trust, 1983.
--- *Hidden Words, The.* Wilmette, IL.: Bahá'í Publishing Trust, 1990.
--- *Kitáb-i-Aqdas.* Haifa: Bahá'í World Centre, 1992.
--- *Prayer for Shaykh Kázim Samandar.* A provisional translation. Haifa: Bahá'í World Centre, 2001.
--- *Prayers and Meditations.* Wilmette, IL.: Bahá'í Publishing Trust, 1987.
--- *Proclamation of Bahá'u'lláh, The.* Haifa: Bahá'í World Centre, 1967.
--- *Tablets of Bahá'u'lláh revealed after the Kitáb-i-Aqdas.* Haifa: Bahá'í World Centre, 1978.
Bahá'í News, The. National Spiritual Assembly of the United States. August 1963, December 1984.
Bahíyyih Khánum. *Bahíyyih Khánum, The Greatest Holy Leaf: A Compilation from Bahá'í Sacred Texts and Writings of the Guardian of the Faith and Bahíyyih Khánum's Own Letters.* Haifa: Baháí World Centre, 1982.
Baker, Dorothy and Collins, Amelia. *Because We Love the Faith.* A taped recording. Wilmette, IL.: Bahá'í Publishing Trust, 1984.
Balyuzi, H.M. *'Abdu'l-Bahá, The Centre of the Covenant of Bahá'u'lláh.* Oxford: George Ronald, 1971.
--- *Bahá'u'lláh, The King of Glory.* Oxford: George Ronald, 1980.
--- *Eminent Bahá'ís in the Time of Bahá'u'lláh: with some Historical Background.* Oxford: George Ronald, 1985.
Beales, Brigitte Ferraby. *John Ferraby.* An article prepared for the author, 2003.
Butler, Rupert. *An Illustrated History of the Gestapo.* Osceola: MBI Publishing Company, 1992.
Cameron, Glen, and Momen, Wendi. *A Basic Bahá'í Chronology.* Oxford: George Ronald, 1996.
Chamberlain, Isabel Fraser. *Divine Philosophy.* Boston: The Tudor Press, 1918.
Chapman, Anita Ioas. *Leroy Ioas: Hand of the Cause of God.* Oxford: George Ronald, 1998.
Collins, Amelia. *A Tribute to Shoghi Effendi.* Wilmette, IL.: Bahá'í Publishing Trust, 1958.
Coker, Nancy. *Experience with 'Alí Muḥammad Varqá.* In an email to the author, 1998.

Developing Distinctive Bahá'í Communities: Guidelines for Spiritual Assemblies. Wilmette, IL.: Bahá'í Publishing Trust, 1989.

Development of the Institution of Ḥuqúqu'lláh. Prepared by the Research Department of the Universal House of Justice. March 1987, Revised April 2002.

El Ruisenor/The Nightingale. San Fernando: Casa Editora.

Esslemont, John. *Bahá'u'lláh and the New Era.* Wilmette, IL.: Bahá'í Publishing Trust, 1980.

Faizi, A.Q. *Milly: A Tribute to Amelia E. Collins.* Oxford: George Ronald, 1977.

Featherstone, Madge, and Waterman, Kaye. *The Dunns - Keys to Their Success.* Australia: The Association for Bahá'í Studies, 1996.

Featherstone, Madge. *Letter to Mother Dunn,* 1952.

Films of Hand of the Cause of God A. Q. Faizi. Spiritual Assembly of the Bahá'ís of San Francisco, 1975.

Fitzner, Harold and Florence. Notes about Hyde Dunn.

For the Celebration of My Praise. Wilmette, IL.: Bahá'í Publishing Trust, 2003.

Freeman, Dorothy. *From Copper to Gold.* Oxford: George Ronald, 1984.

--- *From Copper to Gold,* revised. Oxford: George Ronald, 1999.

Furútan, 'Alí-Akbar. *The Story of My Heart.* Oxford: George Ronald, 1984.

--- *Mothers, Fathers and Children. Practical Advice to Parents.* Oxford: George Ronald, 1980.

--- Letter to the author, 1993.

Gail, Marzieh. *Other People Other Places.* Oxford: George Ronald, 1982.

--- *Summon Up Remembrance.* Oxford: George Ronald, 1987.

Garis, M.R. *Martha Root: Lioness at the Threshold.* Wilmette, IL.: Bahá'í Publishing Trust, 1983.

Giachery, Ugo. *Shoghi Effendi: Recollections.* Oxford: George Ronald, 1973.

--- *Closing Talk by Ugo Giachery as the Guardian's representative at the 1958 Intercontinental Conference in Wilmette.* Provided to the writer by Roger Coe.

Gregory, Mary. From a letter written by Abu'l-Qásim Faizi, 8 September 1998.

Grossmann, Hartmut. *Hermann Grossmann.* An article prepared for the author, 2002.

Haney, Paul. *Hand of the Cause of God Paul Haney at Falls, Church, VA.* Belchertown: Images International, 1982.

Harper, Barron. *Lights of Fortitude.* Oxford: George Ronald, 1997.

Ḥaydar-'Alí, Ḥájí Mírzá. *Stories from the Delight of Hearts. The Memoirs of Ḥájí Mírzá Ḥaydar'Alí,* Los Angeles Kalimat Press, 1980.

Hofman, David. *George Townshend,* revised. Oxford: George Ronald, 1983.

Holley, Horace. *Religion for Mankind.* London: George Ronald, 1956.

--- A Talk by Horace Holley at the 1954 Annual Bahá'í Convention in which Mr Holley's reads the Guardian's message for the appointment of Auxiliary Boards. Provided to the author by

Roger Coe.
Holy Bible. King James Authorized Version. Cleveland and New York: The World Publishing Company.
Hornby, Lenen Bassett. *Lights of Guidance: A Bahá'í Reference File.* New Delhi: Bahá'í Publishing Trust, 1997.
Ḥuqúqu'lláh, The Right of God. Compiled by the Research Department of the Universal House of Justice. Oakham: Bahá'í Publishing Trust, 1986.
In Memoriam, Shu'a'u'llah Ala'i - 1889-1984. A synopsis provided to the author by Shomais Afnan.
Izadinia, Fuad. An email to the author, 1998.
Khadem, Javidukht. An interview with the author about Zikrullah Khadem, 2000.
--- *Zikrullah Khadem, The Itinerant Hand of the Cause of God.* Wilmette, IL.: Bahá'í Publishing Trust, 1990.
Khadem, Zikrullah. *Implementation of Ḥuqúqu'lláh in the West,* a transcribed talk.
--- *Mysterious Power in This Cause,* A taped recording at the 1980 Bahá'í National Convention. Wilmette, IL.: Bahá'í Publishing Trust, 1980.
--- *Sacrifice.* A taped recording provided to the author by Roger Coe.
Khadem-Missagh, Bijan. Memories of Dr Adelbert Mühlschlegel told to author, 2003.
K͟házeh, Jalál. A taped recording of Mr Kházeh speaking in Arlington, Texas, provided by Donald Witzel, 1974.
Koran, The. Translated from the Arabic by J.M. Rodwell, M.A. London: J.M. Dent & Sons Ltd.
Levy, Ben. *Dr Ugo Giachery.* An article written for the author, 2002.
Macias, Shirley. *Conqueror of Hearts. Excerpts from Letters, Talks and Writings of Hand of the Cause of God Abu'l-Qásim Faizí.* An unpublished compilation. Bahá'í Academics Resource Library, 2002.
--- *Abu'l-Qásim Faizi.* An article for the author, 2002.
Mandela, Nelson. *Long Walk to Freedom.* Boston, New York, London: Little, Brown and Company, 1994.
Mayberry, Florence. *The Great Adventure.* Canada: Canadian Cataloguing in Publishing Data, 1994.
McKay, Doris. *Fires in Many Hearts.* Manotick: Nine Pines Publishing, 1993.
Minney, Orville. Letter to author about Zikrullah Khadem, 1998.
Moffett, Ruth J. *Du'á on wings of prayer.* Naturegraph Publishers, 1984.
Momen, Moojan. *Ḥasan M. Balyuzi (1908-1980), A Bio-bibliographical Sketch.*
--- *Dr. John E. Esslemont, Hand of the Cause of God.* London: Bahá'í Publishing Trust, 1975.
Morrison, Gayle. *To Move the World.* Wilmette, IL.: Bahá'í Publishing Trust, 1982.
Ministry of the Custodians, The, 1957-1963: An Account of the Stewardship of the Hands of the Cause. Haifa: Bahá'í World Centre, 1992.
Muhajir, Irán Furútan. *Dr Muhajir, Hand of the Cause of God, Knight of*

Bahá'u'lláh. London: Bahá'í Publishing Trust, 1992.
--- *The Beloved Guardian's Promise.* A video presentation.
Nabíl-i-A'ẓam. *The Dawn-Breakers: Nabíl's Narrative of the Early Days of the Bahá'í Revelation.* Wilmette, IL.: Bahá'í Publishing Trust, 1970.
Nakhjavání, 'Alí. Letter to author about Músá Banání, 2002.
Nakhjavání, Violette. *The Great African Safari: The travels of Amatu'l-Bahá Rúḥíyyih Khánum in Africa, 1969-73.* Oxford: George Ronald, 2002.
--- *Tribute to Amatu'l-Bahá Rúḥíyyih Khánum, A.* Thornhill: Bahá'í Canada Publications and Nepean: Nine Pines Publishing, 2000.
New Freewoman, The. Edited by Ezra Pound, 1 September 1913.
Olinga, Enoch. *Are You Happy?* A recorded talk by Mr Olinga. Wilmette, IL.: Bahá'í Publishing Trust, 1980.
Olinga, Joyce. *Enoch Olinga. Knight of Bahá'u'lláh. Father of Victories. Hand of the Cause of God.* A video presentation of the life of Enoch Olinga. Wilmette, IL: Olinga Productions Associations, 2000.
Pfaff-Grossmann, Susanne. *Hand der Sache Gottes Hermann Grossmann - ein Leben für den Glauben.* Excerpts translated for author, c. 2003.
Pioneering in a World Community, Quickeners of Mankind. National Spiritual Assembly of the Bahá'ís of Canada, 1980.
Rabbani, Rúḥíyyih. *The Guardian of the Bahá'í Faith.* London: Bahá'í Publishing Trust, 1988.
--- *A Manual for Pioneers.* New Delhi: Bahá'í Publishing Trust, 1974.
--- *Pioneering: Challenge to Bahá'í Youth. The second of three talks by Hand of the Cause of God Rúḥíyyih Khánum at the National Bahá'í Youth Conference,* June 19-21, 1970. Wilmette, IL.: Bahá'í Publishing Trust, 1970.
--- *Poems of the Passing.* Oxford: George Ronald, 1996.
--- *The Priceless Pearl.* London: Bahá'í Publishing Trust, 1969.
Randall-Winckler, Bahíyyih, in collaboration with M.R. Garis. *William Henry Randall, Disciple of 'Abdu'l-Bahá.* Oxford, One World, 1996.
Robarts, Audrey. *A recording of Mrs Robarts speaking about John Robarts.* January-February 1995. Tapes 1, 2 and 3.
--- Letter to author, 1996.
Robarts, John A. *Letter to Bahá'ís.* Provided to the author by Mrs Audrey Robarts, 1995.
--- Talk at 1958 Intercontinental Conference in Wilmette.
Root, Martha. *Ṭáhirih The Pure. Introductory essay entitled "With Martha"* by Marzieh Gail. Los Angeles, CA: Kalimát Press, 1981.
Ruhe-Schoen, Janet. *A Love Which Does Not Wait.* Riviera Beach: Palabra Publications, 1998.
Rutstein, Nathan. *Corinne True: Faithful Handmaid of 'Abdu'l-Bahá.* Oxford: George Ronald, 1987.
--- *He Loved and Served: The Story of Curtis Kelsey.* Oxford: George Ronald, 1982.

Samandarí, Ṭarázu'lláh. *Moments with Bahá'u'lláh.* Los Angeles: Kalimát Press, 1995.
Sears, Marguerite. Letters to author, 1992, 2000.
Sears, William. *All Flags Flying.* Goodwood: National Spiritual Assembly of the Bahá'ís of South and West Africa, 1985.
--- *A Cry from the Heart: The Bahá'ís in Iran.* Oxford: George Ronald, 1982.
--- *God Loves Laughter.* Oxford: George Ronald, 1973.
--- *The Prisoner and the Kings.* Litho'd in Canada, 1969.
--- *Reminiscences.* Tucson, AZ: Betts Printing, 1999.
--- *The Significance of Covenant Breaking.* A taped recording of a study and deepening session. Wilmette, IL.: Bahá'í Publishing Trust.
--- *Thief in the Night.* Oxford: George Ronald, 1961, 1980.
Sharp, Priscilla Stone. *Shu'á'u'lláh 'Alá'í, Hand of the Cause of God* in Deepen Magazine, Spring '95.
Shoghi Effendi. *The Advent of Divine Justice.* Wilmette, IL.: Bahá'í Publishing Trust, 1990.
--- *Bahá'í Administration: Selected Messages 1922-1932.* Wilmette, IL.: Bahá'í Publishing Trust, 1974.
--- *Dawn of a New Day: Messages to India 1923-1957.* New Delhi: Bahá'í Publishing Trust, 1970.
--- *God Passes By.* Wilmette, IL.: Bahá'í Publishing Trust, revised edition. 1974.
--- *Letters to Australia and New Zealand.* Australia: Australian Baha'í Publishing Trust, 1971.
--- *The Light of Divine Guidance: The Messages from the Guardian of the Bahá'í Faith to the Bahá'ís of Germany and Austria.* 2 vols. Hofheim-Langenhain: Bahá'í-Verlag, 1982.
--- *Messages to America.* Wilmette, IL.: Bahá'í Publishing Trust, 1947.
--- *Messages to the Antipodes.* Maryborough: Australian Print Group, 1997.
--- *Messages to the Bahá'í World.* Wilmette, IL.: Bahá'í Publishing Trust, 1947.
--- *Messages of Shoghi Effendi to the Indian Subcontinent, 1923-1957.* New Delhi: Bahá'í Publishing Trust, 1995.
--- *Principles of Bahá'í Administration.* London: Bahá'í Publishing Trust, 1950.
--- *This Decisive Hour. Messages from Shoghi Effendi to the North American Bahá'ís, 1932-1946.* Wilmette, IL.: Bahá'í Publishing Trust, 2002.
--- *The Unfolding Destiny of the British Bahá'í Community: The Messages of the Guardian of the Bahá'í Faith to the Bahá'ís of the British Isles.* London: Bahá'í Publishing Trust, 1981.
--- *The World Order of Bahá'u'lláh: Selected Letters by Shoghi Effendi.* Wilmette, IL.: Bahá'í Publishing Trust, 1974.
Semple, Ian. Letter to author about Agnes Alexander, 2003.
Sims, Barbara. *Japan will turn Ablaze.* Japan: Bahá'í Publishing Trust, 1992.
--- *Traces that Remain.* Japan: Bahá'í Publishing Trust, 1989.
Star of the West. Reprint. Oxford: George Ronald, 1984.
Stockman, Robert. *The Bahá'í Faith in America, Early Expansion, 1900-*

1912, vol. 2. Oxford: George Ronald, 1995.

Ṭaherzadeh, Adib. *The Child of the Covenant.* Oxford: George Ronald, 2000.

--- *The Revelation of Bahá'u'lláh.* vol. 1. Oxford: George Ronald, 1974.

--- *The Revelation of Bahá'u'lláh,* vol. 2. Oxford: George Ronald, 1977.

--- *The Revelation of Bahá'u'lláh.* vol. 3. Oxford: George Ronald, 1983.

--- *The Revelation of Bahá'u'lláh.* vol. 4. Oxford: George Ronald, 1987.

Tinnion, Nina Roberts. *John A. Robarts memorial Article and Endnotes,* unpublished, 1995.

Tirandaz, Cyril. An email about 'Alí-Akbar Furútan, 1998.

To Follow a Dreamtime, 'Father' and 'Mother' Dunn, The Spiritual Conquerors of a Continent. Commemorating the Fiftieth Anniversary of the Arrival of the Bahá'í Faith in Australia, 18 April 1970. Paddington, New South Wales: The National Spiritual Assembly of the Bahá'ís of Australia, Inc., 1970.

Townshend, George. *Christ and Bahá'u'lláh.* Oxford: George Ronald, 1957.

Tribute to Hand of the Cause Shua Alai on the Tenth Year Anniversary of his Passing. A video presentation. Publisher unknown.

The Universal House of Justice. *A Wider Horizon, Selected Messages of the Universal House of Justice, 1983 - 1992.*

--- *Covenant-breaking and the Hands.* Letter to an individual believer, 4 June 1997.

--- *Eulogy to Hand of the Cause of God Dr 'Alí-Muḥammad Varqá,* 23 September 2007.

--- *In Memoriam.* 'Alí-Akbar Furútan, 27 November 2003.

--- Letter to author, 2002.

--- Letter to the National Spiritual Assembly of the United Kingdom, 19 November 1996.

--- *Mason Remey and Those Who Followed Him.* Provided to the author by Universal House of Justice member Mr Hushmand Fatheázam on his pilgrimage in February 1997.

--- *Messages from the Universal House of Justice 1963-1986.* Wilmette, IL: Bahá'í Publishing Trust, 1996.

--- *Riḍván Message.* Haifa: Bahá'í World Centre, 1997.

--- *Riḍván Message.* Haifa: Bahá'í World Centre, 2000.

--- Statement of Research Department, 2001.

--- *Wellspring of Guidance.* Wilmette, IL.: Bahá'í Publishing Trust, 1976.

The Vision of Shoghi Effendi. Ottawa: Bahá'í Studies Publications, 1993.

Varqá, 'Alí-Muḥammad. *Fundamentals, Hand of the Cause of God and Trustee of Ḥuqúqu'lláh 'Alí-Muḥammad Varqá On the elements of Ḥuqúqu'lláh.* Talk given at the Sixth International Convention on May 1, 1988.

--- An interview about Valíyu'lláh Varqá On the elements of Ḥuqúqu'lláh, 1990.

--- Letter to author about Valíyu'lláh Varqá, 2003.

Victory Promises. A compilation by the National Spiritual Assembly of the

Bahá'ís of the Hawaiian Islands, 1978.
Vreeland, Paul. Letter to the author about Horace Holley in response to questions addressed to Claire Vreeland, 2002.
Waterman, Graham and Kaye. *H. Collis Featherstone*. An 'In Memoriam' article in *Bahá'í World*, vol. 20, 1994.
Whitehead, O.Z. *Portraits of Some Bahá'í Women*. Oxford: George Ronald, 1996.
--- *Some Bahá'ís to Remember*. Oxford: George Ronald, 1983.
Whitmore, Bruce W. *The Dawning Place*. Wilmette, IL.: Bahá'í Publishing Trust, 1984.
Witzel, Donald. Unpublished Article about Dr Rahmat Muhájir, 2002.
--- Letter to author about Agnes Alexander, 2003.
Woodman, Ross. An Article about John Robarts, offered to author by Audrey Robarts, 1995.

Origins

n. Nationality, e. Education, l. Languages, p. Profession, b. Bahá'í declaration, m. Marriage, c. Children, b. Bahá'í birth year (spiritual parent or influence), a. Administrative services (NSA, Auxiliary Board, International Bahá'í Council, Custodian, Ḥuqúqu'lláh), t. Titles, ic. Intercontinental conferences, s. Scholarship, d. Death (where).

Mullá 'Alí-Akbar-i-Shahmírzádí, Ḥájí Ákhúnd (1842 – 1910)
n. Persian (Shahmírzád, Persia). **e.** Religious colleges, Mashhad. **p.** Neither rank nor fortune. **m.** Fáṭimih Khánum (1872). **b.** c. 1861 (Mullá Ṣádiq). **a.** Consulting Assembly of Ṭihrán (1899-) (precursor of NSA of Irán). **t.** Apostle of Bahá'u'lláh. **d.** Ṭihrán, Persia.

Mírzá 'Alí-Muḥammad (Ibn-i-Aṣdaq) (c. 1850 – 1928)
n. Persian. **m.** 'Udhrá Khánum, entitled Ḍíyáu'l-Ḥájíyyih (great-grand daughter of Muḥammad Sháh). **b.** Birth (Father: Ismu'lláhu'l-Aṣdaq). **a.** Consulting Assembly of Ṭihrán (1899-)(precursor of NSA of Irán). **t.** Shahíd Ibn-i-Shahíd (martyr, son of martyr) by Bahá'u'lláh (1882); Apostle of Bahá'u'lláh. **d.** Ṭihrán, Persia.

Mírzá Muḥammad-Taqí (Ibn-i-Abhar) (Mid-19th century – 1917)
n. Persian (Abhar, Persia). **m.** Munírih Khánum (daughter of Ḥájí Ákhúnd). **b.** Early days of Faith (Father: Mírzá Ibráhím-i-Abharí). **a.** Consulting Assembly of Ṭihrán (1899-) (precursor of NSA of Irán). **t.** Apostle of Bahá'u'lláh. **d.** Ṭihrán, Persia.

Ḥájí Mírzá Ḥasan-i-Adíb (1848 – 1919)
n. Persian (Talaqán, Persia). **e.** Religious education, Mashhad. **p.** Divine. **b.** 1889 (Nabíl-i-Akbar). **a.** Consulting Assembly of Ṭihrán (1899-)(precursor of NSA of Irán). **t.** Apostle of Bahá'u'lláh; Adíbu'l-'Ulamá (litterateur of the 'ulamá). **d.** Ṭihrán, Persia.

Mullá Muḥammad-Riḍáy-i-Muḥammad-Ábádí (c. 1814 – 1897)
n. Persian (Yazd, Persia). **e.** Education as Muslim clergyman. **p.** Divine. **b.** c. 1855 (Raḍa'r-Rúḥ). **d.** Ṭihrán, Persia.

Muḥammad-i-Qá'iní (1829 – 1892)
n. Persian (Naw-Firist in district of Qá'in, Persia). **e.** Disciple of eminent mujtahid, Shaykh Murtiḍáy-i-Anṣári, excelling in humanities, philosophy

of Illuminati, teachings of mystics, theology. **p.** Mujtahid. **b.** c. 1853. **t.** Fáḍil-i-Qá'iní (the Learned One of Qá'in); Surnamed Nabíl-i-Akbar by Bahá'u'lláh; Apostle of Bahá'u'lláh. **d.** Bukhárá.

Mullá Ṣádiq-i-Muqaddas-i-Khurásání (1800 – 1889)
n. Persian (Mashhad, Persia). **e.** Disciple of Ḥájí Siyyid Káẓim-i-Rashtí. **p.** Mujtahid. **c.** Ibn-i-Aṣdaq. **b.** c. 1844 (Mullá Ḥusayn). **t.** Ismu'lláhu'l-Aṣdaq ("The Name of God the Most Truthful" by Bahá'u'lláh). **d.** Hamadán.

Mírzá 'Alí-Muḥammad Varqá (1856 – 1896)
n. Persian (Yazd, Persia). **p.** Physician. **m.** Amatu'l-Hagh (divorced), Liqá'íyyih Khánum. **c.** 'Azízu'lláh, Rúḥu'lláh, Valíyu'lláh, Badí'u'lláh. **b.** Birth (Father: Ḥájí Mullá Mihdiy-i-'Aṭrí). **t.** Apostle of Bahá'u'lláh. **d.** Ṭihrán, Persia.

Ḥájí Abu'l-Ḥasan-i-Ardikání (Amín-i-Iláhí, Ḥájí Amín) (c. 1831 – 1928)
n. Persian (Ardikán, Persia). **p.** Trading and writing (for those who could not). **m.** Daughter of a local merchant. **b.** c. 1850 (married into Bábí family). **a.** Trustee of Ḥuqúqu'lláh. **t.** Apostle of Bahá'u'lláh. **d.** Ṭihrán, Persia.

'Abdu'l-Jalíl Bey Sa'ad (? – 1942)
n. Egyptian. **p.** Judge in civil courts. **b.** In days of (Mírzá Abu'l-Faḍl). **a.** NSA of Bahá'ís of Egypt and Sudan. **s.** Translated *The Dawn-Breakers* into the Arabic language. **d.** Cairo, Egypt.

John Henry Hyde Dunn (c. 1858 – 1941)
n. British (London, England). **l.** English. **p.** Travelling salesman. **m.** Fanny (dec.d 1911); Clara Davis (1917). **b.** 1905 (Ward Fitz-Gerald). **t.** Spiritual Conqueror of Australia. **d.** Sydney, Australia.

John Ebenezer Esslemont (1874 – 1925)
n. Scottish (Aberdeen, Scotland). **e.** Bachelor of Medicine and Surgery from Aberdeen University (1898). **l.** English, Esperanto, French, Spanish, German, Persian and Arabic. **p.** Medical doctor. **m.** Jean Fraser (1902). **b.** c. 1915 (Katherine Parker, wife of a colleague). **a.** NSA of British Isles as Vice-President (1923-1924). **s.** *Bahá'u'lláh and the New Era*; Translated *The Hidden Words* with Dr Ḥakím into Esperanto. **d.** Haifa, Israel.

Louis George Gregory (1874 – 1951)
n. African-American (Charleston, South Carolina, USA). **e.** LL.B. degree from Howard University (1902). **l.** English. **p.** Lawyer. **m.** Louisa Mathew.

b. 1909 (Joseph and Pauline Hannen). **a.** Executive Board of Bahá'í Temple Unity; NSA of Bahá'ís of United States and Canada, 1922-1924, 1927-1932, 1939-1946. **d.** Eliot, Maine.

Keith Ransom-Kehler (1876 - 1933)
n. American (Dayton, Kentucky, USA); maiden name: Nannie Keith Bean. **e.** Masters degree from Vassar College (1898); graduate studies at Albion College and Universities of Michigan, Arizona and Chicago. **l.** English, French. **p.** Child psychology. **m.** Guy Ransom (c. 1901- , dec'd); James Howard Kehler (1910-c. -1923, dec'd). **c.** Julia Keith Ransom. **b.** 1921. **d.** Iṣfahán, Persia.

Muḥammad Taqí Iṣfahání (c. 1860 - 1946)
n. Persian (Sidih, Persia). **b.** In the early days of the Declaration of Bahá'u'lláh. **a.** NSA of Egypt. **s.** Helped to translate the *Kitáb-i-Íqán* and *Some Answered Questions* into Arabic. **d.** Cairo, Egypt.

Martha Louise Root (1872 - 1939)
n. American (Cambridgeboro (Cambridge Springs), Pennsylvania, USA); other name: Mattie on birth certificate. **e.** Studied languages, English, psychology, mathematics, and Bible at Oberlin College (1889-1894); Baccalaureate degree from University of Chicago (1895). **l.** English, Chinese, French, Japanese, Spanish, Esperanto. Also studied Latin, Greek, French and German in college. **p.** Journalist. **m.** Single. **b.** 1909 (Roy Wilhelm). **t.** Peerless Herald of the Cause, Leading Ambassadress of Bahá'u'lláh's Faith, the foremost Hand. **s.** *Ṭáhirih the Pure.* **d.** Honolulu, Hawaii.

Muṣṭafáy-i-Rúmí (c. 1846 - 1945)
n. Iráqí (belonged to a noble family of Baghdád, Iráq). **l.** Arabic, Persian, Turkish, Gujarati, Bengali, Urdu and English. **p.** Trader. **m.** Married into prosperous family of traders. **b.** 1877 (Jamál Effendi). **a.** NSA of India and Burma . **s.** Translated into Burmese: *The Hidden Words, The Kitáb-i-Íqán, Some Answered Questions* and *Bahá'í Prayers*; translated into Urdu: *Maoála-i-Sayyáh;* compiled in Urdu: *The True Criterion*; wrote: *Lessons in Religion* in Burmese. **d.** Thingagyun, Burma.

Roy C Wilhelm (1875 - 1951)
n. American (Zanesville, Ohio, USA). **l.** English. **p.** Coffee trader. **m.** Single. **b.** 1907 (Mother: Laurie Wilhelm). **a.** Bahá'í Temple Unity (1909 - 1925); NSA of US and Canada (1925 - 1946, missing one year for illness), serving as treasurer for many years. **d.** North Lovell, Maine.

Agnes Baldwin Alexander (1875 - 1971)
n. American (Honolulu, Hawaii). **e.** Oahu College (c. 1895). **l.** English, Esperanto, Braille in English and Esperanto. **p.** Teacher. **m.** Single. **b.** 1900 (Charlotte Dixon; then nurtured by May Maxwell in Paris). **a.** Auxiliary Board Member in Asia (1954-); NSA of North East Asia (1957-1963). **t.** Mentioned in *Tablets of the Divine Plan.* **ic.** 1958: Sydney and Djakarta-Singapore. **s.** *History of the Bahá'í Faith in Japan 1914-1938.* **d.** Hawaii.

Paul Edmond Haney (1909 - 1982)
n. American (Los Angeles, California, USA). **e.** M.B.A. from Northwestern University. **l.** English. **p.** Economist. **m.** Helen Margery Wheeler (1942) **b.** Birth (Mother: Mary "Mariam" Haney). **a.** NSA of USA and Canada (1946-1948); NSA of USA (1948-1957) as Chairman (1950-1957); Custodian (1957-1963). **t.** 'Abdu'l-Bahá by the Master. **d.** Haifa, Israel.

Jalál Kházeh (1897 - 1990)
n. Persian (Ṭihrán, Persia). **e.** Veterinary medicine at military academy. **l.** Persian, Arabic, English and Spanish. **p.** Army rising to rank of Military colonel. **m.** Jamálíyyih, daughter of Ustád Ḥasan-'Alí Mi'márbáshi-i-Káshání (c. 1916). **c.** Three daughters and two sons. **b.** Birth (Parents: Ghulám-Riḍá and Jamáliyyih, daughter of Jináb-i-Karbilá'í Mihdí Ṭihrání). **a.** NSA of Persia; Custodian (1957-1963). **ic.** 1958: Frankfurt. **s.** Oversaw compilation of a manual for Spiritual Assemblies. **d.** Canada.

Rúḥíyyih Khánum (1910 - 2000)
n. American (New York City, New York, USA); maiden name: Mary Sutherland Maxwell. **e.** General education. **l.** English, Persian, German and French. **m.** Shoghi Effendi Rabanni, 1937. **b.** Birth (Mother: May Bolles Maxwell). **a.** International Bahá'í Council, liaison (1952-1961); Custodian (1957-1963). **t.** Amatu'l-Bahá (Handmaid of Bahá'u'lláh). **ic.** 1953: Chicago-Wilmette and Kampala. **s.** Books: *Prescription for Living, The Priceless Pearl, The Desire of the World, The Guardian of the Bahá'í Faith, Manual for Pioneers,* and *Poems of the Passing, Twenty-five Years of the Guardianship*; compiled and wrote introduction to *The Ministry of the Custodians 1957 - 1963*; Films: *The Pilgrimage* and *The Green Light Expedition.* **d.** Haifa, Israel.

Dr 'Alí Muḥammad Varqá (1912 - 2007)
n. Persian (Ṭihrán, Persia). **e.** PhD in Human Sciences from the Sorbonne. **l.** Persian (native), English (correspondence) and French. **p.** Professor. **b.** Birth (Father: Valíyu'lláh Varqá). **a.** Trustee of Ḥuqúq'lláh (1955-2007); Custodian. **ic.** 1958: Djarkarta-Singapore. **d.** Haifa, Israel.

Dorothy Beecher Baker (1898 - 1954)
n. American (Newark, New Jersey, USA); maiden name: Dorothy King Beecher. **e.** Graduate of Montclair Normal College. **l.** English and Spanish. **p.** Teacher. **m.** Frank Baker, 1921. **c.** Louise and William. **b.** 1912 (Grandmother: Ellen "Mother" Beecher). **a.** NSA of US and Canada. **ic.** 1953: Kampala, Chicago-Wilmette, Stockholm and New Delhi. **d.** Air crash over Mediterranean near Elba island.

Amelia Engelder Collins (1873 - 1962)
n. American (Pittsburgh, Pennsylvania, USA); maiden name: Amelia Engelder. **l.** English. **m.** Thomas H Collins. **b.** 1919?. **a.** NSA of United States and Canada, 1924-1933, 1938-1951; International Bahá'í Council, vice president (1951-1961); Custodian (1957-1962). **t.** Outstanding benefactress of the Faith; Collins Gate leading to Shrine of Bahá'u'lláh. **ic.** 1953: Chicago-Wilmette and Stockholm; 1958: Frankfurt. **d.** Haifa, Israel.

'Alí-Akbar Furútan (1905 - 2003)
n. Persian (Sabzivár, Persia). **e.** Psychology and Child Education degree from Moscow University (1930). **l.** Five languages. **p.** Teacher. **b.** Birth (Father: Karbalá'í Muḥammad-'Alíy-i-Sabzivárí). **a.** NSA of Persia, serving as secretary for many years; Custodian (1957-1963). **ic.** 1953: Kampala, Chicago-Wilmette, Stockholm and New Delhi. **s.** *Majmú'ih Risálát Tarbiyatí, Principles of Education, Scientific Essays, A Glimpse of History, The Story of My Heart;* translation: *Mothers, Fathers and Children* from *Majmú'ih Risálát Tarbiyatí*; compilation: *Stories of Bahá'u'lláh.*

Ugo Giachery (1896 - 1989)
n. Sicilian (Palermo, Sicily). **e.** Doctorate in Chemistry from Royal University of Palermo. **l.** Italian and English. **p.** Teacher. **m.** Angeline (1926). **b.** c. 1926 (possibly wife: Angeline). **a.** NSA of Italy and Switzerland; International Bahá'í Council, member-at-large (1952-1961); Custodian. **t.** Door to Shrine of Báb: Báb-i-Giachery. **ic.** 1953: New Delhi; 1958: Chicago-Wilmette and Frankfurt. **s.** *Shoghi Effendi, Recollections;* translated with wife: *Bahá'u'lláh and the New Era* from English to Italian; treatise: *One God, One Truth, One People: Some thoughts on the Peace Encyclical of Pope John XXIII.* **d.** Samoa.

Hermann Grossmann (1899 - 1968)
n. German (Rosario, Argentina to German parents). **e.** Doctorate of Political Science from University of Hamburg (1923). **l.** German and English. **p.** Management. **m.** Anna Hartmuth (1924). **c.** Susanne Bahíyyih and Hartmut Harlan. **b.** 1920 (Grace Ober). **a.** NSA of Germany. **ic.** 1953:

Stockholm; 1958: Frankfurt. **s.** *The Dawn of a New Age, A Change-over to Unity, God's Covenant in Revealed Religions, What is the Bahá'í Religion?, The Bahá'í Believer and the Bahá'í Community;* translated *The Seven Valleys* and *Paris Talks* into German; Bahá'í magazine: *La Nova Tago.* **d.** Neckargemünd, Germany.

Horace Hotchkiss Holley (1887 - 1960)
n. American (Torrington, Connecticutt, USA). **e.** Majored in literature at Williams College (1909). **l.** English. **p.** Writer. **m.** Bertha Herbert (c.1909 - 1919, divorced) and Doris Pascal (c. 1919). **c.** Hertha and Marcia, by Bertha. **b.** c. 1909 (Future wife: Bertha Herbert). **a.** NSA of United States and Canada (1923 - 1959) serving as secretary every year except two, Custodian (1959-1960). **ic.** 1953: Kampala, Chicago-Wilmette, Stockholm and New Delhi; 1958: Chicago-Wilmette. **s.** *Bahá'ísm - The Modern Social Religion. The Social Principle, Bahá'í, the Spirit of the Age.* Compiled *Bahá'í Scriptures,* later revised as *Bahá'í World Faith.* "International Survey of Current Bahá'í Activities" for every *Bahá'í World* until his death, "American Declaration of Trust of the National Assembly" and "ByLaws of a Local Assembly". Study guides to the *Kitáb-i-Íqán* and *God Passes By.* Introductions to *Bahá'í World Faith, World Order of Bahá'u'lláh, The Secret of Divine Civilization, Foundations of World Unity, The Reality of Man, Messages to the Bahá'í World* and *Bahá'í Administration.* Poetry: *The Inner Garden, The Stricken King, Divination and Creation*; Prose: *Read-Aloud Plays.* **d.** Israel

Leroy C Ioas (1896 – 1965)
n. American (Wilmington, Illinois, USA). **e.** Some commercial training. **l.** English. **p.** Manager in railway industry. **m.** Sylvia Kuhlman. **c.** Farrukh and Anita. **b.** Raised (Parents: Charles and Maria Ioas). **a.** NSA of USA and Canada, International Bahá'í Council, Secretary-General (1952-1961). Custodian (1957-1963). **t.** Octagon door of Shrine of Báb: Báb-i-Ioas. **ic.** 1953: Kampala; 1958: Chicago-Wilmette and Djakarta-Singapore. **d.** Haifa, Israel.

William Sutherland Maxwell (1874 – 1952)
n. Canadian (Montreal, Canada). **e.** École des Beaux Arts in Paris. **l.** English. **p.** Architect. **m.** May Bolles. **c.** Mary Sutherland Maxwell (Amatu'l-Bahá Rúḥíyyih Khánum). **b.** 1909 ('Abdu'l-Bahá). **t.** Southern door of Shine of Báb: Báb-i-Maxwell. **d.** Montreal, Canada.

Charles Mason Remey (1874 – 1974)
n. American (Burlington, Iowa, USA). **e.** Sorbonne. **p.** Architect. **b.** 1899 (May Bolles). **a.** Executive Board of Bahá'í Temple Unity (1909-1910, 1911-1912, 1918-1920, 1921-1924); International Bahá'í Council, President; Custodian. **t.** Covenant-breaker. **ic.** 1953: Chicago-

Wilmette; Stockholm; New Delhi. **s.** William Collins's *Bibliography of English-Language Works on the Bábí and Bahá'í Faiths 1844-1985* lists over 55 separate works (pp. 133-5). **d.** Florence, Italy.

Ṭarázu'lláh Samandarí (1874 – 1968)
n. Persian (Qazvin, Persia). **e.** Tutored by Mullá 'Alí (Mu'allim) who was praised by Bahá'u'lláh. **p.** Caligrapher. **m.** Ṭarázíyyih (1895). **c.** Mihdí Samandarí. **b.** Birth (Father: Samandar). **t.** Ṭaráz-i-Iláhí (The Divine Ornament); Apostle of the Crimson Ark. **s.** 18-volume compilation of Tablets received by the Bahá'ís of Iran. **d.** Haifa, Israel.

George Townshend (1876 – 1957)
n. Irish (Dublin, Ireland). **e.** BA from Oxford University (1899). **l.** English. **p.** Priesthood (1916). **m.** Anna Sarah Maxwell (Nancy) (1918). **c.** Una (1920) and Brian (1921). **b.** 1919 (Louise Finley, librarian at Sewanee). **t.** Canon of St Patrick's Cathedral (1932 – 1945, 1946 – 1947), Archdeacon of Clonfert (1933 -); pre-eminent Bahá'í writer. **ic.** 1953: Stockholm. **s.** *The Altar on the Hearth, The Genius of Ireland, The Heart of the Gospel, The Promise of All Ages, Christ and Bahá'u'lláh, The Old Churches and the New World Faith, The Glad Tidings of Bahá'u'lláh,* "Bahá'u'lláh's Ground Plan for World Fellowship"; Introductions to *God Passes By, The Dawn-Breakers* and *The Hidden Words*; David Hofman listed over 60 separate works. **d.** Dublin, Ireland.

Valíyu'lláh Varqá (1884 – 1955)
n. Persian (Tabríz, Persia). **a.** NSA of Persia (Chairman). **e.** General education followed by college in Beirut. **l.** Persian, English and Arabic. **p.** Secretary and translator. **m.** Bahíyyih K͟hánum. **c.** Ten children including 'Alí Muḥammad, Mihdí, Malíhih, Muníroh, Parvín, Maḥmúd, and Lami. **b.** c. 1904 (Ḥájí Mir Ḥusayn, an uncle). **a.** NSA of Persia; Trustee of Ḥuqúqu'lláh (1938-1955). **ic.** 1953: Kampala, Chicago-Wilmette, Stockholm and New Delhi (1953). **d.** Tübingen, Germany.

S͟hu'á'u'lláh 'Alá'í (1889 – 1984)
n. Persian (Ṭihrán, Persia). **e.** Accountancy. **p.** Accounting and Finance. **b.** Birth (Parents: Muḥammad Náẓimu'l-Ḥukamá and K͟hadíjih ('Bíbí Ján). **a.** NSA of Persia; Custodian. **m.** Furúg͟híyyih 'Alá'í. **c.** Ḥis͟hmat, Mihrangíz, Bihjat, Faraḥangíz and Amír. **ic.** 1953: Kampala, Chicago-Wilmette, Stockholm and New Delhi. **d.** Scottsdale, Arizona, USA.

Músá Banání (1886 – 1971)
n. (Bag͟hdád, Iraq). **l.** Persian and Arabic. **p.** Entrepreneur. **m.** Samíhih; **c.** Violette and Amín. **b.** After 1911. **t.** Spiritual Conqueror of Africa.

ic. 1953: Kampala, Chicago-Wilmette, Stockholm and New Delhi; 1958: Kampala and Frankfurt. **d.** Kampala, Uganda.

Clara Dunn (1869 – 1960)
n. British (London, England); maiden name: Clara Holder. **l.** English. **p.** Nurse. **m.** William Allen Davis (c. 1885-1888), John Henry Hyde Dunn (1917). **c.** Allen Junior (by Davis). **b.** 1907 (John Henry Hyde Dunn). **ic.** 1953: New Delhi; 1958: Sydney. **d.** Sydney, Australia.

Zikrullah Khadem (1904 – 1986)
n. Persian (Ṭihrán, Persia). **e.** Dar-ul-Fonoon College in Ṭihrán. **l.** Persian, Arabic, French and English. **p.** Diplomatic core and entrepreneur. **m.** Jávíddukht Jávíd. **c.** Mozhan, Jena, Riaz, Ramin and May. **b.** Birth (Parents: Mírzá Naṣru'lláh Khádem and Ráḍíyyih Khánum). **a.** NSA of Persia (1938-1960); Custodian (1958). **ic.** 1953: Kampala, Chicago-Wilmette, Stockholm and New Delhi; 1958: Sydney. **s.** Translated portions of *The Advent of Divine Justice, The Promised Day is Come,* and two volumes of *Bahá'í World* from English to Persian; *Registry of Bahá'í Holy Places* (141 volumes). **d.** Chicaco, Illinois; buried Skokie.

Adelbert Mühlschlegel (1897 – 1980)
n. German (Berlin, Germany). **e.** Studied in Freiburg im Breisgau, Greifswald and Tübingen. **l.** German, English, Persian, Esperanto. **p.** Medical doctor. **m.** Herma Weidle (1926-1964, dec'd); Ursula Kohler (1965). **c.** Two girls and three boys by Herma. **b.** 1920 (Mother). **a.** NSA of Germany, sometime Chairman; substitute Custodian. **ic.** 1953: Stockholm; 1958: Frankfurt. **d.** Greece.

Siegfried Schopflocher (1877 – 1953)
n. German. **p.** Businessman. **m.** Florence Evaline 'Lorol' Snyder (1918). **b.** 1921 (Wife: Lorol Schopflocher). **a.** NSA of United States and Canada and NSA of Canada. **t.** The Chief Temple Builder by the Guardian. **ic.** 1953: Chicago-Wilmette. **d.** Montreal, Canada.

Corinne Knight True (1861 – 1961)
n. American (Oldham County, Kentucky, USA); maiden name: Corinne Knight. **e.** Virginia finishing school. **l.** English. **p.** Housewife. **m.** Moses Adams True (1882). **c.** Harriet Merrill, Laurence Knight, Charles Gilbert Davis, Edna Miriam, Arna Corinne, Katherine and Kenneth, Nathanael. **b.** 1899 (a friend). **a.** Bahá'í Temple Unity as financial secretary, 1909 – 1922. **t.** Mother of the Temple. **ic.** 1953: Chicago-Wilmette. **d.** Wilmette, Illnois.

Ḥasan Balyuzi (1908 – 1980)
n. Persian (Shíráz, Persia). **e.** Diplomatic History receiving M.Sc. in Economics from London School of Economics (1935). **l.** Persian, Arabic, English and Urdu. **p.** Broadcasting and writing. **m.** Molly (Mary) Brown (1941). **c.** Hushang, Robert, Felix, Richard and Simeon. **b.** 1925 (Shoghi Effendi). **a.** NSA of British Isles (1933-1960) as Chairman (except years 1943-1944); Custodian (1957-1959). **ic.** 1958: Frankfurt. **s.** *Bahá'u'lláh, King of Glory; 'Abdu'l-Bahá; The Báb; Bahá'u'lláh; Eminent Bahá'ís in the Time of Bahá'u'lláh; Edward Granville Browne and the Bahá'í Faith; Muḥammad and the Course of Islam; Khadíjih Bagum, The Wife of the Báb* and in Persian *The Story of Three Sisters; Half-Brothers;* and *Words in English Derived from Persian.* **d.** England.

Abu'l-Qásim Faizi (c. 1906 – 1980)
n. Persian (Qum, Persia). **e.** Degree in English Literature and Education from American University at Beirut. **l.** Persian, Arabic, French and English. **p.** Teacher. **m.** Gloria 'Alá'í. **c.** May and Naysan. **b.** c. 1921 (Bahá'í classmates at Tarbíyat School). **a.** Auxiliary Board Member for Asia (1954-); Custodian (1957-1963). **t.** Spiritual Conqueror of Arabia. **ic.** 1958: Djakarta-Singapore. **s.** Persian: *Payám-i-Dúst va Bahár-i-Ṣad-u-Bíst, Dástán-i-Dústán*; English: *Three Meditations on the Eve of November the Fourth, Explanation of the Emblem of the Greatest Name, Our Precious Trusts, The Wonder Lamp.* Translations (English to Persian): *The Priceless Pearl* and *Portals to Freedom*; (Persian to English): *Stories from the Delight of Hearts.* **d.** Haifa, Israel.

Harold Collis Featherstone (1913 – 1990)
n. Australian (Quorn, South Australia). **e.** Studied accounting at night school. **l.** English. **p.** Precision engineering. **m.** Madge Green. **c.** Kaye, Margaret, Joan, Mariette and Geoffrey. **b.** 1944 (Bertha Dobbins). **a.** NSA of Australia and New Zealand, sometime Chairman (1949 – 1962); Auxiliary Board Member for Australia (1954 -). **ic.** 1958: Sydney. **s.** Audiotape recording of Clara Dunn; 16mm colour film of 1958 Conclave. **d.** Kathmandu, Nepal.

John Graham Ferraby (1914 – 1973)
n. British (Southsea, England). **e.** Educated at Malvern and King's College, Cambridge on major scholarship. **l.** English. **p.** Statistician with Mass Observation. **m.** Dorothy Cansdale (1943). **c.** Brigitte. **b.** 1941 (mentioned by Victor Cofman, a friend; taught by Hasan Balyuzi). **a.** NSA of British Isles (1941 – 1960) as secretary (1946 – 1960); Custodian (1959-1963). **ic.** 1958: Frankfurt. **s.** *All Things Made New.* **d.** Cambridge, England.

Raḥmatu'lláh Muhájir (1923 - 1979)
n. Persian (Sháh 'Abdu'l-Aẓím, Persia). **e.** Graduated with honours from School of Medicine at University of Ṭihrán (1952). **p.** Medical doctor. **m.** Irán Furútan (1951). **c.** Gisu. **b.** Birth (Parents: Ḥafiẓu'lláh Khán and Iṣmat Khánum). **a.** Regional Spiritual Assembly of South-East Asia. **t.** Knight of Bahá'u'lláh. **ic.** 1958: Djakarta-Singapore. **d.** Quito, Ecuador.

Enoch Olinga (1926 - 1979)
n. African (Abaango). **e.** High school in Mbale District. **l.** Fluent in six languages, including Ateso and English. **p.** Translator. **m.** Eunice (- 1961, divorced); Elizabeth (c. 1963). **c.** George, Patrick, Godwin, Grace and Florence (by Eunice); Lennie, Tahirih and Badi (by Elizabeth). **b.** 1952 ('Alí Nakhjavání). **a.** Regional National Spiritual Assembly of North and West Africa. **t.** Knight of Bahá'u'lláh; Abu'l-Futúh (Father of Victories) by Guardian. **ic.** 1958: Kampala, Frankfurt and Djakarta-Singapore. **d.** Kampala, Uganda.

John Aldham Robarts (1901 - 1991)
n. Canadian (Waterloo, Ontario). **e.** Ridley College in St Catharines. **l.** English. **p.** Entrepreneur and later insurance sales manager. **m.** Audrey FitzGerald (1928). **c.** Aldham Edward, John FitzGerald, Patrick Tempest, Nina Grace. **b.** 1938 (Grace Robarts, an aunt). **a.** NSA of Canada as chairman (1948 - 1953); Auxiliary Board Member for Africa (1954 -); Regional National Spiritual Assembly of South and West Africa (1956 -). **t.** Knight of Bahá'u'lláh; Gooch Ooxú (Wolf Teeth). **ic.** 1958: Kampala, Chicago-Wilmette and Frankfurt. **s.** Introduction to *Messages to Canada, Letter to Bahá'ís*. **d.** Rawdon, Quebec.

William Sears (1911 - 1992)
n. American (Duluth, Minnesota, USA). **e.** University of Wisconsin, no degree. **l.** English. **p.** Broadcasting. **m.** Marguerite Reimer (1940). **c.** Two sons. **b.** 1940 (Wife: Marguerite Sears). **a.** Auxiliary Board Member for Africa (1954-); Regional National Spiritual Assembly of South and West Africa, first Chairman; Custodian (1958, 1961-1963). **ic.** 1958: Kampala. **s.** Television series: "In the Park"; Radio programs: "Meet Mr. Justice" and "That Man Sears"; Cassette recording: *Stories from the Children's Dawn-Breakers;* Books: *Release the Sun, Thief In The Night, God Loves Laughter, Cry From The Heart, Prisoner and the Kings, Prince of Peace, The Wine of Astonishment, The Flame* (with Robert Quigley), *All Flags Flying, Tokoloshe, Run to Glory, The Half Inch Prophecy*. **d.** Tucson, Arizona.

Appointments Of The Hands Of The Cause

APPOINTMENTS BY BAHÁ'U'LLÁH
(Last few years of His life)

Ḥájí Mullá 'Alí-Akbar-i-Shahmírzádí (Ḥájí Ákhúnd) – Persian
Ḥájí Mírzá Muḥammad Taqíy-i-Abharí (Ibn-i-Abhar) – Persian
Mírzá 'Alí-Muḥammad (Ibn-i-Aṣdaq) – Persian
Mírzá Muḥammad-Ḥasan (Adíbu'l-'Ulamá (Adíb) – Persian

REFERRED TO BY 'ABDU'L-BAHÁ

Áqá Muḥammad-i-Qá'iní (Nabíl-i-Akbar) – Persian
Mírzá 'Alí-Muḥammad Varqá – Persian
Shaykh Muḥammad-Riḍáy-i-Yazdí - Persian
Mullá Ṣádiq-i-Muqaddas (Ismu'lláhu'l-Aṣdaq) – Persian

POSTHUMOUS APPOINTMENTS BY SHOGHI EFFENDI

APPOINTED	DATE APPT'D
John Esslemont – Scottish	30 November 1925
Ḥájí Abu'l-Ḥasan Amín – Persian	July 1928
Keith Ransom-Kehler – American	28 October 1933
Martha Root – American	2 October 1939
'Abdu'l-Jalíl Bey Sa'ad – Egyptian	25 June 1942
Siyyid Muṣṭafá Rúmí – Iraqi	14 July 1945
Muḥammad Taqíy-i-Iṣfahání – Persian	15 December 1946
Louis Gregory – American	5 August 1951
Roy Wilhelm – American	23 December 1951
John Henry Hyde Dunn – British	26 April 1952

FIRST CONTINGENT: 24 December 1951

HOUR NOW RIPE TAKE LONG INEVITABLY DEFERRED STEP CONFORMITY PROVISIONS 'ABDU'L-BAHÁ'S TESTAMENT CONJUNCTION WITH SIX ABOVE-MENTIONED STEPS THROUGH APPOINTMENT FIRST CONTINGENT HANDS CAUSE GOD, TWELVE IN NUMBER, EQUALLY ALLOCATED HOLY LAND, ASIATIC, AMERICAN, EUROPEAN CONTINENTS STOP INITIAL STEP NOW TAKEN REGARDED PREPARATORY FULL DEVELOPMENT INSTITUTION PROVIDED 'ABDU'L-BAHÁ'S WILL, PARALLELED PRELIMINARY MEASURE FORMATION INTERNATIONAL COUNCIL DESTINED CULMINATE EMERGENCE UNIVERSAL HOUSE JUSTICE STOP NASCENT INSTITUTION FORGING FRESH LINKS BINDING RISING WORLD CENTRE FAITH TO CONSOLIDATING WORLD COMMUNITY FOLLOWERS MOST GREAT NAME, PAVING WAY ADOPTION SUPPLEMENTARY MEASURES CALCULATED REINFORCE FOUNDATIONS STRUCTURE BAHÁ'Í ADMINISTRATIVE ORDER STOP NOMINATED HANDS COMPRISE, HOLY LAND, SUTHERLAND MAXWELL, MASON REMEY, AMELIA COLLINS, PRESIDENT, VICE PRESIDENT, INTERNATIONAL BAHÁ'Í COUNCIL; CRADLE FAITH, VALÍYU'LLÁH VARQÁ, ṬARÁZU'LLÁH SAMANDARÍ, 'ALÍ AKBAR FURÚTAN; AMERICAN CONTINENT, HORACE HOLLEY, DOROTHY BAKER, LEROY IOAS; EUROPEAN CONTINENT, GEORGE TOWNSHEND, HERMAN GROSSMANN, UGO GIACHERY STOP NINE ELEVATED RANK HAND THREE CONTINENTS OUTSIDE HOLY LAND ADVISED REMAIN PRESENT POSTS CONTINUE DISCHARGE VITAL ADMINISTRATIVE, TEACHING DUTIES PENDING ASSIGNMENT SPECIFIC FUNCTIONS AS NEED ARISES STOP URGE ALL NINE ATTEND AS MY REPRESENTATIVES ALL FOUR FORTH-COMING INTERCONTINENTAL CONFERENCES AS WELL AS DISCHARGE WHATEVER RESPONSIBILITIES INCUMBENT UPON THEM AT THAT TIME AS ELECTED REPRESENTATIVES NATIONAL BAHÁ'Í COMMUNITIES. (BW13 333-4)

APPOINTED	**REPRESENTATING**
William Sutherland Maxwell - Canadian	Holy Land
Charles Mason Remey - American	Holy Land
Amelia Collins – American	Holy Land
Valíyu'lláh Varqá – Persian	Cradle Faith
Tarázu'lláh Samandarí – Persian	Cradle Faith
'Alí Akbar Furútan – Persian	Cradle Faith
Horace Holley - American	American Continent
Dorothy Baker – American	American Continent
Leroy Ioas – American	American Continent
George Townshend - Irish	European Continent
Hermann Grossmann – German	European Continent
Ugo Giachery – Sicilian	European Continent

SECOND CONTINGENT: 29 FEBRUARY 1952

ANNOUNCE FRIENDS EAST WEST, THROUGH NATIONAL ASSEMBLIES, FOLLOWING NOMINATIONS RAISING NUMBER PRESENT HANDS CAUSE GOD NINETEEN, DOMINION CANADA, UNITED STATES, FRED SCHOPFLOCHER, CORINNE TRUE RESPECTIVELY. CRADLE FAITH, D͟HIKRU'LLÁH K͟HÁDEM, S͟HU'Á'U'LLÁH 'ALÁ'Í. GERMANY, AFRICA, AUSTRALIA, ADELBERT MÜHLSCHLEGEL, MÚSÁ BANÁNÍ, CLARA DUNN, RESPECTIVELY. MEMBERS AUGUST BODY INVESTED CONFORMITY 'ABDU'L-BAHÁ'S TESTAMENT TWOFOLD SACRED FUNCTION PROPAGATION PRESERVATION UNITY FAITH BAHÁ'U'LLÁH, DESTINED ASSUME INDIVIDUALLY COURSE TIME DIRECTION INSTITUTIONS PARALLELING THOSE REVOLVING ROUND UNIVERSAL HOUSE JUSTICE, SUPREME LEGISLATIVE BODY BAHÁ'Í WORLD, NOW RECRUITED ALL FIVE CONTINENTS GLOBE REPRESENTATIVE THREE PRINCIPAL WORLD RELIGIONS MANKIND . . . (BW13 334)

APPOINTED	**REPRESENTING**
Fred Schopflocher (Jewish) - German	Dominion Canada
Corinne True (Christian) - American	United States
Dhikru'lláh Khádem - Persian	Cradle Faith
Shu'á'u'lláh 'Alá'í (Muslim) - Persian	Cradle Faith
Adelbert Mühlschlegel – German	Germany
Músá Banání (Jewish) - Persian	Africa
Clara Dunn (Christian) - British	Australia

APPOINTED	**REPLACING**
Rúḥíyyih K͟hánum – American (26 March 1952)	William Sutherland Maxwell (Deceased: 25 March 1952)
Jalál K͟házeh – Persian (7 December 1953)	Fred Schopflocher (Deceased: 27 July 1953
Paul Haney – American (19 March 1954)	Dorothy Baker (Deceased: 10 January 1954)
'Alí-Muḥammad Varqá - Persian (15 November 1955)	Valíyu'lláh Varqá (Deceased: 12 November 1955)
Agnes Alexander - American (27 March 1957)	George Townshend (Deceased: 25 March 1957)

3RD CONTINGENT: OCTOBER 1957

"So marvelous a progress, embracing so vast a field, achieved in so short a time, by so small a band of heroic souls, well deserves, at this juncture in the evolution of a decade-long Crusade, to be signalized by, and indeed necessitates, the announcement of yet another step in the progressive unfoldment of one of the cardinal and pivotal institutions ordained by Bahá'u'lláh, and confirmed in the *Will and Testament of 'Abdu'l-Bahá*, involving the designation of yet another contingent of the Hands of the Cause of God, raising thereby to thrice nine the total number of the Chief Stewards of Bahá'u'lláh's embryonic World Commonwealth, who have been invested by the unerring Pen of the Centre of His Covenant with the dual function of guarding over the security, and of insuring the propagation, of His Father's Faith."

"The eight now elevated to this exalted rank are: Enoch Olinga, William Sears and John Robarts, in West and South Africa; Ḥasan Balyuzi and John Ferraby in the British Isles; Collis Featherstone and Raḥmatu'lláh Muhájir, in the Pacific area; and Abú'l-Qásim Faizí in the Arabian Peninsula – a group chosen from four continents of the globe, and representing the Afnán, as well as the black and white races and whose members are derived from Christian, Muslim, Jewish and Pagan backgrounds." (BW13 334-5)

APPOINTED	REPRESENTING
Enoch Olinga - African	West Africa, black, Pagan
William Sears – American	South Africa, white, Christian
John Robarts - Canadian	South Africa, white, Christian
Hasan Balyuzi – Persian	British, white
John Ferraby – British	British, white, Jewish
Collis Featherstone - Australian	Pacific, white, Christian
Raḥmatu'lláh Muhájir – Persian	Pacific, white
Abu'l-Qasim Faizi – Persian	Arabian Peninsula, white, Muslim

SURVIVING TIME OF PASSING OF SHOGHI EFFENDI: 4 NOVEMBER 1957

APPOINTED	RESIDING	AGE	SPAN
Rúḥíyyih Khánum – American	World Centre	47	1910 - 2000
Charles Mason Remey – American	World Centre	83	1874 - 1974*
Amelia Collins – American	World Centre	84	1873 - 1962
Dr 'Alí-Muḥammad Varqá – Persian	Persia	46	1912 - 2007
Ṭarázu'lláh Samandarí – Persian	Persia	83	1874 - 1968
'Alí Akbar Furútan – Persian	Persia	52	1905 - 2003
Horace Holley – American	America	70	1887 - 1960
Paul Haney – American	America	48	1909 - 1982
Leroy Ioas – American	World Centre	61	1896 - 1965
Agnes Alexander – American	Japan	82	1875 - 1971
Dr Hermann Grossmann – German	Germany	58	1899 - 1968
Dr Ugo Giachery – Sicilian	Italy	61	1896 - 1989
Jalál Kházeh – Persian	Persia	60	1897 - 1990
Corinne True – American	America	96	1861 - 1961
Dhikru'lláh Khádem – Persian	Persia	53	1904 - 1986
Shu'á'u'lláh 'Alá'í – Persian	Persia	67	1889 - 1984
Adelbert Mühlschlegel – German	Germany	60	1897 - 1980
Músá Banání - Persian	Africa	71	1886 - 1971
Clara Dunn – British	Australia	88	1896 - 1960
Enoch Olinga – African	Africa	31	1926 - 1979
William Sears – American	Africa	46	1911 - 1992
John Robarts – Canadian	Africa	56	1901 - 1991
Hasan Balyuzi – Persian	England	49	1908 - 1980
John Ferraby – British	England	43	1914 - 1973
Collis Featherstone – Australian	Australia	44	1913 - 1990
Dr Raḥmatu'lláh Muhájir – Persian	Indonesia	34	1923 - 1979
Abu'l-Qasim Faizi – Persian	Arabia	51	1906 - 1980

* Expelled as Covenant-breaker in 1960

Addendum

THE UNIVERSAL HOUSE OF JUSTICE

26 November 2007

To the Bahá'ís of the World

Dearly loved Friends,

We are moved on the occasion of this Day of the Covenant to reflect on the august Institution of the Hands of the Cause of God in the aftermath of the decease only two months ago of the last remaining Hand of the Cause, Dr. 'Alí-Muḥammad Varqá. It was just a few weeks before the fiftieth anniversary of the passing of Shoghi Effendi that our world community suffered this grievous loss. How sobering, indeed, it is to realize that Dr. Varqá's departure brought to an end the remarkable stewardship of an institution whose legacy is unparalleled in religious history! At so significant a juncture in the Formative Age of the Faith, it is only fitting that an effort be made to understand more deeply than before the significance of the achievements of so outstanding an organ of the Administrative Order—one that proved to be so integral to the evolution of our world community during its nascent years.

We trace the origins of the Institution to Bahá'u'lláh Himself, Who designated four renowned promoters of His teachings as Hands of the Cause of God. In a period before the administrative system of the Faith was inaugurated, they became rallying points for the friends, as much because of the virtuous character of their personal lives as for their unceasing endeavours in proclaiming the Teachings and defending the Faith against its detractors. They remained resolute in such activities despite the severe persecution, including imprisonment in some instances, to which they were subjected by the authorities. These distinguished personages remained active during the ministry of 'Abdu'l-Bahá, Who, in 1899, instructed them to take steps to form the Local Spiritual Assembly of Ṭihrán, on which they all served. The focus of these first Hands on propagation and protection of the Faith, as well as their efforts to edify believers as to the importance of the new Laws, intimated even then the pattern of functioning the Institution would adopt at a later stage in the advancement of the Bahá'í community.

The Master did not Himself appoint Hands of the Cause, but referred to four believers posthumously as such. However, His Will and Testament confirmed the Institution and extended it by authorizing the Guardian of the Faith to appoint consecrated souls to it. At first, over a period of three decades, Shoghi Effendi named ten such souls posthumously; all were distinguished for the constancy, vigour and impact of their efforts to propagate the Cause and promote its best interests. The Guardian's designation in December 1951 of twelve living believers as Hands of the Cause introduced the Bahá'í world to a wholly new dynamic in the operation of the Order of Bahá'u'lláh; through it the Hands exerted an unusual vitality during the Ten Year Crusade, particularly after the sudden passing of the Sign of God. His subsequent appointment of seven more in February 1952 and replacement thereafter of five of those deceased kept the number of living Hands at nineteen until less than a month before his departure, when in his last message to the Bahá'í world he identified an additional eight,

Bahá'í World Centre • P.O. Box 155 • 31001 Haifa, Israel
Tel: 972 (4) 835 8358 • Fax: 972 (4) 835 8280 • Email: secretariat@bwc.org

bringing the total to twenty-seven. Shoghi Effendi's description of them as the "Chief Stewards of Bahá'u'lláh's embryonic World Commonwealth" prefigured the world-shaking reality of the unexpected responsibilities that would be thrust upon them on the morrow of his passing.

The Guardian now forever gone, the Hands' first task, despite the sorrow that overwhelmed them, was to restore the composure of a grief-stricken community. A vital aspect of that task was, of course, to settle the minds of the friends about the direction that the Faith would take. The Hands acted with dispatch. Only sixteen days after the burial of the Guardian, they issued from the Holy Land a proclamation to the Bahá'ís of East and West. Declaring that, after a thorough search, no will or instruction of Shoghi Effendi had been found, they set forth in this message the procedures they would follow in meeting the daunting challenge they faced. It announced that a body of nine Hands, designated "Custodians", was constituted to function at the Bahá'í World Centre to protect the Faith, maintain communications with National Spiritual Assemblies in connection with the prosecution of the Ten Year Plan and on administrative matters, and attend to all issues related to the preservation of the World Centre of the Faith. The friends everywhere derived from this first communication assurance that the ship of the Cause would safely traverse the waters severely troubled by the Guardian's passing. Subsequent messages issued from conclaves of the Hands held in the Holy Land further infused confidence in the believers who arose to meet the goals set before them in the Plan.

The Hands residing outside the Holy Land, in addition to giving close attention to the progress of the Plan in their own regions, undertook extensive journeys to visit and encourage the believers in every clime. Their travels covered the entire surface of the planet as they pursued every opportunity to advance the work of the Plan left by Shoghi Effendi. The obligations of the Hands spelled out in the Will and Testament of 'Abdu'l-Bahá were carried out with the selflessness, fearlessness and zeal characteristic of their activity. To "diffuse the Divine Fragrances, to edify the souls of men, to promote learning, to improve the character of all men"—all these they undertook with outstanding, sometimes astonishing, results. Such travels did not cease with the conclusion of the Ten Year Plan but continued with unabated intensity, the legendary journeys of Amatu'l-Bahá Rúḥíyyih K͟hánum generating immeasurable stimulus. Thus the activities of the Hands demonstrated to a superlative degree the efficacy of Bahá'u'lláh's assertion that the "movement itself from place to place, when undertaken for the sake of God, hath always exerted, and can now exert, its influence in the world."

Among the principal results of their combined labours, these stand out: maintenance of the stature of the Faith as an independent and indivisible Order; protection of the Cause against schism, despite the disloyalty to the Covenant of one among their exalted company, Mason Remey, whom they were obliged to cast out; preservation of the properties and maintenance of the Holy Places and gardens at the World Centre; success in the vast expansion of the Faith. All these hard-won accomplishments prepared the path to the smooth transition that the Hands effected from the ministry of Shoghi Effendi, as head of the Faith, to that of the Universal House of Justice, for whose first election they meticulously prepared the Bahá'í world, especially the fifty-six National Spiritual Assemblies that participated in it. The Hands of the Cause delivered to the House of Justice a community that was so greatly transformed during the Ten Year Plan as to place the Faith of Bahá'u'lláh on the map as a world religion in every legitimate sense. The grand celebration at the World Congress in London attended by Bahá'ís from countries of every continent demonstrated the validity of that claim.

Beyond the World Crusade, the Hands of the Cause threw the full weight of their support behind the newly formed Universal House of Justice, whose creation their valiant efforts ensured. They undertook many missions on its behalf and pursued tasks befitting their continuing obligation to propagate and protect the Faith. As in the absence of the Guardian there was no way further to appoint Hands of the Cause, the Hands in the Holy Land in particular performed what may well be viewed as a distinct and final mark of service: they assisted the House of Justice to extend into the future the functions of propagation and protection in the special character of their institution. Hence, in 1968 Continental Boards of Counsellors were raised up and then in 1973 was created the International Teaching Centre foreshadowed in the writings of Shoghi Effendi. In their tireless support of the House of Justice in the design of these institutions and in the guidance they lent to their development, the Hands left to the Bahá'í world a further legacy that only future generations will be able adequately to appreciate. A shining value of their ultimate exertions is evident in the stature to which the International Teaching Centre has risen in such a short time and the permeating influence of the institution of the Counsellors which reaches every nook and cranny of our worldwide community.

It is highly worthy of note that the body of the Hands, with one exception, remained unbeguiled by the allurements of power that commonly corrupt those who are suddenly thrust by force of circumstances into positions of elevated rank and authority. In this instance, all of creation cannot but bear witness to the integrity of their stewardship, the unblemished virtue of their faithfulness to principle.

A point to ponder as well is the survival to the last of the one who was simultaneously appointed in 1955 to the two offices of Hand of the Cause and Trustee of Ḥuqúqu'lláh. That he was able to shape the latter institution and finally to see to its administrative transition in the formation in 2005 of the International Board of Trustees of Ḥuqúqu'lláh, with branches spread throughout the globe, is yet another sign of the constancy and abundance of the providential confirmations which have attended the evolution of the Administrative Order. Clearly, then, the work of the divinely ordained Institution of the Hands of the Cause of God was indispensable to the progress of the Faith from the Heroic Age to an early period of the Formative Age; its effects are certain to endure as an integral part of the Order of Bahá'u'lláh. The passing of Dr. Varqá marks both the end of a chapter of Bahá'í history and the beginning of a new stage in the unfolding of that Order.

With such thoughts astir in our minds, we recognize with increasing wonder and appreciation the magnitude of the contributions of the Hands of the Cause of God to the growth and consolidation of the Faith in all parts of the world. In our grateful hearts we recite with deep emotion the benediction so eloquently exclaimed by the Lord of Hosts: "Light and glory, greeting and praise be upon the Hands of His Cause, through whom the light of fortitude hath shone forth and the truth hath been established that the authority to choose rests with God, the Powerful, the Mighty, the Unconstrained, through whom the ocean of bounty hath surged and the fragrance of the gracious favours of God, the Lord of mankind, hath been diffused."

The Universal House of Justice

www.ingramcontent.com/pod-product-compliance
Lightning Source LLC
Chambersburg PA
CBHW031132160426
43193CB00008B/118
9781925320114